National Resources and Urban Policy

i

NATIONAL RESOURCES
AND URBAN POLICY

Edited by
DOUGLAS E. ASHFORD

Thomas J. Anton
Ronald Aqua
Douglas E. Ashford
Samuel B. Bacharach
Ian D Ball
Thomas Boast
Stephen L. Elkin
Elliot J. Feldman
Jerome Milch
Michio Muramatsu
Jonathan Reader
Bernd Reissert
George Rolleston
Martin Shefter
Ken Young

Methuen   Croom Helm
New York   Toronto   London

Manufactured in the United States of America

First American edition published by
Methuen, Inc.,
733 Third Avenue,
New York, N.Y. 10017

Published in Great Britain by
Croom Helm Ltd,
2-10 St John's Road,
London SW11

Published in Canada by
Methuen Publications,
2330 Midland Avenue,
Agincourt, Ontario M1S 1P7

Library of Congress Cataloging in Publication Data

Main entry under title:
National resources and urban policy.
Essays presented at a conference held by the
Western Societies Program, Center for International
Studies, Cornell University, in June 1977.
    Bibliography: p.
    1. Urban policy—Congresses. 2. Municipal
finance—Congresses. 3. Federal-city relations—
Congresses. I. Ashford, Douglas Elliott, II. Anton,
Thomas Julius. III. Cornell University. Western
Societies Program.
HT166.N38 1980   336.1'85   77-94185
ISBN 0-416-60181-2

British Library Cataloguing in Publication Data

National resources and urban policy.
    1. Finance, Public 2. Urban policy
    I. Ashford, Douglas Elliot
    336.1'85   HJ192
ISBN 0-7099-0034-1

CONTENTS

PREFACE

The essays in this volume were presented at a conference held by the Western Societies Program, Center for International Studies, Cornell University, in June 1977. The initial stimulus for the meeting was the range of work being done by Cornell scholars on urban decision making and policy. The work involved the United States, several European countries, and Japan. It was agreed that the growing strain among levels of government in allocating funds to cities made a closer examination worthwhile. A number of foreign scholars were invited to join in a discussion of how resource constraints affect urban development and urban policy. Because of limitations of space, the papers in this volume are only part of those presented. Selection is never easy, but the concern is to point out both the macro- and micro-level influences that come to bear on the creation and use of urban resources, particularly the fiscal and financial limitations placed on cities by the political system.

In the process of planning and holding the meeting, ideas about the relationship of cities to states changed. This may be taken as a sign of the fruits of the endeavor rather than of its uncertainty. In the early discussions the city was seen as opposed to the state, possibly even in some kind of irreconcilable conflict. During the meeting and while revising papers, it became clearer that the relationship was an extremely diverse one, placing constraints of particular kinds on particular systems, and one subject to a variety of transformations as urban resources were allocated in different countries. Five of the eleven papers focus on the United States, but they do so at different levels of decision making. The others deal with Britain, France, West Germany, and Japan. The contributors' hope is that the comparative dimension of the volume will illuminate the diversity that exists within the United States (part 1) and in the other countries by showing, first, how investment decisions are influenced by national governments (part 2) and, second, how the transfer of funds to cities is affected by the decisions at lower levels of government (part 3).

Comparison is a method of simplifying diversity and, hopefully, of identifying salient similarities and differences across political systems. Though a general theory has not been constructed, the agreement that emerged may bear formulation before reading the essays. There is clearly a trend towards using fiscal and financial measures to facilitate national-level policy making in all the countries. The importance of politics and policy is underscored by the fact that the search for new ways to make national urban policy has not in all cases been accompanied by the expected increase in funds from the center. In this sense, some national-urban systems are more "controlled" than others, but not simply by size of transfer. One might leap to generalization at this point were it not that the micro-level studies also show the diversity of decision making within cities in the countries. Dependence on national resources may mean only that cities become more ingenious in finding ways to evade, modify, and influence national guidelines and requirements. On the whole, it appears that the European systems are better at doing this than are those of the United States and Japan.

The politics of urban policy making appears to be more a question of how resources are transformed on their way to urban governments than of the simple correspondence of partisan interest and resource use that was once postulated. Several things that have happened become apparent in the essays. The "distance" between cities and national government has increased rather than diminished with the growth of cities. In most cases cities now have much larger bureaucracies than national governments, and the sheer multiplication of decisions estranges cities from states. Until recently the influence of the agrarian sector kept cities off the national agenda, and national governments could resist urban demands and needs by balancing one sector against the other. The political game has now changed and cities find themselves working together across partisan lines in order to extract resources from the central government. At the micro-level, the diverse and often urgent needs of cities means that local partisan interests are not easily fitted into the massive and intricate problems confronting metropolitan areas. The intervention of national government itself tends to remove many of the most controversial distributive decisions from the cities. The politics of parties thus tends to gravitate toward the politics of policy making (part 1).

The politics of resources is an important—possibly the crucial—component in the growing complexity of intergovernmental relationships between cities and central government. Perhaps the turn of the century municipal reformers have achieved their objective of nonpartisan city government for reasons they did not anticipate. The early restrictions on urban control of resources were, of course, the limits placed on municipal enterprise by nearly all the governments studied in the volume. As national government took on the large task of redistributing income with economic growth, it claimed more elastic, progressive taxes. It seems unlikely that the clamor for a more elastic urban fiscal base to urban government will reverse this trend. The paradoxical effect of this transformation has been that politics within cities has not changed very much. Mayors still struggle with diverse, programmatic offers of support and thus become manipulators at a slightly higher level of politics; but they are relatively confined in reordering the political alignment within cities (parts 1 and 3). Local political mobilization does not appear to influence the politics of policy making in significant ways.

Though the participants in the Cornell conference would no doubt interpret these events in different ways, we are commonly indebted to a number of groups for help in making the conference possible. The Council for European Studies provided a generous grant. The Japan Foundation made it possible for us to include in our discussion one of the most urban of industrial nations, one often left out of comparative studies. The Canadian government provided support for several participants from that country. The Western Societies Program of Cornell University also provided support. The Program considers that there is much more to be learned by encouraging American scholars to compare their work with the experience of other industrial democracies, especially in the study of key elements in the policy-making process such as the allocation of resources. We hope that the results will persuade others to do the same.

Douglas E. Ashford, Director
Western Societies Program
Cornell University
July 1979

National Resources and Urban Policy

CHAPTER 1

INTRODUCTION

Douglas E. Ashford

A volume based on how national resources influence cities should begin by considering why this question has become important politically. The simple economic truism that there are no free lunches does not help much, nor would most economists be happy with this reduction of their elaborate concepts and theories. The explanation, in the first instance, must be an historical one. Until the rapid industrialization of the past generation, cities were more homogeneous and self-confined units of government. National governments have always placed constraints on urban finance and determined the acceptable forms of local taxation. In the late nineteenth century the reorganized British local government system explicitly stated that municipal loans could not be used to compete with commercial enterprises, and France took similar measures to curb municipal enterprises in the 1920s. But urban services were much smaller and the social costs of industrial infrastructure were not thought of as part of the price of running cities. Two forces gave the resource problem priority. First, the rapid urbanization of society made the costs more visible and the cities more influential in national politics. The countryside could less easily be played against the cities, and the importance of urban services to industrial growth became unmistakable. Second, national economic policy became inextricably entwined in the fiscal and financial calculations of the cities. As the measures to stabilize economies, provide jobs, and stimulate industrial growth became national problems, national policy converged with urban policy.

In all the countries discussed in this book there has been lively debate about why the government does not have an "urban policy." What is meant by this phrase depends a great deal on where one decides to put the emphasis. There are in fact a multitude of urban policies involved in, say, housing, education, and roads. To determine whether a government needs an overall urban guideline, as suggested by Moynihan (1970), or whether urban policies are so diverse and complex as to escape generalization (Banfield 1970) is not the major purpose of this book. Even in countries providing much more assistance to cities than the United States, one can find numerous complaints that the national government has not decided what to do about cities (Pahl 1970; Crozier et al. 1974).[1] Another way of thinking about urban policies is to ask how the bargaining relationship among levels of government is influenced by systems of taxation and financing local investment. If cities are indeed "unwalled" (Long 1972), perhaps it is misleading to adhere too closely to an older version of urban studies that saw cities as readily separated from national politics and economic policy. Put differently, so long as cities are seen as discrete units of government providing specific services, it may not even be possible to formulate a more general theory of how government and cities interact in an advanced industrial society.

Nearly a decade ago Campbell and Burkhead (1968, p. 638) showed that in the United States the question is not so much that the nation lacks an urban policy but that it has an array of crucially important issues concentrated in cities. So long as governments could easily separate these issues, there were not only multiple urban policies but also no need to examine, from a policy perspective, what cities were about. Urban policies were indeed subject to the marketplace (Mollenkopf 1975), but there was also no pressure to deal globally with their resource problems. Perhaps more important, until societies became more uniformly urbanized, there was no mechanism making generalization about resource problems possible. The interlocking services provided by cities produced the functional specialization (Liebert 1976) that in turn made investments more readily identifiable and their financing more difficult. Many services could no longer be provided economically by individual cities; and water, sewage, and roads, to name a few services, became regional or were managed by groups of cities. As the operating and capital costs of cities became more visible, it is hardly surprising that distribution of these costs became a political issue, and one that by definition could not be resolved at the level of cities. The emergence of the welfare state was based on enlarging indirect taxation and creating an elastic tax base. Thus the reallocation of national revenues and the provision of national credit to cities inescapably

---

[1]In all these countries there was in the 1960s a wave of literature on regions and regional policy, much of which was in fact a national government device to avoid the problems of cities. Reorganization being so time consuming and difficult, governments turned to regions to undertake "rational" planning. With the growth of cities the distinction, except for rural and depressed areas, has gradually slipped away. Hall, et al. (1973) have persuasively argued that Britain actually undertook to avoid the formation of metropolitan areas. French regional policy was initially a Gaullist device to overcome centrifugal tendencies, and similar preoccupations with rational problem solving are detectable in the American literature.

became a formulation of how nations would respond to the new urban environment. The "urban fiscal crisis" is only the most recent chapter in this development; it can be traced to the economic dislocations of the past few years and will no doubt continue in years to come.

While the contributors to this volume do not pretend that a collective work can provide an entirely persuasive theory of how these changes might be studied, it is felt that the emphasis given to urban resources holds the key to building better theories about policy making for cities and states. The existing theories about resource allocation are global and abstract. The choice between the marketplace and class conflict as a way of deciding how resources should be allocated is not a happy one, nor is it very useful in actually deciding what governments at any level should do. The neomarxists have done a great deal to make their social theory relevant to urban questions (Castells 1972; Lojkine 1975, 1977; Pickvance 1977), but the identification of conflict is not the same as specifying what real governments can do or how persistent problems might be dealt with. Nor does the "monocentric" tradition of liberal theories about government (Gregg 1974) seem much better suited to disentangling the use of resources in modern states. To move in the direction of market solutions is not only unacceptable in many modern welfare states, but it is impossible where, as often happens in housing, diverse national policies have virtually eliminated anything similar to a free market situation. Interorganizational analysis also becomes an alternative, but it says little about the parameters of policy making and how policy change might take place. For these reasons, the feeling expressed in this book is that the relationship between national and local governments requires reformulation. One of the least explored issues is how the exchange of resources among levels of government is influenced.

Those who might hope to disentangle the resource problem by using economics are likely to be disappointed. Economists have been aware of the complex problem of transfers among and within governments for many years, well before the transfer problem became a political and social issue. (See, for example, Burkhead 1975; Schmandt & Goldbach 1969.) The counter-cyclical effects of local spending and investment were a critical issue in the application of Keynesian analysis to national spending (Hansen & Perloff 1944). Urban economics is a highly developed discipline,[2] but it has the same problems of dealing with the aggregate estimates in micro-terms that often complicate political and social analysis. (See Margolis 1965; Perloff & Wingo 1968; and Crecine 1970.) The clearest example is the early work on local and state spending (Braser 1959), which

---

[2]Much of the early economists' work such as Sacks and Harris (1964) and Moneypenny (1960) concentrated on the demand structure of local government and has a direct link to the state and local analysis of Dye (1966) and Sharkansky (1970). The more structural economic analysis leads into the similarly designed political analysis of the relationship between reformed urban government and politics, in particular Hawley (1973) and Hayes (1973).

provided the model for the aggregate analysis undertaken by Dye, Sharkansky, and others. Some of the urban economists have indeed concentrated on structural questions such as the economic performance of different types of city government (Campbell & Sacks 1967); but these, like politically oriented community studies, are generally confined to a single level of government.

The most important theme of this book is how resources are affected as they move among levels of government, most often from the center (capital) to cities. Economists have usually been most interested in performance at a single level only, while policy and outcomes are in fact the result of an intricate exchange of information, influence, and goals among a variety of levels of government. Indeed, an economist's critique of one of the famous contributions to the micro-economics of urban spending (Tiebout 1956) notes that it lacks "specification of a political process by which the government policies are formed" (Margolis 1968, p. 548). Every set of aggregate spending figures available for the modern industrial nations shows local spending advancing at a rate higher than national spending, but the explanation of how and why this happens is not satisfactory. The dependence is quite clear (see, for example, Burkhead 1975), but whether dependence is being used to the advantage of the center or the cities remains very unclear. How one approaches this question depends, like most empirical research, on the values and definitions that are presupposed.

Are the political and social theories much better? Unlike the economists, other social scientists are not even decided on the appropriate unit of analysis. In this book units of government are studied. The behavioral vogue of the past decade has tended to concentrate on the individual. The behavioral assumptions of social and political theory appear neatly opposed, but neither is particularly helpful in dealing with problems of intergovernmental relations such as resource allocation. In most sociological theories, and most clearly in the neomarxist ones, the major criterion becomes need. The movement of income and spending in the social fabric should be influenced to see that all persons receive minimal, sometimes equivalent, support. Putting aside the enormous problems of actually calculating what *minimal* or *equivalent* means, the notion that this is not what is happening is hard to defend. Most resource transfers, for example, are linked to specific needs and came about historically to pay for services and benefits that cities could not pay for. The growth of transfers to lower levels of government is perhaps the best demonstration that the modern democracies have a strong commitment to redistribution. The income effects of transfers are also counter to the neomarxist argument. Where local governments are confined to a generally regressive tax base, most notably in Britain, the transfers convert the overall tax effects to be progressive. If one looks closely at the history of grants and transfers, at least in Britain, France, and the United States, it is also hard to argue that socialist or progressive cities were more willing than conservative ones to enact or to demand more progressive local taxes. Though it may be correct to say that economic decision making and industrial organization are no longer rooted in the urban structure (O'Connor 1973), it is also true that the cities themselves contributed to these structural dislocations. Mayors do not enjoy levying taxes and so national governments do so. Where equalization of individual treatment exists in cities, it is largely due to the indirect taxes that national governments collect and then try to redistribute on equity or need principles.

One of the striking paradoxes of the behavioral revolution, at least in American political science, is how similar its interpretation of political behavior is to the sociologist's interpretation of social behavior. Again, the methodological requirements were more easily fulfilled with the development of survey research and attitudinal studies, so that the emphasis was on individual participation and perception of the political process. Valuable as the literature in political behavior has been, it was divorced from the performance of political systems and had little to say about conflict within government. The Eastonian black box (the designation of government in the political system) went unopened. The local level counterpart to this model, the famous community power controversy, went more or less unchallenged until Clark, a sociologist, began to ask about national influences on community power structure (Clark 1974). The political analysis of national economic and budgetary problems, pioneered by Wildavsky (1964), was initially rooted in the incrementalist view of government and confined to studies of national decisions. The early interest in policy analysis (1) tended to concentrate on how demands on government are aggregated and (2) assumed that if the right demands were made, then government would deliver the goods (Sailsbury 1968). Somehow the idea that we are "semi-sovereign" people (Schattschneider 1960) went virtually unnoticed until policy studies came back into fashion a few years ago. The overall effect was that the internal workings of government seemed to have little to do with politics; and, thereby, the immense influence of government and administration on allocating resources among and within levels of government was not pertinent to the discipline. The present volume is only part of a growing literature that has begun to redress this imbalance.

Theories about intergovernmental relations and the resource allocation issue, in particular, are likely to be slow to emerge because we have not explored the complexity of the problem. In social science language, it is difficult to select a promising dependent variable from the array of events and relationships until something is known about the intricacy of these events and relationships. One of the messages of this book is that there is great variance among the ways that national governments go about controlling and influencing how cities obtain a share of the national pie. In absolute terms, the magnitude of dependence varies from the high of Britain and France, which provide respectively about 45 and 40 percent of local revenues from national taxes, to the lows of Germany and the United States, which provide roughly a fourth of local (urban) revenues.[3] No sooner does one embark on the systemic comparison than do the intrasystemic differences begin to loom in importance and threaten to wipe out the more easily established explanations. (See Price 1968.) No two countries, for example, could have more different territorial divisions than Britain, now with about 450 local governments, and France, with over 36,000 (actually, 2,000 account for two-thirds of the population). Similarly, a simple time series shows that Germany has managed to keep the transfer to lower levels fairly constant for the past thirty years, while in the United States the national government was providing only about 10 percent of local and state revenues in 1950. The essays in part 1 of the present volume (Anton, Bacharach, and Boast) describe the intricacy of internal relationships in the United States.

The level of transfer suggests some interesting hypotheses. For example, the countries that are most generous with national revenues in supporting cities are those where the national politics tend to be polarized.[4] France has been governed by the Gaullist and now centrist coalition for twenty years. Since World War II, Japan has had nothing but liberal government. Britain is polarized around urban problems in a different way, but the concentration of Labour support in the cities tends to make urban policy, and particularly the grant system, an instrument of political competition at Westminster. Contrary to the neomarxist view, it may be the exclusion of progressive parties at higher levels of government that brings about readiness for national government to share resources with lower levels of government. This is not to say that the latent social conflict is not present but only that from a policy perspective one does not need to introduce it in order to see how governments respond to cities. These questions are taken up in part 2 of this volume, which deals with national constraints on urban resources (Ashford, Ball, Reissert, and Muramatsu and Aqua). Again, the suggestion is that within the transfer process itself one can detect important political variations. The German government must try to deal with the constitutional limitations on the spatial redistribution of resources, and it encounters provincial politics very different from those of France or the United States. A basic distinction introduced here is whether control will be focused on capital or current spending,

---

[3]Now that revenue sharing has become a political football game, we may forget that it was initially conceived as a macro-economic device for finely tuning the economy. (See Heller et al. 1968.) It was, of course, eventually accepted by President Nixon in hopes of reducing urban influence on national politics (Dommel 1974), but it has become part of the urban presence in the federal system that now will probably never be reduced.

[4]There are, of course, important differences in the division of functions among levels of government that influence such aggregate figures. Nonetheless, the intriguing fact is that, even with formal differences in intergovernmental relationships, growth has been so marked. For additional aggregate cross-national comparison, see Ashford 1978.

which may not be simply a function of the size of the transfer but of how national policy makers choose to implement national economic policy.

The most difficult aspect of the resource transfer problem is how to generalize about the immense number of agencies and programs that are involved in any decision process linking two or more levels of government. Germany and France, for example, have kept transfers at a fairly constant proportion of public spending for the past several decades, but they are also two of the European countries with extremely high spending on welfare and assistance.[5] Is it appropriate to consider only the decisions involved in intergovernmental relationships if one wishes to assess how lower levels bargain for resources, when large amounts may in fact be assigned to localities through important agencies outside government? Japan makes generous allocations to cities and is under severe pressure to give more, but it is much less willing to support welfare programs. A more progressive Britain provides a large share of urban revenues but does so within a relatively stiff set of controls on both current and capital spending.[6] Federal aid to American cities is distributed among 1,000 or more programs, more than double the number in the 1960s. Germany administers fifty-five special grant schemes to support the states, and France differentiates its loan subsidies *(subventions)* in more than a hundred ways and administers them through nine ministries (Intergroupe 1971; Grossman Report 1973).

Existing political theory is not very well suited to deal with such institutional and administrative variations within systems. With varying degrees of distress and delight, the trend toward more complex ways of transferring funds from one level of government to another has been observed by all shades of political opinion. The liberal response favors constructing a "polycentric" urban system that will, it is hoped, reproduce for public goods what the marketplace was to provide for private goods (Ostrom et al. 1961; Olson 1969). The frictions and favoritism of resource allocation are somehow to disappear after a more rational and visible way of assigning social costs is put in motion. The socialist response is more difficult to summarize and more limited among the available cases. Certainly, the periods of Labour party power in Britain have brought as much tinkering with the grant system as have Conservative governments; and, possibly unintentionally, it was Conservative reform

---

[5]The most extreme case appears to be Sweden, where two-thirds of local expenditure comes from the center. See Anton 1977. The other important case omitted from the present volume is Canada, where the transfer system underwent important structural changes in the 1960s. See Smiley 1974 and Maxwell 1974.

[6]The essay in this volume on France (chapter 5) relates only to capital expenditure because this is the most important means of control on local growth. The share of revenues is estimated from the transfer to French local government of the value-added tax (*versement représentatif de la taxe sur les salaires,* or VRTS) on municipal government transactions. (See Guerrier & Bauchard 1972, pp. 94–98.) As might be expected, this transfer has become the subject of a fierce debate between French mayors and Paris.

of the British transfers to local government that facilitated the redistributive use of the grants. There is little doubt that the Democratic
party in the United States is responsible for putting cities on the national
agenda (Gelfand 1975), but revenue sharing was a President Nixon proposal to simplify government (Dommel 1974). Clearly redistributive use
of transfers responds to the objectives of socialist values, but there also
remain a wide variety of ways in which equalization can be implemented, and the choice is often more purely a political advantage than
a value decision. Put differently, within any goal of the transfer structure, there are many ways of seeing that funds respond to their alleged
purposes. The politically determined variation introduced in implementation may even cancel out the initial aims of programs. Part 3 of this
volume (Shefter, Feldman and Milch, Young, and Elkin) sets forth different ways of trying to come to grips with the complexity of decision
processes.

In the language of comparative politics, systemic similarities or differences among countries are meaningful only when it can be shown that
internal variations are roughly alike. The same logic can be applied to each
step of disaggregation in an effort to establish causal links among the
internal variations of governments (Ashford 1975; Prezworski & Teune
1970). For the more general needs of either a liberal- or socialist-inspired
theory, a nominal or directional measurement is often sufficient to study
broad social or political changes. For a policy analysis this does not seem
enough, yet how to go beyond case studies is still not clear. Put differently,
in order to understand the internal interactions of levels of government,
it is important to know whether two countries are moving in the same
direction in different or similar ways. The value differences that separate
the major political and social theories do not help much with the "how"
of governmental decision making. At the abstract level of controversy this
may not matter, but at the empirical application of the theories it matters
a great deal. Both the United States and France, for example, are divided
into a large number of municipal and local units of government. The
allegedly more liberal orientation of American cities, however, has not
made the allocation of social costs easier, even though the highly ar-
ticulated system would suggest a market solution might work. In contrast,
the territorial complexity of France has facilitated the intricate system of
coalitions and bargaining between elected and administrative officials
who, in turn, influence how loans and grants will be forthcoming. Oddly
enough, except for differences about the departmental prefect, the
proposals for local reform of both the left and right in France look remarkably alike.

Where to apply logical and empirical rigor is, of course, in the first
instance an intuitive problem. Assembling these papers was initially in-
spired by the contributors' feeling that resources are likely to become not
only the most controversial issue about cities in the future but also part of

the common language of discourse in urban studies. The simple reason is that none of the advanced industrial states now denies the importance of urban problems on the national political agenda. That one should now speak of the "captive" city (Harloe 1975) after nearly a century of struggle to get political recognition of urban problems is curious in itself. When the first wave of American urbanists descended on Washington during the New Deal, they found President Roosevelt preoccupied with winning the farm vote (Gelfand 1975, pp. 10–25). A generation later the reform mayors like Lee of New Haven and Lawrence of Pittsburgh were still fighting to have national recognition. Urban renewal was the wedge in the door, but in 1959 its appropriation of $300 million was no more than the support for potatoes (Gelfand 1975, p. 288). The combined charm and guile of President Kennedy could not make a place at the cabinet table for cities. It required an astute political manipulator, President Johnson, to create a Department of Housing and Urban Development; and not until the Housing Act of 1972 was there a statutory provision for "the establishment of a national urban growth policy" (Wingo 1972).

Much the same story can be told of the other countries considered in this volume. For two decades after the war a succession of British committees and inquiries were entangled in boundary disputes in hopes of simplifying local government (Wiseman 1970). In a few months, an impetuous minister, Crossman, put the structural issue on the agenda[7] (Jones 1966). In 1969 another step was made by organizing a giant ministry, the Department of the Environment, which became and remains a loosely connected agency composed on older housing, transportation, regional, and local government ministries (Draper 1977). In France the Ministère de l'Equipement emerged in 1966 from a stormy fight among elite groups within the French civil service (Thoenig 1973), and in the most recent change of government it has had environment added to its responsibilities. Like many federal systems, Germany's national government has restricted taxation powers, and an intricate constitutional evasion was worked out to help cities through transfers to the states (Rothweiler 1972; Weiler 1972). In a conservative Japan, the Home Ministry is embarrassed by its own procedure for calculating the "excess burden" of urban spending.

The underlying message of this book, then, is that the politics of policy formation and implementation may be more important to cities than what cities themselves decide. The social differences and political diversity within cities may have done less to produce a national urban policy than the historic trend toward a more homogeneously urban society. Policy making establishes its own imperatives, and these are as much a function

---

[7]These hopes were dashed when the reorganization law actually fell to the Conservatives (see Ashford 1976). One of the fascinating consistencies in the struggle to link national and urban policy has been the tendency for major structural changes to be made by the more conservative party, though this varies greatly with type of party and electoral system.

of the national political system as of the aggregated character of urban government and politics. The reasons for this are outlined in part 1 of this volume: the multiple ways that political actors can indeed influence the implementation of urban funds (chapter 2); the diverse resource base of cities and towns (chapter 3); and the external economic constraints that are placed on cities (chapter 4).

The political environment of cities is found in various levels of policy making, which can be most easily summarized in the politics of resource allocation. Part 2 is more distinctly comparative than part 1, looking at how institutional variations among systems may account for the pattern of resource allocation. If national influence over resources is growing, it is then important to specify more clearly how such influence is exercised. This part describes: the interlocking use of funds and loans to align local investments with national policy objectives in France (chapter 5); the primary concern of Britain with national economic policy leading to a "stop and go" policy toward local borrowing (chapter 6); the intricate system of federal relationships in Germany requiring more astute federal bargaining (chapter 7); and the growth of protest combined with soaring urban costs in Japan that fixes attention on national politics (chapter 8). Each country has had peculiar ways of "nationalizing" urban problems.

The most difficult conceptual and methodological step is how to link differences within decision processes to national policy. Part 3 is no more than a first attempt to do so, viewing several specific decisions affecting cities through a policy lens. To sort them along the lines of the national constraints on urban policy with any reliability would require many more case studies. But cases remain our best way of determining the key actors in decisions. In the New York financial crisis the power of the urban bureaucracy reasserts itself (chapter 9); in the construction of airports the ability of cities to form coalitions with their hinterland appears crucial (chapter 10); in Greater London the conflicting roles of inner and outer borough leaders and officials produces a failure of housing policy (chapter 11); and in the United States the changing relationship of racial conflict to urban policy appears crucial (chapter 12). Cases are essential if we are to link national contraints on urban resources to political actors and roles; but it is only through cases that we can see how successfully lower levels of government can evade, divert, and perhaps change the resource constraints that are being imposed by higher levels of government. The more general theories about social and political change have difficulties explaining the patterns of reciprocity and conflict found in real decisions and outcomes. As more research of this kind is done, we might design a more satisfactory, policy-based theory of how cities deal with resource constraints in a highly urbanized society. Some suggestions along these lines will be provided in the volume's concluding chapter.

REFERENCES

Anderson, Martin. 1976. *The federal bulldozer.* New York: McGraw-Hill.

Anton, Tom. 1977. Governing Greater Stockholm: A study of policy development and system change. Berkeley and Los Angeles: University of California Press.

Ashford, Douglas E. 1975. Theories of local government: Some comparative considerations. *Comparative Political Studies* 8 (April): 90–107.

———. 1976. *The limits of consensus.* Center for International Studies, Western Societies Occasional Paper no. 6. Ithaca, N.Y.: Cornell University Press.

———. Territory vs equality: Politics and policy choice in the modern state. *Political studies,* forthcoming.

Banfield, Edward C. 1970. *The unheavenly city.* Boston: Little, Brown.

Braser, H. E. 1959. *City expenditures in the United States.* Washington, D.C.: National Bureau of Economic Research.

Burkhead, Jesse. 1975. The political economy of urban America: National urban policy revisited. In G. Gappert and H. M. Rose, eds. *The social economy of cities,* pp. 49–68. Beverly Hills, Calif.: Sage.

Burkhead, Jesse, and Miner, Jerry. 1971. *Public expenditure.* Chicago: Aldine.

Campbell, Alan K., and Burkhead, Jesse. 1968. Public policy for urban America. In H. Perloff and L. Wingo, eds. *Issues in urban economics,* pp. 577–649.

Campbell, A. K., and Sacks, Seymour. 1967. *Metropolitan America: Fiscal patterns and governmental systems.* New York: Free Press.

Castells, Manuel. 1972. *La question urbaine.* Paris: Maspero.

Clark, T., ed. 1974. *Comparative community politics.* New York: Halsted.

Connery, Robert H., and Leach, Richard H. 1960. *The federal government and metropolitan America.* Cambridge: Harvard University Press.

Crecine, J. P., ed. 1970. *Financing the metropolis: Public policy and urban economics.* Beverly Hills, Calif.: Sage.

Crozier, Michel, et al. 1974. *Où va l'administration française?* Paris: Editions d'Organisation.

Dommel, P. 1974. *The politics of revenue sharing.* Bloomington: Indiana University Press.

Draper, Paul. 1977. *Creation of the DOE.* London: Civil Service Department, HMSO.

Dye, Thomas R. 1966. *Politics, economics, and the public policy outcomes in the American states.* Chicago: Rand McNally.

Gelfand, Mark. 1975. *A nation of cities:* The federal government in urban America. New York: Oxford University Press.

Gregg, Phillip M. 1974. Limits and levels of analysis: A problem policy analysis in federal systems. *Publius* 4 (fall): 59–85.

Grossman Report. 1973. Les possibilités offertes aux collectivités locales en matière de ressources financières externes (subventions et emprunts). *Journal Officiel* (July 31), pp. 527–51.

Guerrier, P., and Bauchard, D. 1972. *Economie financière des collectivités locales.* Paris: Colin.

Hall, Peter, et al. 1973. *The containment of urban England.* London: Allen & Unwin.

Hansen, N., and Perloff, H. S. 1944. *State and local finance in the national economy.* New York: Norton.

Harloe, M., ed. 1975. *Captive cities.* New York: Wiley.

Hawley, Willis D. 1973. *Non-partisan elections and the case for party politics.* New York: Wiley.

Hayes, S. P. 1973. The politics of reform in municipal government in the reform era. In D. Gordon, ed. *Social change and urban politics.* Englewood Cliffs, N.J.: Prentice-Hall.

Heller, Walter W., et al. 1968. *Revenue sharing and the city.* Baltimore: Johns Hopkins University Press & Resources for the Future.

Intergroupe d'Etude des Finances Locales. 1971. *Rapport.* Paris: Commisariat Générale du Plan.

Jones, G. W. 1966. Mr. Grossman and the reform of local government, 1964–1966. *Parliamentary Affairs* 20: 77–89.

Liebert, R. J. 1976. *Disintegration and political action: The changing functions of city governments in America.* New York: Academic Press.

Lojkine, Jean. 1975. Stratégies de grandes entreprises, politiques urbaines, et mouvements sociaux urbains. *Sociologie du Travail* 12: 18–40.

———. 1977. L'Etat et l'urbain: Contributions à une analyse matérialiste des politiques urbaines dans les pays capitalistes développés. *International Journal of Urban and Regional Research* 1 (June): 256–71.

Long, Norton. 1972. *The unwalled city.* New York: Basic Books.

Margolis, Julius. 1968. The demand for urban public services. In H. S. Perloff and L. Wingo, eds. *Issues in urban economics,* pp. 527–64. Baltimore: Johns Hopkins Press.

Margolis, Julius, ed. 1965. *The public economy of urban communities.* Baltimore: Johns Hopkins University Press & Resources for the Future.

Martin, Roscoe. 1965. *The cities and the federal system.* New York: Atherton.

Maxwell, J. A. 1974. Federal grants in Canada, Australia and the United States. *Publius* 4 (summer): 63–75.

Mollenkopf, J. H. 1975. The post-war politics of urban development. *Politics and Society* 5: 257–85.

Moneypenny, Phillip. 1960. Federal grants-in-aid to state governments: A political analysis. *National Tax Journal* 13 (March): 1–16.

Moynihan, D. P., ed. 1970. *Toward a national urban policy.* New York: Basic Books.

O'Connor, James. 1973. *The fiscal crisis of the state.* New York: St. Martin's Press.

Olson, Mancur, Jr. 1969. The principle of "financial equivalency": The division of responsibility among different levels of government. *American Economic Review* 59 (May): 479–87.

Ostrom, V.; Tiebout, C. M.; and Warren, R. 1961. The organization of government in metropolitan areas: A theoretical inquiry. *American Political Science Review* 55: 831–42.

Pahl, R. E. 1970. *Whose city?* Harmondsworth, Middlesex: Penguin Books.

Perloff, H. S., and Wingo, Lowdon, eds. 1968. *Issues in urban economics.* Baltimore: Johns Hopkins Press.

Pickvance, C. G. 1977. Marxist approaches to the study of urban politics: Divergences among some recent French writers. *International Journal of Urban and Regional Research* 1 (June): 219–55.

Prezworski, A., and Teune, H. 1970. *The logic of social inquiry.* New York: Wiley.

Price, D. 1968. Micro- and macro-politics: Notes on a research strategy. In O. Garceau, ed. *Political research and political theory,* pp. 102–40. Cambridge: Harvard University Press.

Rothweiler, Robert L. 1972. Revenue sharing and the Federal Republic of Germany. *Publius* 2 (spring): 4–25.

Sacks, Seymour, and Harris, Robert. 1964. The determinants of state and local expenditures and intergovernmental flows of funds. *National Tax Journal* 17, no. 1 (March): 75–85.

Sailsbury, R. 1968. The analysis of public policy: A search for theories and roles. In A. Ranney, ed. *Political science and public policy.* Chicago: Markham.

Schattschneider, E. E. 1960. *Semi-sovereign people.* New York: Holt, Rinehart & Winston.

Schmandt, Henry J., and Goldbach, John C. 1969. The urban paradox. In H. J. Schmandt and Warner Bloomberg, Jr., eds. *The quality of urban life.* Beverly Hills, Calif.: Sage.

Sharkansky, Ira, ed. 1970. *Policy analysis in political science.* Chicago: Markham.

Smiley, Donald V. 1974. Federal-provincial conflict in Canada. *Publius* 8 (summer): 8–24.

Thoenig, Jean-Claude. 1973. *L'ère des technocrates.* Paris: Editions d'Organisation.

Tiebout, C. M. 1956. A pure theory of local expenditure. *Journal of Political Economy* 64, no. 5 (October): 416–24.

Weiler, Conrad J., Jr. 1972. Metropolitan reorganization in West Germany. *Publius* 2 (spring): 26–68.

Wildavsky, Aaron. 1964. *The politics of the budgetary process.* Boston: Little, Brown.

Wingo, Lowdon. 1972. Issues in a national urban development strategy for the United States. *Urban Studies* 8 (February): 3–27.

Wiseman, H. Victor, ed. 1970. *Local government in England, 1958–69.* London: Routledge & Kegan Paul.

PART I

POLITICS, POLICY, AND URBAN RESOURCES IN THE UNITED STATES

The papers in this part provide a profile on how resource allocation takes place in the United States and indicate that the political environment of transferring funds to cities is much more complex than our general theories recognize. The aggregate division of resources among levels of government is rarely a single, rationally calculated decision. The interlocking features of the private and public sectors are found at every level of government; and the distinction in the United States, as in most of Europe and Japan, has begun to lose its meaning. The ability of cities and towns to complement external assistance varies immensely. Neither the conventional social categories nor the political models fit well with the interdependence of resources among levels of government and within local governments. In building a theory that better encompasses the complexities of resource allocation in the modern democratic state, a first step is to grasp the variability of these relationships.

CHAPTER 2

FEDERAL ASSISTANCE PROGRAMS: THE POLITICS OF SYSTEM TRANSFORMATION

Thomas J. Anton

The United States is in the midst of a major transformation of the institutional relationships that historically have defined its pattern of delivering and funding public services. When the much publicized fiscal crisis of New York City first became headline news several years ago, it was still reasonable to believe that New York was an exception in its financial practices and difficulties. Massive federal government loans to prevent bankruptcy and the creation of a new state agency—the Municipal Assistance Corporation, known popularly as "Big MAC"—to monitor and supervise the New York City budget could also be reasonably viewed as measures of unusual severity, rarely utilized in a political system committed to the independence of local units of government.[1] Although severe, these measures nevertheless have not "solved" the crisis: New York's fiscal problems continue to grace our front pages, giving rise to considerable speculation about the deeper causes of crisis and increasing popular recognition that many other cities now confront financial problems that differ from the New York problem only in degree, not in kind. According to one current estimate, fully 40 percent (196) of the 489 American cities of over 50,000 persons suffer from above-average conditions of "urban hardship" (Nathan & Dommel 1979). And, despite the apparent "severity" of the measures taken in New York, they reflect what now seem countrywide changes in relationship between lower and higher level units.

Figure 2-1 (lower graph) displays the national dimensions of changes in these institutional relationships. The local government share of domestic expenditures from own funds (i.e., excluding transfer payments) has

---

[1]Aron and Brecher (1976) offer useful views of the New York situation. The same holds true for an earlier work of Brecher on federal, state, and local finances (1974).

Figure 2-1   Graph 1: *Federal Grants-in-Aid as a Percentage of State-Local Receipts from Own Sources, 1960–1977 (in billions of dollars); and* Graph 2: *Growing Federal Role in Domestic Public Sector[d] (percentage distribution)*

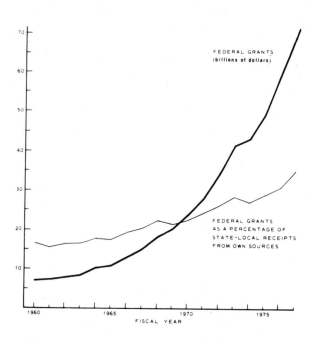

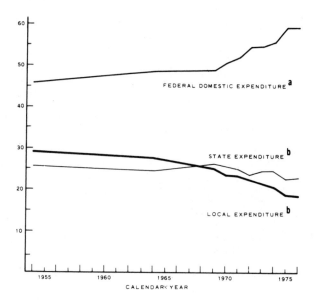

steadily declined for the past quarter century and now amounts to only 18.3 percent of total domestic spending. The state government share of domestic expenditures also has declined, but less markedly, amounting to 22.7 percent of the estimated 1976 total. If we exclude domestic spending by the federal government, the state government share of total state-local spending in fact increases considerably, from 46.7 percent in 1964 to 55.5 percent in 1976. Measured either as a fraction of total domestic spending or as a fraction of only state and local spending, then, local government expenditures from own-source revenue are now dramatically less significant than they once were. State government spending has come to dominate the state and local sector in what appears to be a steady centralization of taxing and spending decisions into state houses and away from city halls. If New York City appears unable to keep pace with requirements for increased spending, other local units seem similarly affected. If the state of New York has assumed increased responsibility for city affairs, so too have other state governments.

Important as they are, these trends are clearly overshadowed by the single most striking revelation of figure 2-1 (upper graph), which is the extraordinary increase in federal government grants-in-aid to state and local governments. Less than $3 billion in 1954, only $7 billion in 1960, and climbing to $24 billion in 1970, federal aid is estimated to be $72.4 billion in 1977: nearly a fivefold increase in the past decade alone (ACIR 1977d, p. 20). Indeed, the increase in federal aid between fiscal year (FY) 1976 and 1977—some $13.4 billion—is more than the *total* amount of federal aid as recently as 1966. At these levels and at these rates of increase, federal grants have come to dominate state and local revenue systems. Federal funds are now the largest single source of state-local revenues (20 percent), exceeding sales and gross receipts taxes (19 per-

Source: ACIR staff compilation based on U.S. Department of Commerce, Bureau of Economic Analysis, *Benchmark Revision of National Income and Products Accounts: Advanced Tables, March 1976; Budget of the United States Government,* various years; and ACIR staff estimates.
[a]Excludes federal expenditure for national defense, international affairs and finance, space research and technology, and the estimated portion of net interest attributable to these functions. Includes Social Security (OASDHI) and all federal aid to state and local governments including General Revenue Sharing payments.
[b]The National Income and Products Accounts do not report state and local government data separately. The state-local expenditure totals (National Income Accounts) were allocated among levels of government on the basis of ratios (by year) reported by the U.S. Bureau of the Census in the governmental finance series.
[c]Partially estimated.
[d]National Income and Products Accounts.

cent), the property tax (18 percent), and the income tax (11 percent) (ACIR 1976, p. 34). Federal grants already amount to 35.3 percent of state and local receipts from own-source revenues, with no foreseeable end to this remarkable outflow of dollars from Washington to lower level governments. The federal government obviously has become the major "bank" for state and local activities, not just in New York but all across the country. Just as obviously, these trends are structural in character and national in scope, however much of our attention has tended to be focused on one major city.

How are we to explain changes of such magnitude? At a very general level, simple observation of the most important categories of federal and state transfers suggests that the increasing pace of fiscal centralization is directly related to equalization efforts. By far the largest "chunks" of federal assistance moneys are devoted to income maintenance, medical insurance, and a variety of welfare and education programs designed to help equalize individual resources (ACIR 1976, pp. 18–23). State assistance programs, similarly, are largely aimed at resource inequalities among school districts, although many other state aid programs, less concerned with equalization, also exist (ACIR 1977c, ch. 1). Using these observations, we might construct an "explanation" that would attribute fiscal centralization to the salience of inequality as a political issue in the past decade, the difficulty lower level units have in dealing explicitly with that issue, and the consequent shift of responsibility upward to higher level governments. We might then seek to examine the "centralization-equalization" relationship in other industrialized nations in an effort to generate a more widely applicable explanation.

Apart from the fact that the data necessary to support such an explanation do not now exist, this entirely plausible set of speculations suffers from two serious flaws. One is vagueness. "Equality" does not just appear out of thin air as an issue; it is proposed and defined by actors, acting for themselves or in organizational roles that permit their proposals to be considered; and the proposals themselves are ultimately translated into programs that, over time, do or do not work to achieve objectives, according to procedures that become more-or-less important in deciding whether and how to continue such programs. These relationships, and the ways they change through time, all would have to be specified in order to give meaning to this kind of explanation. Achieving greater specificity, of course, would require a more explicit theoretical model than has yet been stated. The second and more serious flaw, in fact, is precisely the uncritical acceptance of an *implicit* theoretical model that focuses on problem-solving rationality as the preferred model of explanation. By directing attention to political or program goals (i.e., equality), this model leads us to look for problems in some environment as the cause of action, and at actor intentions as the relevant data *to explain programs.* [2] Intentions and

---

[2] I have elsewhere analyzed the deficiencies of these views (Anton 1976).

goals are surely relevant, but verbal or written program statements may not be the best way to discover them, particularly if changes as large and as rapid as those noted above are occurring.

What we need, obviously, is an explanation or explanations less global in scope, capable of comprehending both change through time and the specific actors, organizations, and programs that structure the character of institutional change. That kind of explanation, unhappily, has yet to be advanced, largely because we have only recently noticed the significance of the changes that have been gathering momentum for the past decade. To assert the lack of a persuasive explanation, however, is not to say that we lack fragments of explanations that have theoretical appeal. Lindbeck (1976), for example, recently has reminded us that there are good theoretical reasons to expect liberal democracies to increase public spending during election periods, an expectation fully borne out by our own recent fiscal history. We also know—or think we know—that Republicans and Democrats tend to spend money on different constituencies. Piven and Cloward (1971, pp. 248–84) and, more recently, Caraley (1976) demonstrate convincingly that Democrats in the White House and in Congress initiate programs that funnel federal funds into the city and urban-area constituencies that provide Democratic votes. Republicans shower their largesse on the midwestern and western small towns and rural areas that vote heavily Republican, as illustrated by General Revenue Sharing, a program that distributes annual allotments of federal funds to thousands of towns that had never before received any direct federal assistance because they were too small or too distant or too well off to care about such assistance (Nathan, Manvel & Calkins 1975). These ideas—let us think of them as fragments of macro-explanations, or macro-fragments—hardly constitute well-rounded theories, but the tendency of Democratic governments to increase spending around election time helps to account for public expenditure growth; and the differing expenditure foci of the major political parties help to account for some aspects of program design. These macro-fragments, in short, are useful if not comprehensive.

We can also identify a number of micro-fragments, of which the most familiar is the "pork barrel" model, in which federal aid programs are attributed to the desire of each congressional representative to generate as much federal spending in his/her district or state as possible.[3] By combining the pork barrel with congressional position, we arrive at a "positional influence" model, which attributes the distribution of federal aid to the ability of powerful committee chairmen to siphon abnormal amounts of federal funds into the districts they represent.[4] Another intriguing micro-fragment was recently offered by Beer (1976), who suggested that congressional representatives try, above all, to avoid being politically

---

[3] An interesting recent review of the venerable pork barrel can be found in an article by Murphy (1974). Equally interesting is Stockman's article on the social pork barrel (1975).
[4] An empirical assessment of this model can be found in Ritt (1976).

disadvantaged in the distribution of federal assistance. Since a major source of political disadvantage is inadequate access to federal money, representatives strive to achieve programs that distribute equal per capita amounts to each district, thus avoiding potentially embarrassing comparisons leading to attacks for failing to "bring home the bacon." Beer refers to this as "distributive localism" and shows its applicability to the passage of General Revenue Sharing, but it seems equally applicable to many other cases of congressional program design, including the recent enactment of a \$4 billion emergency unemployment package (*New York Times* 1977, p. 1).

These macro- and micro-fragments seem insightful in varying degrees, but their inadequacies are apparent. None of them explain why the rate of increase in government spending for *federal aid* should be so explosive, nor do they take us very far in understanding why federal spending should be disproportionately targeted on less-populous, more rural, and more wealthy states (ACIR 1977b). The Beer hypothesis seems clearly inconsistent with these biases in federal programs, while the "positional influence" thesis, which seems to explain why southern states have received so much federal aid, recently has been tested and found wanting by Ritt (1976). More fundamentally, perhaps, none of these fragments tells us much about the mechanisms through which programs are designed; funding is provided; and money is spent. Such mechanisms are preeminently bureaucratic rather than congressional in character. Understanding them is essential if we are to achieve a comprehensive view of federal assistance politics. California's ability to capture some 36 percent of total annual federal spending for social service grants (Derthick 1975), for example, would be quite incomprehensible without some knowledge of both program mechanics and the bureaucrats responsible for spending federal dollars.

Our current theoretical inadequacies suggest the wisdom of a cautious strategy in seeking to understand the meaning of the institutional transformation now under way in the United States. Whatever the "global" significance of these changes may turn out to be, it seems essential at this point to understand something about the temporal meanings attached to federal assistance programs by the actors responsible for bringing them into existence. We can identify these actors easily enough by observing specific programs. And we can find out something about real—as opposed to formal—goals by observing the manner in which these programs change through time. Disaggregating the notion of "system transformation" into specific program components and observing change in those components through time may reveal patterns of thought and behavior that tell us more about structural change than any of the theoretical fragments now available.

DIMENSIONS OF PROGRAM DESIGN

The most recent *Catalogue of Federal Domestic Assistance* lists some 1,030 different federal assistance programs; how are we to choose individual programs for detailed analysis from such a large number? Since we hope to illuminate the nature of program intentions, or goals, perhaps the best method is to select programs that illustrate the major design alternatives faced by policy makers when they create fiscal assistance programs for lower level units. Apart from goals, which for reasons that will become evident below would not constitute useful selection criteria, the design issue that has tended to dominate both bargaining sessions and public political debate during the recent period of federal grant explosion has been the issue of constraint.

Whatever the officially stated purposes of a given aid program, policy makers must determine the extent to which the program shall be constrained by various federal application, accounting, and reporting requirements, typically referred to as "strings." During the 1960s, when Democratic presidents enunciated hopes for reforming society, the principal mechanism for assisting in the achievement of such hopes was a federal grant to which many strings were attached: state or local governments were required to send in thick applications with twenty or thirty copies. If approved by a federal agency the recipient unit was typically required to set up strict accounting procedures to keep track of federal funds received and spent; and a variety of initial, intermediary, and final reports were required to be submitted to the relevant Washington agency. More than 400 new programs of this type were created during the 1960s (Walker 1977); and, because they were available only for carefully limited purposes, they came to be known as "project" or "categorical" grants (Walker 1977). Over time, the flowering of categorical grants led to increasingly widespread and vociferous complaints against the enormous quantity of paper and other procedural "red tape" generated by the strings in such programs.[5]

Program designers responded to these complaints by devising what have come to be known as "block grants," the first of which was enacted in 1966 (Stenberg 1977). Instead of tightly specified purposes, block grants are made available for broadly defined goals: "educational assistance" rather than "support for third grade curriculum development," for example. Instead of multiple applications to secure approval from a federal agency official, block grants typically make money available on the basis of a statutory formula that cannot be affected by bureaucratic action. Instead of multiple and continuing reports, block grants allow considerably more discretion to state and local officials in utilizing federal funds and

---

[5]Project grants allocated by formula, of course, reduced the level of competition and thus reduced paper work as well.

usually require little more than an initial statement (a plan) and a final report. Block grants, in short, contain many fewer "strings" than categoricals, and they presumably free lower level governments from much of the red tape generated by more constrained programs.

Republican assumption of the presidency in 1968 led to a period of increasing popularity for block grants. Indeed, they became a major element in the "new federalism," leading to programs in employment training, social services, and community development that were initially structured as block grants (Stenberg 1977). The ideology of "less federal interference" and "strong state and local government" that defined Republican support for block grants produced, as its logical extension, a program in which federal strings were essentially reduced to zero: General Revenue Sharing. This program, adopted in October 1972 and reenacted in the fall of 1976, distributes approximately $6 billion per year to all state governments and all units of general purpose local government in the country, according to a statutory formula. As originally enacted, recipients were free to spend these moneys on any of eight "priority categories"; but, since these categories included all of the major functional purposes of government (except education), this federal constraint was hardly any constraint at all. Recipient units were required to publicize and submit to the Office of Revenue Sharing (in the Treasury Department) a "planned use report" before they received the funds and an "actual use report" after the funds had been expended. These reports simply certified that the federal dollars had been lawfully expended, however, and were neither intended or treated as constraints on recipient discretion. General Revenue Sharing thus was and remains an essentially unrestricted grant.[6]

At one extreme is a tightly constrained grant program, in which purposes are carefully set out, funds are disbursed only after detailed federal review of lower unit application forms, and actual expenditures are monitored through a variety of periodic reports submitted to Washington. At the other extreme is a program design that permits lower level units to expend funds with essentially no constraint on purpose and minimal reporting requirements. There are, of course, a virtually infinite variety of points in between depending on the kind and specificity of constraints attached to any given program. From a political point of view the issue of constraint is important because its resolution in a particular program defines the extent to which a *national* purpose will be identified and enforced in the distribution of federal funds. From an intellectual point of view the issue is important because each package of constraints can be thought of as reflecting a theory of how the behavior of lower level units can be influenced by federal program design: each program in effect states a hypothesis of how a given range of behaviors can be achieved by a given

---

[6]Among the many volumes devoted to the analysis of General Revenue Sharing, the study edited by Juster (1976) is perhaps the most comprehensive.

Table 2-1   Federal Grant Design, 1967, 1972

Grants	1967			1972		
	no.	$	%	no.	$	%
Project						
Primarily to states	23	1,229	8	36	2,960	8
Primarily to local	10	878	6	19	4,585	13
Formula						
Primarily to states	15	10,235	67	18	23,909	68
Primarily to local				2	755	2
Mixed	41	2,652	18	25	3,195	9
Total	89	15,193*	99	100	35,404	100

Source: Adapted after ACIR 1977b, pp. 27; 30.
*Total reported.

program package. From this perspective, a program such as General Revenue Sharing can be thought of as reflecting no national purpose other than general financial support for state and local governments. Expenditure purposes were not defined in a constrained way, and no reporting or other strings were created to monitor lower unit expenditures. String-bound categorical programs, on the other hand, presumably reflect a more considered definition of national purpose and a more clearly specified theory of what strings will induce lower unit behavior that accords with the national purpose. By observing programs with different mixes of constraints, we can observe different theories as well as different politics. And by observing program change through time, we may well be able to assess the extent to which different theories are in effect "tested" by empirical political realities.

At the outset it may be helpful to have in mind an image of the relative significance of different mixes of program constraint. This is not an easy task, partly because rapid growth has added complexity to an already complex system and partly because political controversy over the "red tape" issue has created public images that may be difficult to change. It is nevertheless possible to provide a reasonable approximation of the system as a whole by observing the distribution among project—or categorical—grants, formula grants, and mixed grants, as is shown in table 2-1 for the years 1967 and 1972. The analysis from which these numbers were drawn is deficient in several respects: data from the two years are not identical; the categories represent a "translation" of more than 1,000 programs (1972) into just 100 categories[7]; and the years shown here may be misleading in failing to deal with later innovations such as General Revenue Sharing or additional block grants. Yet the basic "system" dimensions revealed here seem stable over this five-year period and probably

[7]The translation is explained in ACIR 1977b, p. 26.

remain very much the same today. In particular, these numbers pick up the vast increases in federal aid and they pick up the increases in categorical or project grant programs. Note, however, that while the number of project grants has increased dramatically—to 55 of the 100 shown here for 1972—formula grants in both years account for more than two-thirds of the dollars. Note, too, that most of the dollars (76 percent) *and* most of the grants (72 percent) go to state rather than local governments in both years. Thus, although the dollar amount of federal aid has increased enormously and local governments have become important recipients of direct federal aid, the traditional American pattern of providing funds to *state* governments, on the basis of statutory formulas, remains very much in force. Finally, since grants distributed by formula are often less amenable to federal monitoring and control than the more tightly constrained project grants, these numbers suggest that both politics and theory at the federal level are aimed primarily at providing lower level financial support rather than achieving national purposes. Let us bear these tentative conclusions in mind as we examine the development of three different federal aid programs: a categorical grant, a block grant, and the essentially unrestricted program of General Revenue Sharing.

GENERAL REVENUE SHARING: SUCCESSFUL FAILURE

A brief commentary on General Revenue Sharing illustrates, despite its unusual design, some highly important characteristics of federal assistance politics. Recall that the idea of a federal revenue-sharing program arrived on the national political agenda when Walter Heller, then Chairman of the Council of Economic Advisors, sketched out a plan to reduce the "fiscal drag" caused by surplus federal revenues (Dommel 1974, pp. 40–44). Although President Johnson was initially attracted to the idea, his enthusiasm waned as expenditures in Vietnam consumed the federal revenue surplus, and the "drag" the surplus was supposed to have caused failed to materialize. It remained for President Nixon, eager to find a way to strengthen the capacity of state and local governments while reducing the influence of federal bureaucrats, to put together the coalition that finally passed a revenue-sharing program in October 1972 (Dommel 1974, pp. 129–67).

General Revenue Sharing was an unusual program in several respects. To begin with, it was not, strictly speaking, a revenue-sharing program at all; it was a five-year appropriation of some $30.2 billion, to be distributed (in roughly equal annual amounts) to all state and local units of general purpose government. State allocations were determined by statutory formula, state governments received one-third and local governments, two-thirds of each state allocation, and distribution among local units within a state was achieved through application of a similar formula. All general purpose units were entitled to their share of the annual allotment, and nothing was required of recipients save reports that they had legally expended the funds. Universal eligibility and automatic disbursement of an existing appropriation made this program as immune from bureaucratic or congressional tinkering as any federal program can be. At the same time, establishment of a direct and lasting financial relationship between the federal government and all local governments in the country was a radical departure from past assistance practices, one that some thought could lead to more rather than less federal control.[8]

One answer to the question, Why was this kind of program enacted in late 1972? leads to a very important insight about federal aid politics; namely, that federal assistance programs are seldom, if ever, designed to serve clearly defined and consistent objectives. Indeed, programs of this kind can hardly be said to be "designed" at all; they are just passed. Consider the political maelstrom out of which this "program" emerged. The Nixon administration's belief that "no strings" federal money would increase the "capacity" of state and local governments seems genuine enough; but to pass the program President Nixon first had to persuade congressional liberals that the program would supplement, rather than substitute for, existing urban assistance programs. Then he had to persuade congressional conservatives that just the opposite was the case. These dubious activities quite likely would have been fruitless had not Congressman Wilbur Mills, in his effort to secure the support of state and local officials for his own presidential ambitions, given up his long-standing opposition to revenue sharing (Dommel 1974, pp. 138–39). Nor is it likely that the state and local officials who so intensely wanted the program— assuming that it would mean additional money—would have been successful had they not agreed to President Nixon's insistence that a ceiling be placed on federal expenditures for state social service spending (Derthick 1975, pp. 71–76). Ultimately, neither the Senate nor the House could agree on which of two formulas to use in distributing money to the states; so they passed both, with a provision that states could use whichever formula gave them the most money. Given this tangle of confused and contradictory intentions, reactions, and choices, any assertion about "the purpose" of General Revenue Sharing could be regarded only as dishonest or silly, or both. Analysis of nothing more than the language of the bill yields sixteen different and sometimes conflicting purposes (Larkey 1975).

One important reason why clear statements of purpose are seldom found, of course, is that such statements impede formation of the coalitions necessary to pass programs through the Congress. Dommel's analysis (1974, pp. 148–55), for example, shows that House liberals joined with conservatives to pass revenue sharing. But it is highly unlikely that liberals could or would have supported the program had President Nixon been clear about his intention to dismantle other urban assistance programs

---

[8]Wilbur Mills is reported to have described revenue sharing as a "Trojan horse." Dommel (1974) gives an extended treatment of his position.

once revenue sharing was on the books. Nor is it likely that conservatives would have been as supportive as they were if they had been clearly aware of the limited significance revenue sharing was ultimately to assume. Muddled programs, in short, often make good politics.

From an intellectual rather than political point of view, however, muddled programs become muddled theories and muddled theories are extremely difficult to evaluate (a consideration that may itself be a political virtue). Perhaps because of its unusual design characteristics, General Revenue Sharing attracted a great deal of attention from a large number of researchers.[9] Much good research has established that revenue sharing has had little or no effect on programs, processes, or structures at the state and local level; lower level governmental strength, capacity, innovativeness, or vitality all seem to have been largely unaffected by this program.[10] Despite evidence of this kind, it cannot be said that the program has "failed," for there are other specified purposes that have in fact been met. The program has provided the "fiscal assistance" mentioned in its title,[11] it has provided that assistance at a time when inflation and tax resistance among local voters have exaggerated the longer term fiscal difficulties of many local governments, and the program is strongly supported by virtually all lower level public officials (Juster 1976, p. 7). Judging "success" or "failure" in programs for which there is no clear statement of purpose therefore cannot be accomplished on the basis of "evidence"; muddled or multiple purposes will always lead to "evidence" that can be given a variety of interpretations.

By the pragmatic political test of survivability, the program seems to be a "success." The program was renewed in 1976—with few changes and at a roughly similar funding level—for another three and one-half years. Recall, however, that other grant programs have continued their remarkable increases in the past five years, including many programs that are more tightly constrained than revenue sharing. Funding and program stability in this environment may therefore be less a mark of "success" than it seems, perhaps because revenue sharing lacks the political incentives available in other program designs, an issue to consider as a classic "categorical" program is examined.

701: THE RISE AND FALL OF "TECHNICAL" ASSISTANCE

Although it is often alleged that the United States lacks an urban policy, we have in fact had a variety of implicit urban policies ranging from tax

---

[9]The National Science Foundation, RANN Division, stimulated much of this work; but the Brookings Institution, the General Accounting Office (GAO), and many universities also provided major studies.

[10]See, for examples of good research, Nathan, Manvel, and Calkins (1975); Juster (1976); and Anton, Larkey, and Linton (1975).

[11]The program's title is the State and Local Fiscal Assistance Act of 1972.

deductions for mortgage interest payments to the federal reserve discount rate. At the federal level there has also been a coherent, increasingly pervasive, and quite *explicit* urban policy that dates back to 1954, when urban renewal was introduced by the Housing Act of that year. To qualify for urban renewal support, communities had to indicate that they met seven conditions of a federally defined "workable program," which included the requirement that the community have a master plan to guide its development. Federal officials knew, of course, that few local governments had developed master plans. To encourage them to do so, section 701 of the 1954 Housing Act created a program of local planning assistance through which the federal government agreed to provide for communities that undertook the task 50 percent of the cost of developing a master plan. Since a plan was required for an acceptable "workable program," communities that wanted urban renewal assistance could not avoid the effort, but the 50-percent local contribution was not required to be made in hard cash, meaning that many communities were able to generate a plan at little or no cost to them (U.S. Housing and Home Finance Agency 1954, p. 451). The federal desire for local plans and local planning reflected judgments about what was required for best use of federal dollars as well as the capacities of most local governments. In this sense, 701 may rightfully be regarded as a technical assistance program, designed to encourage and support lower level capabilities rather than to distribute political goodies through the classic "pork barrel."

What pattern of growth might be anticipated for a technical assistance program? Plausibly, one might anticipate that program growth would be related to technical achievements, monitored through careful estimates of expenditure and performance over time, with spurts resulting from technical breakthroughs or new problem discoveries. Careful performance monitoring and goal achievement might be the major justifications for program growth. Figure 2-2 charts the growth in federal appropriations for the Comprehensive Planning Assistance Program from 1954 to 1974 and in doing so casts considerable doubt on the "technical" model of program growth. For the entire period, the familiar rachet of public expenditure increase is apparent: a period of slow or moderate growth is followed by a large increase, which is in turn followed by another relatively stable period, and so on. Note, however, the timing of the major increases. Appropriations more than double in 1960 and again in 1962; a very large increment is achieved in 1968; and appropriations are again more than doubled in 1972, when funds appropriated exceed $100 million for the first time. This is hardly a large federal program—total accumulated appropriations through 1974 amounted to barely $.5 billion— and it is nominally a purely technical assistance program. But three of the years in which a major appropriations increase occurs are presidential election years, and the fourth happens to be a congressional election year. One is led to suspect that this pattern is more than coincidental.

Closer examination of the program changes associated with appropria-

Figure 2-2   *Comprehensive Planning Assistance Grant Program, 1954–1974 (in thousands of dollars)*

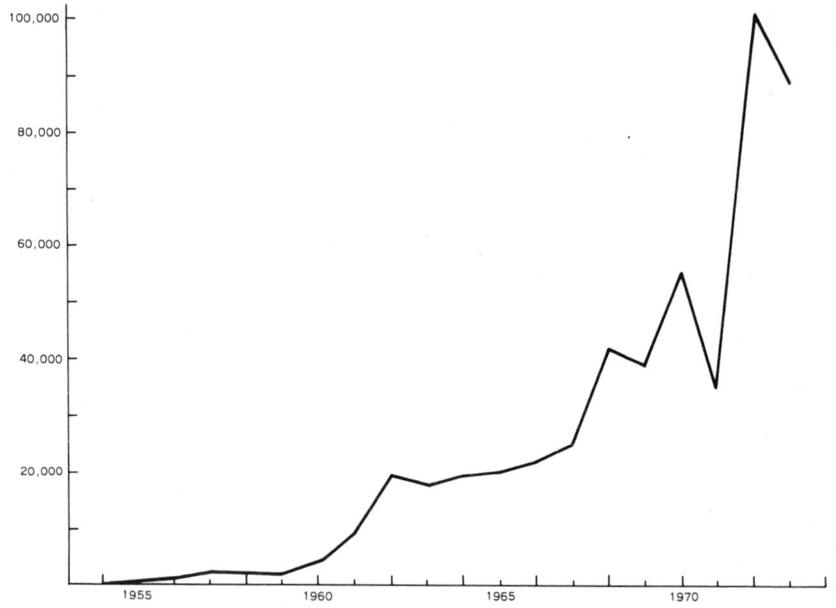

Source: Appropriations based on figures from *The Budget* of the United States, 1954–74 (Washington, D.C.: Government Printing Office), 1956–74, for fiscal year ending June 30 (actual expenditure).

tions increases offers some insight into the character of this pattern. As originally enacted, 701 provided planning assistance funds for communities of 25,000 or fewer persons and for state, metropolitan, or regional agencies that were, or desired to be, engaged in urban planning work. In 1959 eligible recipients were broadened to include cities of less than 50,000 population, groups of adjacent municipalities with less than 50,000 persons, and state planning agencies "for state *and* interstate comprehensive planning." Other amendments increased the federal share from one-half to two-thirds (1961) and authorized grants for: all counties (regardless of size); agencies established by interstate contract; Indian tribes; regional agencies; the Appalachian Regional Commission; areas affected by growing federal installations; areas affected by *declining* federal installations; and even for areas affected by international treaties.[12] By 1970 it was difficult indeed to find an agency that was *not* eligible for 701 assistance. The most plausible explanation of this expansion of eligible units is that 701 program managers, like other experienced federal bureaucrats, were

---

[12]This information can be found in the *U.S. Code Congressional and Administrative News* for 1957, p. 318; 1959, pp. 2865–66; 1961, p. 1954; 1964, pp. 343, 3457–58; and 1965, pp. 5–24. See also U.S. Housing and Home Finance Agency 1964, p. 331.

eager to expand the constituency of the program in order to insure continued political support. As one clientele group was exhausted, another was added or earlier constituencies were redefined to expand the operative base of support. More than 6,000 of the nation's 38,000 general purpose local units had received 701 support by 1970, along with a myriad of other county, state, regional, and interstate organizations (U.S. HUD 1970, pp. 67–70).

Bureaucratic cultivation of clientele groups is of course an old story in Washington, and it is typically associated with the equally solicitous cultivation of congressional relations. A preliminary review of 701 grants to states represented on the relevant House and Senate appropriations committees makes clear that bureaucratic budget planners are careful about "whom" when they plan "how much." Table 2-2 provides a cumulative summary of 701 expenditures in the states and the District of Columbia through 1974, the last year for which adequate data were available. In each of these years, the average grant to states represented on congressional appropriations committees was considerably higher than the cumulative average for the fifty states, and the gap appears to be widening. In 1970, 1972, and 1974 the average accumulated grants to states whose representatives were actually present at appropriations hearings was moreover considerably higher than grants to states whose representatives were not present and far exceeded the all-state average. Since these are cumulative figures and since the number of states represented changes somewhat over time, it seems clear that program managers give very careful consideration to the concerns of committee members and that sensitivity to those concerns tends to increase over time. Of the 1972 appropriation of some $102 million, more than $56 million went to the eleven states represented on HUD, Space, Science, and Veterans Subcommittee—including substantial grants to "urban" states such as Mississippi, Indiana, Maine, and Nebraska (U.S. HUD 1972, pp. 75–79). The Senators on that 1972 Appropriations Committee for these states were John Stennis of Mississippi, Margaret Chase Smith of Maine, Birch Bayh of Indiana, and Roman Hruska of Nebraska, all long-term and powerful members of the Appropriations Committee.

Congressional participation in the reshaping of 701 thus appears to have been structured primarily by congressional interest in obtaining as many dollars as possible from a program that appeared to have relatively unrestricted dollars available for the asking. Until the mid-1960s congressional scrutiny of 701 appropriations was largely pro forma; not until the late 1960s were serious questions raised, usually about overlapping "planning" responsibilities between HUD and other federal agencies. Questions of achievement or impact at the state and local level appear infrequently in the public record, and there is no evidence of sustained congressional concern for developing information that might lead to such evaluations. From one year to the next, appropriations hearings

Table 2-2 701 Grants to All States and "Represented" States

Year	All States & Territories[a]	U.S. Only[a]	Members on Appropriations[a]	Members at Hearings[a]
1968	54 states & terrs. $3,614,203 $191,271,000[b]	50 states & D.C. $3,778,627	25 states $4,335,800 $108,395,000[b] (55%)	11 states $3,942,720 $43,369,920[b] (22%)
1970	54 states & terrs. $5,292,629 $285,802,000[b]	50 states & D.C. $5,522,294	21 states $6,268,714 $131,642,944[b] (46%)	7 states $9,483,140 $66,381,980[b] (23%)
1972	55 states & terrs. $7,718,018 $424,491,000[b]	50 states & D.C. $8,196,784	18 states $10,102,500 $181,845,000[b] (43%)	7 states $13,556,570 $94,895,900[b] (22%)
1974	55 states & terrs. $10,726,200 $589,941,000[b]	50 states & D.C. $11,398,607	18 states $14,944,111 $268,944,000[b] (46%)	10 states $15,981,200 $159,812,000[b] (27%)

[a]Average federal grant.
[b]Cumulative total.

produce much the same kinds of interactions: HUD secretaries or under-secretaries stress the value of 701 in increasing coordination and efficiency in urban government, report the number of governments now participating in the program, and request more money; senators and representatives repeatedly ask for a program justification and examples of success (but not for evidence of success), and they occasionally criticize some minor grant or minor policy priority. "Next questions" such as, What is the evidence for that assertion? are almost never asked; when they are, bureaucrats have difficulty answering them and often respond by offering a statement that can be inserted into the record later, thus avoiding all questions that might follow from additional information. On the public record, congressional "review" of the 701 program appears to be almost totally characterized by ritualistic verbal fencing.[13]

It is entirely possible that congressional participation is only poorly reflected in these public exchanges. Congressional staff personnel and 701 program managers may have worked out a structure of relationships that permits considerably more detailed congressional participation in program evaluation and reform. This possibility is clearly worth exploring, but there is reason to doubt that such relationships, if they exist, have much impact; 701 appropriations are rather small relative to the total HUD budget, and there may be little incentive for major congressional attention. Had such interactions moreover become structured, it seems likely that they would have produced some public evidence in the form of questions "planted" at hearings. As already indicated, however, questions raised on the record tend to be few and quite similar from one year to the next, suggesting strongly that staff personnel may not pay much attention to this small program.[14]

What, then, are we to conclude about the quality of congressional concern for federally assisted "urban planning" programs? A tentative conclusion, consistent with the above record, is this: most senators and representatives think that something called "urban planning" is probably a good thing; they realize, however, that the concept changes over time in order to provide justifications for appropriations increases. They continue to support the *program* rather than these changing definitions because it provides federal jobs and general financial aid to lower level units. It also provides opportunities for congressional representatives to "announce" grants, thus helping themselves politically. Precisely because "purposes" are so muddled, representatives do not expect clear-cut or hard evaluations; it is enough if money is delivered to state and local units. Except for those rare occasions when they can place someone in a federal

---

[13]This conclusion is based on a review of congressional appropriations hearings for 1963–65, 1967–70, 1972–74.

[14]There are exceptions, however. The most recent major changes (1974) were in fact initiated by a legislative assistant to Senator Stevenson (Illinois).

job or help to deliver a grant to a home town supporter, congressional support is entirely symbolic: *this program is a good thing and the federal government should be involved in it, whatever it is now taken to mean.* A formal justification is of course necessary each year in order to maintain congressional responsibility. But the real congressional purpose is to determine if enough interests believe a program is worth supporting and, if so, to provide funds. Period.

Similar conclusions might easily be offered for a number of federal programs. What is interesting here is that it can be made so easily for a program of technical assistance in which there is (was) presumably some known technology to exploit and a great many "strings" attached. With hindsight it seems evident that the technology—"planning"—was never in fact clear and was always expandable to meet new political imperatives. There is more than a little irony in this, since the federal government has devoted two decades to encouraging state and local activities that the federal government itself can neither define coherently nor impose upon its own operations.[15] Nevertheless, planning requirements have been widespread in other federal assistance programs, usually in conjunction with other kinds of technologies. A quick review of one such combination, in the form of a block grant, may suggest something about the underlying significance of the planning strategy as a response to the federal assistance dilemma.

LEAA: DESIGN FOR A MONEY SHOVEL

In many respects the Law Enforcement Assistance Administration (LEAA) program, created in 1968, contrasts sharply with 701. Whereas 701 began as a small appendage to a larger and broader program (urban renewal), LEAA was itself the larger and broader program at the focus of attention. Whereas 701 was introduced without fanfare or much public notice, LEAA emerged from the currents of presidential politics in which one attorney general was charged with "softness" and promises made to bring in a tougher approach and a tougher man to deal with the wave of urban riots that had become a national issue in a presidential year. Whereas 701 was in a sense a "classical" categorical grant program, requiring formal application, extended negotiations with HUD, and extensive

---

[15]"The Advisory Commission on Intergovernmental Relations reported in 1973 that more than 4,000 multijurisdictional program areas had been created by the 24 Federal programs the Commission identified as assisting in areawide planning. The most common geographic program areas included 247 air quality regions, 481 law enforcement planning regions, 198 comprehensive areawide health planning regions, 124 economic development planning districts, and 501 manpower planning areas. OMB estimated in 1974 that 2,000 areawide agencies received Federal planning assistance. A 1975 study prepared by the city of Seattle, Washington, reported that any metropolitan area might have as many as 20 federally sponsored bodies planning on a multijurisdictional basis" (U.S. Government Accounting Office 1977, p. 7).

reporting after receipt of the grant, LEAA was basically a block grant program. Some 85 percent of Action Grant funds, the largest grant category in the program, were to be made available to state and local governments according to population, with the remainder available to national officials as discretionary money. Within each state, funds were to be disbursed by State Planning Agencies on receipt of local applications, but the only control available to national officials was a statewide comprehensive plan, prepared annually, that required federal approval before grants could be made available to states. (We shall see in a moment that federal plan approval has not been a major hindrance.) Finally, whereas 701 was and remained a small program, LEAA appropriations began at just over $60 million and increased dramatically to more than $850 million in just five years (figure 2-3). Later appropriations increases confirmed that Congress and the federal bureaucracy (Justice Department) were serious about spending money to "fight crime."[16]

These differences aside, LEAA seemed in many respects similar to 701. Lacking an operational definition of what it meant to "fight crime," apart from a vague list of eligible activities that seemed all-inclusive, the statute placed heavy emphasis on a "planning" strategy. Since, according to Congress, crime could be dealt with effectively only by state and local officials, the national policy was to

> ... assist state and local governments in strengthening and improving law enforcement at every level by national assistance. It is the purpose of this title to (1) encourage states and units of general local government to prepare and adopt comprehensive plans based upon their evaluations of state and local problems of law enforcement; (2) authorize grants to states and units of local government in order to improve and strengthen law enforcement; and (3) encourage research and development directed toward the improvement of law enforcement (U.S. Congress 1968, p. 237).

Since most states did not have the State Planning Agencies required by the act, the first appropriation provided $19 million to get them started. Announcement of these funds produced a reaction that surprised Charles Rogovin, first LEAA administrator:

> When the planning funds were made available by the act, an astonishing thing happened. Every one of the 50 States, plus Washington, D.C., Puerto Rico, and the Virgin Islands, said they wanted to take part. All $19 million in planning funds available this fiscal year has been given and every State has created a high-level commission and all are busily at work (U.S. House Subcommittee of the Committee on Appropriations 1969, p. 1033).

---

[16]For an analysis of LEAA, see ACIR 1977a.

Figure 2-3   Comparative Summary of Distribution of Funds (in thousands)

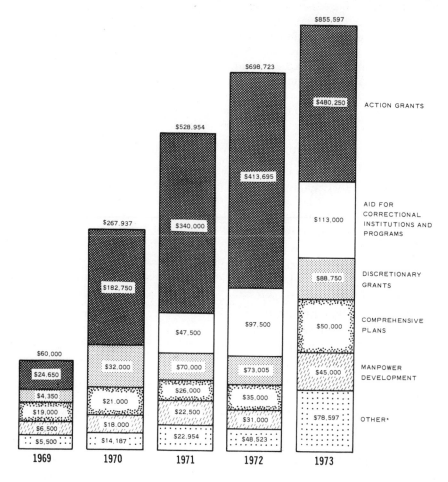

*Includes Administration, Technical Assistance, Data Systems and Statistical Assistance, and National Institute of Law Enforcement with Criminal Justice.

Rogovin might have added at a later point that LEAA proved to be highly efficient in approving the results of that busy work. Within six months of the time when all states were reported to have created planning agencies, all state plans had been approved, including one in excess of 6,000 pages submitted by the state of California (U.S. LEAA 1971a, p. 4). Within another six months nearly $250 million in "encouragement" was on its way to states and local governments, surely an impressive display of federal ability to "move money." In its third annual report (1971), LEAA described the great revolution that had taken place:

Three years ago there were among the states no broad scale programs of the kind envisioned by the Congress when it established the LEAA. There were no substantial federal funds available for law enforcement assistance. There were no State Criminal Justice Planning Agencies to plan and carry out large-scale programs. There was no significant state or federal research under way to advance the state of the art of law enforcement. There were no concentrated efforts to apply statistics research or systems analysis to the operation of the Criminal Justice System. In short, there was no working blueprint to improve the Criminal Justice System, whose focus and objective it was to reduce crime and delinquency in America.

Today, all of these things are realities in the United States—all generated by federal funds channeled to the states by LEAA.

While LEAA program managers were focusing on agencies created, salaries paid, and money spent, some in Congress were noticing that crime rates continued to increase. Either failure of LEAA funds to affect this obvious impact indicator or perhaps the size of the program and the difficulty of using formula-based grants for "cultivation" produced more spirited congressional inquiry. From the beginning, individuals such as Senator McClellan (Arkansas) expressed concern over the capacity of states to use these large sums effectively. Questioning Attorney General Mitchell, McClellan wondered whether the states had "sufficient" experience: ". . . In other words, are they prepared to utilize more money . . . or had we better watch it and make them demonstrate the effectiveness of their plans before we give them more money?" (U.S. Senate Subcommittee of the Committee on Appropriations 1969, p. 140). Mitchell and later program managers repeatedly insisted that grants would be used "for the requisite purposes," but how were LEAA program managers to know? The original point of leverage, approval of a state plan, comes before rather than after expenditures are made, providing nothing more than verbal assurances that are easily forgotten once federal dollars are in hand. In a knowledgeable exchange with the third LEAA Administrator, Jerris Leonard, Congressman Smith clarified the problem:

> . . .What I am really getting at is this—and other members tell me that they hear the same thing—it's not a matter of illegal expenditure of funds. In fact, the act itself is very vague. The guidelines are rather loose. If you are too strict in enforcing guidelines, they complain about red tape. If you are not strict enough, anybody who wants some money comes in under the name of law enforcement and makes application. This is what has been happening. . . . What goes on is that they find out the big money now is coming from LEAA. So if they need some money, they figure out an application which can be put under that program. These local people know

where the money is coming from and where the big increases are. They try to get in under it (U.S. House Subcommittee of the Committee on Appropriations 1972, p. 1126).

In the LEAA case, local efforts to "get in under" this particular program led in time to changes that undermined the original block grant idea. Since the state agencies that distributed LEAA monies were themselves coalitions of the more prominent components of each state's criminal justice system, it was inevitable that the more powerful components would wind up with disproportionate shares of a given state's allocation. This, in turn, led to demands from the less-advantaged components for "their own" funds, protected against more influential groups. Just as inevitably, representatives responded through a series of actions that have been called "creeping categorization": between 1970 and 1976 Congress either added new programs or earmarked portions of LEAA funds for corrections (i.e., prisons), juvenile justice, and neighborhood crime prevention activities.[17] Thus, instead of a block grant program, LEAA had by 1976 become a general grant program in which separate allocations were set aside for the various components of criminal justice systems—something quite like a categorical program. The opportunities for developing constituencies by responding to specific group requests through specific (categorical) programs are powerful incentives for congressional representatives and bureaucrats alike. Block or unrestricted grants, which remove such incentives, are unlikely to become very popular in Washington.

A MODEL OF FEDERAL AID POLICY DEVELOPMENT

Three programs among more than 1,000 hardly provide a firm base for generalized conclusions, even if the programs were selected to illustrate the differences among tight, loose, and no federal constraints. Taken together with the substantial work that either has been completed or is under way at the Brookings Institution, the ACIR, the Urban Institute, and elsewhere,[18] it is possible to state some preliminary generalizations that have reasonable if not conclusive, support. Other studies, as well as the three reports offered here, suggest that formal statements of program purpose are always ambiguous and highly unstable through time—the reason why such statements are of very little use in distinguishing among programs. Other studies, as well as those reported here, also suggest the extraordinary difficulty of even classifying, let alone measuring, the effects of different mixes of "strings." While string-bound programs such as 701 planning assistance may generate more paper reports, it is not clear that statements in such reports are of any different quality than the "actual

---

[17]See, for example, the Omnibus Crime Control Act of 1970, the Crime Control Act of 1973, and the Juvenile Justice and Delinquency Prevention Act of 1974.
[18]See ACIR (1976; 1977a; 1977b; 1977d) and Nathan, Manvel, and Calkins (1975).

use" reports of the unstrung revenue-sharing program or the 6,000-page "plans" of LEAA. Strings are combined in ways far more complicated than the "categorical," "block," and "unrestricted" classification we conventionally use; the combinations of strings change through time, and we have yet to find a way to determine the impact of such dynamic combinations of constraint.

The implications of these conclusions can be stated more systematically in the following political "model" of federal policy making for financial assistance programs:

1. *Advocacy, not analysis, is the source of programs.* Federal programs to assist state and local units seldom arise from careful consideration of research reports that investigate some "problem" and propose alternative solutions. They come into existence because some group or individual effectively advocates the desirability or necessity of the program. Crises, particularly if they are of national scope, provide a convenient occasion for advocacy: thus national publicity about crime, abetted by opportunistic use of a national political campaign, generates LEAA; or national publicity about the urban fiscal crisis encourages support for a revenue-sharing program that will not, in fact, have a measurable impact on that crisis. Crises, however, are hardly the sole occasions for effective advocacy. Bureaucrats in key positions—as in the case of Walter Heller and revenue sharing—can quietly mobilize support for programs; and public interest groups can be effective advocates even when few people know or care about what the groups are doing. See Steiner's discussion of the 1962 social service programs (Steiner 1966).

It goes without saying, of course, that persuasive politicians such as John F. Kennedy (economic development) or, more recently, Edmund Muskie (water resources), to say nothing of Lyndon B. Johnson, have many ways to generate support for programs they advocate. Programs conceived in advocacy relationships may sometimes use studies or research as justification, but they are often enacted quickly (the necessary coalition may be very temporary) and thus bear the imprint of coalition politics more than any research or analysis that may be mentioned.[19]

2. *Program design is atheoretical.* Above it was suggested that every program could be thought of as a "theory" of influence: we want lower units to accomplish X, therefore we design this program with Y and Z characteristics because Y and Z cause X to occur. In fact, however, there is little evidence to suggest that such calculations actually take place. Indeed, since there is normally so much calculated ambiguity regarding program objectives, it is difficult to envision how these calculations could take place. To the extent that instrumental theory exists at all, it appears to focus on the belief that forcing recipient units to "match" federal dollars with their own, will encourage or guarantee program achievement. There is, in fact, considerable evidence that programs that require high levels of matching do stimulate higher levels of recipient expenditure than no-

---

[19]The diffusion of model cities from a target group of 12 cities to 150 communities is another good example. See Frieden and Kaplan (1975).

match or low-match programs. This evidence is admittedly crude, confined as it is to per capita spending variables rather than to program performance variables, but it is at least something (ACIR 1977b, pp. 47–51). It is all the more striking, therefore, to observe that most program designs require little or no "matching": more than $30 billion (86 percent) of the $35 billion in grants ACIR was able to classify for 1972 contained either "low" or "no" state-local matching requirements (ACIR 1977b, p. 28). Even at this crude level, then, program designers clearly are reluctant to impose conditions that might encourage performance. From an instrumental point of view, most designs are simply atheoretical.

3. *Program design is political and pragmatic.* The absence of instrumental theories does not imply the absence of organizing principles, for there does seem to be a set of operating ideas that, for want of a better term, we may call *political.* Both congressional representatives and bureaucrats share an interest in being "responsive"; thus when a program is advocated there is an inclination to be supportive if the problem to which the program responds is made to sound important and if the proposed solution is made to sound reasonable. In the absence of good instrumental theories, being "responsive" can only mean appropriating funds, an act that allows representatives to claim that they are "doing something" about problem X and bureaucrats to claim they "are working on it." Being "responsive" in Congress also means that programs have to be shaped to cover at least enough congressional districts or states to generate the votes necessary for program approval; hence the ubiquity of what Beer (1976) calls "distributive localism." These political incentives mean that, for a great many programs delivered in what might be called the "see-what-happens" syndrome, a program is advocated; money is appropriated to do "something"; and plans are made to call in witnesses in twelve to eighteen months to find out what that "something" was and, depending upon who testifies and what he/she says, to modify the program with the next appropriation. At this level, the "strings" attached, either in legislation or in the writing of regulations, respond primarily to the need politically to be protected against illegal expenditure of funds (accounting strings) and the appearance of irresponsible money throwing (reporting or planning strings). The strings do not and probably cannot insure performance or program quality. As a former designer, then user, of the LEAA program recently has testified:

> . . . Congress consistently fails to take an active interest in the quality of the programs it creates. It is always surprising to me to listen to the passionate debates of Congress in the process of creating a federal program—the care taken about the shape of the program, its statement of purpose, and appropriation. Two years after its creation, Congress is prepared year after year to fund it, but take[s] no interest at all in its record.

There is no oversight of LEAA and its programs, and there never has been (U.S. House Subcommittee on the City of the Committee on Banking, Finance, and Urban Affairs 1977, p. 33).

4. *"Successful" programs generate their own constituencies.* Nothing guarantees that a program, once enacted, will continue to exist. Those that survive tend to follow the pattern so well illustrated by the 701 program: bureaucratic program managers energetically buy support by spreading their funds around to clientele groups while simultaneously cultivating members of Congress who can influence the next appropriation. Absent clientele and/or congressional support, program activities can be ended —as the demise of the "new communities" program, among others, makes clear (Connerly 1977). With clientele and congressional support, programs can withstand even the determined opposition of the president, as Richard Nixon learned and Jimmy Carter is learning. The influence of these three-cornered "systems"—bureaucratic program manager, congressional group, clientele groups—challenges the received wisdom about scarcity and the budget constraint; for there is always enough money for favored programs, whatever the asserted condition of the public purse. Programs that minimize the significance of these inherently political alliances are not as popular as those that encourage them, hence the lack of growth in General Revenue Sharing. Grants that are appropriated rather than allocated by formula provide greater opportunities for political alliances, but, again, success in alliance building is not guaranteed: it must be pursued. Because of widespread clientele support, orchestrated by politically sensitive program bureaucrats, 701 survived the determined opposition of two presidents. As the present paper is being written, researchers at the American Institute of Planners and at International City Managers' Association (ICMA) are busily compiling a list of "success stories" in the use of 701 funds that can be used during the next round of appropriation hearings. This research is supported by a grant from HUD.

5. *Program goals are inherently unstable through time.* Programs with muddled goals—conceived in advocacy and continued through alliance building—can hardly be expected to demonstrate much consistency of purpose. Indeed, initial statements of purpose are probably more accurately viewed, on the one hand, as symbolic affirmations of support for a cause on the part of Congress and, on the other hand, as political fishing licenses that authorize program managers to test their skill at generating public and congressional support for their activities. Since problems and congressional representatives change, there can be no surprise in observing changes in program activity, some of which will be formalized in new statutory symbols, some of which will be detected only through careful review of annual reports and other statements of activity. This suggests that symbols and practice will tend to follow "hot" issues over time regardless of original intent. For example, we should expect a variety of pro-

grams in a variety of different federal departments to provide verbal and financial support for state-local "energy" programs in 1977–78, since, as the saying goes, "that is what they are calling money in Washington this year." In time, this pattern leads to duplication and overlap among different programs, administered through different departments. So long as the tripartite alliance structure supporting the program holds up, however, any given program will continue to enjoy its changeable feast.

FEDERAL AID AND SYSTEM TRANSFORMATION

The present discussion began with some rather large questions about both the nature of institutional change in the United States today and the theories we use to comprehend that change. In conclusion, let us explore the kinds of answers generated by a dynamic analysis of specific programs, as opposed to a more conventional, cross-sectional view of global issues. One conclusion that seems clear, if tentative, is that patterns of policy making for federal aid programs are identifiable and seem similar from one program to the next. More precise specification of that pattern can come only from further analysis; but vague objectives, goal change through time, a political imperative to "spread out" benefits, and bureaucratic leadership in alliance building are all illustrated by the programs examined here as well as by reports of other programs. It also seems clear that the remarkable fiscal centralization we have experienced has *not* yet led to significant program centralization. Programs seldom change because "evaluation" has revealed "failure" or, for that matter, "success." Such judgments are precluded by both ambiguous goals and federal inability to monitor the use of federal dollars once those dollars leave Washington. Programs generally change because a new problem has been defined and a coalition powerful enough to pass a program to deal with the problem has emerged. In choosing "strings," designers of federal programs exhibit neither much interest in nor an ability to achieve recipient unit program control. The basic federal aid program is money, "legal expenditure" remains the most fundamental evidence of "success," and lower level units thus retain their traditional power to divert external funds to their own uses.

It would nevertheless be wrong to believe that nothing is changing, for the truly staggering amount of federal dollars now being pumped into state and local budgets—with the promise of much more to come—is both new and consequential. For one thing, these federal dollars have helped to fuel the increased volume of public sector activity at the state-local level: between 1955 and 1974, when private sector employment was increasing by 39 percent and federal government employment, by only 19 percent, state-local employees increased by 125 percent, from 4.1 to 9.3 million (ACIR 1976, p. 4). There are now more state and local analysts, bureau heads, directors, and other staff personnel than ever before. Their needs are, as a consequence, greater and their ability to press those needs is also greater. These officials moreover now can utilize their own lobby organizations, the so-called public interest groups (or PIGS), to organize pressure when necessary.[20] Having helped to create these new officials and new organizations, vast sums now available in Washington encourage their activity: the stakes have become higher and the activity, more intense. Federal government agencies are themselves changing in response to these developments. A full-time presidential advisor for intergovernmental affairs now exists, and major federal agencies are even now in the process of creating specialized offices to handle their liaison activities with states and localities. The magnitude of federal assistance, in short, has helped to create new political actors, it has focused attention on a new political arena, and it has created the strongest possible incentive for participation: money.

These changes in the public bureaucracy have occurred at a time when a major reorientation among congressional representatives also has taken place. Party identification among voters in congressional elections appears to have declined, the number of marginal districts has fallen, and incumbency appears to have become more powerful in determining congressional elections. Fiorina (1977), noticing the conjunction between these trends and the expansion of the public bureaucracy, has suggested that, as a result, members of Congress are gradually being transformed from national policy makers to caseworkers, responsible chiefly for expediting bureaucratic action for their constituents. "The nice thing about casework, . . ." he notes,

> . . . is that it is mostly profit; one makes many more friends than enemies. In fact, some congressmen undoubtedly stimulate the demand for their bureaucratic fixit services. Recall that the new Republican in district A says, "I'm your man in Washington. What are your problems? How can I help you?" And in district B the demand for the congressman's services presumably did not rise so much between 1962 and 1964 that a "regiment" of constituency staff became necessary. Rather, possessing the regiment, the new Democrat did his damnedest to create the demand to which he could apply his regiment.
>
> In addition to profitable casework let us remember too that the expansion of the federal role has also produced a larger pork barrel. The pork barreler need not limit himself to dams and post offices. There is LEAA money for local officials; and education program grants for the local education bureaucracy. The congressman can stimulate applications for federal assistance, put in a good word during consideration, and announce favorable decisions amid great fanfare (Fiorina 1977, p. 180).

---

[20]Beer (1976) analyzes this phenomenon.

The "I'm your man in Washington, how can I help you?" orientation seems to be an important clue to the motor force behind the recent expansion of federal aid, in part because it can only strengthen the commonality of interest between politicians eager to "help" and bureaucrats eager to expand their programs. But the implications of bureaucratic and congressional change extend considerably further. As more people compete for more federal dollars through more-and-more specialized roles, we can anticipate much greater sophistication about federal aid issues. With a constantly growing intelligence network made up of academics as well as practitioners all across the country, we can anticipate more public disputes about issues, particularly formula issues, that a short while ago would have been thought to be beyond official (to say nothing of public) understanding. There is already considerable evidence that more sophisticated discussions of federal aid programs will tend to change the major "face" of the political question from, What is this program for? to, What organizations, in what districts, in what regions will get how much from formula X or formula Y? It is entirely conceivable, therefore, that a rhetoric of national purpose will come to be replaced by a rhetoric of institutional support, with outcomes determined by regional rather than party or ideological cleavages. What we now think of as local or regional questions would become major agenda items for our national legislature, and various regional cleavages would gain a prominence that might well organize further institutional changes among states and localities. Other scenarios are possible, but this one is enough to suggest the potential power of forces already at play in the American polity.

REFERENCES

Advisory Commission on Intergovernmental Relations (ACIR). 1976. *Significant features of fiscal federalism.* Washington, D.C.
——. 1977a. *Safe streets reconsidered: The block grant experience, 1968–1975.* Washington, D.C.
——. 1977b. *Federal grants: Their effects on state/local expenditures, employment levels, wage rates.* Washington, D.C.
——. 1977c. *The state and intergovernmental aids.* Washington, D.C.
——. 1977d. *Intergovernmental Perspective* 3 (spring). Washington, D.C.
Anton, T. J. 1976. The imagery of policy analysis: Stability, determinism, and reaction. In Phillip M. Gregg, ed. *Problems of theory in policy analysis,* pp. 91–101. Lexington, Mass.: D. C. Heath.
Anton, T. J.; Larkey, P. D.; and Linton, T. 1975. *Understanding the fiscal impact of General Revenue Sharing.* Ann Arbor: University of Michigan Institute of Public Policy Studies.
Aron, Joan, and Brecher, Charles. 1976. State-local relations in New York: A functional-fiscal-political overview. In S. Cole, ed. *Partnership within the States: Local self-government in the federal system,* pp. 103–24. Urbana: University of Illinois Press.
Beer, S. H. 1976. The adoption of General Revenue Sharing. *Public Policy* 24 (spring): 127–95.
Brecher, Charles. 1974. *Where have all the dollars gone?* New York: Praeger.
Caraley, Demetrios. 1976. Congressional politics and urban aid. *Political Science Quarterly* 91 (spring): 19–45.

Connerly, C. 1977. Planning as rhetoric: The Title VII New Communities Program. Ann Arbor, Mich.: Institute of Public Policy Studies, 1977 Seminar paper. Mimeographed.

Derthick, M. 1975. *Uncontrollable spending for social services grants.* Washington, D. C.: Brookings Institution.

Dommel, P. 1974. *The politics of revenue sharing.* Bloomington: Indiana University Press.

Fiorina, M. P. 1977. The case of the vanishing marginals: The bureaucracy did it. *American Political Science Review* 71 (March).

Frieden, B., and Kaplan, M. 1975. *The politics of neglect.* Cambridge, Mass.: MIT Press.

Juster, F. T., ed. 1976. *The economic and political impact of General Revenue Sharing.* Ann Arbor, Mich.: Institute for Social Research.

Larkey, P. D. 1975. Process models and program evaluation: The impact of General Revenue Sharing on municipal fiscal behavior. Ph.D. dissertation, University of Michigan.

Lindbeck, Assar. 1976. Stabilization policy in open economies with endogenous politicians. *American Economic Review* 66 (May): 1–19.

Murphy, J. T. 1974. Political parties and the pork barrel: Party conflict and cooperation in the House Public Works Committee decision making. *American Political Science Review* 68 (March): 169–85.

Nathan, R. P., and Dommel, P. R. 1979. The cities. In *Setting national priorities: The 1978 budget,* ch. 9. Washington, D.C.: Brookings Institution.

Nathan, R. P.; Manvel, A. D.; and Calkins, Susannah E. 1975. *Monitoring revenue sharing.* Washington, D.C.: Brookings Institution.

New York Times. 27 April 1977.

Piven, F. F., and Cloward, R. A. 1971. *Regulating the poor.* New York: Random House.

Ritt, L. G. 1976. Committee position, seniority, and the distribution of government expenditures. *Public Policy* 24 (fall): 463–89.

Steiner, G. Y. 1966. *Social insecurity.* Chicago: Rand McNally.

Stenberg, C. W. 1977. Block grants: The middlemen of the federal aid system. *Intergovernmental Perspective* 3 (spring): 8–13.

Stockman, D. A. 1975. The social pork barrel. *The Public Interest* 39 (spring): 3–30.

U.S. Annual. *The Budget.* Washington, D.C.

U.S. Congress. 1957. *U.S. Code Congressional and Administrative News.* Vol. 1. St. Paul, Minn.: West.

——. 1959. *U.S. Code Congressional and Administrative News.* Vol. 2. St. Paul, Minn.: West.

——. 1961. *U.S. Code Congressional and Administrative News.* Vol. 2. St. Paul, Minn.: West.

——. 1964. *U.S. Code Congressional and Administrative News.* Vol. 3. St. Paul, Minn.: West.

——. 1965. *U.S. Code Congressional and Administrative News.* Vol. 1. St. Paul, Minn.: West.

——. 1968. *U.S. Code Congressional and Administrative News.* Vol. 1. St. Paul, Minn.: West.

——. 1974. *U.S. Code Congressional and Administrative News.* Vol. 1. St. Paul, Minn.: West.

U.S. Department of Housing and Urban Development (HUD). 1970. *Annual Report of the Department of HUD.* Washington, D.C.

——. 1972. *1972 HUD statistical yearbook.* Washington, D.C.

U.S. Government Accounting Office (GAO). 1977. *Federally assisted areawide planning: Need to simplify policies and practices.* Washington, D.C.

U.S. House. Subcommittee of the Committee on Appropriations. 1965. *Supplemental appropriations for 1966.* Washington, D.C.

——. 1968. *Independent offices and Department of HUD appropriations for 1969,* pt. 3. Washington, D.C.

——. 1969. *Hearings.* Departments of State, Justice and Commerce, the Judiciary, and Related Agency Appropriations FY 1970. Washington, D.C.

——. 1972. *Hearings.* Departments of State, Justice and Commerce, the Judiciary, and Related Agencies for FY 1973. Washington, D.C.

U.S. House. Subcommittee on the City of the Committee on Banking, Finance, and Urban Affairs. 1977. *Toward a national urban policy.* Washington, D.C.

U.S. Housing and Home Finance Agency. 1954. *Eighth annual report.* Washington, D.C.
———. 1964. *Eighteenth annual report.* Washington, D.C.
U.S. Law Enforcement Assistance Administration (LEAA). 1971a. *Second Annual Report of the LEAA, FY 1970.* Washington, D.C.
———. 1971b. *Third Annual Report of the LEAA, FY 1971.* Washington, D.C.
U.S. Senate. Subcommittee of the Committee on Appropriations. 1969. *Hearings.* Departments of State, Justice and Commerce, the Judiciary, and Related Agency Appropriations for FY 1970. Washington, D.C.
Walker, D. B. 1977. Categorical grants: Some clarifications and continuing concerns. *Intergovernmental Perspective* 3 (spring): 14–19.

CHAPTER 3

AUTONOMY AND DEPENDENCE: THE MAZE OF LOCAL GOVERNMENT REVENUES

Samuel B. Bacharach
Jonathan Reader
George Rolleston

Over the last twenty years, increasing attention has been paid by political scientists and sociologists to public policy issues. Academic interest in these issues may be traced back to the New Deal. What began as a series of governmental responses to the problems generated by an historically specific crisis—the Great Depression—subsequently became institutionalized as policy and program responses to various social and economic problems. In effect, the New Deal changed the federal government's role in that it was no longer confined to regulatory activities; instead, the government took on the responsibility for providing various services both for the general population and specific population groups (Buenker 1973; Hofstadter 1955). This commitment to the delivery of services signaled a shift in federal policy, for it meant that under certain conditions the government would establish service programs designed to redistribute social and economic resources, redressing the inequities in resource distribution perpetrated by the private sector.

CENTRALIZATION AND DEPENDENCE

Beginning with the New Deal, the adoption by the federal government of this service role with its redistributive functions has raised the issue that American government, by spurning its grass roots tradition, may have become overly centralized. Stephens, among others, has traced this tendency toward centralization back to the turn of the century: "In terms of things we can measure for the recent past or from the turn of the century, power has apparently evolved upward from local to state and from local and state to national" (Stephens 1974, p. 47). With regard to cities,

Schmandt and Goldbach (1969) have divided this trend in centralization into three stages. Specifically, they maintain that since the turn of the century cities have evolved from politically independent entities to ones that administer policies formulated at the state or national level and then finally to dependent cities; that is, cities where both allocation of resources and policy determination are handled by larger governments. There is empirical evidence furthermore that appears to support the contentions of Stephens and Schmandt and Goldbach concerning the increasing dependence of states and cities on the federal government. Federal grants--in-aid to state and local governments, for example, rose from 1.8 billion in 1948 to 30.3 billion in 1972. The sheer number of federal grants has increased dramatically. Since 1960, 424 grant-in-aid programs have been implemented (Reagan 1972, p. 65). The threat of centralization has given rise in the 1960s and 1970s to considerable debate concerning the status of local governments: Are they functioning in the autonomous manner envisioned by de Tocquevillean democracy or as subunits of the federally administered welfare state?

It may be argued that the centralization of the American policy seems more pervasive than it actually is, for the concept has been applied so indiscriminately that it bears only a tenuous relationship to the phenomenon. The issues implicit in this concept cannot be addressed directly until certain definitional and operational questions are resolved. There are different types of centralization, each having several dimensions; and although it is not the intention of the present paper to present an elaborate taxonomy of centralization, several examples drawn from community research may serve to crystallize some of the conceptual difficulties.

In the most general sense, *centralization* has been used to refer to the locus of power to make specific types of decisions. Hunter (1953) and Dahl (1961), in their research on Atlanta, Georgia, and New Haven, Connecticut, used the case study method to identify which community leaders were influential with regard to specific community decisions. The theoretical limitation of this perspective is that it views community power in highly individualized terms, ignoring its structural sources. The primary weakness of the case study method is that it prevents the examination of decision-making patterns across communities.

In response to the individualized orientation and the case study method, the comparative structuralists such as Clark (1973), Aiken and Alford (1970a; 1970b), Lineberry and Fowler (1967), and Crain and Rosenthal (1967) viewed the community as an aggregate system rather than confining their examination to its component parts such as community leaders (Eyestone 1971). In an effort to determine whether communities are centralized or decentralized, they concentrated on the relationship between systemic characteristics such as community size and the ratio of managers, proprietors, and officials in the civilian labor force (Hawley 1963; Aiken 1970).

Recently the comparative structuralists have become concerned with the relationship between community centralization and policy outputs (Lincoln 1976; Smith 1976). They are interested in determining whether centralized or decentralized communities have higher levels of expenditures. This approach assumes that community characteristics by themselves lead to either a high or low degree of centralization, which, in turn, has consequences for community expenditures. In effect, this approach views the community as a closed system, for it neglects the relationship of the community to the larger political economy in which it is embedded (Alford & Friedland 1975). Given the federal system of American government, this oversight is particularly striking. Both legally and fiscally, communities have interdependent relationships with state governments and the federal government. Since the acquisition of resources is, moreover, the primary consideration, communities are dependent both locally and nationally on institutions in the private sector.

If an open systems perspective is adopted, centralization can no longer be defined solely in terms of the locus of community power; the community's relationship with the larger society must be taken into consideration. An open systems view of centralization entails determining those segments of the polity and the economy with which the community has direct linkages.

One variant of an open systems perspective of communities typified by the work of Clark (1973, pp. 5–6) holds that these linkages may be established through an examination of expenditures. The emphasis on expenditures has two distinct limitations: First, while expenditures shed some light on local decision making, they provide few insights into extra-local sources of control. Second, expenditure data often contain revenues, confusing the economic issue of supply and demand. In effect, the perspective adopted by Clark and others reveals considerable information on how monies are distributed but offers few clues as to how they are obtained. When the concept "linkage" has been used in conjunction with expenditures, it has often failed to specify the types of fiscal relationships communities must enter into with institutions in the larger society. This concept furthermore has failed to elucidate either the dependent nature of these relationships or the control mechanisms that govern them. To understand such fiscal relationships between communities and the larger society, within both the public and private sectors, revenues prove to be a more fruitful concept, for they permit analysis of the twin issues of control and dependence. By concentrating on revenues, expenditures in addition become more comprehensible because revenues make the political basis of the supply-and-demand relationship between communities and the larger political economy more salient.

Linkages must be treated conceptually in terms of the degree of dependence; that is, the more dependent X is on Y, the stronger the linkage between X and Y. In effect, Y has considerable control over X. The concept "revenue" provides a means for determining how diffuse or concentrated the extra-local sources of control over community resources are. From an open systems perspective, revenues are useful in determining how centralized a community is because they facilitate the identification of community dependence on extra-local sources and, therefore, the degree of control these sources exercise. The fewer the alternative sources of revenue, for example, the more centralized is the control of that community.

Since a basic tenet of critical political theory (O'Connor 1973) holds that the one who controls the purse strings inevitably controls the decision-making process, it seems ironic that political scientists have paid so little attention to revenues. Mosher and Poland have described the interrelationship between revenues and expenditures: "Revenues are the cutting edge, the sharp political edge of public spending programs, for the bulk of expenditures must normally be paid from public revenues" (Mosher & Poland 1964, p. 61).

Until now, most of the research on public revenues has not attempted to compare different units of government; instead, it has confined itself to specific units of government such as states or cities (Maxwell & Aronson 1977; Mosher & Poland 1964; Campbell & Sacks 1967). This approach gives the impression that the unit of government under consideration is an isolated entity rather than an integral part of the federal system. To understand the issue of governmental centralization/decentralization, in general, as well as the specific case of public revenues, both the federal system and the economy must be taken into consideration. This observation takes on added significance in a capitalist economy, where local governments are frequently dependent on resources from both the private sector (e.g., borrowings) and the public sector (e.g., federal aid). In fact, it is the mixed nature of the capitalist economy that, in part, accounts for the competition among local governments for revenues.

Previous research on American local government has been plagued by the tendency to confine the scope of analysis to one level of government. Such a truncated perspective overlooks the federalist nature of the American system. The empirical consequence of adopting this type of perspective is either to ignore the web of intergovernmental relationships or to take them for granted. Since the Constitutional Convention of 1787, however, the debate on how centralized or decentralized the American system of government should be has persisted in both academic and political circles. Who has the responsibility for resolving domestic problems such as crime, housing, welfare, and health: local government, state government, federal government, or some combination of each? In a different vein, this debate has surfaced in the controversy between cities and suburbs over annexation. As the longevity of this debate attests, consensus has yet to emerge as to what constitutes the appropriate set of intergovernmental relationships. It may be assumed, therefore, that while a spate of legislation has sought to define both functionally and jurisdictionally the relationships among various units of local government in the federal system, the unceasing competition among these units for resources subjects their functional and jurisdictional claims to constant challenge and frequent change.

The research imperative embodied in this assumption is that the interdependent nature of the federal system is basically problematic and must be taken into consideration when investigating as central an issue as the acquisition of revenues by local governments. To examine empirically the question of local government autonomy or dependence, New York State will serve here as the research site; it is therefore necessary to provide a brief description of its various units of local government.

NEW YORK STATE LOCAL GOVERNMENT UNITS

The aim of the present research is to determine, for the period 1959–75, where various local governmental units obtained their revenue. While the scope of analysis is confined to New York State and is, therefore, limited, there are distinct reasons for using one state. Under the American federal system, local governments are creations of the state; namely, they owe their existence to various acts of state legislatures. As a result local governments, both in terms of organization and authority, exhibit a high degree of variation from one state to the next. The responsibility for the delivery of services varies. In some instances, the state is chiefly responsible; in others, local government must bear this burden. Recent data on governmental finance (Maxwell & Aronson 1977, p. 32) reveal that Hawaii relies heavily on the state government for the delivery of services, accounting for 80 percent of the expenditures, whereas New York relies primarily on local government, the state accounting for only 22.5 percent. Since in New York, the state's contribution accounts for one-fifth of the total amount, local governments must rely on other sources of support, either local or national. Consequently, unlike Hawaii, how New York local governmental units acquire their revenues is not so readily understandable and, therefore, warrants investigation. The present research includes the following local governmental units: counties, cities, towns, villages, school districts, and New York City (NYC), which, because of its size, fiscal importance, and unique organization, has been categorized individually.

Counties

Counties in New York are defined as "municipal corporations that are established to carry out various governmental functions that are authorized by law" (New York State 1976, p. 69). Historically, counties were political subdivisions of the state; however, in the early 1960s, as an increasing number of counties have adopted home rule charters, their authority no longer derives solely from state law.

Technically, New York State consists of 62 counties. The 5 counties, however, that comprise New York City have been stripped of their official governmental functions. In effect, New York State is divided into 57 counties. These may be placed into two categories: (1) those that operate under county law and (2) those that have adopted home rule charters. Forty counties fall into the former category and 17 into the latter. In the counties that operate under county law, the legislative and executive functions are combined, whereas in most charter counties these functions have been separated. All the charter counties except Tompkins and Herkimer have either elected or appointed administrators.

Cities; New York City

A city in New York State is a creation of the state legislature. Aside from New York City and Albany, which owe their status to colonial charters, the remaining 60 cities in New York State owe their existence to various legislative acts. Population size has little to do with these designations. For instance, 171 of the state's 556 villages have populations greater than that of the smallest city. The 62 cities in New York State range in population size from 3,000 to almost 7,900,000. The Municipal Home Rule Law of 1963 grants cities considerable power to amend their own charters or to adopt new charters without authorization from the state legislature. Thus cities have some discretion in changing their basic organizational and administrative structures to accommodate the needs of their citizens.

New York City, as it exists today, represents the consolidation of various counties, cities, towns, and villages. Thus, in contrast to the rest of the state, New York City diverges from the multitiered structure of local government. Hence there are five counties but no county government; nor are there any villages, towns, or other subcity units of government. The chief executive officer is the mayor, who is elected to a four-year term; and the chief fiscal officer is the comptroller, also elected to a four-year term. The legislative authority resides with the city council, which consists of 43 members; 33 are elected on a district basis, and 10 are elected from at-large boroughwide districts, 2 from each borough. The Board of Estimate acts as a second legislative body whose responsibility is limited to certain fiscal matters such as the budget, leases, franchises, contracts, and capital budgets. The board consists of the mayor, the council president, the comptroller, and the five borough presidents. In actuality, none of the members of the board is directly elected. The interests of the five boroughs are represented by their respective presidents, who are elected to four-year terms. (The borough president once had considerable administrative power on the board, but it has been transferred to the mayor by the most recent charter revision.)

Towns

Town may be defined as "a municipal corporation comprising the inhabitants within its boundaries and formed with the purpose of exercising such powers and discharging such duties of local government and administration of public affairs as have been, or may be conferred or imposed upon it by law" (New York State 1976, p. 98). In New York State, there are 930 towns. The governing authority for these units resides in the town board, which performs both executive and legislative functions. It should be noted that the executive power in towns is quite circumscribed. Any existing executive power is delegated by the councilmen to the supervisor. All members of the town board are directly elected.

The composition of these boards varies with population size. According to the Town Law of 1932, towns in New York State fall into two classes, primarily on the basis of population size. In the larger towns, the board usually consists of a supervisor and four councilmen, and in the smaller ones it normally consists of a supervisor, two town justices, and two councilmen. From this description it is evident that in the larger towns the judiciary functions have been separated from the legislative and executive ones; this is not the case in smaller towns. Like cities, towns enjoy some degree of autonomy because, as of 1964, they have been legally granted home rule powers.

Villages

Village may be defined as "a municipality that has satisfied the statutory requirements for incorporation as they were established and modified by the State Legislature" (New York State 1976, p. 116). As the last phrase implies, criteria for incorporation vary over time. The most recent legislation sets forth certain geographic and demographic criteria for incorporation; specifically, a territory of 500 or more inhabitants may incorporate as a village in New York State, provided that territory is not already part of a city or village. New York State has 556 villages, ranging in size from the Village of Dering Harbor with a population of 24 to the Village of Valley Stream with a population of 40,413. Most villages have populations of under 5,000. A village is governed by a board consisting of five elective officials: the mayor and four trustees. It should be noted that the board can increase or decrease the number of trustees subject to ratification by a mandatory referendum. Historically, a village board combined both legislative and executive functions. As the 1972 revision of Village Law attests, however, the trustees have become primarily concerned with legislative matters, and the mayor has increasingly assumed the executive responsibilities.

School Districts

In New York State in 1973, there were 759 local school districts. These are separate units of government with the power to levy taxes and to incur debts. There is an exception to this general tendency. In the five largest cities—New York, Buffalo, Rochester, Syracuse, and Albany—school districts are part of the municipal government.

School districts in New York may be divided into three categories: common, union free, and city. Common school districts provide education through eighth grade; they contract with neighboring districts for secondary education. They are governed by a single elected trustee or an elected three-member board of trustees. In contrast to common school districts, union free districts may operate high schools when granted a charter by the board of regents. These districts are governed by a board of education. Depending on the size of the district, these boards consist of three to nine members elected on a regular basis. If a district satisfies certain criteria, including those for size, the board may appoint a superintendent of schools.

City school districts—aside from those in the five largest cities—constitute separate units of government. These are governed by a board of three, seven, or nine members. In most instances, board members are elected; however, they are sometimes appointed. Common school districts and many union free districts are not able to appoint a superintendent. These districts are administered by a superintendent who is, in effect, the local representative of the commissioner of education. The superintendent, in this case, has jurisdiction over a varying number of school districts, a jurisdiction referred to as a "supervisory district."

FINDINGS

As is evident from the above description, there is a representative array of local governmental units included in the present analysis. Discussion will make clear, moreover, that the research also includes the standard types of revenue. Consequently, by not having restricted the scope of analysis to one type of governmental unit or to one source of revenue, the concept of centralization/decentralization can be examined from a differentiated perspective instead of a monolithic one. The assumption is that a differentiated view of this concept is more congruent with its empirical manifestations. To elaborate, the concept of centralization—which has been operationalized as the degree of local government's dependence on one or more sources of revenue—casts doubt on the zero-sum assumption that underlies the more traditional, monolithic notions of centralization. In at least two respects, there is empirical justification for presenting an alternative to the monolithic view. First, contrary to what this view implies, there is no arbitrary ceiling on how much revenue a local government may raise annually. This is not to dismiss the constraining influence exerted by various political, legal, and economic factors. A county board of representatives, for example, may decide to generate more revenue by substantially increasing its sales tax. Legally this action is permissible; however, mobilizing political support for such a measure may prove quite difficult. Also, since there is no prescribed ceiling, acquiring revenues from one source—such as procuring a loan from a bank—does not preclude acquiring them from other sources—such as state or federal aid. It may be inferred that local governments can usually avail themselves of a number of different sources of revenue. The degree of dependence or autonomy that local governments enjoy is determined by the source of the revenue and the amount that the source supplies. The source and the amount are affected, furthermore, by the competition among local governmental units for revenues. Thus competition, in part, determines a local government's autonomy or dependence. To conclude, such a differentiated perspective of centralization views the American system of public finance as a negotiated order based on competition for, and exchange of, resources; it also accentuates the fact that local governments differ according to the sources and the amount of revenue at their disposal.

As argued above, the sources of revenue reveal to what extent the various units of local government in New York State are dependent on various constituencies for resources. The relationship between each unit of local government and each of its constituencies implies a different type of dependence. Specifically, the type of dependency refers to the degree to which each local government either controls or is controlled by each of its constituencies in obtaining revenues. The following examples will serve to illustrate this point: a local government that depends primarily on locally generated revenues—whether they are in the form of local taxes or vendor charges—is relatively autonomous, for it depends mainly on local constituencies over which it has some degree of control. A local government primarily dependent on state resources may be viewed as less autonomous because frequently it has less control over the state legislature than it does over its own citizens. This nonetheless does not imply that a local government has no control over the state legislature; for, through its elected representatives and local interest groups, it can exert considerable political pressure. When a local government is primarily dependent on federal revenues, it has less control over this relationship than it does over its relationship with the state. This is because the amount of political influence that a single local government can exert through its political representatives and local interest groups at the federal level is relatively modest. The relationship between a local government and the state government, furthermore, is more institutionalized. For example, the amount of state aid allocated to a local government is often determined by population size. The state revenue-sharing program is a case in point. Federal revenues are frequently allocated in the form of grant-in-aid programs, which entail considerable bargaining between a local government and the federal government. The annual level of grant support is often subject to negotiation. When a local government is primarily dependent on borrowing and the sale of bonds for revenues, it has the least control over its relationship with a constituency because the relationship is essentially that of a debtor. Given this perspective, revenue becomes a means of examining the autonomy and dependence of local government.

Summary data on the sources and amounts of revenue raised by different units of local government have been obtained from New York State's *Special Report on Municipal Affairs,* which the state comptroller prepares and submits annually to the legislature. The data used in the present research spans the period 1959–75. Information pertaining to six general revenue categories has been included in the analysis of the revenue structure of different units of local government. These categories are borrowings, real property and nonproperty taxes, special activity revenues, and state and federal aid.

CHANGES IN TOTAL REVENUE BY UNIT OF LOCAL GOVERNMENT, 1959–1975

Table 3-1 provides a profile of the distribution of public revenues for New York local governments between 1959 and 1975.* During this seventeen-year period, county revenues increased the most, reflecting a 486-percent gain. New York City follows with a 366-percent increase; then towns, with 267 percent; school districts, with 252 percent; villages, with 194 percent; and cities, with 172 percent. It is evident that during this period there was considerable but not uniform growth in local government revenues; for example, counties evidenced the most disproportionate gain.

As table 3-1 reveals, from 1962 county revenues grew at a faster pace than the revenues of other local governments. The total county revenues for 1968–70 exceeded those for 1965–67 by 75 percent. By contrast, dur-

---

*To make the comparisons in table 3-1 more meaningful, an observation concerning the relationship among the various jurisdictional boundaries of local government should be made. These units are not always organized so that their boundaries are mutually exclusive. In some instances, the jurisdiction of one unit overlaps that of another. This is particularly true in the case of school districts; in other instances, the jurisdictions of two units—such as a village and a school district—may coincide. Finally, the jurisdiction of one unit—such as a county government—may encompass the jurisdiction of several smaller units such as towns, villages, cities, and school districts. An important consequence of such jurisdictional arrangements is that, since taxes often account for a significant proportion of local government revenues, local governments frequently share the same tax base. This shared relationship makes the raising of revenues a distinctly political issue. If school districts in a given county increase their tax assessments, for example, it is unlikely that the county government, although manifesting a similar need for additional revenue, could simultaneously increase its taxes by the same amount because the taxpayer would probably balk at having to accept two such increments at once.

Table 3-1   *Total Revenue by Type of Local Government, 1959–1975*

Type	1959–61	% Change	1962–64	% Change	1965–67	% Change	1968–70	% Change	1971–72	% Change	1973–75
Counties	$1,946,544	23	$2,395,378	42	$ 3,397,265	75	$ 5,935,643	60	$ 6,338,880	20	$11,412,018
Cities	1,229,771	19	1,458,946	11	1,614,613	29	2,075,104	49	2,057,930	9	3,349,653
Towns	896,360	32	1,181,634	24	1,461,110	41	2,066,790	29	1,775,858	24	3,292,404
Villages	441,229	15	507,812	21	616,250	32	812,679	36	738,355	17	1,297,382
School districts	4,035,277	26	5,090,860	38	7,004,385	40	9,805,472	32	8,656,161	9	14,197,152
New York City	5,844,879	26	7,381,839	40	10,315,763	43	14,797,952	46	14,451,350	26	27,211,359

Source: Adapted from data in New York State 1975.
Note: In calculating the annual rate of change of revenue, the number of years in a given period has been controlled.

ing the same period, the total revenue for New York City, towns, and school districts increased by 43 percent, 41 percent, and 40 percent, respectively. Villages and cities experienced substantially smaller changes: 32 percent and 29 percent. Paradoxically, despite the dramatization of the urban crisis by politicians and the media, cities were relatively unsuccessful in translating this purported social concern into increased revenues.

Between 1968–70 and 1971–72, county governments evidenced an increase of 60 percent; this increase is considerably more than that experienced by other units of government. Although these aggregate figures do not indicate what contribution was made by the federal government, it may be inferred that the change in administration did not have an adverse effect on the growth of county revenues. During the same period, cities experienced a sizable increase in revenues over the previous period, 1959–67, while New York City continued to experience modest revenue growth. It may be speculated that federal and state aid had begun to offset the decrease in tax revenues created by the flight of business, industry, and the middle class to the surburbs during the 1960s. By comparison, villages, towns, and school districts registered significant but, nonetheless, smaller increases in revenue: 36 percent, 29 percent, and 32 percent, respectively. It can be generally stated that up until the 1973–75 period counties, New York City, cities, and villages reflected an overall pattern of steady growth in revenue, while the growth of town revenues and school district revenues followed fairly erratic patterns.

Though it had been widely heralded that the federal revenue sharing program would bolster local government revenues, examination of the 1973–75 period in table 3-1 reveals that the rate of revenue growth for all types of local government actually dropped sharply during the early years of the revenue sharing program. While the actual dollar amount of revenues continued to grow during the period, the rate of revenue growth for counties, cities, and school districts proved to be the lowest for any of the periods examined in table 3-1. The rate of revenue growth for counties during the 1973–75 period was 20 percent, while cities and school districts experienced only a 9-percent increase in revenues over the 1971–72 period. Noticeable drops in the rate of revenue growth were also experienced by towns, villages, and New York City. Towns experienced the lowest rate of revenue growth of 24 percent since the 1965–67 period, while the revenue growth of villages dropped to 17 percent—the lowest since the 1962–64 period. After nearly a decade of continuous growth in the rate of revenue collections, New York City experienced a decline of 20 percent in the rate of revenue growth over the 1973–75 period. The rate of revenue growth for New York City during the 1973–75 period was 26 percent, its lowest rate of growth since the 1962–64 period.

Given the aggregate figures presented in table 3-1, it is only possible to speculate as to why the sudden change in the rate of revenue growth occurred during the 1973–75 period. One plausible explanation for the lower rate of revenue growth experienced by local governments during the 1973–75 period is the cutback of federal funds in other grant programs. Nathan, Manvel, and Calkins (1975) and Stolz (1974) have pointed out that just when the federal revenue sharing program was being enacted, the era of the Great Society social welfare assistance programs were being phased out by the Nixon and Ford administrations. The withdrawal of federal dollars from the domestic programs of the 1960s coupled with the impoundment of funds carried out by the Nixon administration would affect the rate of revenue growth of local governments in two ways.

First, direct grants from the federal government to local governments would be reduced as federal support of these programs diminished. Second, the federal government imposed ceilings on the amount of money provided by federal grant-in-aid programs to states. These ceilings indirectly affect the amount of extra-local revenue available to local governments, for if the amount of federal aid to states is reduced, states must begin to economize. One means of economizing is to reduce the amount of state aid to local governments. To gain a better understanding of the various patterns and shifts in local government revenue growth for the entire period as well as the 1973–75 period, it is necessary to discuss the data reported in table 3-2 below.

Borrowings

In New York State, as in other states, there are constitutional limits on the type and the amount of debt that local governments can incur. Prohibitions against both short-term and long-term indebtedness, however, have been made less restrictive with the adoption of home rule policies. As Moak and Hillhouse point out, ". . . the role of borrowing is that of supplying ready funds for immediate use through the anticipation of future revenues . . . borrowing permits the leveling out of the burden of payment which cannot be easily achieved by the pay as you acquire" (Moak & Hillhouse 1975, p. 91). Borrowing, more than any other source of revenue, is more sensitive to fluctuations in the national economy.

In the present study, *borrowings* includes issuance of bonds and tax, revenue, and bond anticipation notes, and any premiums and accrued interest on such borrowings. As table 3-2 indicates, dependence on borrowing by all local government units was relatively stable during 1959–75. Cities, towns, and villages relied on borrowing as a source of revenue more than the other units of local government. Despite its fiscal difficulties, New York City relied on borrowing less than other units of government. Table 3-2 also reveals that as county government grew—both in terms of scope and number of services—it increasingly relied on borrowing. The reliance on borrowing by all units of local government, however, decreased between 1971–72 and 1973–75. This decrease may be attributable to two factors. First, it may reflect an increased reliance on funds made available to local governments by the Federal Revenue Sharing Act of 1972. Sec-

Table 3-2   *Percentage of Total Revenue by Type of Local Government,*
             1959–1975

Categories	1959–61	1962–64	1965–67	1968–70	1971–72	1973–75
Borrowings						
Counties	16	14	14	16	21	12
Cities	23	27	22	20	27	18
Towns	26	30	29	30	26	20
Villages	21	20	20	23	26	18
School districts	19	16	14	12	13	5
New York City	16	17	17	11	19	12
Real property tax						
Counties	39	37	34	26	22	23
Cities	40	38	38	33	26	25
Towns	33	30	27	28	29	30
Villages	43	43	41	38	36	37
School districts	39	39	36	36	38	44
New York City	31	27	23	19	14	13
Nonproperty tax						
Counties	2	2	3	9	10	12
Cities	7	6	8	10	9	12
Towns	0	0	2	2	3	3
Villages	2	2	2	3	4	4
School districts	1	1	1	1	1	1
New York City	27	27	24	22	20	21
Special activity revenues						
Counties	15	17	15	14	11	12
Cities	21	20	20	22	19	22
Towns	27	27	28	28	28	30
Villages	28	29	29	27	28	28
School districts	4	3	5	5	5	6
New York City	9	9	9	7	6	7
State aid						
Counties	19	18	21	20	17	17
Cities	7	6	8	12	12	13
Towns	13	11	13	11	11	10
Villages	5	5	6	7	6	6
School districts	36	40	41	43	40	41
New York City	11	12	17	24	23	23
Federal aid						
Counties	8	11	13	15	19	24
Cities	2	3	4	3	7	10
Towns	0	1	1	1	3	7
Villages	1	1	2	2	3	7
School districts	1	1	3	3	3	3
New York City	6	7	9	17	18	24

Source: Some data adapted from New York State 1975.
Note: Due to errors in rounding, the columns in these tables do not always add up to 100 percent.

ond, it may indicate that many local governments have reached their constitutional debt limit (Billings 1974). While local governments' dependence on borrowing during this period was substantial, it did not increase significantly; and, therefore, local governments' dependence on the national private sector did not increase.

Real Property Taxes

For many years property taxes have been considered the backbone of locally generated revenues; however, recently there has been some indication that property taxes as a source of revenue are becoming less important. This is often attributed to the exodus of business and industry from the cities and metropolitan areas. This raises the question, Which level of government has been most affected? The dependence of towns, villages, and school districts on property taxes has remained relatively constant. While there have been yearly fluctuations, the basic level of dependence has not changed. Towns showed a 3-percent decrease for the period, school districts a 5-percent increase, and villages a 6-percent decrease.

Due to the purported diminishing tax base, the issue of city government dependence on property taxes is of particular interest. Hence it seems appropriate to compare New York City's dependence on this type of revenue with that of other cities. From 1959–61 to 1973–75, New York City shows a steady decline in the amount of revenue derived from property taxes. Specifically, in 1959–61 New York City derived 31 percent of its revenues from property taxes; by 1973–75, however, only 13 percent of its revenue came from that source. This decline occurred at the same time that demands for public services were increasing, forcing New York City to look elsewhere for sources of revenue. The other cities in the state did not follow New York City's pattern. From 1959 to 1967, these cities' dependence on property taxes for revenue decreased slightly, from 40 percent to 38 percent; however, from 1965–67 to 1973–75, their dependence on these taxes decreased by 13 percent, from 38 to 25 percent.

During this period counties experienced a steady decline in property taxes as a source of revenue: a drop of 16 percent, from 39 percent in 1959–61 to 23 percent in 1973–75. Although the data are not conclusive, it may be inferred that businesses and industries not only moved out of the cities but also out of New York State, in general, relocating in southern and western states, where the commitment by local government to the delivery of services is considerably less and, therefore, the taxes are lower.

Despite the decline in revenue from property taxes, local governments did not attempt to compensate for the loss in revenue by increasing their dependence on borrowing from the private sector; to offset the effect of a shrinking property tax base, local governments had at their disposal the four other options for generating revenues mentioned above: (1) nonproperty taxes; (2) special activity revenues; (3) state aid; and (4) federal aid.

The remainder of this discussion attempts to discover which option or options local governments selected (see also table 3-2).

Nonproperty Taxes

Due to legislation passed in 1947, New York State local governments have considerable nonproperty taxing authority. The category "nonproperty tax" consists mainly of local sales taxes, income taxes, and user taxes; sales taxes usually produce the greatest amount of revenue. Despite the legislative mandate, raising revenue through nonproperty taxes often presents local government officials with political problems, for it is difficult to gain popular support for increases in sales and income taxes. New York City, however, due to its income and sales taxes, is more dependent on nonproperty taxes than other units of local government. From 1959–61 to 1973–75 this dependence nonetheless decreased slightly. In 1959 nonproperty taxes accounted for 27 percent of New York City's revenue, in 1973–75 they accounted for 21 percent. This slight decrease may be attributed to two factors: First, during the 1960s a large number of middle-class families left New York City for the suburbs, reducing the amount of taxable income. Second, raising nonproperty taxes has become increasingly unpopular politically because it tends to penalize those income groups that can least afford it.

During this period the amount of revenue derived by cities other than New York increased slightly. In 1959–61, cities obtained approximately 7 percent of their revenue from nonproperty taxes, whereas by 1973–75 nonproperty taxes accounted for 12 percent of their revenue. As these percentages attest, cities depended on nonproperty taxes for only a small portion of their revenue. Counties exhibited a similar pattern. Their dependence on nonproperty taxes for revenue increased from 2 to 12 percent. Towns, villages, and school districts depended on nonproperty taxes for only a small fraction of their revenue, and this dependence remained relatively stable, increasing slightly for towns and villages and decreasing slightly for school districts. It is evident from table 3-2 that cities, counties, and New York City did not depend on nonproperty taxes to compensate for the loss of revenues resulting from the diminishing property tax base. All units of local government moreover were *minimally* dependent on nonproperty taxes as a source of revenue.

Special Activity Revenues

Special activity revenues are derived primarily from the user charge that local governments place on certain public services and facilities. Through the implementation of user charges, local governments have been able to provide public services that might otherwise be provided by private interests. These revenues are derived from special service functions such as public transportation, hospitals, cemeteries, stadiums, auditoriums, docks, markets, golf courses, and airport facilities. They also include local government-operated water, electric, gas, and steam utility systems, as well as miscellaneous charges such as interest and penalties on taxes; licenses and permits; fines, fees, and forfeited bail sales; rentals and reimbursements; and departmental fees and charges.

Of all the units of local government, villages were the most dependent on this type of revenue (see table 3-2). Although there was a slight decrease, villages obtained approximately 30 percent of their revenue from special activity revenues. For cities, revenues obtained from special activities remained relatively constant. By contrast, New York City depended less on these revenues. In 1959–61 it obtained approximately 9 percent from special activity revenues; however, by 1973–75, these contributed only 7 percent to its total. During this period, town and village dependence on special activity revenues was approximately the same; it remained moreover relatively constant. Counties' dependence was even less than towns', fluctuating between 11 and 17 percent. This contribution moreover has changed little over time. As might be expected, school districts are the least dependent on special activity revenues; for, unlike other units of local government that provide an array of services, some of which require user charges, school districts are constituted to provide a specialized service: education. There are also legal constraints on the types of vendor relationships in which school districts can enter, thereby limiting the number of user charges that can be levied.

Up to this point, the present paper has examined local governments' dependence on revenues generated either in the private sector through borrowing or in the public sector through taxes. What now must be examined is *intergovernmental transfers,* money that comes to local governments either from the state or the federal government.

Intergovernmental Transfers

State Aid. Revenues derived from state aid consist of state revenue sharing; highway, traffic, and transportation; urban renewal; social service assistance; youth projects; plans for sewer studies; maintenance and construction of sewage treatment facilities; health care; libraries; mental health services; loss of railroad tax compensation; and state mortgage taxes. It has been argued that a significant proportion of state aid is derived from federal sources, since federal aid is closely tied to state spending because of matching formulas (Roeder 1976). Since these revenues are essentially mandated for state programs and are administered by the state, however, they have been treated in this study as state aid. Of the units of local government in our sample, New York City and other state cities turned increasingly to the state as a source of revenue during 1959–75. As table 3-2 indicates, county dependence on state aid increased slightly between 1959–61 and 1968–70, from 19 to 20 percent. Between 1968–70 and 1973, however, county dependence on state aid dropped 3 percent, from 20 to 17 percent. It may be speculated that this decline may be attributed to increased federal support due to revenue sharing. New York City's pattern differed markedly from that of the counties. Between 1959–61 and 1973–75 the city's dependence on state aid increased by 12 percent; specifically, in 1959–61, it accounted for 11 percent of the city's revenues; and by 1973–75 it accounted for 23 percent.

The other cities in New York State also increased their dependence on state aid but not as dramatically as New York City. Between 1959–61 and 1973–75, this dependence increased by 6 percent. By 1973–75, however, cities, when compared to New York City and counties, derived a much smaller portion of their revenue from New York State, receiving approximately 13 percent. Of all the units of local government, school districts were the most dependent on the state for revenue, receiving approximately two-fifths from that source. Between 1959–61 and 1973–75, this dependence gradually increased from 36 percent to 41 percent. It may be inferred from these percentages that although, with the exception of the five largest cities, New York State school districts functioned politically as autonomous units, fiscally they were highly dependent on the state. Thus, the state's commitment to elementary and secondary education has a considerable effect on school districts' revenues; and, therefore, it affects to some degree how they spend their money. Towns and villages, when compared with the other units of government, are much less dependent on state aid. Between 1959–61 and 1973–75, moreover, this dependence remained relatively constant, decreasing slightly for towns and increasing almost imperceptibly for villages. Hence it may be inferred that since towns and villages provide fewer services than the other units of government, they can rely on locally generated revenues—specifically property taxes and special activity revenues—to underwrite the costs of providing services. To recapitulate, parsimony in service insures some degree of fiscal autonomy. Conversely, as the number of services delivered by cities, counties, and New York City have multiplied, the more these units of government have had to shift from locally generated to externally generated revenues: the state and federal government and the private sector.

Federal Aid. In the present analysis, federal aid includes grants to local governments for purposes such as public health, social service assistance, hospital construction, sewage treatment works, public works planning, urban renewal programs, and civil defense equipment. The data in table 3-2 regarding federal aid are particularly interesting in light of the public policy debate concerning federal aid to local governments, especially the cities. Some critics have argued that despite massive doses of federal aid, the problems of the cities have grown both in magnitude and severity. Advocates of urban areas have countered this criticism by contending that the amount of federal aid is still inadequate. As table 3-2 attests, New York

City's dependence on federal aid as a source of revenue increased markedly—by 18 percent—from 1959–61 to 1973–75. Ironically, the larger gains were made under the Republican and not the Democratic administrations, despite the latter's sponsorship of the War on Poverty.

Counties' dependence on federal aid increased similarly: it went from 8 to 24 percent of total county revenue. Unlike New York City, however, counties did not make their sharpest gains under the Republican administrations; instead, the pattern was one of steady increases throughout the period. The relative growth may be attributed to two factors: (1) increased urbanization and (2) the gradual assumption by counties of increased responsibility for delivering social services. Aside from New York City, the other cities' dependence on federal aid increased rather modestly, from 2 percent in 1959–61 to 10 percent in 1973–75. It may be speculated that not only does New York City have a greater need for federal aid, but it also has the political clout necessary to obtain it. Another inference to be drawn from these percentages is that, despite the outcry concerning the extravagant waste of federal resources on cities, in fact the federal government's contribution to cities has been relatively modest. Thus it may be concluded that federal aid to cities including New York City is more a response to political pressures than to actual needs.

Prior to the Republican administrations towns and villages received virtually no federal aid. Beginning in 1968, there was a small but noticeable increase. It may be inferred that the concept of the "New Federalism" introduced by the Republicans led to more support for these smaller units of government than did the War on Poverty, which was intended primarily for urban populations. As might be expected, school districts, which more than other units of local government are legally tied to the state, were virtually independent of federal support during this period.

SUMMARY

As stated, the aim of this research was to determine whether local governments in New York State between 1959 and 1975 exhibited the autonomy that de Tocqueville (1953, pp. 61–64) hailed as one of the primary virtues of American democracy or whether their dependence on the state and federal government had transformed them into administrative appendages of the national welfare state. Using New York State as a research site, the attempt was made to ascertain whether there was merit in the oft-repeated criticism that the American federal system has become too centralized. The assumption was that previous research, due to its conceptual framework and methodology, was not equipped to evaluate properly—whether the system was centralized or decentralized—because it frequently limited the scope of its analysis to one level of government within the multitiered federal system. An important consequence of adopting this assumption has been to exaggerate the role of local government in the decision-making process and to minimize the role that other levels of government and private institutions play in this process. As a result, local government looms more self-sufficient than, in fact, it is; and the federal system appears more decentralized than, in fact, it is.

Another factor that contributed to this image of the federal system was that previous research often focused on decisions that were confined to one level of government. It concentrated on output measures such as program innovations and expenditures. This perspective ignores the fact that local governmental units have increasingly had to rely on either larger governmental units or the private sector for resources to handle the problems. Concentrating on policy outputs such as expenditures and program innovations puts the cart before the horse because it ignores the significance of inputs, specifically revenues. The amount of revenue and the source from which it is obtained can influence, to a greater degree, a local government's pattern of expenditure and level of innovation. Revenues provide a better means for determining local governments' autonomy or dependence because the raising of revenues frequently requires considerable negotiations among levels of government and between the public and private sectors. To address this issue, the present paper examined where various units of local government in New York State obtained their revenues between 1959 and 1975. The six revenue categories used reflect varying degrees of autonomy and dependence. Local governments that rely primarily on property taxes, special activity revenues, and nonproperty taxes may be characterized as autonomous, while local governments—which primarily acquire their revenues through state aid, federal aid, and borrowing—may be termed *dependent*.

County government was neither wholly autonomous nor wholly dependent. It derived approximately two-fifths of its revenues from federal aid and property tax. The remaining three-fifths was spread relatively evenly among nonproperty taxes, special activity revenues, borrowings, and state aid. Despite its growing need for services due to urbanization and the increased availability of federal funds due to revenue sharing, county government avoided becoming solely dependent on the federal government for assistance. By the same token, it had no illusion of self sufficiency. Property taxes are declining due to the exodus of the middle class, business, and industry from the Northeast. Owing to various political, economic, and legal constraints, nonproperty taxes and special activity revenues furthermore could not generate enough income to underwrite the cost of rapidly expanding services.

By contrast, New York City, plagued by both fiscal problems and service needs, turned increasingly to the federal government for assistance. The city experienced a more precipitous decline in revenues obtained from property taxes than did the county governments (see table 3-2). Similarly, the amount of revenue generated by nonproperty taxes between 1959 and 1975 decreased steadily, from 27 to 21 percent. The amount contributed by special activity revenues also dwindled. In 1959, this category of revenue accounted for almost 10 percent of New York City's total, but by 1975 it accounted for only 7 percent. It may be inferred that New York City's reliance on local sources of revenue is rapidly diminishing. The shift to extra-local sources nevertheless has not been without its difficulties. Namely, the state government, the banks, and the federal government—all are reluctant to be saddled with the responsibility for regularly supplying revenue to New York City. As the recent fiscal crisis demonstrated, there are legal and economic constraints on the amount of aid that New York City can request from either the private sector or the state government. Hence, by process of elimination, the federal government becomes the most desirable source of support; and, as noted previously, between 1959 and 1975, the size of its contribution to New York City's total revenue substantially increased. For a variety of political, economic, and social reasons, the federal government is not eager to adopt New York City as its ward. The trends in the data nonetheless indicate that New York City, when compared with other units of New York State local government, is more vulnerable to the threat of centralization.

Other cities in New York State relied mainly on locally generated revenues: property taxes, nonproperty taxes, and special activity revenues. Between 1965 and 1975, this contribution ranged from 67 percent in 1965 to 59 percent in 1975 of the total for cities. Of these three sources of local support, only the revenue produced by property taxes declined, dropping from 38 percent in 1965 to 25 percent in 1975. From 1959, special activity revenues remained constant, contributing between 19 and 22 percent, and nonproperty taxes increased from 7 percent in 1959–61 to 12 percent in 1975. In contrast with county governments and New York City, other New York State cities' main source of extra-local revenue was borrowings, although their dependence on state and federal aid increased, so that by 1975 the combined contribution of these two categories of revenue to the total amount was approximately 23 percent. In effect, by relying mainly on local sources of revenue, these cities retained a considerable degree of autonomy. Faced with the dilemma of growing service needs and a shrinking tax base, however, they may have to relinquish their autonomy in exchange for external support.

Towns and villages depended, for the most part, on local sources for their revenue: primarily property taxes and special activity revenues. The amount contributed by nonproperty taxes was negligible. Their main extra-local source of revenue was borrowing. As table 3-2 shows, towns and villages, when compared with counties, New York City, and cities, derived a much smaller amount of revenue from the state and federal government. Their acquisition of revenues tended to follow the same pattern as New York State cities (with the exception of New York City). Unlike the cities, however, towns and villages are not faced with the dilemma of a rising demand for services and a rapidly dwindling tax base. Either by design or accident, towns and villages tend to attract residents who are accustomed to purchasing most of their services from the private sector. In fact, it may be argued that their location in rural areas and suburbs reflects a desire to escape the high taxes and endless queues associated with urban government. In sum, there are not enough incentives for towns and villages to trade their cherished autonomy for the additional resources that the state and federal governments can supply.

School districts, which are the most specialized type of local government in this study, relied on property taxes and state aid for approximately four-fifths of their total revenue. Despite their dependence on state aid, school districts are relatively autonomous. Since American culture places a premium on education, the value of the service provided by these districts is relatively unchallenged by both other units of government and the public. As a result school districts, unlike other units of local government, do not have to enter into protracted negotiations to establish the legitimacy of their requests for aid. The state furthermore is willing to comply with their requests for aid because it can rationalize that an investment in education saves money elsewhere. Specifically, it reduces the welfare costs and obviates the need for additional programs in job training and placement. Since the tangible value of an education moreover has been demonstrated, the public is more willing to bear the burden of increased taxes than it is for other services such as health and welfare, whose value remains unproven. Hence the relative autonomy that school districts have is attributable to the service they provide rather than to the sources of revenue.

Despite the concern about an overly centralized federal system, the local governmental units in New York State included in this study did not exhibit a high degree of centralization. In fact, the reverse appeared to be the case: namely, most of the local governmental units seemed to be relatively autonomous in their acquisition of revenues. There was variation, of course: towns, villages, and, to some degree, cities enjoyed more autonomy than New York City and counties. It may be inferred that towns, villages, and, to a lesser extent, cities still subscribe to the Jeffersonian notion that the best government is the least government. By contrast, since their constituencies expect them to deliver a wide array of services (e.g., both to the general population and to specific population groups such as blacks, women, and the poor), New York City and counties are more committed to a redistributive notion of government. As discussed above, to meet these rising service needs, locally generated revenues are no longer adequate. Consequently, New York City and county governments must contemplate sacrificing their autonomy and appealing to extra-local sources, primarily the federal government, for assistance. Pursuing this strategy of course would enhance the likelihood of centralization. As the recent fiscal crisis in New York City illustrated, however, the federal government is loath to provide massive amounts of aid on a regular basis to local governments. Therefore, although federal aid to New

York City and counties is increasing, it is not dispensed prodigally; local governments must demonstrate their commitment to efficiency by reducing unnecessary services and by eliminating superfluous jobs. Thus—contrary to what critics have alleged—the federal government is, perhaps, more eager than some local governments to avoid centralization.

Although the revenue data for local units of New York State government between 1975–78 are not available, it is possible to make some speculations regarding the main sources of revenue on which these governmental units are now relying and will probably continue to rely in the near future.

As the data in table 3-2 indicate, between 1959–75 state aid to New York City doubled and federal aid quadrupled. Yet, as the data in table 3-2 affirm, between 1971–72 and 1973–75 the rate of revenue growth in New York City began to decline. When viewed from the perspective of the past seventeen years, New York City has become increasingly dependent on extra-local sources of support, suggesting a trend toward centralization. The recent decline in the rate of revenue growth, however, suggests that the amount of state and federal aid has either stabilized or begun to decrease, signifying that the trend toward centralization has either stalled or begun to reverse.

There are several reasons why state aid to New York City over the next five years is unlikely to increase. The fiscal crisis of 1975 revealed that New York State's financial problems were possibly of greater magnitude than New York City's. First the state debt had risen from $3.1 billion in 1961 to $13.4 billion in 1975. Second, among the fifty states, New York has the highest per capita state-local taxes. Third, since 1969 New York State has lagged far behind other states in personal income and industrial employment growth (Haider 1976, p. 207). Fourth, state emergency aid to New York City and Yonkers in 1975 and Buffalo and Niagara Falls in 1976 put a severe strain on both its resources and fiscal structure. The effects of this strain have yet to be remedied. Since 1975, New York State has embarked on a three-year austerity plan to balance its budget and to improve its credit rating. Part of this plan entailed substantial reductions in social services and aid to local government. Both these measures tended to circumscribe New York City's capacity to deliver services. This policy, albeit modified, is likely to continue, for Governor Carey, facing a tough election, is promising tax cuts. By the same token, New York City's political clout, coupled with its demonstrable social and economic needs, makes drastic cuts in state aid unlikely. As a result of these factors, state aid to New York City over the next five years will decline no more than 5 percent.

Overall federal aid to New York City will decline somewhat over the next five years. The city, in the wake of the 1975 fiscal crisis, was able to secure support until June 1978 through loans authorized by the New York Seasonal Financing Act of 1975. Both federal and New York City policy makers recognize that loans are essentially a stopgap measure. The Carter administration is caught in a dilemma. As President Ford discovered, an abrupt termination of the loan program is politically hazardous, especially when a presidential election is imminent. Pursuit of this loan policy is economically and politically undesirable. Economically, the federal government lacks the resources to provide loans indefinitely to New York City. If this loan policy continues, it establishes a dangerous political precedent, for it obligates the federal government to offer similar assistance to other financially troubled cities. Given those considerations, it seems likely that loans to New York City will be gradually terminated and, therefore, overall federal aid to New York City will decrease.

The other major source of federal aid to New York City is General Revenue Sharing. This program was initially designed to enable local governments to supplement existing services, fostering expansion and innovation. Cities such as New York that are confronted with a growing demand for services and a dwindling tax base, however, are using the funds supplied by this program to fill the gap in revenues caused by decreasing local resources. Federal policy makers are attempting to monitor this practice, for if it is pursued to excess, it will beget the same type of unwanted dependence by New York City on the federal government as a long-term loan policy would. Since General Revenue Sharing is designed to allow local officials considerable discretion on how the money is spent, federal officials can only curb this practice of substitution as opposed to the desired one of supplementation by controlling the amount of revenue-sharing money allocated to New York City. As a result, over the next five years, New York City's portion of revenue-sharing money is not likely to increase substantially (Nathan et al. 1975).

The anticipated decrease in extra-local sources of support means that New York City will have to rely on local sources of revenue such as borrowings, real property and nonproperty taxes, and special activity revenues. Although the Municipal Assistance Corporation has experienced some success in the sale of bonds, it has not produced the amount needed to make up for revenue shortages. The fiscal crisis of 1975 severely undermined buyer confidence, especially since many of these buyers are individual investors (Haider 1976, p. 212). The exodus of residents and industry to the suburbs and the Sunbelt states has reduced the amount of revenue that can be obtained from real property taxes. Given the prevailing political climate epitomized by the approval of Proposition 13 in California, the generation of more revenues through increased income taxes does not seem likely. The contribution made by special activity revenues has been so insignificant that in practical terms, it must be discarded as a source of revenue. Given these projections, New York City over the next five years is not likely to experience substantial growth in revenues; and, therefore, barring financial collapse, increased centralization is unlikely. As the report of the Temporary Commission on City Finances (1977) suggests, the long-term remedy for New York City's financial woes is economic development. Specifically, it must expand its tax base by attracting new businesses and industries while preventing the exodus of its present businesses and industries. In the short run, this means cuts in business taxes and reduction in the present level of municipal services (Adams 1978, p. 135).

Due to its precarious financial situation, New York State, since 1975, has not increased significantly the amount of aid to counties, cities, towns, villages, and school districts. This trend will probably continue over the next five years. In fact, Governor Carey's proposed tax cuts signal a reduction in state-sponsored services. By the same token, state aid to local governments will be selectively reduced but not drastically cut. It may be argued that this selectivity will depend on whether the program has powerful political advocates. Programs that have failed to develop such advocates are more likely to experience reductions. As Bailey et al. (1970) indicate in their study of state aid to education in the Northeast, school district officials have been quite successful in building coalitions consisting of state legislators, local party officials, teachers, and business and community interests. In New York State, these coalitions over the past decade have tended to grow in number and to gain in political strength, thus diminishing the likelihood that local school districts will suffer severe cutbacks in the near future. By contrast, the constant debate over the eligibility requirements for state public assistance attest to the fact that welfare recipients have not been effective in creating a powerful coalition of sympathetic advocates.

The chief source of federal aid to New York State local governments will be the General Revenue Sharing program, which in 1976 was renewed until 1980. In the counties and larger cities, revenue-sharing funds will be used to fill the gap in revenues created by the erosion of the local tax base. In the smaller cities, towns, villages, and school districts that are not confronted with the same fiscal problems as the larger units of government, these funds will be used to supplement existing services. While federal policy makers support the purposes and design of this program, they are eager to prevent revenue sharing from nurturing excessive dependence on the federal government. The amount of General Revenue Sharing funds allocated to New York State government over the next four years will not increase substantially.

It may be concluded that all units of local government in New York State will remain highly dependent on local sources of revenues. In the case of New York City, other large cities, and many counties, local resources may not be adequate to meet growing service needs. While they can anticipate some assistance from the state and federal governments, they will probably be compelled to adopt fiscal policies that emphasize reductions in the level of service expenditures and tax cuts. The smaller cities, towns, villages, and school districts, however, will continue to provide the same level of services.

CONCLUSION

The present study sought to achieve two objectives: (1) to determine, using New York State as a research site, how autonomous or dependent local governments are in terms of their acquisition of revenues and (2) to demonstrate the complexities involved in studying this question. Regarding the first objective, the finding is that the centralization of local government in New York State was more feared than real. Regarding the second, the attempt was made to demonstrate that most previous research on local government centralization/decentralization, both in terms of its conceptual framework and methodology, has ignored the dynamic nature of the federal system and, as a result, has depicted local government as being unduly centralized. A systematic examination of the full range of relationships produced by the interaction between types of local government and sources of revenue reflects a more accurate image of local government as an integral part of the federal system. This research illustrates that a comparative—rather than a case study—approach is more suitable for such an examination.

REFERENCES

Adams, J. R. 1978. Anatomy of a fiscal crisis. *The Public Interest* 50 (winter): 132–37.
Aiken, M. 1970. The distribution of community power: Structural bases and social consequences. In M. Aiken and P. E. Mott, eds. *The structure of community power*, pp. 487–525. New York: Random House.
Aiken, M., and Alford, R. R. 1970a. Community structure and innovation: The case of urban renewal. *American Sociological Review* 35 (June): 650–65.
———. 1970b. Community structure and innovation: The case of public housing. *American Political Science Review* 64 (September): 843–64.
Alford, R. R., and Friedland, R. 1975. Political participation and public policy. *Annual Review of Sociology* 1: 429–79.
Bailey, S., et al. 1970. A study of state aid to education in the Northeast. In M. Kirst, ed. *The politics of education at the local, state and federal levels*. Berkeley, Calif.: McCutchan.
Billings, C. D. 1974. The impact of revenue sharing in the United States of America on local credit. *Local Finance* 3: 11–14.
Buenker, J. D. 1973. *Urban liberalism and progressive reform*. New York: Scribner's.
Campbell, A. K., and Sacks, Seymour. 1967. *Metropolitan America: Fiscal patterns in government systems*. New York: Free Press.
Campbell, C. D., and Campbell, R. G. 1976. *A comparative study of the fiscal systems of New Hampshire and Vermont, 1940–1974*. Mishawaka, Ind.: Wheelabrator.
Clark, T. N. 1973. *Community power and policy outputs*. Beverly Hills, Calif.: Sage.
Crain, R. L., and Rosenthal, D. B. 1967. Community status as a dimension of local decision-making. *American Sociological Review* 32 (December): 970–84.
Dahl, R. A. 1961. *Who governs?* New Haven: Yale University Press.
de Tocqueville, A. 1963. *Democracy in America*. Ed. P. Bradley. Trans. H. Reeve. Vol. 1. New York: Vintage.
Eyestone, R. 1971. *The threads of public policy: A study in policy leadership*. Indianapolis, Ind.: Bobbs-Merrill.
Frieden, B. J., and Kaplan, M. 1975. *The politics of neglect*. Cambridge, Mass.: MIT Press.
Haider, D. H. 1976. Fiscal scarcity: A new urban perspective. In L. H. Masotti and R. L. Lineberry, eds. *The new urban politics*. Cambridge, Mass.: Ballinger.
Hawley, A. 1963. Community power and urban renewal success. *American Journal of Sociology* 68 (January): 422–31.

Hofstadter, R. 1955. *The age of reform.* New York: Vintage.

Hunter, F. 1953. *Community power structure: A study of decision-makers.* Chapel Hill: University of North Carolina Press.

Lincoln, J. R. 1976. Power mobilization in the urban community: Reconsidering the ecological approach. *American Sociological Review* 41 (February): 1–15.

Lineberry, R. L., and Fowler, E. P. 1967. Reformism and public policies in American cities. *American Political Science Review* 61 (September): 701–16.

Maxwell, J. A., and Aronson, J. R. 1977. *Financing state and local governments.* 3d ed. Washington, D.C.: Brookings Institution.

Moak, L., and Hillhouse, A. 1975. *Concepts and practices in local government finance.* Chicago: Municipal Finance Officers Association.

Mosher, F., and Poland, Q. 1964. *Costs of American governments.* New York: Dodd, Mead.

Nathan, Richard P.; Manvel, A. D.; and Calkins, Susannah E. 1975. *Monitoring revenue sharing.* Washington, D.C.: Brookings Institution.

New York State. Department of Audit and Control. 1959–75. *Special Report on Municipal Affairs.* 17 vols. Albany.

————. Department of State. 1976. *Local government handbook.* Albany.

O'Connor, J. R. 1973. *The fiscal crisis of the state.* New York: St. Martin's.

Reagan, M. D. 1972. *The new federalism.* New York: Oxford University Press.

Roeder, P. W. 1976. Stability and change in the determinants of state expenditures. Sage Professional Papers in American Politics 3, Series no. 04-027. Beverly Hills, Calif.: Sage.

Schmandt, H. J., and Goldbach, J. C. 1969. The urban paradox. In H. J. Schmandt and W. Bloomberg, Jr., eds. *The quality of urban life.* Vol. 3. Urban Affairs Annual Review Series. Beverly Hills, Calif.: Sage.

Smith, R. A. 1976. Community power and decision-making: A replication and extension of Hawley. *American Sociological Review* 41 (August): 691–705.

Stephens, G. 1974. State centralization and the erosion of local autonomy. *Journal of Politics* 36: 44–75.

Stolz, Otto G. 1974. *Revenue sharing: Legal and policy analysis.* New York: Praeger.

Temporary Commission on City Finances. 1977. *The city in transition: Policies and practices for New York City.* New York: Columbia Graduate School of Business.

Torrence, S. W. 1974. *Grass roots government: The county in American politics.* Washington, D.C.: Luce.

CHAPTER 4

URBAN RESOURCES, THE AMERICAN CAPITAL MARKET, AND FEDERAL PROGRAMS

Thomas Boast

The effect of the American capital market on urban[1] resources in the United States results from a federal polity that is embedded in nationally and internationally integrated economics. The market supplies approximately 90 percent of urban capital funds from external sources, while the central government provides only a tenth. Since the urban capital market is national in scope, cities must compete against each other. Those that create conditions conducive to private economic prosperity can compete successfully on the market, while those that have declining local economies are less able to attract market investment funds. If a local government does not guarantee financial returns to the suppliers of capital, the concentrated nature of the market allows a veto over urban politics. Thus the mobility of resources in the private sector creates conditions to which declining cities must react, but on their own and without the assistance of the central government. Cities are a residual in a federal political system at the same time that they are strongly influenced by private market financial decisions.

The political structure of local government in the United States, where there is competition for private wealth both between special and general governments within metropolitan areas and among governments in various regions of the country, provides an analog to the market. Subnational jurisdictions compete so that investment decisions will obtain the most

---

[1] As used in this paper, *urban* means the same as *state and local.* Neither states nor cities in the United States can exercise deficit spending, given the necessity of national economic steering. The "urban capital market" therefore includes debt issued by both states and cities; it is commonly called the "municipal bond market" in the United States. While aggregate statistics include both states and localities, a major focus later in the paper is cities. Much of the discussion is therefore phrased in terms of cities.

efficient allocation of resources among localities. The efficiency addressed by the political and economic markets, however, is not the only value that could be considered. If the two markets operate to exclude notions of equitable distribution among classes or among cities, then the markets exclude these values from an already established political agenda.

The dual markets of local government and capital resources in the United States create opportunities for horizontal lateral movement of economic enterprises and vertical policy redress for organized interests from the federal government (Scheiber 1975).

> . . . it remains an inescapable fact of federalism that if localities try to redistribute income to a much greater extent than the other localities, or if they run abnormally large deficits and incur subsequent high interest and debt retirement costs, there is a good risk that the taxpaying population will simply pick up stakes and leave the locality in a fiscal situation that is much more precarious (Gramlich 1976, pp. 417–18).

But it is not federalism alone that leads to this constraint on local resource uses. In addition, the municipal capital market provides opportunities to influence political choices in a particular city. Because the central government does not supply urban capital resources, private economic decisions can set boundaries around local government undertakings. If a city jeopardizes investment returns through deficit spending or large expenditure programs that do not directly generate private taxable wealth, market decisions can withhold credit. The reliance on the private capital market provides opportunities to enforce "fiscal equivalence" (Olson 1969). Local expenditure decisions can be dominated not only by taxpayer constituents but also by private investors seeking secure financial returns. Minorities lack the opportunity to expand the arena of conflict to more inclusive jurisdictions where coalition politics may be more successful (Schattschneider 1960).

The structure of political institutions has important consequences for the substance of political decisions (Offe 1974, pp. 36–37). City efforts to redistribute resources from haves to have-nots can be checked. Local politicians can borrow and displace costs into the future to provide benefits to organized clienteles without jeopardizing taxpayers' support. The New York City fiscal situation in the 1970s, for example, involved the expansion of borrowing and spending until capital market creditors suddenly refused to extend more loans. Organized clienteles such as labor unions and banks retained political access in the particularized bargaining arenas that were established to supply capital resources; but service users and unorganized community groups lost some influence over electoral coalitions. New York City politicians could point to the market during campaigns and shrug off responsibility with a "sorry, folks, but we have to regain access to the market." The market is not only a constraint but also an excuse.

Local politicians have had few incentives to organize and lobby for increased federal capital allocations. Unlike members of a functional interest group such as labor, agriculture, or business, cities compete against each other rather than against another sector. No issues unite local political leaders except the expansion of noncategorical, or unrestricted, federal funds such as General Revenue Sharing (GRS) or counter-cyclical aid grants. But the short-term strengthening of local current budgets has made cities only more reliant on the private capital market for long-term funds.

The federal government, instead of creating redressive resource flows, has narrowed, authorized, stabilized, and absorbed the risks of the market. Federal programs undergird, not undermine, the market. These programs of market support, which replicate the ideology of competition in American politics, avoid conflictual decisions in the political order. By not actively intervening in capital allocations, the state does not threaten its legitimacy, as it might if it replaced the market with political allocation and distribution decisions.

The first section of the present paper describes the sources and uses of urban capital in the United States. Then the capital market features that help create the opportunities to affect cities' political decisions are identified. The third section shows that market allocations have adversely affected cities in the northern and eastern United States. Next, the federal programs for the market are described. The conclusion identifies a dilemma of policy in a liberal state.

CITIES AS PRODUCTIVE ENGINES: DIRECTION AND FUEL

Cities provide the public services that make possible the continued prosperity of the economic machine in the United States. Public infrastructure promotes private economic enterprises by supplying utilities and transportation facilities that no single producer has an incentive to create. Educational and health facilities supply services that reproduce society in its own image. Subsidies are extended to reduce the "public bads" of private enterprise and to promote the "public goods" that are not profitably supplied by private entrepreneurs. By undertaking these activities, local politicians must be entrepreneurs, too. Low tax rates satisfy electoral constituents and attract private enterprise; market borrowings reduce current costs and provide economic infrastructure that promotes private prosperity. The symbiosis among borrowing, private wealth, and low tax rates makes cities part of the "competitive" capital sector (O'Connor 1973, pp. 13–15). In contrast to oligopolistic entities that can plan, set prices, and accumulate capital surpluses from retained earnings, the competitive local government sector must rely upon the marketplace for directives, prices, and capital (Galbraith 1973).

Urban capital consumption and saving play a considerable role in the national economy. State and local governments in the United States accounted for 88.3 percent of all general government gross capital formation and for 12.2 percent of all capital formed from 1961 through 1975 (U.N. 1977). It has been estimated that by 1980 nearly 10 percent of the Gross National Product will be spent on public facility expenditures (U.S. Congress 1969, p. 30). Thus, local government investments contribute a great deal to national wealth.

Private financial investors supply the bulk of the funds for public investment goods. State and local governments in the United States receive capital from two external sources: the federal government and the private capital market. During the decade from 1966 through 1975 the market supplied $193 billion of the $257 billion in long-term capital derived from sources outside cities, while federal government supplied $64 billion as "additions to state and local assets" (Moody's Investors Service 1976; U.S. Office of Management and Budget 1976). The market loaned the entire $187 billion in short-term funds. But since the federal government's $64 billion in long-term capital is a large sum with which to guide urban capital expenditures, a potential for public leverage seems to exist. The character of these federal additions, however, diminished the potential federal influence. Over two-thirds ($43 billion) of the federal funds were earmarked for highway construction, financed through the Highway Trust Fund. Appropriated federal capital for nonhighway purposes amounted to only $21 billion during the decade; over nine times as much capital derived from the market.

The federal government guaranteed only 4 percent ($15 billion) of the total market funds through federal "debt service grants" for urban renewal and public housing bond offerings. In effect, these grants assured investors that municipalities would retire debt as contracted. If the proceeds from housing project rentals or the resale price of urban renewal property did not meet the total costs of the projects, the federal government paid the difference (U.S. ACIR 1970, pp. 5; 18; 51–52). Even the very small percentage of market offerings that were guaranteed by the federal government therefore were used to promote particular private interests.

Rather than consciously reshaping the character of cities, federal grant programs have been oriented toward particular beneficiaries who receive the contracts and subsidies. During the New Deal, the Urbanism Committee of the National Resources Committee made efforts to coordinate federal programs (U.S. National Resources Committee 1937); but the federal government did not contrive an institutional mechanism for creating an "urban policy." Instead, professionals in various agencies defined the program goals: building highways to suburbs, guaranteeing housing mortgages in suburban but not central city areas, and tearing down uneconomic housing in central cities and replacing it with urban renewal. The

consequences for cities could not have been more complete, even if the
various programs had been coordinated. Cities were indirectly reshaped
from Washington.

Each federal agency served its particular clientele: commercial
redevelopers wanting profitable urban renewal land value "writedowns";
homeowners wanting the privacy and income protection provided by
suburban plots of land; commuters wanting individual comfort and mobile
convenience; contractors wanting more public works; bankers wanting
guarantees for already safe mortgages; home builders wanting easy financing terms for new construction. The "clients" of public housing, meanwhile, were excluded from the organized jockeying for federal aid. Federal urban programs helped cities facilitate private economic growth,
which is what cities did in the nineteenth century without federal aid
(Warner 1968, pp. 213–14).

The two primary uses of the capital supplied by the federal government—building highways and subsidizing commercial redevelopment—
are the opposite uses that one might expect of public financing. These
uses, especially highway projects, directly promote private economic enterprise. Since highways are economic infrastructure uses, it might be
expected that the market would supply the funds without the federal
policy involvement.[2] From 1966 through 1975, however, the market did
not primarily finance economic infrastructure. Instead, it supplied over 90
percent of the funds for social reproduction and subsidy purposes. More
than half of the market capital was used as subsidies. In contrast, states and
localities used 77 percent of all federal capital additions to assets for economic infrastructure, even though state and local governments used only
35 percent of all their total capital from external sources for infrastructure
purposes. In supplying 54 percent of all infrastructure funds, the federal
government—which could use a broader calculus than does the market in
determining the need for subsidy or social reproduction uses—abdicated
to the market the responsibility for these uses' financing. As a result, if a
city was creating too many educational or health services or providing too
many subsidies to particular sectors, the market could step in and call a
halt. Investor financial returns had to be protected first.

MARKET REACTIONS: MEANS AND PURPOSES

The market can have a direct influence on urban policy because of its
particular structure of ownership and manner of operation. The market
for state and local debt obligations is narrow—composed of only three

---

[2]*Economic infrastructure* uses include water, sewer, gas, electric, highway, bridge, and
tunnel facilities. These purposes contrast to *subsidy* uses (veterans, housing, industrial, pollution, and unidentified facilities) and *social reproduction* uses (education and health facilities).
The author tabulated the figures for these categories out of the specific purposes listed in
The Bond Buyer (1976, p. 8) and the U.S. Office of Management and Budget (annual).

main types of lenders—and is structured so that each new bond issue must pass numerous veto steps. These two factors have induced fluctuations in the demand for municipal securities (depending on the current strength of the national economy) and have provided opportunities for shutting a particular issuer out of the market altogether. Cities as a group lie on the bottom of the credit ladder, and individual cities remain vulnerable to particular market decisions.

Ninety percent of the municipal market is composed of only three sectors: commercial banks, fire and casualty insurance companies, and households. During prosperous economic periods, banks, insurance companies, and high-income households purchase tax-free municipal bonds to decrease their tax liabilities. The lower yields of municipals are offset by the large tax savings that these buyers achieve. When a recession occurs, however, banks' and insurance companies' profits ordinarily decline, eliminating the incentive to purchase tax-free bonds. Without these two major purchasers, cities must create large inducements for new buyers.

From 1961 through 1968 banks and insurance companies usually accounted for over 70 percent of the net flow of funds into municipal securities. From 1970 through 1972 the two sectors provided over 80 percent of the net new purchases. During the recessionary years of 1969 and 1973 through 1976, however, the two sectors contributed only 18, 57, 41, 20, and 38 percent of the net flow (Huefner 1972, p. 147; U.S. Board of Governors 1973, pp. 47–48; idem 1977, pp. 36–37). The remainder of the funds had to be obtained from the other sectors; households, for example, supplied 92, 57, and 50 percent of the net new purchases in 1969, 1974, and 1975. Yet in 1975 and 1976 these three main sectors left about a quarter of the net flow to the other sectors that ordinarily purchase less than 10 percent of the new municipal assets. In order to attract other types of lenders, borrowers have had to pay higher interest rates. The impact on cities' costs has been accentuated furthermore because (1) municipal bond interest rates fluctuate more widely than do those of federal securities and (2) localities cannot delay the issuance of short-term debt, no matter what the price (Phelps 1961, pp. 287–90; Tanzer 1964). Recessions, then, have a disproportionate impact on cities in relation to other borrowers.

The concentrated structure of the market also offers opportunities to veto particular cities' debt offerings. Commercial banks' holdings of municipal bonds are grouped in the few largest banks. In 1975, for example, the 187 insured commercial banks with more than $500 million in deposits held 49 percent of all deposits in insured commercial banks and received over 40 percent of all the interest on state and local debt paid to all insured commercial banks (U.S. Federal Deposit Insurance Corporation 1975, pp. 151; 187). Because commercial banks as a whole held nearly 50 percent of all outstanding municipal securities, these 187 commercial banks held about 20 percent of *all* municipal bonds. Decisions by a few banks to liquidate their bond portfolios can have a strong effect on the market.

In addition, new municipal bond issues must pass four independent evaluation stages, any one of which can decisively influence a city's access to the market. First, a prospectus must be prepared, usually by one of six nationally recognized financial consultants (U.S. Congress 1966, vol. 2, p. 9). Second, a bond counsel must register an opinion on the legality of the issue; without a favorable opinion, the issue virtually cannot be made (U.S. Congress 1966, vol. 2, p. 208). Third, only two major rating agencies—Standard and Poor's and Moody's Investors Service—provide ratings on municipal bonds. The rating decision affects both the cost and the marketability of a bond issue (Twentieth Century Fund 1974). Fourth, an underwriting syndicate must agree to market large bond issues to the secondary market; almost half of all bonds underwritten are picked up by the ten largest dealers and banks (Twentieth Century Fund 1976, p. 40). If an underwriting syndicate balks at picking up a new issue, anticipating that the secondary market may not buy the bonds, few alternative market sources exist for the issuer of a large transaction. No single bank can undertake the task of selling huge issues. Without the organization offered by the underwriter, therefore, the securities cannot be traded.

This structure creates strategic opportunities for reactions to individual issues. Recent New York City experience provides the extreme and more visible examples. In spring 1975, after the default of the New York State Urban Development Corporation (a revenue bond housing authority), the eleven New York City clearinghouse banks jointly refused to bid for New York City securities; the city was completely blocked from the market. In spring 1976, before a consortium of banks would lend funds to the state, New York officials had to satisfy three demands of the California-based Bank of America. First, the state comptroller was to impound revenues and place them in special debt service reserve funds; second, state political leaders were to promise not to enact another debt moratorium[3]; and third, federal mortgage guarantees for state housing projects would have to be obtained (*The New York Times* 1976, p. 46). When New York City attempted to reenter the credit market with a $200 million note issue in November 1977, the low rating Moody's gave the issue made underwriters back away from the sale. The underwriters determined that only

---

[3]The New York State legislature enacted a moratorium on the repayment of outstanding New York City short-term debt in November 1975 as part of the state's effort to aid the city (N.Y. Unconsolidated Laws, ch. 22 (Consolidated Laws Service)). A year later the New York Court of Appeals declared the moratorium invalid as an unconstitutional abrogation of the state's "full faith and credit" pledge to municipal bondholders (*Flushing National Bank v Municipal Assistance Corporation for the City of New York*, 40 N.Y.2d 731 (1976)). This court decision parallels a similar April 1977 Supreme Court finding that the New Jersey and New York legislatures' retroactive repeal of a bond covenant between the Port Authority of New York and New Jersey and creditors was an "impairment of contract" invalid under Article I, Section 10 of the United States Constitution (*United States Trust Company of New York v State of New Jersey*, 431 U.S. 1 (1977)).

a small amount of notes could be sold to the public at a very high interest rate, and the underwriters were not willing to purchase the notes for their own accounts (*The Fiscal Observer* 1977, p. 5).

In addition to the generalized low status of cities on the credit ladder and the specific strategic position that a few market sectors hold, the use of the market created an even more general influence on urban resources. The potential for generating surplus funds from city enterprises is reduced by the prior existence of the market and the heavy reliance on market funds. Indirect incentives are created for local politicians to maintain property in private ownership, to build up the value of private taxable property, and to tax that property at low rates. Because cities must compete with each other for resources from the market and because the strength of a city's economy is largely gauged by its assessed valuation of taxable property, those cities that most successfully develop economic enterprises are rewarded with lower cost and more accessible market capital. Conversely, cities that pay for expanded public services with a declining tax base are penalized with higher market costs and less access.

This combination of federalism with use of the capital market, conditions the policies pursued by local governments. Thus, perhaps Schumpeter's "The Crisis of the Tax State" more directly applies to urban communities in America than to the national government. Cities cannot extract resources from the private sectors too heavily because individuals would "lose financial interest in production or at any rate cease to use their best energies for it" (Schumpeter 1954, p. 20). Conversely, if a city does not rely on taxes but instead attempts to undertake its own productive enterprises, that city must operate within capitalist boundaries. A city must

> . . . work with money capital just as any other entrepreneur and since it can raise this money only through loans, it is unlikely that the remaining profit will be much larger than what could have been extracted from the same industry by direct and indirect taxes including taxes on the income of this industry (Schumpeter 1954, p. 24).

Whichever route to production a city takes, whether nominal taxation or minimal enterprise, it remains a business not a polity. In the U.S. federal system, no city can be entirely maverick. Other cities' participation in the capital market will draw back nonconforming local policy into a singular mold: the creation of infrastructure and avoidance of "nonproductive" public services.

THE FEDERAL POLITY OF CITIES AND CAPITAL

A basic tenet of the American polity is that local governments are the most efficient means to satisfy individual preferences. Just as consumers in the economic market can choose their desired goods and services, the federal structure provides individuals with maximum choice to live with their most preferred bundle of collective goods (Ostrom, Tiebout & Warren 1961). The ideology is reflected in the law in that cities are treated like corporations but states and the national government are not. For example, municipalities are subject to antitrust laws. Further, citizen taxpayers have standing in the courts to challenge the constitutionality of local spending programs but not federal or state expenditures except in the most limited circumstances. The rationale is that a municipal taxpayer has a direct and immediate interest in local expenditures, much as does a stockholder in a private corporation.[4] The taxpayer owns part of the city; the theory is that of contractual government.

Cities are also like enterprises because cities' effects on each other are as widespread as the externalities created in the private marketplace. Cities competing for economic growth and resources have just as decisive effects on political development as do corporations on economic development. Growth is multipoled and disjointed; presumably unbalanced growth is the propellant of innovation. The competition among cities means however that what one city gains, another loses; the game on the market is zero-sum.

The consequence is similar to that which resulted from the competition among states for economic growth in the nineteenth century, when state policy intervention provided the "base, guarantee, defense, and take-off" for the Lockean man of property (Berle 1955, p. 79). During the nineteenth century the federal market among states provided an opportunity for those opposed to governmental intervention to use the states as excuses to promote laissez-faire ideology or to create public intervention in support of producer interests. Which strategy was used depended upon the particular problem presented by a state's policy. Those who believed in "states' rights" in principle did not necessarily oppose governmental action by the states; but those who believed in "states' rights" in order to stop governmental intervention counter to the interests of business, from whatever jurisdiction,

> . . . often found it convenient to resist action at the federal level in the name of states' rights rather than in the name of *laissez faire*. When states did attempt to take action, this latter group even supported the federal government against the "offending" states in order to serve the same ends of nonintervention (Elazar 1962, p. 77).

---

[4]See *Crampton v Zabriskie*, 101 U.S. 601 (1879). The sole recognized federal exception is a challenge to an expenditure arguably in violation of the establishment of religion clause in the First Amendment to the United States Constitution. See *Flast v Cohen*, 392 U.S. 83 (1968). In 1978, the Supreme Court determined in *City of Lafayette, Louisiana v Louisiana Power & Light Co.*, 435 U.S. 389 (1978), that federal antitrust laws can apply to a municipal electric utility.

The federal structure provided a dual laboratory in which the interests of producers could overcome those of consumers.

During the twentieth century the same sort of competition has occurred among cities. Each is a locus of production, and economic growth is promoted when central cities compete against suburbs, when cities compete against special districts, and when cities in the Frostbelt compete against those in the Sunbelt. If these forms of competition serve local preferences, the metropolitan and regional disparities are only "natural" consequences of free market forces. If local policy uses national resources without standards and burdens minorities, that is a small cost to pay for the federal market. If the existence of a variety of jurisdictions provides producers an opportunity to shop for the least restrictive regulatory schemes, economic dynamism justifies the inchoate costs of wasteful or unguided resource use.

Although cities are the engines of production, they are not expected to create their own fuel; they (or general governments[5]) may be like corporations, but they are not-for-profit ones. Special districts and public authorities, not general governments, typically have operated profitable infrastructure-oriented activities for which user prices can be charged. Not only do the functional departments established within city governments at the impetus of federal programs contribute to problems of coordination within cities, but also additional functional agencies outside the city governments create competition among different types of local government. The local political order is fragmented into a multiplicity of organizations, each of which monopolizes a particular program.

One indication that special districts are profitable, self-sustaining operations is that special district revenues provide funds sufficient to cover the districts' current operations, while general governments' current operations increasingly have been paid with intergovernmental revenues.

General governments' revenues from their own sources provided 87 percent of the funds to pay for their current operations in 1957, but 84 percent in 1962, 79 percent in 1967, and 75 percent in 1972. In contrast, special districts' own general revenues paid for over 90 percent of all current operating expenditures in each of the four years (U.S. Bureau of the Census 1959; 1964; 1969; 1974). Intergovernmental revenues have constituted a greater share of each type of jurisdiction's current expenditures (up from 38 percent in 1957 for general governments to 46 percent in 1972, and up from 16 percent in 1957 for special districts to 39 percent

---

[5]As used here, "general" governments include incorporated and unincorporated municipalities, counties, and school districts. School districts have been distinguished from special districts because schools supply social reproduction goods rather than infrastructure or subsidies to particular sectors. Schools traditionally have been less autonomous than have special districts such as water or sewer districts. All citizens furthermore can vote in school district elections, while no "one person-one vote" rule applies to special district elections. Instances of this distinction appear in *Kramer v Union Free School District No. 15*, 395 U.S. 621 (1969) and *Salyer Land Co. v Tulare Lake Basin Water Storage District*, 410 U.S. 719 (1973).

in 1972), but the nonlocal revenue share for general governments was larger than that for special districts in each of the four years. Special districts have been able to maintain a more balanced current budget sheet.

This aggregate relationship between general governments and special districts exists for the fifty-five largest cities in each of five regions of the nation.[6] The average ratio of current budget surpluses (or deficits) to capital expenditures for special districts was positive in all five regions in 1962, 1967, and 1972. The average ratio for general governments was negative in all five regions in the three years. The difference between special district and general government average ratios in each region increased during the decade in the Northeast, however, while in other regions it generally decreased. Thus general governments in the Northeast operate with larger deficits and in greater contrast with the special districts in their metropolitan areas than do cities in other regions in the nation.

The problems of declining industrial cities are reflected in their access to and use of the urban capital market. Because special district revenues more closely match current expenditures, which include debt service charges, investors may perceive special district bonds as safer investments than bonds issued by cities facing current fiscal deficits. The amount of special district borrowing has increased faster than the amount of general government borrowing. In 1957 special districts issued only 10 percent of all local long-term debt; fifteen years later special districts issued a fifth (21 percent) of all local debt and accounted for somewhat less than a fifth of all local capital outlays (U.S. Bureau of the Census 1959; 1964; 1969; 1974). Special districts have financed a greater share of their capital outlays from the market than have general local governments. Market debt issues have amounted to about three-quarters of special district capital outlays, but only about two-thirds of general government capital outlays.

But in the major cities in the Northeast, special districts have undertaken smaller shares of all local capital outlays between 1962 and 1972, in contrast to the generally rising share in other regions of the country. The average ratio of special district and general government capital outlays in the nine largest cities in the Northeast was 0.29 in 1962, but only 0.15 in 1972. The average ratio in the eleven largest southwestern cities increased from 0.06 to 0.18, and in the ten largest Pacific cities, from 0.16 to 0.27 (U.S. Bureau of the Census 1964a; 1969a; 1974a). The general city governments that were less favored in the credit market because they had larger current deficits, were also the jurisdictions that took greater responsibility

---

[6]The fifty-five cities with populations greater than 250,000 in 1970 include nine cities in the Northeast, fifteen in the North Central, ten in the Southeast, eleven in the Southwest, and ten in the Pacific region. The author compared data for all general and special district governments in the "central county component" of each city's Standard Metropolitan Statistical Area (U.S. Bureau of the Census 1964a; 1969a; 1974a). For more detail, see Boast (1977, ch. 7).

for capital expenditures. Because of this reversal of capital expenditure role and fiscal capability, northeastern cities may not be effective bidders for private capital.

This disadvantage is illustrated by the declining credit ratings received by northeastern cities and the improved ratings registered by cities in the South and West (Moody's Investors Service, annual). Eight of the 55 largest cities in the nation received lower credit ratings from Moody's Investors Service in 1976 than they had in 1957, and all of these cities were in the Northeast and North Central regions. In contrast, 27 of the 55 cities received higher ratings in 1976 than they had in 1957, and 21 of these cities were in the South and West. Between 1957 and 1976, 20 of the 55 cities received a rating at least two levels different from their 1957 rating. Six of these were multiple decreases—all in the Northeast and North Central regions. The other 14 were multiple rating increases—all but 2 in the Southeast, Southwest, or Pacific regions.

Thus cities' requirements for private capital, the structure of the credit market, the competition between special and general governments, and the variable private economic strength of cities in different regions of the nation have reinforced each other. Declining older industrial cities cannot expect to recover their fiscal strength with the aid of the capital market, which more likely exacerbates declining conditions.

As cities have competed for federal outlays—grants and purchases the federal government spreads throughout the nation—the effects of the capital market could be redressed. The distribution of federal outlays among the fifty-five cities, however, has reinforced the market distribution. The average ratio of federal personal income tax payments to federal outlay receipts in 1969 for the southwestern cities (0.52) and Pacific cities (0.45) were smaller than the ratios for the southeastern (0.67), northeastern (0.63), and North Central cities (0.73), indicating that northern cities were "overtaxed" or "underrewarded" in relation to western cities (U.S. Department of the Treasury 1972; U.S. Office of Economic Opportunity 1970). The result is consistent with a progressive federal income tax structure and federal spending patterns tilted toward the South and West. But the distribution of both market capital and federal outlays has disadvantaged northern and eastern cities.

THE FEDERAL PROGRAM FOR THE MARKET

Federal policy does not directly allocate capital, nor does it redress the flow of capital to cities through current spending. But a federal program undergirds and stabilizes the urban capital market. The clientele of these federal urban programs is market investors rather than producers of highways or office buildings, but the impact on cities' resources is just as great. The programs affect the market in four ways: (1) by creating tax incentives to condition who will purchase municipal bonds; (2) by authorizing two of the market stages; (3) by stabilizing the market during periods of credit contraction; and (4) by absorbing the risks of investment in cities by supplying automatic, unrestricted current grants-in-aid that can be used for debt service payments. Each of these efforts has an impact on the entire capital market not just on the urban renewal or public housing bonds that were guaranteed by federal "debt service grants."

First, federal tax policy creates incentives for high-income households and for banks and insurance companies to purchase municipal bonds during periods of prosperity. Not only is the market narrowed by the treatment of interest on municipal debt as tax-free income, but also there is an implicit subsidy to investors. The savings achieved by state and local governments from the lower interest rates are less than the taxes foregone by the federal treasury (Huefner 1972, ch. 10; Twentieth Century Fund 1976, pp. 147–54). Without the tax-exempt interest status of municipal securities, the market would behave much differently. The range of investor incentives would be broader if, for example, low- or middle-income households or nontaxable pension funds were attracted to the municipal market.

Second, federal rules authorize some private market operations. The market is narrowed—but strengthened at the same time—by a 1938 agreement, which continues in effect, among the Controller of the Currency, the Federal Deposit Insurance Corporation, the Board of Governors of the Federal Reserve System, and the Executive Committee of the National Association of Supervisors of State Banks. Only bonds with a rating in the top four categories are considered "Grade I" or "investment grade" securities that can serve as "net sound capital" in fulfillment of bank reserve requirements (Twentieth Century Fund 1974, pp. 65–66; U.S. Congress 1966, vol. 2, pp. 234–36). In 1964 savings and loan associations were authorized to buy municipal bonds in the top four rating categories. Amortization requirements of the Committee on Valuations of the National Association of Insurance Commissioners stipulate that insurance companies cannot buy revenue bonds rated below the top four grades (Dougall & Gaumnitz 1975, pp. 71; 96). In effect, ratings "have become tools of financial regulation used to influence portfolio structure, to evaluate bank liquidity and capital adequacy, and to determine eligible forms of collateral" (Twentieth Century Fund 1976, p. 110).

Federal policy also indirectly legitimates another market stage. Bond counsel opinions on the legality of a bond issue are determinations by a professional group that exercises self-licensing supported by public policy. Further, in 1975 Congress created the Municipal Securities Rulemaking Board, which is "essentially an industry self-regulatory body with the power to adopt binding rules," though subject to oversight by the Securities and Exchange Commission (Twentieth Century Fund 1976, p. 118). Thus underwriters and accountants are active definers of the rules governing market operations, which bond counsels must use. A portion of public policy is "privatized" to particular professional groups (Lowi 1969, pp. 86–93; Beer 1973, pp. 65–66; 76).

Third, federal policy also stabilizes investors' expectations by creating and altering municipal bankruptcy laws.[7] Investors can have a structured legal recourse to protect their rights as creditors. The federal bankruptcy laws were first extended to municipalities in 1934 during the depression when 4,770 local governments defaulted on about 16 percent of all local debt (Hempel 1971, p. 22). Creditors holding two-thirds of the claims in each debt class and three-quarters of all claims would have to assent to any debt restructuring (Public Law no. 73-251, sec. 80, 48 stat. 798 (1934)). Without negotiation rules over the payment of debt obligations, investors would be more reluctant to invest in municipal bonds. By eliminating any need for unanimous consent, the original federal municipal bankruptcy chapter facilitated negotiations over debt obligations. Further, because of the voting rules, small claim holders would have less influence under these rules than would large claim holders such as institutional investors.

It was not until 1976 that Congress made the first substantial change in the municipal bankruptcy chapter. After 1976 final approval had to be given by creditors holding two-thirds of the dollar volume of all voting creditors and by one-half the number of voting creditors (Public Law no. 94-260, sec. 92(b), 90 stat. 315 (1976)). The level of approval was reduced, since nonvoting creditors were eliminated from the threshold requirements. The 1976 revision also deleted the requirement that notice of the negotiations be supplied to all creditors. Thus, given the current context of the capital market, the new bankruptcy law facilitates negotiations. The larger investors can still dominate the negotiations because institutional investors have more intense interests than do individuals and more likely will be aware that a repayment plan is under consideration; but all investors are given assurance that, given a municipal default, an inability to reach a unanimous agreement among creditors will not completely stymie negotiations. The changing nature of federal municipal bankruptcy laws, then, illustrates one of the fundamental functions of the liberal state: Providing laws so that exchanges can occur under stable expectations that contractual obligations between parties will be enforced.[8]

---

[7]Contractual rights can also be upheld by the courts, as in the debt moratorium and bond covenant cases mentioned in footnote 3, above. The consistency of court decisions is not certain, however, since jurists may change the balance between creditors' rights and the state's power to promote the general welfare. A legislative protection of creditors' position therefore is a more conclusive illustration of the public program for the market.

[8]States may also stabilize expectations in *particular* exchanges by setting aside public revenues to meet debt service costs. When the market shut the credit spigot off for New York City in spring 1975, the state established the Municipal Assistance Corporation (MAC), which would issue, on behalf of the city, bonds backed by state revenues specially diverted from the city. The law placed the proceeds of the state stock transfer tax and the city-derived portion of state sales tax under MAC control (N.Y. Public Authorities Law, art. 10,

Fourth, federal policy indirectly undergirds the market supply of capital to cities by reducing investors' risks through subsidization of current local budgets with an automatic, formula-based distribution of funds that are not tied to particular purposes. After GRS began in 1973, about one-seventh of all federal current grants were unrestricted. The $20 billion in GRS grants distributed during 1973, 1974, and 1975 almost equaled the amount of federal capital additions-to-assets for nonhighway purposes from 1966 through 1975 (U.S. Office of Management and Budget, annual). The requirement that localities spend GRS grants on specific "priority" social expenditures was abandoned when Congress extended the program in 1976, showing that GRS grants were truly unconditional in nature. In addition, Congress added a counter-cyclical aid program to the Public Works Employment Act of 1976. This program authorized the distribution over a fifteen-month period of $1.25 billion to states and cities with high unemployment rates. These were the same areas that had declining tax bases and difficulty obtaining either short- or long-term capital from the market.

The New York City Seasonal Financing Act (1975) represented an extreme extension of the subsidy program for the market (Public Law no. 94-143, 89 stat. 797 (1975)). From December 1975 through June 1978, the U.S. Treasury loaned short-term cash to New York City, but this was only an interim measure until the city could regain market access, anticipated to occur in 1978. In October 1975 William Simon, then Secretary of the Treasury, said the federal government would "build a bridge to the capital markets" (U.S. House 1975, pt. 3, 1834–47). The major issue, Simon maintained, was

> ... whether our system of financing state and local government credit needs—a system which has served this country well for more than a century—will be replaced by a system of federal financing and by federal control of fiscal and financial decision-making at the state and local level (U.S. House 1975, part 3, p. 1823).

Simon feared that the Seasonal Financing Act started down that path of federal control. The first two-and-one-half years' operation of the program indicated, however, that the city's desire to reenter the municipal bond market was much greater than the potential for federal control. The federal government no more constructed a bridge away from the market than it built a bridge to it. Instead, the federal government merely sup-

---

sec. 3012.1(c) and sec. 3012.6 (Consolidated Laws Service)). MAC soon exhausted its credit. In September 1975 the state established a second state agency, the Emergency Financial Control Board (EFCB). The board had oversight over all city revenues and could establish a special debt service repayment account (N.Y. Unconsolidated Laws, ch. 22, sec. 9.1 and sec. 9.4 (Consolidated Laws Service)). The law mandated that the city pay contractual obligations before other expenses (sec. 9.5). When the state extended the life of the EFCB in 1978, the amendments required debt service accounts to be administered by the New York State comptroller (*The Fiscal Observer* 1978, p. 13).

plied a boat to cross the river just one more time, but that boat did not reach the other shore. After the New York City note issue failed to gain market acceptance in November 1977, the city did not try to reenter the market again before the Seasonal Financing Act expired on June 30, 1978.

The short-term loan program spawned another federal effort to build a bridge to the market for the city, the New York City Financial Assistance Act of 1978, which passed Congress in July 1978 (Public Law no. 95-339 (1978)). City officials said the city needed at least $4.5 billion in long-term financing in 1979–82 gradually to regain financial credibility. But the city's state financing authority, the Municipal Assistance Corporation, could not issue the entire amount to the public and neither the city pension funds nor the major New York banks would accept unguaranteed private placements of a sufficient amount. If the federal government, however, would guarantee the city bonds to be placed with the city and state pension funds, the city said, it might be able to round up enough commitments from the banks and sell enough bonds to the public to regain investor confidence. The plan was almost as hypothetical as the hope in 1975 that short-term federal seasonal loans would bring the city back to the market by 1978. But the goal in both programs was the same: Prop up the city temporarily and get it back to the market.

BEYOND PROGRAMS TO POLICY?

Many of the program-oriented grants during the 1960s—such as the Job Corps, the Appalachia Commission, the Community Action Program, and Model Cities—represented the "pervasiveness of subsidy" (Ripley 1972, pp. 534–37). And GRS, counter-cyclical aid, and temporary loans and loan guarantees to New York City represented subsidy to an extreme. The federal government has transformed mayors into another functional interest group. Any standards for use of new federal benefits have been more lenient than they were in the Model Cities Program. A new political subsystem of generalist urban lobbyists had been strengthened. Under the program grants, each city competed against every other one for project funds; few incentives for intercity cooperation existed. With GRS and counter-cyclical aid, the incentives for initial organizing increased, since the competition for project grants was eliminated; but local politicians achieved unity only so long as they lobbied for more unrestricted funds. Cohesion broke down over the creation of the distribution formulas. As a result, everyone received something, but this policy was one of "distributive localism" (Beer 1976, pp. 147–49; 172–74). To get seasonal loans in 1975 and loan guarantees in 1978, New York members of Congress traded votes on public works programs in other regions.

Although urban lobbying increased under the "new federalism," it is not certain what the new local lobbyists in Washington want other than more distribution (Farkas 1971; Reagan 1972; Dommel 1974). Local politicians have no interests in common except maximum discretion, expandable revenues, and lower taxes. Federal subsidy programs can be politically useful to political entrepreneurs in cities, since they allow greater autonomy in pursuing local budget policy; but that consensus over obtaining greater discretionary revenues from the federal government does not constitute an "urban policy." Mayors cannot create an urban policy through lobbying in their own interests. What is in each mayor's interest does not necessarily coincide with a policy that distributes federal resources among cities in a planned and purposive way. It is inescapable that cities must compete against each other in a federal polity. When they are faced with limited resources from the capital market, they compete for funds by keeping tax rates low and property values high. Federal subsidies of current local budgets disguise the competition for scarce governmental resources at the same time that the subsidies help assure investors that a city will not declare bankruptcy.

Cities may have greater independent public resources than they did under "cooperative" or "creative" federalism, but that does not mean that cities have greater choice. Mayors may have regained political leverage that they had lost to bureaucrats receiving federal program grants, but cities are no more "sovereign." The potential for bargaining with the capital market is less than that for lobbying in Washington. While market use contributes to local politicians' short-term political gain by disguising costs from electoral constituents and financing benefits to clienteles,[9] that symbiosis breaks down when investors' financial interests no longer match politicians' electoral ones. Then both the substance and the process of urban politics can be influenced by market decisions.

Were a federal "urban policy" to be formulated, the independence of both cities and the market could not be maintained. Instead a greater centralization of authority in Washington would be required. A more "unitary bias" might be necessary in order to reframe the "terms and rules of competition" (Dyckman 1966, p. 42; Rodwin 1970, p. 273). A more centralized public loan machinery might determine priorities that differ from those held both by local politicians and by financial investors, a situation that would threaten the deep-seated value of local autonomy. For instance, the supply and distribution of both human and capital resources might be manipulated among regions of the nation (Wingo 1972, p. 25; Thompson 1972, pp. 114–16). The interrelationships among programs would have to be recognized and the values would have to be balanced against one another. For instance, it might be determined that public investments generate extra profits for speculators, who hold onto

---

[9] Justice Brennan's characterization of the municipal bond market as "a goose that lays golden eggs" for local politicians intimates this benefit from the market. See Brennan's dissent in *United States Trust Company of New York v State of New Jersey*, 431 U.S. 1 (1977).

property in anticipation of an improved market price (Burkhead 1975, pp. 58–59; Wood 1972, pp. 85–88). Then surplus profits on land sales would be taxed as unearned income.

Such results may change the individual economic incentives that it is thought drive the market system. Public policy would substitute for market allocation decisions and would subvert individual choice. Not only the capitalist economic market but also the federalist political market would be weakened, but the loss of either would threaten the legitimacy of the American political order. Capitalism and federalism, which have shaped the development of cities in the United States, involve processes widely perceived as vital to growth and social learning. We may not like the results of the two markets in every instance, but we regard the individually oriented procedures as the least worst alternative. The automaticity of the market and the illusions of freedom of federalism are strongly entrenched. Even a critic who calls for "comprehensive government control" qualifies this recommendation by advocating the replacement of the market by a "decentralized planning process" (Harvey 1973, pp. 113; 115–16). But whether *any* planning is possible is debatable, because

> . . . the degree of concreteness demanded of state policy suddenly becomes more rigorous. . . . This in turn requires a process of political consensus-building, from which an agreed definition of "the quality" serving as the criterion of qualitative growth can be derived. This implies the need for an operable consensus regarding priorities, the distribution of costs, employment effects, incentives, subsidies, price and tax incidence, regional allocation and distribution problems, and so on. *The more concrete a policy, the more acute and multiple the effects of polarization and the conflicts it entails* (Offe 1973, p. 112).

Perhaps no liberal regime could withstand the choices and crises created by such a conflictual allocation mechanism. Instead the "state apparatus vacillates between expected intervention and forced renunciation of intervention," between an independence from bureaucratic clients and a subordination to producing interests (Habermas 1975, pp. 58–64).

When the urban capital market in the United States is threatened, public policy does not achieve a level of concreteness in reallocating resources. Instead urban capital dislocations are smoothed by supplying temporary loans or guarantees and current budget subsidies. Public policy stabilizes rather than replaces the discipline of the market. A planning process from Washington does not uproot the value of localism. Instead when Washington supplies additional public resources to cities, conflict occurs; but it is isolated to local decision making, structured more by the capital market and interlocal competition than by national public policy. Neither a national system of cities nor a replacement of the market becomes an object of public policy. In the United States, cities are left to cope as best they can.

REFERENCES

Beer, S. H. 1973. The modernization of American federalism. *Publius* 3 (fall): 44–95.

————. 1976. The adoption of General Revenue Sharing: A case study in public sector politics. *Public Policy* 24 (spring): 127–95.

Berle, A. A. 1955. Evolving capitalism and political federalism. In A. W. MacMahon, ed. *Federalism: Mature and emergent,* pp. 68–82. Garden City, N.Y.: Doubleday.

Boast, T. H. 1977. A political economy of urban capital finance in the United States. Ph.D. dissertation, Cornell University.

The Bond Buyer. 1976. *Municipal Finance Statistics, 1975.* Vol. 14. New York: The Bond Buyer.

Burkhead, Jesse. 1975. The political economy of urban America: National urban policy revisited. In G. Gappert and H. M. Rose, eds. *The social economy of cities,* pp. 49–68. Beverly Hills, Calif.: Sage.

Dommel, P. K. 1974. *The politics of revenue sharing.* Bloomington: Indiana University Press.

Dougall, H. E., and Gaumnitz, J. E. 1975. *Capital markets and institutions.* Englewood Cliffs, N.J.: Prentice-Hall.

Dyckman, John. 1966. The public and private rationale for a national urban policy. In S. B. Warner, Jr., ed. *Planning for a nation of cities,* pp. 23–42. Cambridge, Mass.: MIT Press.

Elazar, D. J. 1962. *The American partnership.* Chicago: University of Chicago Press.

Farkas, Suzanne. 1971. *Urban lobbying: Mayors in the federal arena.* New York: New York University Press.

The Fiscal Observer. 1 December 1977. Vol. 1, no. 10. New York: New School for Social Research.

————. 15 June 1978. Vol. 2, nos. 12; 13. New York: New School for Social Research.

Galbraith, J. K. 1973. Power and the useful economist. *American Economic Review* 63 (March): 1–11.

Gelfand, Mark. 1975. *A nation of cities: The federal government and urban America, 1933–1965.* New York: Oxford University Press.

Gramlich, E. M. 1976. The New York fiscal crisis: What happened and what is to be done? *American Economic Review* 66 (May): 415–29.

Habermas, Jürgen. 1975. *Legitimation crisis.* Boston: Beacon Press.

Harvey, David. 1973. *Social justice and the city.* Baltimore: Johns Hopkins Press.

Hempel, G. H. 1971. *The postwar quality of state and local debt.* National Bureau of Economic Research General Series no. 94. New York.

Huefner, R. P. 1972. *Taxable alternatives to municipal bonds.* Federal Reserve Bank of Boston Research Report no. 53. Boston.

Lowi, T. J. 1969. *The end of liberalism: Ideology, policy, and the crisis of public authority.* New York: Norton.

Moody's Investors Service. Annual. *Moody's municipal and government manual.* New York: Moody's Investors Service.

The New York Times. 21 March 1976.

O'Connor, James. 1973. *The fiscal crisis of the state.* New York: St. Martin's Press.

Offe, C. 1973. The abolition of market control and the problem of legitimacy. *Working Papers on the* Kapitalistate 1: 109–16.

————. 1974. Structural problems of the capitalist state: Class rule and the political system. On the selectiveness of political institutions. Vol. 1. In K. von Beyme, ed. *German political studies,* pp. 31–57. Beverly Hills, Calif.: Sage.

Olson, Mancur. 1969. The principle of "fiscal equivalency": The division of responsibilities among different levels of government. *American Economic Review* 59 (May): 479–87.

Ostrom, V.; Tiebout, C. M.; and Warren, R. 1961. The organization of government in metropolitan areas: A theoretical inquiry. *American Political Science Review* 55 (December): 831–42.

Phelps, C. D. 1961. The impact of tightening credit on municipal capital expenditures in the United States. *Yale Economic Essays* 1 (fall): 275–321.

Reagan, M. D. 1972. *The new federalism.* New York: Oxford University Press.

Ripley, R. B. 1972. Political patterns in federal development programs. In H. Hahn, ed. *People and politics in urban society,* pp. 531–55. Beverly Hills, Calif.: Sage.

Rodwin, L. 1970. *Nations and cities: A comparison of strategies for urban growth.* Boston: Houghton Mifflin.

Schattschneider, E. E. 1960. *The semi-sovereign people.* New York: Holt, Rinehart & Winston.

Scheiber, H. N. 1975. Federalism and the American economic order, 1789–1910. *Law and Society Review* 10 (fall): 57–118.

Schumpeter, Joseph. 1954. The crisis of the tax state. *International Economic Papers* 4: 5–38.

Schussheim, Morton J. 1974. *The modest commitment to cities.* Lexington, Mass.: Lexington Books.

Tanzer, M. 1964. State and local government debt in the postwar world. *Review of Economics and Statistics* 46 (August): 237–44.

Thompson, W. R. 1972. The national system of cities as an object of public policy. *Urban Studies* 9 (February): 99–116.

Twentieth Century Fund. 1974. *The rating game.* New York: McGraw-Hill.

———. 1976. *Building a broader market.* New York: McGraw-Hill.

U.N. Department of Economic and Social Affairs. Statistical Office. 1977. *Yearbook of national accounts statistics, 1976.* New York: United Nations.

U.S. Advisory Commission on Intergovernmental Relations (ACIR). 1970. *Federal approaches to aid state and local capital financing.* Washington, D.C.: Government Printing Office.

———. Board of Governors of the Federal Reserve System. 1973. *Flow of funds accounts 1945–1972 (adjusted): Annual total flows and year-end assets and liabilities.* Washington, D.C.: Federal Reserve System.

———. Board of Governors of the Federal Reserve System. 1977. *Flow of funds accounts: 1st quarter, 1977.* Washington, D.C.: Federal Reserve System.

———. Bureau of the Census. Census of Governments. 1959. 1964. 1969. 1974. *Government finances compendium of government finances.* Washington, D.C.: Government Printing Office.

———. Bureau of the Census. Census of Governments. 1964a. 1969a. 1974a. *Local government in metropolitan areas.* Washington, D.C.: Government Printing Office.

———. Congress. Joint Economic Committee. Subcommittee on Economic Progress. 1966. *State and local public facility needs and financing, study.* Vol. 2. 89th Cong., 2d sess.

———. Congress. 1969. *Public facility requirements over the next decade, hearings.* 90th Cong., 2d sess.

———. Department of the Treasury. Internal Revenue Service. 1972. *Statistics of income . . . 1969: Zip code area data.* Washington, D.C.: Government Printing Office.

———. Federal Deposit Insurance Corporation. 1975. *Annual report.* Washington, D.C.: Federal Deposit Insurance Corporation.

———. House. Committee on Banking, Currency, and Housing. Subcommittee on Economic Stabilization. 1975. *Debt financing problems of state and local government: The New York City case, hearings.* 3 parts, 1 app. 94th Cong., 1st sess.

———. National Resources Committee. Research Committee on Urbanism. 1937. *Our cities: Their role in the national economy.* Washington, D.C.: Government Printing Office.

———. Office of Economic Opportunity. 1970. *Federal outlays in* [selected states]. Springfield, Va.: National Technical Information Service.

———. Office of Management and Budget. Annual. *Special analyses of the budget of the United States.* Washington, D.C.: Government Printing Office.

———. Senate. Committee on Banking, Housing and Urban Affairs. Subcommittee on Housing and Urban Affairs. 1973. *The central city problem and urban renewal policy, study.* 93d Cong., 1st sess.

Warner, S. B., Jr. 1968. *The private city: Philadelphia in three periods of its growth.* Philadelphia: University of Pennsylvania Press.

Wingo, Lowdon. 1972. Issues in a national urban development strategy for the United States. *Urban Studies* 8 (February): 3–27.

Wood, R. C. 1972. *The necessary majority: Middle America and the urban crisis.* New York: Columbia University Press.

PART II
NATIONAL CONSTRAINTS ON URBAN RESOURCES

An important innovation in urban studies in recent years has been the recognition that national governments often set the parameters for urban policy. The next step in the investigations in this volume is to describe in more detail how the decision processes relating to these issues indeed take place. Cities are not uniformly opposed to national policy objectives, nor are national governments uniformly hostile to the needs and preferences of cities. There are some separable policy objectives at each level of government, and there are some that overlap. The papers in this part look more deeply into how national institutions pattern the flow of resources to lower levels of government.

In many instances, such institutions are not those that have been conventionally associated with government. France has an elaborate network of financial institutions that are closely linked to ministries and national planning. Britain has surprisingly firm control of capital spending and has tried to devise ways of regulating borrowing in line with national economic policy. Germany offers an interesting case of a national government whose first problem was to establish how it could penetrate federal complexities in order to move funds to lower levels of government. Japan is a curious mixture of a national government that has indeed made substantial contributions to urban development but now finds that rapid industrialization has both imposed severe costs on cities and also fed urban protest.

CHAPTER 5
LA TUTELLE FINANCIÈRE: NEW WINE IN OLD BOTTLES?

Douglas E. Ashford

Conflict between cities and the state is not new to France, whose revolutionary fathers were torn between their concern that the communes become "small republics" and their fear that the communes might indeed elude the control of the state. To reconcile the potential conflict the French constructed an elaborate state apparatus well before the other modern industrial democracies did so. An essential element of this machinery was the prefect, who was to represent the state in the departments and communes. Among his formidable battery of weapons was the *tutelle* (supervisory power). The decisions of the communes were to conform to the elaborate system of administrative law and procedure coming from Paris.

So long as the mayor was *patron* of a rural community (half the French population was rural until the 1930s), the system worked fairly well; but the rapid growth of cities since World War II has meant that the *tutelle*, if it was not to disappear, would have to change in content. A complex urban society could not be governed by examining each decision step by step, and the supervisory power had to be generalized in some way. However much we may argue about the success of French administration, it is seldom without proposals. Though not a formal decision, the supervision of French cities has been transformed over the past two decades into a financial instrument of the state and its officials.

One of the more difficult problems in understanding the changing relationship between national and local governments is the role of intergovernmental agencies. France has many of these and nearly all are connected to the administration. The crucial issue in following such an institutional transformation is, of course, how it relates to policy change. The French cities were desperately in need of capital and, unlike many of the mixed economies, it had well-developed financial institutions within its orbit. Though a conservative regime, the Gaullists saw that a massive construction program was needed as millions of the French moved to cities in the 1960s. As in most complex problems, institutional adjustment had to come from many levels. In Paris control over urban policy and programs tended to slip away from the old ministries and move toward the semipublic financial institutions of the state. There was a huge controversy within the administration (Bloch-Lainé 1977). At the intermediate levels of government, decisions had to be better coordinated and ways found to deal with integrated projects for the new cities. The influence of the planners and financial officers of the state naturally increased. Locally the issue was how the funds were to arrive in cities while also preserving the old controls on smaller towns and villages. Thus the issue in France was neither whether the aid would be forthcoming, for it was fairly high on the agenda, nor whether new industrial centers would receive it, for this fit with the French industrial strategy. The issue was how to make such a massive change without dismantling a crucial element in the national political system. A new form of state supervision, the *tutelle financière,* became a way of changing the content of center-local relations in France without endangering the state.

The transformation of the center-local relationship into a financial rather than a regulatory one has been noted by a number of French writers (Médard 1968, p. 793; Bernard 1969, p. 232; Conseil Economique et Social 1973, p. 534). One of the clearest statements appears in the Bourrel report.

> So long as communes and departments were limited to essential activities, activities of management or administration and furnishing *(pré-station)* of services, their intervention only posed problems of legality to the superior administration. The modest role played by local administration in the growth of cities, the slow development of public services, the few credits for infrastructure *(équipment)* left little place to put to work an original municipal policy, hence little occasion for the supervisory administration to exercise a control of opportunities and provide incentives. . . . With urbanization, the pressure of investment needs, and the necessity to order urban development, the role of the local collectivities is considerably increased and transformed. The enlarged domain of their economic, social and urban interventions cannot be minutely regulated like their administrative or management activities. . . . The legal control applies only to the most routine and least vital part of the activities of the local collectivities. The arsenal of procedures and powers of the *tutelle* often appears poorly adapted to the evolution of concrete problems that face the local collectivities daily (Bourrel 1965, pp. 112–13) (Ashford translation).

Preoccupation with local and national finance is not, of course, a wholly new concern of the French political and administrative system. Guerrier and Bauchard (1972, p. 287) list eight investigations of local finance since 1892, not including the most recent Guichard Report (1976). What distinguishes the changes of the past twenty years is that the financial burden has become so great that the state can no longer manage investment and debt at the local level through the old supervisory system. From 1964 to 1974 the debt of communes and departments tripled to become 61 billion francs. Oddly enough, during this period the center reduced its support to cities and towns, initially seeking fiscal reform (increasing revenues) and only later turning to financial reorganization (manipulating resources). The sequence is a natural one in a highly centralized state and probably in any highly industrialized one. The increased dependence of the local governments on the center had the reciprocal effect of strengthening their demands for more resources; i.e., control over investment. The developmental impact, then, has not necessarily been to increase central control but rather to force the center to look for new means to influence local decisions. The short-term, cash-flow supervision became unworkable with the growth of an urban society. The *tutelle financière* is a form of mutual adjustment.

To a surprising extent, the central government paved the way for the present fiscal and financial conflict, possibly believing in the early years of the Gaullist regime that the state could always assert its power over local governments. The Fifth Plan increased local credits for infrastructure by 50 percent: twice the rate of growth planned for the private sector (Bourrel 1965, p. 21). By 1967 half the infrastructure investments made by the state were located in the communes and departments (Intergroupe des Finances Locales 1971, p. 104). Excluding the semipublic agencies, the local collectivities accounted for roughly two-thirds of the infrastructure investment in France. One should not, of course, underestimate the ingenuity of the French *grands corps,* particularly under the impulse of the Gaullist desire for a prosperous and powerful France.

There were essentially three devices put in place to control the rapid growth of urban debt and investment. All of them were technocratic inventions, and all of them failed. The first—and no doubt essential—reform was to set in motion a standard accounting system for both local and central government. This transformation went on from 1959 to 1969. French local accounts now appear in the familiar operational and investment format of the national budget rather than the simple *actif* and *passif* accounts of the old cash-flow budget. (For details see Guerrier & Bauchard 1972, pp. 160–66.) The effect was to make the economic discrimination against local government more visible than under the old system. A second device was to organize infrastructure credits around regional authorities, where they could be more readily influenced. By 1967, 70 percent of credits for urban development were part of the regional budget—which is part of the state budget—rather than being allocated to the local budget-

ing and financial apparatus (Bernard 1969, p. 280). While partially successful, this strategy failed with the regional referendum of 1969. The new
regional arrangements of 1972 made provision for local representation on
the regional bodies, but the region's financial role has not grown. The third
innovation was the establishment of the *Fonds National de l'Aménagement Foncier et de l'Urbanisme* (FNAFU) to lend money to cities for
industrial development. The fund was to be administered by the Caisse
des Dépôts et Consignations (CDC), whose decisions are heavily influenced by the technical studies done by other parts of the French government (Guerrier & Bauchard 1972, pp. 71–72). Had the center been
able to keep the upper hand in administering local credits for infrastructure through technical supervision, this tactic might have worked; but
before the decade was out the machinery for providing state credits to
localities became so cumbersome that it was under heavy attack by the
cities and towns.

Considering that President de Gaulle was not particularly interested
in local level problems, it is surprising that many changes were indeed
being made in the midst of his regime. The year 1966 was crammed with
innovations and can be considered the turning point in the redefinition of
the *tutelle.* The long and complex problem of fiscal reform began with the
suppression of the *patentes,* a direct local tax, laying the groundwork for
fiscal relief through a national value-added tax (TVA). A decree fixed
permissible rates of interest for private loans to local government. Lending by the CDC was liberalized by creating the *Caisse d'Aide à l'Équipement des Collectivités Locales* (CAELC). Most important in changing the
relationship between Paris and towns and cities was the reorganization at
the prefect level. A decree sought to increase the prefect's power to
coordinate local spending and investment (see Machin 1974), and the
Direction Départmentale d'Equipement (DDE) was added in each prefecture to provide planning and coordination for the growing infrastructure
needed at the local level. (See Thoenig 1973, pp. 73–86.)

Whether the strategy for changing the *tutelle* was clearly conceived at
these early stages is not known, but the crucial links between financial
incentives and local reorganization became increasingly clear. A system
for diverting subsidies *(subventions)* to infrastructure needs was announced by decree in 1964. An interministerial commission was established, and in its first three years of activity 166 requests for additional
subsidies were granted (Bernard 1969, p. 263). Most of these benefits went
to communes, which formed multipurpose syndicates (SVMs), but a few
also went to urban districts, a planning unit for urban development
created in 1959, and to communes that underwent a fusion process. This
tactic continued with the formation of *communautés urbaines* under a
1966 law that essentially forced four cities—Bordeaux, Lille, Lyons, and
Strasbourg—to form unified city governments. The urban communities
were also given special incentives through subsidies (Médard 1968; Hour-

ticq 1974). Launched in a typically autocratic manner, the question became whether this new policy instrument would indeed remain in the
hands of the central administration.

Thus by the mid-sixties the instruments and procedures for the revised
tutelle were in place and being used. The full complexity of the task the
administration undertook at this time should be made quite clear. With
diminishing subsidies for urban infrastructure (Intergroupe des Finances
Locales 1971, p. 20), the state set out to influence the localities to abandon
the communal structure itself, to direct investments into those cities and
regions where growth seemed desirable, and to undertake a variety of
changes in planning procedures, land use control, and the local tax system.
One may charge the French administration with arbitrary behavior and
manipulative tendencies, but one must also recognize that the early Gaullist government set in motion a series of reforms that most industrialized
nations of Europe were only beginning to contemplate at that time. In
fact, the fiscal, financial, and organizational problems of local government
are interlocked; but few governments undertook such comprehensive
efforts in 1966. As we shall see, the administration underestimated the
complexity of urban development. Neither of these errors would seem
unique to the French system.

The *tutelle financière* should not be thought of simply as a new procedure governing center-local relations. First, the increased reliance on
subsidies as a means of control also implied new relations within the
central government, most dramatically revealed in the formation of the
Ministère d'Equipment. The nature of interministerial rivalry and of competition among the *grands corps* was changed. Second, the relation between local administrators and the communes was changed as Thoenig
(1973) has made abundantly clear. Thus the new form of the *tutelle* is
more than a simple administrative device; it is a restructuring of policy-
making relationships at several levels of government and within government itself. Before examining the various effects, we should take a closer
look at the subsidy system itself and how it has developed.

LA SUBVENTION: A STATE WITHIN A STATE

The great virtue of the subsidy is its flexibility as a policy instrument. This
may also become its major disadvantage if conflicting requirements are
imposed on the urban structure. There are at least three objectives to the
use of subsidies in France. They are, first, an instrument of economic
policy at both the macro- and micro-levels. The subsidies are a major
device to control investment levels and to guide individual city plans and
choices. In the complex world of French urban fiscal and financial policy,
it has also become a central issue in fiscal and financial reform. One of the
most heated controversies in French urban policy is the relation of the

subsidy and its subsequent effects on local investment and tax reform. Its third objective is to encourage the regrouping and fusion of communes. (See Knaub 1974.) All of these policies—economic control, fiscal and financial reform, and local reorganization—overlap, of course, with many other state policies, but the subsidy is a key element in each.

Perhaps the first thing to understand about the use of subsidies in France is their immense size and scope. Though this paper concentrates on the relationship of subsidies to local government, financial incentives are a common policy instrument. In 1969, for example, the state provided over 43 million francs in subsidies, almost half of which went to enterprises (*Les Comptes de la nation 1969* 1970, p. 45). The state budget contained 19 million francs in subsidies for governmental activities of which over 7 million went to the communes, departments, and regions in connection with public programs. The 2.5 million in local level investment subsidies provided by the state is by far the largest single investment incentive administered by government. Put differently, the local investment subsidies represent roughly a sixth of all such subsidies and a third of those within the public sector. The ability of national agencies and ministries successfully to influence the use of the funds is crucial to achieving their objectives at the local level. Competition at the national level to acquire investment subsidies for key programs is no less keen than competition at the local level to acquire new local projects.

The ubiquitous quality of the subsidies in French government makes it almost impossible to generalize about their use. The major instrument is the interministerial fund or the agency fund from which local investments for infrastructure are underwritten. These transfers are for both operational and capital spending, but the latter becomes the major device for control of the communes and departments. Without technical endorsement of a project that carries some government funds, the commune or department has little chance of getting its project approved and funded by national lending agencies. In 1975 seventeen such funds can be identified.

Although an interministerial committee usually administers the funds, they tend to be within the domain of particular ministries and more often than not used to promote programs and projects that fall within the ministry's orbit. In the case of investment subsidies for local public works and urban development, the most important is FNAFU, which is heavily influenced by decisions within the Ministry of Infrastructure and its network of field administrators at the regional, departmental, and communal levels. Another major fund affecting urban policy is the Fonds d'Intervention pour l'Aménagement du Territoire (FIAT), organized to support regional projects of particular interest to the national government. FIAT is closely aligned with the policies of the regional planning agency, the Délégation à l'Aménagement du Territoire et à l'Action Régionale (DATAR). The Ministry of the Interior acquires financial influence from the Fonds d'Equipement des Collectivités Locales (FECL), which redistributes the value-added tax on local projects to more needy areas of the country. Similar funds exist for agriculture, sports and leisure, culture, and tourism as well as for massive national programs for superhighways and water. In this way, every ministry dealing with local affairs has its own claim on resources, which are used to manipulate and bargain with the cities and to compete among the ministries for influence over urban development and policy.

DATAR has been one of the major agencies developing the use of subsidies over the past decade. Although the DATAR fund, FIAT, is one of moderate size, about 286 million francs in 1975, using this money as an investment subsidy enables the multiplication of its influence. Though we know a good deal about DATAR's use of its funds (see Prud'homme 1974, pp. 46–55; Isaac and Moliner, 1975, pp. 363–89; Prud'homme et al. 1975), the regional literature barely touches on the intergovernmental network that regulates the flow of subsidies to the communes. In its most recent report, DATAR claims that about 22 percent of infrastructure funds from the state are funneled through its programs (*Project de loi de finance* 1975, p. 80), but this tells us little about how decisions are actually made, particularly since DATAR merged with the Ministry of the Interior in 1972. Its activities are now subordinated to a number of programs to aid cities and towns formed at high levels of government.

The critical agency in the management of subsidies is the CDC, which serves as the banker for the local government system. In the CDC's operations one begins to see the complexity of the administrative state as it has developed in France. The CDC was formed in 1816 to assist in the repair and rebuilding of French towns and cities following the Napoleonic wars, though its history can be traced back to the *ancien régime* through the Caisse d'Ammortisements (Priouret 1966). Under the conservative pressures of the Restoration, parliament did not want deposits to be subject to treasury control and decided to establish an independent agency to hold local government funds. Communes and departments are still required by law to deposit their funds in the CDC. Until the formation of the CAECL —the subsidiary deposit bank of CDC—in 1966, the localities received no interest.

To understand the role of the CDC and the entire superimposition of the administrative state on French politics requires some description of the financial relationship between localities and the center. In nineteenth-century France finance was looked upon primarily as a problem of guaranteeing a fixed return. Finance capital as one thinks of it today—that is, investment return calculated in terms of equity and growth—emerged late in the century. The mentality of the *rentier* controlled the CDC and most state financial institutions, though it was denounced by Saint Simon and others (Priouret 1966, p. 56; Duplouy 1967, p. 74). Only under extreme pressure from the government, for example, did the CDC agree to assist in the very profitable enterprise of building railroads in the mid–

nineteenth century. Not until the huge pressures of urbanization follow-ing World War II did the CDC become a banker in the modern sense.

The CDC has been described as "a state within a state" (D'Arcy 1968, p. 237). The projects nurtured by subsidies from the various funds must pass through its procedures as well as arrive at the CDC with ministerial approval of technical and legal qualifications. Though the ministries re-main in direct contact with the localities, it is the CDC that has final decision-making power over infrastructure loans. These are rarely given without the ministerial assurance of a subsidy. Linked to the CDC are all the major institutions for public finance in France. The Crédit Foncier, founded in 1860, handles loans for land acquisition and housing. The Crédit Agricole, linked to the Ministry of Agriculture, handles rural im-provement projects of many kinds. The CAELC was formed with strong resistance from the CDC in 1966 (Duplouy 1967, pp. 153–57) to provide the localities with loans on slightly more favorable terms and to restore a small interest payment for deposits from localities. The financial resources concentrated within the CDC organization are further augmented by a variety of other deposits less directly related to local government: the Caisse Nationale de Retraite des Agents des Collectivités Locales and the Caisse de Securité Sociale.

The government statistics that permit one to gauge the power of the CDC are collected for a variety of reasons, but all point to the immense financial power concentrated in one financial institution of the state. Fixed capital formation, including both private and public sector credits, was estimated to be about 9 billion francs in 1965. Roughly 60 percent of this amount was private loans and largely within the private industrial section; 30 percent was state credits; and 10 percent was credits derived from local savings (Duplouy 1967, p. 19). The state budget itself provides a second indicator. The Intergroupe des Finances Locales (1971, p. 104) for the Sixth Plan found that in 1967 about 48 percent of infrastructure credits went to local authorities; about 35 percent, to state investments; and the remainder, to semipublic agencies and hospitals. An even finer measure can be derived from fixed capital formation and land acquisition (direct investment) by the state alone, which shows that about two-thirds of these investments under state auspices take place through the local government system (Ashford 1978). Local government has become more dependent on credit from the national government. In 1962 the state provided 72 per-cent of local credit, while in 1973 it provided 94 percent (Duplouy 1967, p. 8; Conseil Economique et Social 1973, p. 535).

The massive lending power organized around the CDC has become a major issue in center-local relations in France over the past decade. The underlying causes relate to the nature of the administrative state as it is developing in France and, the present author would argue, in many other modern democracies. The immediate reasons for the conflict are found in the financial institutions of France itself and the relation of this structure to the localities. French communes and departments have three basic means for raising investment funds: self-financing *(autofinancement)*, public and private loans, and the subsidy. The amount of loans raised on the private market is very small in France, probably no more than 10 percent of annual investments. Despite frequent complaints about the state's financial institutions, the low rates of interest combined with the subsidies keep local governments within public sector borrowing. This is all the more remarkable given the steady decline in the percentage of investments covered by subsidies, as shown in table 5-1.

Though not central to the role of subsidies, the declining capacity of the communes to finance their own investments increases state control. This is largely due to ever-increasing interest payments of large towns and cities, estimated for 1970 to be nearly 70 percent of new loans *(Rapport technique* 1973, p. 31). The cumulative effect has been to make communes increasingly dependent on loans, even though these remain tied to the subsidies. The effect is even more striking when calculated in constant francs. From 1970 to 1974 loans increased by 7 percent, while self-financing actually diminished by 2 percent and subsidies increased only 5 percent.

The importance of the subsidy as a control over the local governments has grown because the detailed budgetary control once exercised by prefects and departments has diminished. In 1959 the entire system of budgetary approval was softened by allowing communes of over 9,000 persons to incur loans without approval if their budgets were balanced and if interest on existing loans did not exceed 10 percent of their income (Guerrier & Bauchard 1972, pp. 63; 145). In 1970 another law extended this choice to all communes. An examination of the revenues of communes in 1974 shows that all communes fall within this limit; so that, technically speaking, borrowing is uncontrolled *(Statistiques des comptes pour l'exercice* 1974, p. 56). The laws also specify, however, that this choice can be exercised only where the loans are coming from the CDC, CAECL, and the other major sources of credit outlined above. In effect, a new form of supervision replaced the old one. Administrative control has shifted from the local level to the financial decision-making authority of the central financial institutions on advice from the various ministries.

By the 1970s France had in place a remarkable structure for the control of local finance and investments. Though built on old institutions, there had been substantial expansion and reorientation of many key institutions such as the CDC. The early efforts to reorganize communes had on the whole been a failure, although there were important reforms to organize the growth of large cities and to restructure local fiscal policy. Given the intransigence of the local government system, the manipulation of subsidies, whether conscious or not, appears to have been the only alternative. Detailed control was no longer possible and financial control met the needs of the state to oversee growth and development. The

Table 5-1   Investment Funds of Communes, 1964–1974

	Self-finan.		Subsidies		Loans		Other		
	Amt.*	%	Amt.*	%	Amt.*	%	Amt.*	%	Total Amt.*
1964	939	16	1,482	25	3,287	56	109	2	5,817
65	907	14	1,810	28	3,613	56	151	2	6,481
66	1,301	17	1,881	25	4,153	55	141	2	7,476
67	1,241	15	2,161	25	4,991	58	113	1	8,506
68	847	10	2,249	27	4,989	60	286	3	8,371
69	821	9	2,501	28	5,260	59	316	3	8,898
70	874	9	2,560	27	5,817	61	316	3	9,597
71	804	8	2,518	26	6,437	64	215	2	10,054
72	1,452	10	2,683	18	10,057	69	334	2	14,526
73	1,718	11	2,855	19	10,494	68	290	2	15,307
74	1,144	7	3,479	22	10,641	68	329	2	15,593

Source: Data from *Statistiques des comptes pour l'exercice* 1974, p. 43; 1973, p. 40; 1972, p. 35; 1970, p. 24; 1969, p. 42.
*In millions of francs. Because of rounding all totals are not 100 percent.

weakness of the *tutelle financière* was that it coexisted with the old system itself, which the administration was unable to dismantle. At the center the individual ministries kept a veto power over financial decisions. At the local level urban governments found themselves increasingly hamstrung with the new array of procedures and regulations.

REVISING THE *TUTELLE FINANCIÈRE*

The urban structure of France is fairly complex. In addition to Paris there are 37 cities of over 100,000 persons and 60 cities from 50–100,000. Together they include about 13.5 million persons, slightly more than one-fourth of the French population (*Statistiques et indicateurs* 1975, p. 344). The new urban units best suited for utilization of the infrastructure subsidies were the new *communautés urbaines,* the districts and the *syndicats* of communes for particular services. In 1973 these new organizations created to deal with urban growth included nearly half the French population. Thus, the *tutelle financière,* though suited to circumventing the complexities of the communal system, remained an ambitious administrative device.

Criticism of the evolving structure for the control of urban investment has come from all quarters. To avoid underestimating the ability of the system to assess its own problems, it should be first noted that the Bourrel report (1965, pp. 112–22) itself recognized the shortcomings of the new form of the *tutelle* and excessive budgetary restrictions placed on communes. The most telling criticism came from the Intergroupe des Finances Locales in its study for the Sixth Plan, which identified the major problem areas (1971, pp. 154–56). The procedures relating urban needs to central subsidies were both "rigid and fragmentary." The commission noted that the sixty procedures involving nine ministries made the system unworkable and failed to take into account the financial needs of the cities. Lastly, there was no way to design an overall urban policy at either the national or local levels of government. (See also Barberye 1973; Grémion 1974; and Fréville 1973.)

Partly under the impulse of Pompidou, the government tried to restore confidence between the local governments and the center. In late 1970 and early 1971 the new president of France made three speeches assuring the *notables* and the cities that he intended to work through the existing structure of local government (de Préneuf 1971, p. 47). Clearly the period of forced draft local reorganization was at an end, giving even more significance to the indirect measures to affect urban growth that survived the Gaullist regime. Efforts to reorganize the *tutelle financière* came quickly. In December 1970 a new law on local budgeting was passed classifying local investments into four categories: national, regional, departmental, and communal. The prefect at the regional or departmental levels was authorized to approve loans under the latter two categories. (See Conseil Economique et Social 1973, pp. 531; 542.) The second important change was enacted by decree in November 1970, enabling the administration to enter into *contrats de Plan*. These were essentially specific authorizations to subsidize integrated proposals for urban development in cities over 20,000 in population (Guerrier & Bauchard 1972, pp. 273–74; Duport 1973; Flecher-Bourjol 1976).

The contracts are a device to enable the communes and other local bodies to (1) integrate their requests for loans and subsidies and (2) provide a simplified procedure for approval. Though a step forward in overcoming the complexities of the subsidies, the contracts did not reach a large number of cities and are under fairly strict administrative control. These arrangements were encouraged by a decree in early 1971 permitting the Caisse d'Epargne and other more liberal lending institutions to enter into special arrangements with the local governments (Conseil Economique et Social 1973, p. 536). The second and most important effort to soften the effects of the *tutelle financière* and to remove the complications obstructing local requests for assistance was the unification of subsidies (*globilisation des subventions*) initiated by decree in March 1972 (Hourticq 1974).

The decree was designed to meet many of the severe criticisms leveled against the subsidy system. First, localities were not prevented from initiating projects that qualified under existing rules until final approval emerged from the administration; second, the conditions for breach of agreement were reduced; and, third, the procedures for application were simplified (Moreau 1976, pp. 33–34; Conseil Economique et Social 1973, pp. 542; 544). The credits for the subsidies to be administered under this plan were to be allocated to the budget of the Ministry of the Interior and were expected eventually to include roughly one-third of all subsidies given to the localities. Given previous experience, the problems of simplifying applications should not be underestimated. The CDC would itself need to adjust its methods of approving loans. The various ministries that control approval of subsidies would need to relinquish their veto powers over components of larger investment proposals. The 1972 decree was intended to reduce the disparities among subsidies for various kinds of projects that had complicated development at the local level and made the subsidy system unintelligible to local mayors and officials (Fréville 1973, p. 730; Bernard 1969, p. 263). To do this assumed considerable cooperation among ministries as well as the capability of localities to depart from their established procedures of working through ministerial agents at the departmental level. While the results of this effort are not clear, it appears from the present author's interviews that the unification effort is being downgraded by central officials in favor of the more specific contracts that fit more easily within administrative procedures. There is some evidence that the Ministry of Finance resisted the reforms that gave longer term and more general forms of assurance to the cities (Flecher-Bourjol 1976). The Grossman Report (Conseil Economique et Social 1973, p. 551) concludes that fourteen years after the initial efforts to soften the *tutelle*, programs affecting the cities and towns are still not "united."

LIVING WITH COMPLEXITY

As noted above, the French state has had basically three objectives in guiding investment in urban infrastructure: to achieve the relatively conservative economic goals of the state itself, meaning to emphasize growth; to achieve these goals despite a complex and overarticulated local government system; and to provide sufficient resources to the localities to maintain essential services. The latter objective is complicated by the fiscal and tax reforms that have been enacted since 1968 and it cannot be fully explained, but these reforms do affect investment through the self-financing procedures. The context for formulating and executing policies related to these goals is enormously complicated by the commune system itself, which has resisted continued efforts to consolidate and merge small communes.

According to the 1968 census, about 55 percent of the French population lived in 37,029 communes of under 2,000 persons (*Statistiques et indicateurs* 1975, p. 344). Many small communes, of course, were densely populated suburban communities, but nonetheless they remained legally autonomous units within the French system. There were 582 communes with 10 to 50,000 inhabitants, representing 26 percent of the population, and 97 communes of over 50,000 persons—24 percent of the population.

Because efforts to simplify this structure have been blocked by mayors and by the inflexibility of the administrative system itself, the subsidies become a key element in ordering the social and economic life of the cities. The centralization of the system notwithstanding, the most important direct lever of local policy in the hands of the state is the subsidy.

The elastic nature of much local level expense means that even with such apparent control financial and fiscal relationships cannot be changed precipitously. An objective appraisal of the local system would, in the present author's opinion, indicate that a remarkable amount of resources has been given to the larger, more needy communes despite the overarticulation of the system. The overall picture is given in table 5-2. The 37,000 small communes have received about 50 percent of the subsidies and 40 percent of the loans. The small towns and cities (10–50,000) have received about a quarter of the subsidies and 30 percent of the loans. The larger cities over 50,000 have received about 26 percent of the subsidies and 32 percent of the loans. Thus it is impossible to argue that the system has been completely unresponsive to the growing urban needs of France. In population terms, about 20 percent of the population has received nearly a third of the infrastructure assistance. Of course, these estimates do not take into account differences in need or resources at the local level, though these can be inferred from the ability of each category of communes to generate surpluses.

Table 5-2 also shows that 45 percent of the direct investment—that is the purchase of land and buildings—has been going to the 697 communes of over 10,000 persons. Thus the system has responded to the needs of the larger towns and cities, where urban infrastructure is needed and more costly; but the larger communes have also born the brunt of the costs associated with heavy urban investment. Indirect investment is the repayment of loans and interest, of which over 60 percent falls to the larger communes, as does debt service, itself. The economic logic is naturally inescapable. The larger communities have the bulk of resources, but the figures also reflect urban development in France. The costs of urban growth are being shifted to the cities.

The overall structure tells us something about the general problems of the French local government system and reflects the basic economic constraints of every mixed economy. To uncover how, if at all, the decision-making structure itself has acted, one must examine changes in the use of subsidies over time. From a political perspective the choice is, of course, rather different from that represented by income and expense statements. The economic behavior of the communes is itself the product of two major forces: (1) the designs of the central administration and its political leadership and (2) the influence that local officials and administration bring to bear on the system. Economic and political constraints can never be wholly separated, but the trends over time help us uncover how the systemic pressures of a political and administrative nature operate. To do

Table 5-2   *Financial Transactions of All Communes, 1973, in Percentages and by Size*

	Under 2,000	2–10,000	10–50,000	50,000 & Over[a]
Sources				
Self-finan.	27	20	25	28
Subsidies	30	20	24	26
Loans	18	20	30	32
Investments				
Direct	23	21	26	29
Indirect	18	16	27	39
Debt service[b]	22	19	26	33

Source: Data from *Statistiques des comptes pour l'exercice* 1973, p. 48.
Note: Because of rounding some totals are less than 100 percent.
[a]Includes *communautés urbaines* but not Paris.
[b]Debt reimbursement includes payments of both interest and principal.

this, assembled here are two tables (5-3 and 5-4) that assess the importance and impact of the subsidies on the variously sized communes over the past decade.

The first and simplest measure is how the subsidies have been distributed according to size (table 5-3). Provided is more detail for the larger towns and cities, for that is where one would expect increased assistance to be given. The most interesting finding is that this relationship is curvilinear. The percentage of subsidies going to the smaller communes did decrease by 10 percent from 1964 to 1969; but in the years since de Gaulle's departure, the proportion going to the small communes increased but did not reach the earlier levels. The small towns and cities between 20,000 and 100,000 persons seem to have been losers in the changes of the past decade. Until 1975, their proportion of the investment subsidies steadily fell for a net loss of 6 percent. More relevant to our immediate objectives is the shift to the larger towns and cities. Including cities of over 100,000 and the urban communities, there has been a net gain of 8 percent in the percentage of subsidies going to them. Investment subsidies to Paris have been cut in half. Though there are many other factors influencing these changes, the overall pattern has been one of giving more subsidies to the rapidly growing cities.

Another test of the ability and intentions of the administrative system is the percentage of direct investment that has been provided by subsidies from 1964 to 1974, which has been calculated from the same sources. On this basis, there is little change over the decade. Communes under 20,000 received 56 percent of their direct investment as investment subsidies in 1964 and 51 percent in 1974. The changes are in the direction of more support for larger towns and cities. These findings are interesting at both ends of the spectrum of size. The smaller communes have more savings

Table 5-3   Percentage Allocation of Subsidies by Size of Communes, 1964–1975

	Under 20,000	20–100,000	Over 100,000	Urban Com.[a]	Paris	Total[b]
1964	63	23	10		4	1,536
65	60	22	13		5	1,891
66	56	20	14		8	2,002
67	54	22	14		9	2,308
69	53	24	13	3	8	2,631
70	54	23	14	2	6	2,648
71	54	21	12	5	7	2,703
72	53	21	12	5	9	2,873
73	56	19	11	5	8	3,091
74	62	17	12	6	4	3,635
75	57	21	13	5	4	5,237

Source: Data from *Statistiques des comptes pour l'exercice* 1975, p. 59; 1974, p. 57; 1973, p. 51; 1972, pp. 52–53; 1971, pp. 30–31; 1970, pp. 36–37; 1969, pp. 34–35. The report for 1968 is not available. Where totals differ in more recent accounts of previous years, the last figure is used. Error due to small amounts (2–3 percent of subsidies) given to overseas territories. Because of rounding all totals are not 100 percent.
[a]The urban communities were not formed until 1966 and do not appear in accounts until 1969.
[b]In millions of francs.

Table 5-4   Percentage Allocation of Subsidies by Level of Government, 1967–1974

	Comm.	Dept.	Paris	Régie[a]	Syn.	Other[b]	Total[c]
1966	61	11	6	1	20	1	3,519
67	60	10	5	1	22	1	3,713
69	56	8	5		21	9	4,453
70	53	9	3		22	13	4,777
71	54	9	4	1	24	8	4,822
72	50	7	5	1	26	10	5,281
73	44	6	4	1	25	20	6,433
74	48	8	2	1	30	10	7,225
75	53	8	2	1	26	9	10,461

Source: Data from *Statistiques des comptes pour l'exercice* 1975, p. 21; 1974, p. 21; 1973, p. 15; 1972, p. 15; 1971, p. 31; 1970, pp. 46, 55, 67; 1969, pp. 71, 83; 1967, pp. 7, 71; 1966, pp. 8, 11, 37, 44. A complete accounting by level of local government cannot be extracted from the earlier accounts.
[a]For part of the time series (1969–71) the regional commuting system under construction in Paris was included under *régies* (Régies Autonome des Transports Parisiens). The *régie* amount and the totals have been adjusted to remove this expenditure.
[b]*Other* includes mainly the Caisse des Ecoles and the Bureau d'Aide Sociale, two centrally administered accounts for assistance to school construction and local social services.
[c]In millions of francs. Because of rounding, all totals are not 100 percent.

but have not lost investment subsidies. The larger cities, having the greatest need for urban infrastructure, have been forced to rely more heavily on loans.

The distribution of investment subsidies among communes, however, does not exhaust administrative choice. The central government also influences which level of government within the subnational structure receives subsidies. Under the French system, departments, locally operated enterprises *(régies)*, *syndicats* of communes, and other minor activities of the local government system qualify for investment subsidies. One indicator of increasing centralization and control of subsidies would be to shift them to higher levels of the subnational structure. The choice among levels also permits the administration to encourage regrouping of communes, most frequently providing additional incentives for communes prepared to pool services in the syndicates. This has been by far the most common way to coordinate services, reaching nearly half the communes in 1973 and involving about a third of the French population. In 1973 there were 1,633 syndicates *(Statistiques et indicateurs* 1975, p. 346). The allocation of investment subsidies among levels of the system is given in table 5-4, which shows that there has indeed been a shift of the subsidies away from the communes. In 1967, the first year for which complete data by level is available, the communes received 61 percent of the subsidies; and in 1974 the proportion was reduced to 48 percent. Curiously, the shift has not been toward the department, where urban problems of a large area might be coordinated. In fact, the departmental share of the subsidies has slightly diminished. The large increases are for the *syndicats,* increasing from 20 percent of the subsidies in 1967 to 30 percent in 1974. Clearly, the administrative system has shown itself capable of moving financial incentives to those local units that provide more efficient local services and that tend to decrease the complications of the overarticulated communal structure. The other large increase has been under "Other," which includes, for the most part, assistance for building primary schools and providing local social assistance. Because these investments are concentrated by population, it is reasonable to infer that these services have been concentrated in the more highly urban areas.

In pursuit of its three major objectives—growth, local reorganization and financial control—the state has made some adjustments. Although the total level of subsidies has decreased in response to fiscal and financial pressures on the French system, there has also been some redistribution of subsidies. The larger cities and towns are somewhat favored in acquiring aid, but the distribution of subsidies remains heavily constrained by the articulation of the communal system itself. The adjustments do not begin to meet the investment costs of the large cities, which have turned increasingly to private loans and have accepted less-well-subsidized state loans to finance their needs.

FINANCIAL CRISIS OR FINANCIAL CRUNCH?

Though *crisis* is a term commonly used in describing nearly every aspect of the French political system, it is not all that apparent that the cities are indeed in a state of crisis. True, economic adversity over the past few years has led central governments to withdraw support, especially for infrastructure construction that can be postponed and that often leads to new and unavoidable operating costs. The total figures, however, in tables 5-3 and 5-4 also show that investment continued to grow in the seventies. The total investment expenditure for 1975 was almost 23 billion francs, double the sums invested by the communes in 1967. Despite inflation and the decreasing subsidies, the communes have been able to invest huge amounts, and they continue to account for about two-thirds of all investment by the state. Their financial importance in the system has not diminished, though it may be more troublesome in relation to national economic policy.

In a period when many industrial nations were drastically reducing local government investments, French local government maintained its share of the investment. The central government accounted for 5 percent of fixed capital formation in 1970 and in 1974; the local government share also remained the same, 8 percent (U.N. 1976, pp. 458–60; 452). True, the debts of communes have increased enormously, from 18 billion francs in 1964 to 61 billion in 1974; but these changes are in proportion to increases in operating and investment budgets over the same time period. Direct investments have multiplied slightly less than three times in this period, while debt has multiplied slightly more than three times. The ratio of debt to direct investment has changed very little in a decade; and, if the investments have been wisely made, the debt burden does not appear out of line with the actual increases in infrastructure (*Statistiques des comptes pour l'exercice* 1974, pp. 47, 61; 1969, pp. 21, 37). Given the high proportion of local debt that in fact is held by the central financial agencies of the state, debt may as easily be interpreted as a way of increasing the communes' claim on the public sector than as a way of making them more dependent on the state.

The arguments of the mayors are much more about the tax system and the conditions under which loans are made than about the burden of debt itself. Like typical good managers of local interests, they complain about interest rates, although the state provides loans below market rates. The more specific complaints are about the cumbersome process imposed by the state and the obligatory deposit of local surpluses in the state treasury (Association des Maires de Grandes Villes 1976, pp. 79–89). In fact, it appears from the mayors' statements that they would prefer to invest even more and to increase the debt burden of the cities and towns. Whether this procedure is well advised or even possible involves macro-economic decisions. All that can be said here is that, while the state has followed a conservative financial policy of debt management (the national debt was 75 billion francs in 1966 and 77 billion in 1972), the communes have tripled their debt. They do not appear to be severely deprived of funds, even with the objectionable constraints of the *tutelle financière.*

NATIONAL URBAN POLICY AND LOCAL FINANCE

The industrial democracies have had great difficulties in forming a coherent urban policy. France is no exception. (See, for example, Grémion 1974, pp. 75–100.) Much of this difficulty results from the differences within the growing metropolitan areas themselves. Even countries with much less differentiation in local government structures such as England have found it nearly impossible to shape a comprehensive urban development policy. A national policy presupposes that the complexities of land zoning, taxes and revenues, industrial growth, and transportation—to name only a few problems—have a uniform solution across widely varying circumstances. In a curious way, emphasis on quantitative analysis in both urban decision making and in the disciplines has tended to minimize the role of the state. Those in the discipline are just beginning to realize that current methods may have contributed to this bias in urban studies.

If a "national" urban policy means finding a general definition of what is needed or how services can be best provided, then the relation of the state to urban problems will always be a secondary consideration. There are, of course, powerful forces within mixed economies and pluralist political systems that favor a system where local choice and autonomy are maximized (Gregg 1974). At the same time, studies are also appearing that suggest how constraints and limitations are placed on cities by the larger political and social system (Castells 1972; Gale & Moore 1975). The examination of the French pattern of local finance and use of subsidies begins to provide a firmer foundation for more general theoretical interests. While France has no national urban policy, the state has placed real constraints on the urban response to new problems, and it has moderated the political and social conflicts that might occur without constraints.

The analysis of the French *tutelle financière* bears on these more general questions in several ways. A unified national urban policy may well be an impossibility for any modern state. Given the complexity of the modern city, a much more likely response may well be to develop other institutional channels that enable the state to monitor and possibly to influence those city policies that are considered essential to the system itself. The French efforts to transform the supervision of cities and towns into a financial control are an illustration of this. France has always had one of the more closely supervised urban substructures. What is new over the past decade is the restructuring of the financial links between the state and the cities. For France itself what is most remarkable is how a new system of constraints appears to have emerged while the state is in fact doing less to support urban investments.

The French experience suggests that the capacity of the industrial democracy to respond and to adjust to new environments may be underestimated. Despite the angry mayors, investment funds have increased at the same rate over a period with severe economic dislocations. The procedural and administrative complications of the subsidies are real and troubling, but they should not blind one to institutional adjustment. Huge transfers are made and will, in all likelihood, continue to be made. The complex network linking ministries, the Caisse des Dépôts, and local administration is itself an institutional reality whose role and influence have grown in the past decade. Very similar changes could be pointed to in England and the United States (Layfield 1976; Beer 1976). The formation of such para-institutional devices may in fact be the most interesting development in the modern state. They are neither the product of the cities themselves nor of central governments. Of immense political importance, their political implications are little understood. Thus the *subvention*, though it may take a familiar form, may denote a major change in the relation of cities to the state.

REFERENCES

Ashford, Douglas E. 1978. French pragmatism and British idealism: Financial aspects of local reorganization. *Comparative Political Studies* 11 (July): 231–54.
Association des Maires de Grandes Villes de France. 1976. *Livre blanc sur les finances locales; Les grandes villes devant l'avenir.* Paris.
Barberye, René. 1973. Les interventions financières de la Caisse des Dépôts dans le domaine de l'équipement local et du logement social. *Bulletin Economique et Financière,* pp. 139–68.
Beer, S. H. 1976. The adoption of General Revenue Sharing: A case study in public sector politics. *Public Policy* 24 (spring): 127–95.
Bernard, Paul. 1969. *Le grand tournant des communes de France.* Paris: Colin.
Bloch-Lainé, François. 1977. *Profession: Fonctionnaire.* Paris: Editions Seuil.
Bouinot, Jean, et al. 1976. *L'influence des finances municipales sur le processus de croissance urbaine.* Paris: Centre National de la Recherche Scientifique.
Bourrel, Vincent. 1965. *Rapport de la Commission d'Etude des Finances Locales à Monsieur le Premier Ministre.* Paris: Imprimerie Nationale.
Castells, Manuel. 1972. *La question urbaine.* Paris: Maspero.
Les Comptes de la nation 1969. 1970. Notes et Etudes Documentaires no. 3725–26. Paris: Documentation Française.
Conseil Economique et Social (Grossman Report). 1973. *Journal Officiel,* no. 12, 31 July, pp. 527–51.
D'Arcy, François. 1968. *Structures administratives et urbanisation: La Société Centrale pour l'Equipement du Territoire.* Paris: Berger-Levrault.
D'Arcy, François, and Jobert, Bruno. 1975. Urban planning in France. In J. Hayward and M. Watson, eds. *Planning, politics and public policy: The British, French and Italian experience,* pp. 295–315. Cambridge: At the University Press.
Duplouy, Joseph. 1967. *Le crédit aux collectivités locales.* Paris: Berger-Levrault.
Duport, J. P. 1973. L'expérience des contrats du plan. *Bulletin de l'Institut International de l'Administration Publique,* no. 25, January/March, pp. 161–75.
Dupuy, G., and Prud'homme, Rémy, et al. 1975. La planification des équipements collectifs en France: Mythe ou réalité? *La Vie Urbaine* 50 (December): 15–30.

Flecher-Bourjol, Dominique. 1976. Essai de typologie fonctionelle des contrats passés entre l'Etat et les collectivités locales et établissements publics territoriaux. *Bulletin de l'Institut International de l'Administration Publique,* no. 38, April/June, pp. 57–90.

Fréville, Yves. 1973. L'évolution de finances de grandes villes depuis 1967. *Revue de Science Financière* 4: 725–58.

Gale, Stephen, and Moore, Eric G., eds. 1975. *The manipulated city.* Chicago: Maaroufa Press.

Gregg, Phillip M. 1974. Limits and levels of analysis: A problem policy analysis in federal systems. *Publius* 4 (fall): 59–85.

Grémion, Pierre. 1974. L'administration territoriale. In M. Crozier et al. *Où va l'administration française?* pp. 75–100. Paris: Editions d'Organisation.

Guerrier, Paul, and Bauchard, Denis. 1972. *Economie financière des collectivités locales.* Paris: Colin.

Guichard Report (Rapport de la Commission de Developpement des Responsabilités Locales). 1976. *Vivre ensemble.* Paris: Documentation Française.

Hourticq, J. 1974. La réforme des régimes des subventions d'investissement de l'Etat aux collectivités locales. *Revue Administrative* 26 (January/February): 65–68.

Intergroupe des Finances Locales. 1971. *Rapport.* Commissariat Générale du Plan. Paris: Documentation Française.

Isaac, Guy, and Moliner, Joel. 1975. L'exercice par les nouvelles institutions régionales de leurs pouvoirs financiers. *Bulletin de l'Institut International de l'Administration Publique,* no. 34, April/June, pp. 341–403.

Knaub, G. 1974. De l'incidence des regroupements de communes sur leur autonomie financière. *Revue du Droit Public* 90 (January/February): 155–68.

Layfield Report. 1976. *Local Government Finance.* London: HMSO, cmnd. 6453.

Leruste, Philippe. 1975. *Le contrat d'aménagement de villes moyennes.* Notes et Etudes Documentaires no. 4234–36. Paris: Documentation Française.

Machin, Howard. 1974. The French prefects and local administration. *Parliamentary Affairs* 27 (spring): 237–50.

————. 1974. Local government change in France—The case of 1964 reforms. *Policy and Politics* 2 (March): 249–65.

Médard, Jean-François. 1968. Les communautés urbaines: Renforcement ou déclin de l'autonomie local? *Revue de Droit Public* 84 (July/October): 737–800.

Moreau, Jacques. 1976. *Administration régionale, locale et municipale.* 3d ed. Paris: Dalloz.

de Préneuf, Jean-Marc. 1971. Finances locales: Les projets Pompidou. *Revue Politique et Parlementaire,* no. 818, February, pp. 46–55.

Priouret, Roger. 1966. *La Caisse des Dépôts.* Paris: Presses Universitaires de France.

Projet de loi de finances pour 1976. 1975. Régionalisation du Budget d'Equipement et d'Aménagement du Territoire pour 1975. Vol. 1. Paris: Imprimerie Nationale.

Prud'homme, Rémy. 1974. Regional economic policy in France, 1962–1972. In N. M. Hansen, ed. *Public policy and regional development,* pp. 33–63. Cambridge, Mass.: Ballinger.

Prud'homme, Rémy, et al. 1975. La répartition spatiale des fonds budgétaires. *Revue d'Economie Politique* 65: 38–59.

Rapport technique sur les projections associées au VIe Plan. 1973. Collections de l'INSEE, série C, no. 24–25. Paris: Documentation Française.

Statistiques des comptes pour l'exercice. 1964–75. Le secteur public local: Les communes, les départements, les établissements publics locaux. Paris: Direction de la Comptabilité Publique, Ministère de l'Economie et des Finances.

Statistiques et indicateurs des régions françaises. 1975. Collections de l'INSEE, série R, no. 19–20. Paris: Documentation Française.

Thoenig, Jean-Claude. 1973. *L'ère des technocrates.* Paris: Editions d'Organisation.

U.N. 1976. *Yearbook of national accounts statistics: 1975.* New York: United Nations.

CHAPTER 6

URBAN INVESTMENT CONTROLS IN BRITAIN

Ian D. Ball

Debate concerning the actual, and proper, relationship between central and local government in Britain has a long history. Much of this debate has centered on two competing views of central-local relations. These are described by Hartley:

> There are two traditions in Britain of the relationship between central and local government. One views local government as an administrative device for the provision of national services within a given area, a field administrative agency in which the relation between local authorities and central government is that of agent and principal. The other sees local government as a system of local independent bodies, each having its own rights and duties, in which the relationship between the two elements is that of partnership (1971, p. 439).

Although, as Hartley acknowledges, there is no consensus as to which view is correct, either descriptively or normatively, these two views stand as the principal alternative positions in the continuing debate. There is however in the relationship a further element that has received much less attention: the element of conflict. Both the partnership and the principal and agent traditions stress the fact that the two levels of government are working together, though with differing degrees of independence. Griffith recognizes the inevitability of conflict:

> It is a pleasant and comforting evasion of the problems created by the existence of these two political groups—the departments and the local authorities—to say that they act as partners. In the broadest terms their interest may be the same; to promote the public welfare. But they are also stationed in opposition to one another. . . . On many

matters, the idea of partnership can be valuable and certainly the interests of both should always be subordinated to the interests of those for whom the services are provided. But to the extent that the interests of the two groups inevitably conflict, there can be no partnership but only a decision (1966, pp. 18–19).

Griffith concludes, however, that while divergent interests may lead to conflict and public dispute, "The public dispute is . . . largely superficial while the private co-operation is fundamental" (1966, p. 506). It is the element of conflict in the central-local relationship that is the subject of the present study, though it will examine conflict only within a certain aspect of the overall relationship.

Conflict, as the term will be used in the present paper, refers to covert or overt dissension between the two parties. This dissension may be manifested in a variety of actions by either party, ranging on the local authority side from mutterings of discontent to outright rebellion. Neither of these two forms of dissension warrants detailed study. The former is so common and so weak an expression of local authority resentment as not to be evidence of serious conflict. An instance of the latter was the refusal of the Clay Cross Council to implement central government policy on council house rentals, even though the policy was enshrined in statute. Such vigorous expressions of local independence are, however, insufficiently common to allow any general conclusions to be reached. Such expressions tend also to be of very limited duration. The evidence of conflict that will be examined in this paper lies at neither of these extremes—it is conflict that can be described as active opposition to central government wishes within the framework of law. It is local authorities obeying the letter of the law but struggling to evade its spirit. It is the spirit of resistance that resulted in Boaden finding evidence that "Small authorities not only defy central wishes, but many do so in a systematic way in a number of different services" (1970, p. 182). Their defiance is active, but not so as to bring the full weight of the law onto their heads.

There are a number of reasons why conflict is to be expected between central and local government in the area of this study, local authority capital expenditure. The reasons derive from differing objectives pursued by the two levels of government. From the standpoint of local government it is clearly of very great importance that it have control over its own capital expenditure. Capital expenditure incurred by local government is a reflection of the services it performs. It is incurred in the acquisition of schools and roads, houses and libraries, water and sewage disposal systems, plus the capital facilities required for health, social, police, and fire services. While this list is not exhaustive it should indicate that local authority capital expenditure is of vital importance in shaping a community. Indeed, so vital is this expenditure that it can reasonably be argued that whoever controls local authority capital expenditure controls urban development. This assertion has greater validity in countries like Britain, where the majority of the services alluded to above are provided solely or very largely by local authorities. In the British context, the only major local authority service in which the private sector has a significant role is housing, and even here the local authority role is greater than in most mixed economies. If local authority capital expenditure is so vital it is hardly surprising that local authorities should wish to be able to exert substantial control over it. This being the case it can reasonably be hypothesized that local authorities will resist attempts by central government to control local authority capital expenditure unless the rationale for such actions is very strong.

What then are central government's objectives in regard to local authority capital expenditure? First, central government is concerned with insuring that the long-term development of the economy is orderly, implying that local authority capital expenditure should not be allowed to increase in a way such that it places an unreasonable burden on other sectors of the economy. Central government perceives that this is more likely to occur with respect to local authority capital expenditure than with respect to current expenditure:

> Capital expenditure presents different problems [than current expenditure]. There is a much greater possibility that, without central government controls, aggregate expenditure could substantially exceed the tolerable level. The local democratic concern may be with the immediate impact—the relatively small interest charges—rather than with the massive capital expenditure itself (Great Britain 1971, p. 6).

The distinction that has been made between capital and current expenditure has a further, important implication that will not have been lost on central government. Capital expenditure can be regarded as a determinant of future current expenditure in that capital expenditure commits the authority to servicing the capital facilities created (for instance, the construction of a school commits the authority to meeting teachers' salaries and other maintenance and running costs). Assuming the capital expenditure to have been loan financed, the local authority is also committed to meeting debt servicing costs.

Second, central government wishes to manage the economy in the short-term so as to minimize the effect of business cycles; i.e., it wishes to implement a counter-cyclical fiscal policy. As the Plowden Committee recognized:

> The Government are required by public opinion to seek to manage the national economy with only small variations in the level of employ-

ment. It is natural, therefore, to explore the possibilities of using variations in public expenditure to help in this task (Great Britain 1961,
p. 10).

Given that central government does wish to vary the level of public
expenditure in order to achieve short-term economic objectives, it must
decide on the least costly and most effective form of control. Again the
distinction between capital and current expenditure is significant. As a
broad generalization it can be asserted that current expenditure is related
to the existing level of service provision; while capital expenditure, as has
been noted, is a determinant of future levels of service provision. In other
words, to cut current expenditure implies a reduction in existing levels of
service, while a cut in capital expenditure merely delays improvements
to the standard of service provision. From the political viewpoint, that
makes capital expenditure a more likely target of expenditure cuts than
is current expenditure; and, as local authority capital expenditure is a
major component of total public investment, it follows that it will be a
prime target for the short-term economic actions of central government.

While central government does have this rationale for its attempts to
control local authority capital expenditure, the use of public investment
as an instrument of counter-cyclical policy is not without its objections.
The two principal objections are that (1) to accelerate or retard capital
programs once they are under way is uneconomic and (2) the time lag
between the taking of counter-cyclical action and that action's being effective (assuming for the moment that such actions are effective) may be so
long as to make the action counter-productive; i.e., it may aggravate the
cyclical variation it was intended to overcome:

> In view of the number and variety of bodies immediately concerned
> . . . , and the impracticability in most cases of varying the rate of work
> on projects already in progress, a decision to stimulate or restrain the
> rate of expenditure must be made in good time if it is to have a
> counter-cyclical effect. It may be six months until significant results
> begin to become apparent and the full effect may not make its impact
> until a year after that (Great Britain 1960b, pp. 6–7).

If central government did not see the implications of this time lag, they
were spelled out by the Plowden Committee:

> Experience shows that at least six to nine months (and often more)
> must elapse before short-term changes in either direction take full
> effect. In the two-year period from high to low, which seems to charac-
> terise post-war fluctuations in the economy, the effect of the action
> taken may well appear at the very moment when the economy is
> already on the turn. The remedy may, therefore, be worse than the
> disease (Great Britain 1961, p. 10).

Central government is, then, aware of the problems associated with the use of public investment (including local authority capital expenditure) as an instrument of short-term economic management. In 1964 the Organization for Economic Cooperation and Development (OECD) pointed out the gap between the apparent attitude of the central government and its actions:

> The United Kingdom authorities consider that the public capital pro gramme is not a very flexible instrument for use as part of an active demand management policy. Once programmes have been launched it is considered that they cannot be cut back by more than a marginal amount without a prohibitive waste of resources or an excessively long time-lag before reductions become effective. Despite these difficulties, there have been attempts on various occasions in the past to restrict public investment when the economy was becoming overloaded (Great Britain, OECD 1964, p. 19).

Table 6-1   Summary, Fiscal Policy Measures Announced by Government That Relate to Local Authority Capital Expenditure

Date	Details
October 1949[a]	Cuts in the level of public investment plans, intended to come into effect from July 1950
April 1950	Revocation of the cuts to planned capital expenditure on housing, announced in October 1949
July 1955[a]	Local authorities requested to hold back the implementation of their capital programs, intended to reduce expenditure in the financial years 1955–56, 1956–57
October 1955[a]	Local authorities requested to hold capital expenditure in 1956–57 to the level of 1954–55 (also monetary measures with tighter conditions of borrowing from the PWLB)
February 1956[a]	Loan sanctions and grants "drastically curtailed" in all areas of local authority capital expenditure save that of housing
October 1956[a]	Restrictions extended to 1957–58
November 1957[a]	Existing restrictions continued into 1959–60 and local authority capital expenditure on housing limited to 80 percent of the existing level
July/October 1958[b]	Restrictions progressively relaxed over the four-month period
November 1958[b]	Local authorities requested to bring forward projects able to be completed in 1959
June 1960[a]	Public investment limited in 1961–62 to the level of 1960–61

[a]Intended impact: restrictive.
[b]Intended impact: expansionary.

Table 6-1—Continued

Date	Details
August 1961[a]	A request to restrain local authority capital expenditure, intended to be effective from 1962
October 1962[b]	Local authorities allowed an extra £60m for capital expenditure in the years 1962–63 and 1963–64, approximately 80 percent relating to 1963–64
November 1962[b]	A further increase in the level of 1963–64 capital expenditure by local authorities
July 1965[a]	Loan sanctions for local authority capital expenditure restricted and projects deferred; intended impact of approximately £200m in a full year
July 1966[a]	Further restrictions on loan sanctions
April 1967[b]	In the budget a sharp rise in public expenditure generally announced for the year 1967–68
December 1967[a]	Local authorities requested to postpone capital expenditure where unacceptable damage would not result, intended to apply in 1968 and 1969
January 1968[a]	Further severe restrictions announced and cuts in the level of house building planned for 1968 and 1969
October 1970[a]	Cuts in the planned level of public expenditure
November 1971[b]	A number of public investment schemes brought forward, though most went to the nationalized industries and relatively little to local authorities
May 1973[a]	Some cuts in public expenditure generally, intended to be effective in 1973–74 and 1974–75[c]
December 1973[a]	Further, more severe cuts in public expenditure[c]

[c]These actions cannot be expected to have any impact on the level of local authority capital expenditure during 1973, the last year covered in this study. The first action could however be expected to impact on the level of local authority capital expenditure during the financial year 1973–74.

The frequency with which central government has nevertheless attempted to manipulate local authority capital expenditure in the interests of short-term economic management is detailed in table 6-1. It is a frequency that belies the above statements. This presents the curious picture of central government on the one hand admitting that its attempts to manipulate local authority capital expenditure in the short-term are likely to be costly, ineffective, and possibly counter-productive and on the other hand proceeding with such manipulations on virtually every occasion during the post–World War II period when the economy appeared to need either restraint or stimulation. As the costs associated with these actions by central government are borne by local authorities (in the form of disruption to capital programs and ineffective capital planning), it is perhaps to be expected that local authorities will make efforts to resist such central government actions.

These then are the reasons why local and central government, respectively, should wish to control local authority capital expenditure. In both cases, viewed from the particular level of government, the objectives being pursued are laudable; but the differing objectives are not compatible, and the implication is that the two levels of government will be in conflict as a result.

THE MECHANISMS OF CONTROL

Having established the potential for conflict, with local and central government both having strong reasons for wishing to control the capital expenditure of local authorities, the administrative arrangements that govern the relationship must be specified. The intention here is to specify the means by which central government can control only local authority capital expenditure; other forms of control will be ignored. The Chartered Institute of Public Finance and Accountancy (the CIPFA, formerly Institute of Municipal Treasurers and Accountants) identifies five direct methods by which central government may exercise control over local authority capital expenditure, to which one can add two indirect methods.

The five *direct* methods are:

1. *Control through revenue expenditure.* "Certain statutes limit revenue expenditure on individual services and thereby capital expenditure reflected in debt charges and running expenses is restricted, though such restrictions rarely present any problem in practice" (CIPFA, ch. 2, par. 17).
2. *Control through regulation.* "In addition to control over capital expenditure the government has control over borrowing methods by the application of specific regulations to certain types of borrowing, mainly to control demands on the money market" (CIPFA ch. 2, par. 19).
3. *Control through cost limitation.* This form of control has been exercised principally in relation to capital expenditure on housing, education, and health and social services. The stringency with which this form of control has applied has varied, being most restrictive in the housing field (since 1970).
4. *Control through general consents.* This control operates in relation to the various sources of local authority borrowing and applies to the actual raising of the loan; i.e., it operates *after* loan sanction has been given. Certain forms of loan may be used only within specified restrictions; for example, foreign loans may be raised only with treasury approval, while bill issues and temporary borrowing may be resorted to only up to a limit specified by Treasury.
5. *Control through loan sanctions.* In order to finance capital expendi-

ture through loan finance, local authorities must receive loan sanction from central government. This gives approval to borrow with respect to a particular project and lays down a maximum period for loan repayment. Sanction was needed for virtually all loans (with only very minor exceptions) until 1970. At that time loan sanctions ceased to be needed for projects in certain areas, though they remained necessary for what were deemed "key sectors." As the key sector includes housing, education, major roads, and police and social services, the exercise of control through loan sanctions remains important. Corden and Curley argue that "The weight of the key sector within the total prevents the exercise of real freedom [by local authorities]" (1974, p. 231).

The two *indirect* methods of control are:

6. *Control through the regulation of Public Works Loans Board (PWLB) interest rates.* The thinking behind this control is that if the interest rates charged by the PWLB can be manipulated, then local authorities should respond in the manner suggested by classical micro-economic theory: decreasing their borrowing when interest rates increase, and vice versa. As an instrument of control this method has declined in importance with the decline in the volume of loan finance received from the PWLB. It was, however, seen as an important instrument of control in 1955, when interest rates were raised four times.
7. *Control through appeal.* On numerous occasions central government has attempted to influence the level of local authority spending, both capital and current, by issuing appeals to local authorities for restraint (usually) or expansion in their spending. Although this form of "control" appears weak, the appeals were presumably issued with serious intent and some expectation that they may influence the level of expenditure. The efficacy of this method must however remain subject to more than a little doubt.

The appearance conveyed is one of central government having a whole battery of weapons with which to control local authority capital expenditure. One may be left with the impression that with such an arsenal, any conflict between central and local government in this area would quickly be settled in favor of the center. This is not necessarily the case. In a broader context Boaden notes the distinction between formal and effective control:

It could be that many of the current views about central control result from the preoccupation with formal relationships which marks so much of the literature. If all the mechanisms of control were fully operated there would be little question about the effective determination of local service provision (1970, p. 184).

In the particular case it is clear that the strength of an arsenal is not determined solely by the variety of weapons. Of the central controls over local authority capital expenditure mentioned above, most are very weak in their application. Some apply only to specific minor services (e.g., control through revenue expenditure); others apply to only a specific source of capital finance (e.g., control through regulation over foreign borrowing); and yet others apply to only certain specific categories of building (e.g., cost limitations on housing and schools). While each of these controls may be effective with respect to individual projects or sources of finance, they are not regarded by central government as being effective controls over the bulk of local authority capital expenditure. An examination of the official literature and a perusal of central government actions over the post–World War II period make it clear that with only minor departures central government sees as its principal instrument of control the loan sanction procedures. The extracts below, from different times during the postwar period, are illustrative of the central government position.

> The [Ministry of Housing and Local Government Circular no. 55/56] indicated how the general policy [of economic restraint] would be applied to those services coming within the Department's responsibility. It was explained that except where risk to health, safety or other vital interests rendered it impracticable, the Minister would drastically curtail loan sanctions or grants for new projects or expansion of existing schemes for water, sewerage and sewage disposal, refuse disposal, coast protection, burial grounds and crematoria; that loan sanction for housing will not be affected; and that in respect of other services within his responsibility he would not propose for the time being, except in cases of special urgency, to authorise any new loans for capital expenditure whatsoever (Great Britain 1957, p. 1).

It is clear that central government sees the loan sanction procedure as the means by which it can achieve its economic objectives. The following describes the aim of central government in introducing a modification to the loan sanction procedures:

> The arrangements are, according to [Department of the Environment] Circular 2/70 aimed at firstly, providing greater freedom to local authorities in planning their capital expenditure, secondly, simplifying the procedure for loan consents and the application of capital receipts and thirdly to improve the Government's ability to monitor

and regulate the total level and main trends of local authority capital investment (CIPFA, ch. 2, par. 47).

This makes clear that (1) while government may be prepared to forego some of its detailed control of capital expenditure, it wishes to retain as close as possible a control over the aggregate and (2) it sees the loan sanction procedures as the means of achieving that control.

Because the loan sanction procedure is not in its immediate impact a control of capital expenditure but rather a control of capital finance, one has further cause for doubting that central government control of expenditure is as strong as at first appears. Borrowing is only one source of capital finance, albeit the major one. If central government lacks control over other sources of finance and does not have effective control of capital expenditure per se, then reliance by central government on the loan sanction procedures may be misplaced. In 1975 approximately 65 percent of finance for capital expenditure was from loans and 5 percent was from central government grants, while the remaining 30 percent was the surplus on current account. Even assuming that control over loan finance through the sanction procedure is effective, there remains 30 percent of total capital receipts that is very substantially within the control of local government. Yet some doubt must also be cast on the effectiveness of control over capital expenditure funded from loans. Central government approves or rejects an application to raise a loan, and in this sense it has total control; but having obtained the sanction the local authority does not have to raise that loan immediately: it may time the raising of the loan to suit itself. Given that one of the major objectives of central government in relation to local authority capital expenditure concerns short-term economic management, the ability of local authorities to vary the timing of their borrowing may represent an opportunity for local authorities to frustrate the wishes of central government. It would therefore seem to be the case that while central government might appear to have the means of controlling local authority capital expenditure and all that implies, in fact local authorities have at least some discretion. The divergence in objectives provides the rationale for possible conflict between central and local government, the distribution of control being not so unequal as to make the possibility of conflict implausible.

Before proceeding briefly to delineate the institutional background against which the evidence must be viewed, one point must be made that is fundamental to an appreciation of precisely why the loan sanction procedure and its application are so critical in any study of the constraints on local authority capital spending. This point is that, in general, local authorities do *not* experience any real difficulty in raising loans; their problem lies in getting from central government the approval that allows them to borrow. Effectively, the financial market does not restrain local authorities. This is despite the fact that in the mid-1950s the facilities of the PWLB were substantially withdrawn from local authorities for precisely the reason that it was thought that this would impose a discipline on local authorities. The outcome was recently described by the Bank of England:

> Experience since 1955, when PWLB facilities were virtually withdrawn, indicates that local authorities have been able to satisfy their market borrowing requirements even when the general financial climate has been particularly stringent (1976, p. 1).

The emphasis in the present paper, therefore, will be on the relationship between central and local government rather than on the market experience of local authorities. Further, since the principal concerns of central government in this area are with economic aggregates and since central government determines the level of loan sanctions, the evidence presented will be at the aggregate level.

Over the period covered by this study there has been some variation in the roles of the various institutions that participate in the determination of local authority capital expenditure levels. The variation has its principal source in the economic philosophy of the government of the time, which is reflected in the policies of the government both as to the appropriate degree of control over local authority capital expenditure and the most effective method(s) of implementing that control. What is less clear, however, is that there has been any significant shift in the general relationship between central and local government in the area of local authority capital expenditure. In broad terms, power has remained with central government and has been exercised through the loan sanction procedures throughout the period of this study. The variation has been in marginal areas such as the role of interest rates as a means of exerting control over local borrowing, the extent to which central government should finance local authority borrowing through the PWLB, and, conversely, the extent to which local authorities should be forced to borrow in a competitive market.

For the purposes of this paper one can distinguish two levels of interaction between the central and local levels of government. The higher level involves the creation and modification of the framework within which decisions are reached on individual local authority capital projects. At this level local authorities, local authority associations, and professional bodies of local authority officers will negotiate with, as necessary, individual departments of central government (especially the Department of the Environment (DoE) and the Treasury but also spending departments with local government responsibilities such as the Department of Education and Science, the Department of Health and Social Security, and the Ministry of Transport), the Bank of England, and the PWLB, as well as members of cabinet and parliament. Such negotiations normally (though not always) precede changes in the overall structure within which local authorities must operate their capital programs. When, in October 1955, the then chancellor of the exchequer announced that thenceforth the PWLB would become a lender of last resort only to local government, the storm of surprised protest from local government suggests that there was little or no prior consultation. When in 1963 the government took action to limit the volume of temporary borrowing by local authorities, however (as detailed Great Britain 1963), this followed negotiation with a group of local authority treasurers who extracted from central government a reversal of the 1955 policy on PWLB lending, enabling local authorities once again to obtain a significant proportion of their borrowing from the PWLB. In general, such changes in administrative and institutional relationships *are* preceded by negotiations between the two levels of government.

The second level of interaction is at a lower level and is of primary concern to this study. It is the interaction that occurs between central and local government when a local authority is seeking to carry out a specific capital project. At this level there is little negotiation between the levels of government. The local authority evaluates the alternative capital projects it might wish to carry out and ranks them according to priority. It then approaches the appropriate spending department of central government (the DoE or, prior to its establishment, the Ministry of Housing and Local Government, the Department of Education and Science, etc.) for loan sanction. The sanction may or may not be given; the spending departments have their own priorities and are themselves limited by the Treasury as to the total value of loans that they may sanction in a given period. The Treasury takes as its first consideration the state of the national economy and, on the basis of this assessment, reaches a decision on the aggregate level of loan sanctions. The allocation to sectors of the economy and to central government departments of this aggregate is an outcome of the political process in central government, with major decisions being made at the cabinet level. It should be clear from the process here described that local authorities may fail to get a loan sanction for a project to which they assign a high priority, yet they may succeed with respect to a project to which they assign a lower priority. The reaction engendered by this outcome was expressed in a heartfelt manner by an eminent local authority treasurer:

> When we then seek loan sanction for say, our old people's home, we are told that the government's allocation of sanctions for this purpose is exhausted, but that they have a ration available for a health centre —which is perhaps lower on our lists of priorities—if we cared to apply for it.
>
> This is highly frustrating. We accept without question that some omniscient overlord should decide how much the local authority capital investment should be for the year and we will even accept that

someone in Whitehall shall have the power to allocate this to local authorities on the basis of a case stated as to need. But who is more competent than ourselves to decide whether the needs of our area are greater for old people's welfare than for health, to take services quite at random? (Page 1968, p. 14).

At this level the situation faced by local authorities is quite clear, if somewhat bleak. They have very little say, jointly or collectively, as to the overall level of loan sanctions or to distribution among sectors of the economy. The local authorities apply for loan sanctions for individual projects; they may or may not get them. The best they can do is to shape their capital programs with the priorities of central government in mind, an orientation that is hardly consistent with the rationale for local democracy. It has already been noted, however, that local authorities do have some scope for evading the control exercised by central government through the loan sanction procedure. They can to some extent vary the timing of their borrowing, they can finance capital expenditure from the rates or from capital receipts, they can vary the rate at which work is undertaken on existing projects, and they can enter lease arrangements that are in substance installment purchases.

AN EMPIRICAL ASSESSMENT OF CONFLICT

The present paper examines evidence relating to the postwar period, with the cut-off periods of 1950 and 1973. The aim of the paper is not to establish that there presently exists conflict between central and local government but that conflict has been a major element in the relationship over a longer period of time. Indeed, given the existing pressures on local government spending in Britain, the absence of conflict (as earlier defined) might be regarded as the more surprising. The specific dates were chosen because 1950 is the year in which economic life was seen to have returned to normal after World War II, while the major local government reorganization of 1974 would raise issues of comparability if figures subsequent to 1973 were used.

The evidence is divided into three sections (see below). In the first, the effectiveness of central government's actions in pursuance of its countercyclical fiscal policy are examined. This section is essentially concerned with central control over local authority capital expenditure in the short-term. In the second section the loan sanction procedure is evaluated for its effectiveness in controlling local authority borrowing in the longer term. Finally, the behavior of the surplus on local authority current account is considered, this being the major source of capital finance outside the control of central government. This evidence, when considered as a unity, should enable some general conclusions to be reached concerning the extent of conflict between the two levels of government and the degree of control over local authority capital expenditure exerted by each level.

A. Fiscal Policy Measures and Local Authority Capital Expenditure

Central government has, on many occasions during the period 1950–73, taken action to modify the level of local authority capital expenditure in order to restore short-term balance to the economy. One test of the effectiveness of control exercised by central government and the effectiveness of local authority resistance will be to determine whether local authority capital expenditure moved in the manner suggested by the central government action. The first step is to specify the occasions on which central government has taken such action (these are listed in table 6–1, above). On the basis of this listing, and after incorporating certain lag assumptions (see the chapter appendix), it is possible to classify each year during the period 1950–73 according to whether the *anticipated* impact of central government actions on local authority capital expenditures is restrictive, expansionary, or neutral (where central government has taken no action). If then the *actual* growth rates of local authority capital expenditures are computed for each year, it can be determined whether the mean growth rates reflect the central government action. It will be noted that in order to minimize the risk of distortion that may result from a particular, unrepresentative measure of the growth rate of local authority capital expenditure being used, three different measures have been used in this analysis. The first is the percentage increase in local authority capital expenditure (more correctly, local authority gross domestic fixed capital formation) at current prices. The second is the percentage increase in local authority capital expenditure expressed as a proportion of the gross national product (GNP). (See table 6-2 for these two measures.) The final measure (see table 6-3) differs from the first two in that it relates (1) to financial rather than calendar years and (2) to England and Wales, alone, not to the whole of the United Kingdom.

With each of the three measures the result is essentially the same. When the intent of central government is to increase local authority capital expenditure, that result is clearly achieved; but when the aim is to restrict the growth of local authority capital expenditure, it can be seen that in such periods the rate of growth is not significantly different from what it is when central government has taken no action at all. In other words, local authorities go along with central government when they see it to be to their advantage, but attempts to restrict their capital expenditure programs are resisted and appear not to be effective. The most obvious explanation of the ineffectiveness of fiscal policy measures in restricting local authority capital expenditure lies in the mechanism of control. It is certainly easy to point to instances where attempts to limit local

Table 6-2   *Impact of Fiscal Policy Measures on Local Authority Capital Expenditure*

Year	Expansionary[a] 1[b]	Expansionary[a] 2[c]	Insignificant[a] 1[b]	Insignificant[a] 2[c]	Restrictive[a] 1[b]	Restrictive[a] 2[c]
1950					6.01	0.29
51			13.30	2.61		
52			17.39	8.47		
53			12.41	4.69		
54			−5.27	−10.45		
55			−2.09	−8.33		
56					0.71	−6.97
57					0.35	−5.54
58					−4.39	−8.28
59	6.99	1.50				
60			3.78	−2.22		
61					16.23	8.71
62					15.95	10.80
63	8.48	1.89				
64	25.93	16.05				
65			6.56	−0.27		
66					13.50	7.20
67	16.58	10.70				
68					9.18	2.02
69					2.63	−2.42
70			5.35	−4.06		
71					5.89	−5.88
72	14.08	1.75				
73	23.21	6.88				
Mean	15.88	6.46	6.43	−1.20	6.61	−0.01

[a]Growth rate of local authority capital expenditure, with anticipated impact of fiscal policy measures.
[b]Represents the percentage increase in local authority gross domestic fixed capital formation at current prices (U.K. figures).
[c]Represents the increase in the proportion of the GNP accounted for by local authority gross domestic fixed capital formation (U.K. figures).

authority capital expenditure growth have been spectacularly unsuccessful. One such instance is the attempt of June 1960 to limit expenditure for the financial year 1961–62 to the level of 1960–61. The actual outcome was an increase of approximately 20 percent for the financial year 1961–62. Of the mechanisms of control specified above, the one most favored and most used by central government is the loan sanction procedure, yet it is a method of control that is totally ineffective in relation to projects that have been commenced and even to projects that may not have been, assuming that the loan sanction has been given. In other words it is completely useless in relation to a large proportion of capital expenditure in the immediate future; i.e., in the short-term. Yet if the measures are to be of any use in implementing fiscal policy, it is precisely that time span over

*Table 6-3   Impact of Fiscal Policy Measures on Local Authority Capital
Expenditure Using a Financial Year Basis*

Year	Expansionary*	Insignificant*	Restrictive*
1950–51			11.30
51–52		15.96	
52–53		16.81	
53–54		9.12	
54–55		−3.97	
55–56			2.29
56–57			2.18
57–58			−6.15
58–59		−4.01	
59–60	10.59		
60–61		8.56	
61–62			20.29
62–63		5.75	
63–64	23.41		
64–65	25.52		
65–66			5.32
66–67			8.92
67–68	9.81		
68–69			2.04
69–70			8.16
70–71		19.84	
71–72			8.48
72–73	25.20		
Mean	18.91	8.51	6.28

*Growth rate of local authority capital expenditure for England and Wales, with anticipated
impact of fiscal policy measures.

which central government needs control. So a case can be made that it is
the mechanisms of control adopted that prevent the effective implementation of government fiscal policy.

The above argument is given added strength when considered in conjunction with another possible explanation, that the inability of central
government to restrain local authority capital expenditure in the short-
term is the result of resistance to the measures on the part of the local
authorities. From their viewpoint there are good reasons to attempt to
frustrate the intentions of central government. The most obvious one is
that attempts to modify local authority capital expenditure programs in
the short-term are disruptive, and in the view of the Plowden Report:

> There is no doubt from the evidence that we have received that chop-
> ping and changing in Government expenditure policy is frustrating to
> efficiency and economy in the running of the public services. It impairs
> cost-consciousness and financial discipline at all levels. . . . The experi-
> ence of recent years, both in the Treasury and in the Departments, and

in the wide circles of local government and nationalised industry outside them is that short-term "economy campaigns" and "stop-and-go"
are damaging to the real effectiveness of control of public expenditure
(Great Britain 1961, p. 9).

If this view is shared by local authorities—and it is—then it is significant
that the means by which central government attempts to restrict capital
expenditure is able to be outflanked by local authorities. If central government restricts the loan sanctions, that does not prevent local authorities
from increasing expenditure on projects already given sanction or on
those that are under construction. In this manner the level of capital
expenditure can be kept up in the short-term in the not-unreasonable
hope that by the time the effect of the reduction in loan sanctions might
start to be felt, policy would have entered a "go" phase. Local authorities
can also thwart the intentions of government by financing capital expenditure from revenue or by disposing of assets no longer required as another
source of capital finance. It should be stressed however that all of these
means of overcoming central government policies can be used only over
a relatively limited period—sources of finance other than from loans are
limited—and can be used only where there is the presumption that a "go"
phase will follow the "stop" phase within two or three years.

The contention that central government's fiscal policy measures are
ineffective because of local government resistance presupposes that local
authorities have the means of frustrating the wishes of central government, a means that the loan sanction procedures afford. The inadequacy
of the loan sanction procedures as an instrument of control over the
short-term pattern of local authority capital expenditure allows local authorities to express their dissatisfaction with the manner in which central
government exercises control, and it provides evidence of conflict between the two levels of government. One must presume that if local
authorities wished to vary their capital expenditure in the manner indicated by central government, it would be within their power to do so.
They demonstrate this to some degree by the speed with which they
respond to requests to bring forward capital programs and increase their
expenditure.

B. The Loan Sanction Procedure as a Means of Controlling Local Borrowing

In the present section the loan sanction will be evaluated for its effectiveness in controlling local *borrowing,* whereas above the concern was with
central government's short-term control over local authority capital *expenditure.* The distinction is important in relation to the objectives of
central government. In order to implement its counter-cyclical fiscal policy, expenditure must be varied; but in order to insure that in the longer
term the growth of local authority capital expenditure is at a rate that the

economy can sustain, central government needs only to insure that it has control over borrowing. This is because of the importance of borrowing as a source of capital finance. Other sources may be able to be used in the short-term to vary expenditure, but the extent to which other sources are available in the long-term is very limited. Rates are perceived to be sufficiently high in most local authority areas without attempting to finance large capital projects directly from the rates.

The relationship between loan sanctions and local borrowing will be examined in two ways: first graphical evidence (see figures 6-1 and 6-2) and then some statistical evidence (see unnumbered tables, below) will be considered. Loan sanctions and local borrowing are depicted in figure 6-1. In both cases the figures are on a financial year basis (1948–49 through 1972–73) and for England and Wales only. (Data relating to loan sanction levels were surprisingly difficult to obtain when one considers that central government sees this as a major instrument of control over local government. The DoE could not supply figures on a calendar year basis; nor, incidentally, could it supply a functional analaysis of total sanctions.)

Figure 6-2 displays the percentage annual increase in loan sanctions and local authority borrowing. The two graphs point to a close relationship between the level of loan sanctions and that of local authority borrowing. This implies that central government does have a high degree of control over local authority borrowing. There are, however, points at which the level of borrowing does not move in the manner suggested by the trend in loan sanctions, notably in the periods 1949–50 and 1950–51, and 1968–69 and 1969–70. These instances suggest that the pattern of local authority borrowing is not completely determined by central government. It should be noted that where the two series diverge it is local authority borrowing that has the more stable growth trend. Bearing in mind (1) that local authorities do have some discretion in relation to their borrowing (i.e., as to the timing of the borrowing once sanction has been obtained) and (2) that local authorities have reason to desire a stable pattern of capital expenditure growth, then the implication is that local authorities have on occasion used the timing of their borrowing to evade attempts by central government to effect short-term variations in their capital expenditure programs.

The picture suggested by the graphical evidence is supported by the statistical evidence. First, the close relationship between the growth patterns of loan sanctions and local authority borrowing is supported by comparing mean growth rates for the two series. The mean growth rate of loan sanctions over the period was 8.06 percent, while the mean growth rate in local authority borrowing was 8.45 percent. In order to determine whether the patterns of growth of the two series were similar, the periods were analyzed into those with respectively low, average, and high growth rates in loan sanctions (arbitrarily defined as negative growth, a growth

Figure 6-1   Loan Sanctions and Local Authority Borrowing in England and Wales (current prices, financial year basis)

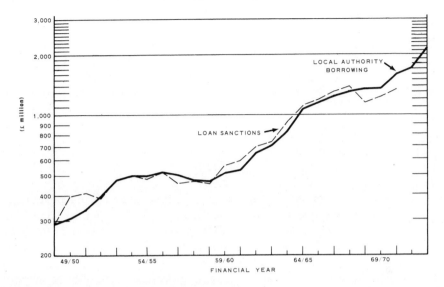

Figure 6-2   Annual Increase in Loan Sanctions and Local Authority Borrowing in England and Wales (current prices, financial year basis)

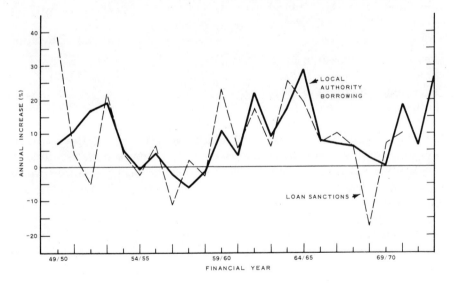

rate of 0 percent to 15 percent, and a growth rate in excess of 15 percent). Having divided the periods in this way the mean growth rate in local authority borrowing for each classification of loan sanction growth rate can be calculated:

	Mean increase in local authority borrowing during periods in which the rate of increase in loan sanctions is:		
	Low	Average	High
Mean percentage increase in local authority borrowing (current prices)	3.05	5.91	17.62

While the mean increase in borrowing is little higher during periods in which there is average growth in the level of loan sanctions than it is during low growth in loan sanctions (5.91 percent as against 3.05 percent), the most striking effect is in relation to periods in which there is high growth in the level of loan sanctions. In these periods local authority borrowing also increased markedly, with an average rate of over 17 percent. These figures, having less of a spread than the growth in loan sanctions, suggest that borrowing has a more stable pattern of growth than loan sanctions. The suggestion is borne out by a comparison of the standard deviations from the mean growth rates of the two series:

	Mean	Standard Deviation
Percentage increase in loan sanctions	8.06	12.79
Percentage increase in local authority borrowing	8.45	8.93

The graphical and statistical evidence, when taken together, provide evidence that the level of local authority borrowing is quite rigidly controlled by central government. The freedom of local authorities would seem to be limited to controlling the timing of their borrowing and thereby attaining a more stable pattern of growth in local authority borrowing than is exhibited by the pattern of growth in loan sanctions.

While this section has examined evidence that suggests that central government has a close control over the level of local authority borrowing, however, this does not mean that it has an equally close control over local authority capital expenditure. Other sources of local authority capital finance are not under the control of central government, and local authorities may be able to achieve a different pattern of growth in their capital expenditure from that implied by the actions of central government with respect to borrowing. Evidence on this point will be examined in the next section, but it must be considered in terms of conclusion reached here: that central government has significant control over local authority borrowing.

C. The Surplus on Local Authority Current Account and Local Authority Borrowing

Apart from borrowing, the major source of finance for local authority capital expenditure is the surplus on current account. In 1973 borrowing provided 70 percent of capital finance, while the surplus on current account provided 24 percent. If, then, local authorities are to be able to incur capital expenditure in a manner contrary to the wishes of central government, such expenditure is likely to be financed through the current surplus.[1] Further, if such conflict does exist between central and local government, then it is likely to be reflected in the relationship between the growth patterns of local authority borrowing and the surplus on local authority current account. Specifically, it can be hypothesized that if local and central governments are in conflict over local authority capital expenditure, then there will be an inverse relationship between the growth patterns of local authority borrowing and the surplus on local authority current account.

The analysis involves a comparison of growth rates with the intention of determining the manner in which the surplus on local authority current account varies with the growth in local authority borrowing. The method adopted involves initially defining the twenty-four years within the study according to whether the growth rate of local authority borrowing was low, average, or high. This was done on an arbitrary basis; the eight years with the lowest rates of increase in borrowing being defined as low growth, the eight years with the highest rates of increase in borrowing being defined as periods of high growth, with periods of average growth being similarly defined.[2] Having thus divided the periods according to the rate of growth in borrowing, the mean rate of growth in the surplus on current account can be calculated for each of the three categories of growth in borrowing. The arbitrary split is made with respect to borrowing because it is seen as being the prior variable, with local authorities having the possibility of modifying the level of the current surplus in response to the permitted level of borrowing:

---

[1]Local authorities have a further means of avoiding the intentions of central government. Capital facilities can be acquired either by purchase or leasing. If loan sanction cannot be obtained, the capital services can still be acquired through some variety of leasing arrangement. Lease payments are, however, classified as current expenditure, and this enables local authorities to disguise their acquisition of capital facilities.

[2]Growth in local authority borrowing is obtained from the series of local authority borrowing as a proportion of the GNP rather than the percentage increase on the absolute figure, thus making some allowance for price level changes.

	The rate of increase in current surplus during periods in which the growth rate of local authority borrowing is:		
	Low	Average	High
Mean annual percentage increase in:			
1. Current surplus at current prices	19.67	13.56	0.65
2. Current surplus as a proportion of GNP	11.68	6.11	−7.48

Whether the surplus on current account is expressed as an absolute figure or as a proportion of the GNP, the result is the same. On the average, the increase in the level of the current surplus is greatest when the rate of increase in local authority borrowing is lowest, and vice versa. The hypothesized inverse relationship is supported by these figures. In other words, it does appear that local authorities use the surplus on their current account to frustrate the intentions of central government.[3]

SYNTHESIS

The evidence presented in the three sections above lends support to the idea that conflict is a significant feature of the relationship between central and local government. Supporting the existence of conflict is the finding that the current surplus and local authority borrowing have inversely related growth patterns. This suggests strongly that local authorities use the current surplus as a means of opposing restrictions placed on their capital expenditure through central government control of their borrowing. A dramatic example of local authority current surpluses being used to counter restrictions on borrowing occurred in 1957. In that year local authority net borrowing declined by over 12 percent from the figure in the previous year. The aggregate surplus on local authority current account in the same year evidenced a spectacular increase of 32.5 percent. Conversely, when in 1961 local authority borrowing was permitted to rise by 49 percent, local authorities had no reason to finance capital works out of current income, and the aggregate surplus on current account declined by slightly under 25 percent. These two cases illustrate the manner in which local authorities have used the current surplus to achieve a different

---

[3]While the figures above indicate the existence of an inverse relationship between the surplus on current account and the growth of local authority borrowing, the consistency of the relationship over time is not established by this analysis. Further analysis of the direction of movement of the two series over the period of the study reveals that the effect described above *has* occurred consistently during the postwar period.

pattern of growth in local authority capital expenditure from that desired by central government.

Further evidence of conflict between central and local government was found in the fact that while borrowing does reflect the growth pattern of loan sanctions, borrowing is phased by local authorities to achieve a smoother growth pattern than is implied by the growth pattern of loan sanctions, thereby avoiding the sudden declines in the growth rate of local authority capital expenditure that central government appeared to desire. This is illustrated by the pattern of loan sanctions and borrowing revealed in figure 6-1. In particular, when the level of loan sanctions declined in the financial year 1968–69, the level of borrowing actually increased, indicating that local authorities will, up to a point, anticipate the future level of sanctions and borrow accordingly. Such a course of action may conflict with the present policy of the government. Fiscal policy actions taken by central government to restrain local authority capital expenditure appear not to be effective, while action to stimulate expenditure is.

The general picture conveyed is one in which central government does, ultimately, control the long-run growth rate of local authority capital expenditure, but within that constraint local authorities have consistently opposed attempts by central government to take short-term action that local authorities deem to be undesirable. If the short-term action is expansionary, local authorities respond in a manner that tends to confirm the impression of central government that, without their exercising control, the aggregate level of local authority capital expenditure would reach a level that they would regard as intolerable.

The actions taken by local government in opposition to the wishes of central government are in conflict within the framework of law. Central government can respond effectively only by changing the law or by applying it more rigorously where that is possible. One would not expect that central government would take action against individual authorities who were, quite legally, financing capital expenditure from their current surplus. What one might expect to find is an increasing tendency for central government to look for controls over total capital expenditure rather than control over borrowing. There is some evidence that central government is responding in this fashion. The arrangements established with the creation of the Greater London Council were the first step in this direction, arrangements whereby central government approves the capital program of the council and does not seek control over the aggregate through the loan sanction procedures. It must be concluded however that if central government did envisage a significant change in its method of control over local authority capital expenditure, then it is being extremely cautious in implementing such a change. The Layfield Committee (Great Britain 1976, p. 242) recognized that the loan sanction procedure is still the most important control central government possesses over local authority spending, and the committee did not bring forward proposals that might shift attention from borrowing to expenditure. It would therefore seem likely that the present system of control will continue, however ineffective it is.

CONCLUSIONS

In drawing conclusions from the evidence a caveat must be stated. This study is concerned solely with the capital expenditure of local authorities, and generalizations regarding the behavior of local authorities with respect to current expenditure should be made with great caution, if at all. The two expenditure categories are subject to different central controls, and it is generally recognized that central government has greater control over capital expenditure. If this is an accurate view then there is less reason to expect conflict with respect to current expenditure, local authorities possessing a greater degree of control in this area. Although it has been noted that central government has the means of controlling local authority current expenditure, a recent study indicated that "The heavy financial dependence of British local authorities on central government has not produced a demonstrable effect on policy choice in the sub-national system" (Ashford 1974, p. 320). This does suggest that a different situation obtains with respect to current expenditure, for central government does have significant, though not uncontested, control over capital expenditure. Capital expenditure however is significant in determining the nature and level of local authority activity and is, in the sense described by Oliver and Stanyer (1969), the major determinant of the long-run growth in current expenditure. To this extent only does the present study have implications for current expenditure.[4]

Conflict has been a characteristic of central-local relations throughout the postwar period. It is not a recent phenomenon, though it may have increased in recent years. The contrast between capital and current expenditure indicates that conflict is more likely where the constraints on local government are tighter. This being the case it would not be surprising to find that conflict had increased significantly in recent years, in line with restrictions on local authority capital expenditure.

---

[4]The data used is in aggregate form; the figures relate to total local authority capital expenditure in the United Kingdom (except as otherwise stated). Without further analysis one would not wish to be categorical, but the evidence suggests that the conflict referred to has existed throughout the broad spectrum of local government. Whether it has been more intense in larger authorities or in the more politicized authorities cannot be determined. Boaden (1970, p. 182) found evidence of intergovernmental conflict in smaller authorities. The present study does nothing to refute Boaden's findings, suggesting that the existence of conflict is not necessarily related to the size and power of the local authority.

APPENDIX: THE LAG STRUCTURE

The measures announced by central government and detailed in table 6-1 cannot be expected to take effect immediately. There will be a time lag between the announcement of the fiscal policy measures and the impact of the measures on local authority capital expenditure.* In this appendix certain assumptions will be made concerning the duration of the time lags. It should be stressed that the analysis is based on assumed lags, not actual lags, which may differ in duration. The assumptions made here derive from the objective of central government in taking the actions; i.e., to bring about short-term changes in the economic situation. If the measures taken by central government are not effective in the short-term, then clearly they cannot bring about the desired improvement in the economic situation. Central government, in taking the actions specified in table 6-1, will expect the measures to be effective in the short-term. It will therefore be assumed that

[1] *The initial impact of fiscal policy action on local authority capital expenditure should occur within approximately one year of the measures being announced.* This assumption will be made more specific in assumptions [3] and [4], below.

Also, if the measures are taken purely for fiscal policy reasons (and there is no reason to think they are not), then government will wish to take measures the impact of which is largely felt in the short-term. Therefore it will also be assumed that

[2] *The major impact of fiscal policy actions on local authority capital expenditure will occur in the first two years in which it is effective.*

These two assumptions reflect the desire of central government to take fiscal policy action that operates swiftly and for only a short duration.

The speed with which action by government to stimulate or restrain the level of local authority capital expenditure impacts upon that level cannot be assumed to be constant. Two factors in particular militate against this possibility. The first is based upon the distinction between action taken to increase local authority capital expenditure and action taken to restrain it. Government perceives it to be undesirable to attempt to halt progress on projects already under construction, so action to restrain expenditure is limited to deferring projects that have not been started and to limiting loan sanctions for future projects. If the desire of

---

*This lag should be distinguished from the time lag involved in the planning and implementation of an individual project. The lag referred to is the time taken to modify the level of *aggregate* local authority capital expenditure.

government is to increase expenditure, however, local authorities will almost invariably have projects that can be brought forward. The implication is that local authorities will be in a position to increase expenditure more rapidly than they could decrease it. Support for this contention is found in a report of the Ministry of Housing and Local Government:

> The measures taken in 1956 to restrict capital investment, which had an immediate effect on loan sanctions, . . . had a delayed effect on the level of capital payments; but the figure for the first half of 1959/60 of £244.3m, compared with £255m for the first half of 1958/59, shows that the recovery in the level of capital payments followed nearly as quickly as the increase in loan sanctions (Great Britain 1960a, p. 28).

The second reason for expecting an irregular lag structure is that the speed with which the effect of the action is felt will depend to some extent upon the situation prevailing prior to the action's being taken. If over a period there has been tight restraint on local authority capital expenditure, a relaxation may result in a more immediate and more substantial increase than if the prior situation had been rather freer. Similarly, a cut in expenditure is likely to impact differently if it follows a period of rapidly increasing expenditure than if it follows a period of restraint. Other factors will also influence the speed with which actions impact upon the level of expenditure; for instance, the method used to implement the policy, the seriousness of the economic situation that provokes the action (or, more correctly, the perceived seriousness of the situation), and the severity of the action actually taken. It can therefore be concluded that the length of time taken for fiscal policy measures to impact upon local authority capital expenditure will not be constant.

In considering the account to be taken in this analysis of the variable time lag, attention must be given to the nature of the analysis. The lag structure is significant only as a means of allowing the classification of each year as being one in which the anticipated impact of local authority capital expenditure would be restrictive, expansionary, or insignificant. In order to achieve this a highly specified lag structure is not necessary. The two most important factors stated above are the two mentioned first: (1) the different impact of expansionary as opposed to contractionary action and (2) the impact of the situation prevailing at the time the fiscal policy measures are taken. The first of these implies that where the fiscal policy measures are intended to increase the level of local authority capital expenditure, it will take less time for those measures to have their effect than if the measures were contractionary. It will therefore be assumed that

[3] *Action taken to restrict the level of local authority capital expenditure will not be effective until the year following such action, unless the action is taken within the first three months of the year.*

Thus if fiscal policy action aimed at restricting local authority capital expenditure is taken in March of a calendar year, it is assumed that the action will be reflected in the growth rate of local authority capital expenditure in that year. If on the other hand the action were not taken until April, its impact is assumed to be first felt in the year following.

[4] *Action taken to increase the level of local authority capital expenditure will have an impact on the growth rate of local authority capital expenditure in that year if it occurs within the first six months of the year. Action taken in the second half of the year will not impact until the following year.*

These assumptions apply in the situation where the fiscal policy action taken is in an opposite direction to that previously prevailing; i.e., where an attempt to increase expenditure follows a period of restraint (or a period of no significant fiscal policy measures in relation to local authority capital expenditure). Where action is taken that merely continues or reinforces existing action, there is no need to make further assumptions, as the existing action will have the same implications for the anticipated outcome of fiscal policy action that further measures in the same direction will have. It is therefore possible to restrict the assumptions that need to be made concerning the lag structure to the four given above.

REFERENCES

Ashford, D. E. 1974. The effects of central finance on the British local government system. *British Journal of Political Science* 4: 305–22.

Bank of England. 1976. *Local authority market borrowing.* Report of the Committee of Inquiry into Local Government Finance. Appendix 6, pp. 1–5.

Boaden, N. T. 1970. Central departments and local authorities: The relationship examined. *Political Studies* 18: 175–86.

———. 1971. *Urban policy-making.* London: Cambridge University Press.

Boaden, N. T., and Alford, R. T. 1969. Sources of diversity in English local government decisions. *Public Administration* 47 (summer): 203–23.

Brittan, S. 1969. *Steering the economy: The role of Treasury.* London: Secker & Warburg.

Chartered Institute of Public Finance and Accountancy (CIPFA). *Financial information service.* Vol. 4, *Capital finance.* (This publication is continually updated.)

Chester, D. N. 1951. *Central and local government: Financial and administrative relations.* London: MacMillan.

Cordon, I. A., and Curley, J. M. 1974. Control over the capital investment of local authorities. *Public Finance and Accountancy* 1: 231–33.

Dow, J. C. R. 1964. *Management of the British economy.* Cambridge: At the University Press.

Great Britain. 1957. Report of the Ministry of Housing and Local Government for the year 1956. *Parliamentary command papers.* London: HMSO, cmnd 193.

———. 1960a. Report of the Ministry of Housing and Local Government 1959. *Parliamentary command papers.* London: HMSO, cmnd 1027.

———. 1960b. Public investment in Great Britain. *Parliamentary command papers.* London: HMSO, cmnd 1203.

———. 1961. Control of public expenditure (Plowden Report). *Parliamentary command papers.* London: HMSO, cmnd 1432.

————. 1963. Local authority borrowing. *Parliamentary command papers.* London: HMSO, cmnd 2162.

————. 1971. The future shape of local government finance. *Parliamentary command papers.* London: HMSO, cmnd 4741.

————. 1976. Local government finance. Report of the Committee of Enquiry (Layfield Report). *Parliamentary command papers.* London: HMSO, cmnd 6453.

————. Organization for Economic Cooperation and Development (OECD). 1964. *Economic survey: United Kingdom.* London: OECD.

Griffith, J. A. G. 1966. *Central departments and local authorities.* London: Allen & Unwin.

Hartley, O. A. 1971. The relationship between central and local authorities. *Public Administration* 49 (winter): 439–56.

Oliver, F. R., and Stanyer, J. 1969. Some aspects of the financial behaviour of county boroughs. *Public Administration* 47(summer): 169–84.

Page, H. R. 1968. Capital finance: Practices and problems. Pt. 2. *Local Government Finance* 72, no. 1: 10–15.

CHAPTER 7

EFFECTS OF FEDERAL AND STATE GRANTS ON LOCAL GOVERNMENT INVESTMENT EXPENDITURES IN WEST GERMANY

Bernd Reissert

In the Federal Republic of Germany, more than 60 percent of public investment expenditures are spent by local governments. Since 1962, both the eleven state *(Länder)* governments (including the city states of Hamburg, Bremen, and West Berlin) and the federal government have been limited to less than 20 percent of public investment (Scharpf et al. 1978, p. 59). These aggregate statistics, which suggest a highly decentralized pattern of public investments, of course do not indicate the extent to which local investment decisions might be influenced through direct or indirect controls exercised by the national or state governments. In fact, there is no doubt that both federal and state governments attempt to exercise such controls. The federal government has a strong interest in correcting the clearly procyclical pattern of local investment expenditures, and both federal and state governments are interested in influencing the spatial (and sometimes even the sectoral) distribution of local public investments.

How are these federal and state controls over local public investment decisions exercised, and what is their effect on local investment expenditures? The most obvious control is federal and state grants-in-aid for local government investments. The German literature on grants-in-aid for local investment has mainly focused on the constitutional aspects of federal and state grants with respect to local government autonomy and on the formal organization of authority with respect to grants-in-aid. This literature has stressed the argument that the right of "local self-administration" guaran-

The author is indebted to Beate Hesse, Fritz W. Scharpf, Peter Georgieff, Benny Hjern, Salomon Klaczko, Günther F. Schäfer, and Winfried Seeringer for helpful comments made throughout the course of his research.

teed by article 28 of the Basic Law tends to be violated by grants-in-aid for local investments (Fuchs 1969, pp. 145, 169; Krumsiek 1969; Zeitel 1970; Gellen 1971; Evers & Lehmann 1972, p. 218; Hesse 1974; Zielinski 1975; Tillmann 1976, pp. 72–74). The argument, however, seems to lack any well-founded empirical evidence on which it might be based. It has mainly been derived from studying the formal organization of grant programs and aggregate data. Up to now there has been little empirical work to analyze the degree to which, and the conditions under which, local government investments are in fact influenced by grants-in-aid (exceptions being Hesse 1973; Scharpf et al. 1974; Grüner 1976; Schäfer et al. 1977a; Petri 1977; Baestlein et al. 1978). The present study will bring the existing empirical evidence to bear on this question. It will first describe the constitutional and institutional framework in which intergovernmental grants operate. After introducing a more general concept of state control, an empirical analysis will be made using both cross-sectional and longitudinal analysis.

BACKGROUND: MULTISOURCE BUDGETING

Unlike in most federal systems, local government in the Federal Republic of Germany has never been able to cover most of its expenses through revenues. The 1949 Basic Law did not allocate a specific tax base to the local communities but instead left it to the states to share their taxes with the local units. In 1956 and in 1969 subsequent tax reform acts were passed that provided for a more ample local tax base, including property, business, and trade taxes as well as several user taxes and a share of the income tax (Meyer 1969, pp. 85–88; Boldt 1975). These changes however did not alter the pattern of local government income in a significant way. Since 1956, taxes have never provided more than one-third of local income, and this share has decreased to about 26 percent in recent years (Reissert 1978, p. 18).

For the system of West German local finance this has meant that local governments have had to rely on other financial resources like intergovernmental grants, fees, contributions, fines, and, increasingly over recent years, borrowing. Federal and state grants account for more than 22 percent of total local government income (Reissert 1978, p. 18). Intergovernmental grants to local governments, however, do not constitute a uniform body of transfers. They are a complex system of general (untied) grants similar to revenue sharing and of specific (categorical, earmarked) grants. Because the Basic Law does not allow direct financial interactions between the federal government and the communities, all grants to local governments are administered by the states, even if the funds were originally provided by the federal government. Within the states a clear distinction is made between general and specific grants, and a share of every state's taxes is legally reserved for general distribution to communities. The distribution formula for these general grants varies from state to state (as well as the tax share from which they are drawn), but it is generally a population formula with other factors that account for a community's needs and specific burdens, factors such as rapid population growth, unfavorable geographical situation, and number of school children. (See Deutscher Städtetag 1973; Gerhardt 1976.) Another share of every state's taxes is normally reserved for specific (earmarked) grants to the communities and supplemented by additional funds out of the state's normal budget. Because the operating budget is not fixed by law, it can be varied more easily than the general grant funds. Since 1956, the specific grants have always been higher than the general grants. Specific grants have accounted for about 12 to 13 percent of local income, general grants have provided 10 to 12 percent (Reissert 1978, p. 18). Specific grants from the states to the communities are appropriated annually and administered through innumerable specific grant programs (Wright 1973, pp. 15–18; Gellen 1971, pp. 20–35). There are programs for most investment and other purposes. About 55 percent of all specific grants are used for local investment projects, and they are the focus of the present paper.

Investment grants account for only about one-third of all intergovernmental grants received by local communities. Nevertheless, within the ongoing West German debate on "state intervention into local self-government" (Baestlein et al. 1978, p. 115), for several reasons most attention has been paid to investment grants. First, the role local governments play within total public investment expenditure is much more important than their role within total current expenditure, and they are therefore critical in the accomplishment of stabilization or regional policy goals. Second, specific grants have become an increasingly important factor for the financing of local government investment over the period beginning in 1962. The share of grants and even the share of investment grants as sources of local government income have remained relatively stable since the early sixties. Yet the importance of investment grants as a source of investment expenditures has almost steadily increased. Due to the declining share of investment expenditures within the overall scope of local expenditure, the share of local investments financed out of investment grants rose from 17.7 percent in 1962 to 26.3 percent in 1973 (Reissert 1978, pp. 18–27). Under these circumstances, the assumption seems plausible that investment grants may have become one of the most important instruments of state control over local communities.

How are grant programs for local government investments administered? The role of the federal government in these processes is highly restricted. The federation is only entitled to pass specific grants to the states, where they are integrated into the state budget and then distributed to the communities under the state's control. The program areas in which the federal government is allowed to give specific grants to the states furthermore are restricted by the Basic Law. According to articles 91a, 91b, and 104a of that law, federal grants-in-aid for local government investments may be spent only on infrastructure programs for agriculture, local transport, urban renewal, low-cost housing, and hospital construction or on short-term stabilization or regional aid programs. Within these areas, the federation may specify the amount of grants it will spend and the exact definition of the program areas the grants may be used for, but it can in no way influence the distribution of funds within the states (Scharpf et al. 1976).

The process of funding the different grant programs forms part of each state's general budgetary process. The amount of funds allocated to the different programs is only partly determined by the amount of grants from the federal government and by the legally fixed share of the states' taxes that has to be reserved for investment grants. During budgetary negotiations each state's ministries submit their proposals to their finance ministry. These proposals, in turn, are based on proposals from the district administrative offices within the states. (Most states have divided their territories into several administrative districts, *Regierungsbezirke*, in which district administrative offices, *Regierungspräsidien*, act as state government field offices. Their task is to coordinate the various departmental activities within the district and to perform legal supervision of local government activities.) The allocation of funds to the various grant programs is thus based on planning processes within the district offices (Hesse 1973; Scharpf et al. 1976, pp. 221–27; Baestlein et al. 1978).

The process of allocating grants to individual local government investment projects is also very much dependent on the district offices. Funds for the different programs are normally distributed to the district level according to an acceptable distribution formula; e.g., the number of registered cars as a formula for distributing grants-in-aid for local road construction. The district offices then allocate grants to individual projects upon applications from the local governments (Hesse 1973; Scharpf et al. 1976). In doing so, the district offices have to follow state guidelines for funding local government investments. Regulations in the state of Baden-Württemberg, for example, require the district offices to consider the following characteristics of a community: financial strength; community functions, especially central functions for a certain region; and the community's share of general grants from the state level (Gerhardt 1976, sec. 10, p. 42).

Because these categories cannot be easily operationalized and because the amount of applications normally exceeds the amount of funds available for investment grants, the district offices have considerable discretion over allocation decisions. The same holds true for decisions on matching grants. In some programs the share of investment costs that may be covered by grants is fixed by law, but in other programs the matching requirements may vary among different cases. Even within the same type of program there seem to be differences among the states. For example, the states of Hesse and North Rhine-Westphalia (NRW) often apply a flexible matching standard, whereas most of the others prefer fixed ratios. (See Scharpf et al. 1976, p. 227.) In most cases where flexible standards are applied, the district offices fix ratios for the individual projects. In doing so, the district offices are required to consider the financial strength of the communities and, eventually, political priorities set by the state government. Even so, discretionary powers of the district offices are relatively strong.

STATE CONTROL OVER LOCAL GOVERNMENT INVESTMENT EXPENDITURES VIA GRANTS-IN-AID

Having described the constitutional and institutional framework in which intergovernmental grants are operating, the present paper will now examine empirical evidence to see under what conditions local government investments are in fact influenced by grants-in-aid. To do this, first an attempt will be made to define *influence* (or *control effects*) and the conditions under which the control effects of grants on expenditures may vary. Specific grants for local public investments may serve different purposes and thus have different control effects upon local investments. One can distinguish four different effects of grants: "level," "allocative," "redistributive," and "technical" effects (Oates 1972, pp. 65–118; Wright 1973, pp. 35–38; Maxwell 1975; Reissert & Hesse 1976).

Grants have *level effects* if they tend to influence the overall level of local investment expenditures without regard to their regional or sectoral distribution. Following neo-Keynesian orthodoxy the level effect is intended to control business cycles. The *allocative function* of grants affects the level of expenditures within specific sectors of local investments and thus influences the priorities for specific investment projects on the local level. The *redistributive effect* of grants is achieved if grants favor "poorer" communities at the expense of "richer" ones. Finally, grants influence the nature and attributes of a single investment project and thus have a *technical effect* if the guidelines specify how projects have to be carried out.

In West Germany, grants for local government investments have been used with the aim of exercising all four types of control upon local investment, although not simultaneously. In order to correct the clearly procyclical level of local government expenditures, intergovernmental grants have been varied by federal and state governments in an anticyclical way (Haller 1960; Krämer et al. 1966; Wilms 1968; Timm 1969; Voigtländer 1970; Evers & Lehmann 1972; Biehl et al. 1974; Kock 1975; Knott 1977). By means of grants for specific types of local investments (e.g., pollution control), federal and state governments have tried to influence local priorities in favor of certain sectors (Ehrlicher 1967, p. 61; Bertram 1967, p. 58; Krumsiek 1969; Hansmeyer 1970; Zeitel 1970; Gellen 1971, p. 45; Scharpf et al. 1974). Specific investment grant programs have been drawn up in order to have a redistributive effect among communities (Ehrlicher 1967; Littmann 1968; Barbarino 1969, 1972; Voigtländer 1969), and central guidelines have tried to influence the technical characteristics of the sponsored projects (Demny 1966).

From the view of the communities, one may suppose that these control effects, if they actually operate, lead to different consequences for local decision making. If level controls are effective they will change local decisions with respect to the time when investment projects are initiated. Allocative controls will make local governments change their sectoral investment priorities in order to favor investments in those sectors for which grants are available and neglect investment in other sectors for which grants are not. This pattern of behavior has been characterized as a "supplier's dictatorship," or *Angebotsdiktatur* (Ehrlicher 1967, p. 61; Bertram 1967, p. 58; Gellen 1971, p. 45). Redistributive control effects will affect timing or priorities only in the communities favored by redistribution. Technical controls will restrict local choice of the characteristics of a single project. The question is not just one of esthetics or construction safety. Construction regulations for schools, hospitals, or youth centers may very well impose requirements based on certain educational or social principles, thereby influencing the later use of a project.

Within a single essay it seems impossible to consider all four different types of control effects. This paper will therefore focus on the allocative control of grants; i.e., their ability to affect the level of expenditures within local investment sectors. This control seems to be a necessary condition for other types of controls to be effective. Controls of levels, redistribution, and techniques will be effective only if grants influence allocation within investment sectors. One must assume of course that the effect of grants upon investment expenditures will not be the same for all communities, grant programs, and investment sectors. The degree to which local government investment expenditures are in fact influenced by specific grants will vary under certain conditions. This analysis therefore asks, Under which conditions are variations in grants closely linked to variations in investment expenditures (thus suggesting a control effect) and, Under which conditions do investment expenditures vary regardless of the amounts of grants involved?

Control effects of grants upon local investment expenditures may vary considerably among different types of grant programs, different states, and different types of local communities (Ewringmann 1971, pp. 53–54; Reissert & Hesse 1976). One may hypothesize, first, that control effects vary among different investment sectors and, hence, among different specific grant programs. In this respect, it seems plausible to suppose that control effects are higher—i.e., that investment expenditures are more likely to follow variations in grants—within those investment sectors in

Table 7-1 *Intergovernmental Grants for Investments as Percentages of Income for Local Government Investment Expenditures, 1973*

State	Real Investment (mil. DM)	Investment Grants
Baden-Württemberg	5,429.2	20.6
Bavaria	5,128.6	32.6
Hesse	2,872.6	30.8
Lower Saxony	3,173.0	20.0
NRW*	7,720.7	37.0
Rhineland-Palatinate	1,786.5	30.8
Saar	419.1	24.5
Schleswig-Holstein	967.3	32.3
All states	27,497.0	29.6

Note: Author's calculations from Statistisches Bundesamt 1973. Percentages of Investment Grants also include intergovernmental loans for local investments, which account for only a small share of local income (about 0.4 percent) but which may be regarded as functional equivalents of grants and may therefore be incorporated into the analysis of grant control effects (Gellen 1971, p. 10). The three city states are not included in this analysis.
*North Rhine-Westphalia.

which local investments have uncompensated positive externalities and where communities would invest little or nothing without external incentives (e.g., pollution control and schools and hospitals open to surrounding communities). (See Break 1967, pp. 62–87; Oates 1972, pp. 65–78.)

Second, one should also suppose that control effects can be different within different states. This seems plausible because the states are almost completely autonomous with regard to organizing their financial relations with the local communities and, hence, their grant programs for local investments. Correspondingly, the patterns of local government income vary widely from state to state. In some states, intergovernmental grants account for a higher share of local income than in others. Some states rely heavily on general (unconditional) grants, while others seem to prefer specific grants for investments or current expenditure (Reissert 1978, pp. 11–13, 18–26). Table 7-1 indicates that these differences in state behavior lead to significantly different shares of local government investments financed out of categorical investment grants and loans. In North Rhine-Westphalia, Bavaria, Schleswig-Holstein, Rhineland-Palatinate, and Hesse, the share of specific grants and intergovernmental loans as a source of finance for local investments is considerably higher than in Saar, Baden-Württemberg, and Lower Saxony. The extreme cases are (1) North Rhine-Westphalia, where state efforts to control local investment spending via grants seem to be the highest, and (2) Lower Saxony, where the share of local investments financed out of grants is only about half of that in North

Rhine-Westphalia. This suggests that there may also be a difference in control effects between these states.

Third, one may also hypothesize that control effects vary among different types of communities. Control effects, for example, may vary according to the relative wealth of communities; i.e., the impact of grants on investment expenditures may be lower for "wealthier" communities than for "poorer" ones. Richer communities will not necessarily have to follow priorities set by grants, whereas poorer ones will have to do so. Control effects may also vary according to the size of local communities. One would expect control effects to be lower for larger communities than for smaller ones because bigger cities with large investment portfolios can "mix risks" and are not as heavily dependent on grants for individual projects as smaller communities, for which investing in one project regardless of grants is a higher risk.

SOME EMPIRICAL EVIDENCE

As a first step towards the identification of conditions favoring or restricting the influence of grants on local investment expenditures, this study will now present the results of a quantitative analysis of the impacts of investment grants upon local investment expenditures under the conditions of different types of grant programs, different states, and different types of communities. These analyses are based on the annual financial records of all 255 West German cities of more than 20,000 inhabitants for the period from 1956–70.[1] Quantitative analyses alone, however, will not provide unambiguous measures of the control effects of grants or of the conditions under which these control effects tend to vary. The measures will not indicate the direction of causality between grants and investments; i.e., they will not reveal whether the availability of grants affects the amount of investments spent (control from "above") or whether investment opportunities affect the use of grants (resource mobilization from "below"). (See Porter 1973.) Similarly, hypotheses that try to explain the variance of control effects among cities, states, and programs as well as quantitative analyses based on them may omit important factors and would thus leave a great deal of variance unexplained.

The aim of the following analyses is therefore not only to test the hypotheses but also to explore the data as a basis for further case studies. On this basis it should be possible to classify cities and programs with respect to their reactions to grants; to strengthen or reformulate hypotheses that attempt to explain different reaction patterns in terms of program,

---

[1]The financial records contain all income and expenditure data of local investment budgets (außerordentliche Haushalte). These data have been collected by the German Association of Cities (Deutscher Städtetag) and transcribed on computer tape by Krupp GmbH. Data analysis has been restricted to the period 1956–70 because territorial reforms initiated in most states after 1970 have made most recent data incomparable to those before 1971.

Table 7-2   *Grant-Investment Ratios for Cities by Sector and by States,*
1956–1970

State	Schools	Cultural Affairs	Social Affairs	Health	Roads & Housing	Public Installations	All Sectors
Baden-							
Württenberg	18.2	10.9	8.7	12.4	27.1	16.5	14.0
Bavaria	12.9	6.8	11.2	18.0	24.5	11.3	15.8
Hesse	39.6	10.7	26.0	32.2	30.0	7.7	19.4
Lower							
Saxony	11.8	3.5	9.7	17.0	15.9	7.0	9.7
NRW	36.9	12.0	28.9	35.4	27.2	13.6	20.6
Rhineland-							
Palatinate	33.3	24.8	16.6	7.9	26.8	12.2	16.7
Schleswig-							
Holstein	36.8	43.5	21.3	35.1	30.9	15.9	21.9
All							
cities	28.2	10.8	21.0	24.5	26.1	12.3	17.6

Note: Author's calculations from unpublished financial records of 255 cities, as described in footnotes 1 and 2 of the present chapter. Saar and the three city states are not included because the city sample does not contain cities in these states.

state, and community characteristics; and to identify "extreme" cases that are not explained by these hypotheses. Out of these cases and classifications those cities whose reaction patterns seem to need further explanation will be selected for more detailed case studies. The following analysis shows how investment expenditures are linked to investment grants and whether different patterns of interdependence between grants and expenditures can, at least partly, be explained by the characteristics of different investment sectors, different states, and different types of cities.

The simplest indicator of control is the share of investment costs financed out of investment grants. A city that has only a small share of investment covered by grants is able to invest without much regard to grants, whereas a city with grants covering a high share of investment costs is either dependent on grants or has been able to mobilize grants even though it did not really need them. For all 255 cities the grant-investment ratios for six sectors were calculated. The grant-investment ratio is the share of local investment expenditures (for the years 1956 through 1970) financed out of investment grants.[2] The aggregate grant-investment ratios for all cities within a state are given in table 7-2. It shows

---

[2]For the purposes of this analysis, *grants* are all federal and state grants and loans contained in the investment budgets; *investments* are all expenditures of the investment budgets. Investment *sectors* are defined as follows: *schools*—all kinds; *cultural affairs*—theaters, concert installations, etc.; *social affairs*—youth centers, installations for social assistance, homes for the aged, etc.; *health*—hospitals and other public medical installations; *roads and housing*—road, bridge, and waterway construction and public housing; *public installations*—wastewater treatment plants, street cleaning, garbage collection, fire protection, slaughter houses, parks, swimming pools, etc. (See Statistisches Bundesamt 1954a.)

almost the same state patterns as table 7-1, with North Rhine-Westphalia, Schleswig-Holstein, and Hesse well above the average, and Baden-Württemberg and Lower Saxony well below it. Table 7-2 also indicates that there are important differences in the grant-investment ratios among investment sectors.

This study has, then, analyzed how and under which conditions grant-investment ratios of different cities deviate from these state averages. Following the hypotheses listed above, the paper has examined whether the grant-investment ratios vary according to city size and wealth. The results of this analysis are given in table 7-3.

Grant-investment ratios tend to be negatively associated with city size and wealth. Although most correlations are not very high, the trend seems to be clear. Larger and richer cities tend to be more able to invest, even if grants are low or nonexistent. This seems to confirm the above hypotheses. A glance at the original data and scattergrams shows that most of these relationships tend to be curvilinear, so that much stronger negative relationships should appear if nonlinear measurements were applied. In fact, the relationship between grant-investment ratios and wealth is most visible for the extreme cases. The richer cities tend to spend almost their total investment budgets without grants, and the poorer ones tend to have the highest grant-investment ratios.[3] Thus in the school investment sector the lowest ratios are those of Wolfsburg and Schweinfurt. According to the wealth indicator these cities are at the same time the richest ones of Lower Saxony and Bavaria. Within those states whose aggregate school grant-investment ratios are above average (see table 7-2), again one finds most of the lower grant-investment ratios with the richer cities; e.g., Leverkusen and Düsseldorf. On the other hand, within the states whose aggregate ratios in the school sector are below average, the highest ratios are those of Heidelberg, Neuburg, Amberg, and Konstanz. All these cities are among the three poorest of their respective state.

The same constellations of cases can be found within the other investment sectors. The cases thus seem to indicate that the role grants play in local investments is negatively associated with city size and wealth. There seems to be an exception for road and housing investments (see table 7-3). One explanation may be the fact that West German cities can ask road neighbors to contribute to road construction costs, which account for most of this investment sector. Road construction investments can therefore also be made by smaller and poorer cities even if grants are not available.

This essay also has examined to what degree cities that receive more grants also spend more than other cities and whether these relationships

---

[3]Negative relationships between grant-investment ratios and city wealth may in part be explained by the facts (1) that financial strength is a factor to be considered by the district offices when grants are allocated and (2) that flexible matching requirements may also be adapted to a city's financial strength. These facts, however, are not likely to explain all the extreme cases found in the present analysis.

Table 7-3   Correlations of City Sectoral Grant-Investment Ratios with City Size and Wealth

State	City Size[a]							City Wealth[b]						
	Schools	Cultural Affairs	Social Affairs	Health	Roads & Housing	Public Install.	All Sectors	Schools	Cultural Affairs	Social Affairs	Health	Roads & Housing	Public Install.	All Sectors
Baden-Würt.	-.13	.07	.26	.31	.32	.16	.13	-.19	-.16	-.19	-.13	-.30	-.23	-.36
Bavaria	-.24	-.11	-.08	-.07	.03	-.29	-.04	-.38	-.23	-.06	-.18	-.13	-.33	-.36
Hesse	-.21	-.06	-.40	.16	.45	-.17	.21	-.31	-.18	-.41	.06	.14	-.41	-.03
Lower Saxony	-.37	.02	-.16	.19	.11	-.16	-.08	-.54	-.11	-.01	-.29	-.31	-.25	-.49
NRW	-.31	.15	-.13	-.13	.10	-.37	-.29	-.37	-.08	-.10	-.23	-.15	-.29	-.44
Rhineland-Pala.	-.39	.16	-.07	-.13	.69	.08	-.11	-.64	-.38	-.27	-.46	.32	.15	-.10
Schles.-Hols.	-.22	.75	-.12	.50	.48	-.29	.01	-.51	.23	-.03	.01	-.13	-.77	-.65
All cities	-.10	.04	-.07	.01	.16	-.22	-.05	-.35	-.15	-.13	-.19	-.16	-.22	-.37

Notes: Also see footnotes 1, 2, and 3 of the present chapter. Author's calculations from unpublished financial records of 255 cities, as described in footnotes 1 and 2 of the present chapter. *Size* is defined as city population in 1970 (Deutscher Städtetag 1971, vol. 58). *Wealth* is defined as *Realsteuerkraft* in 1969 (idem 1971, vol. 58). *Realsteuerkraft* is an index of local property and business tax revenues. It is widely accepted as an indicator for local financial strength.

Correlations are Pearson correlations. Interpretations of results for Hesse, Rhineland-Palatinate, and Schleswig-Holstein are restricted by the fact that numbers of cases are less than twenty for these states.

[a]Inhabitants.
[b]*Realsteuerkraft.*

*Table 7-4   Correlations of Grants and Investments in Cities, by Sector and
State*

State	Schools	Cultural Affairs	Social Affairs	Health	Roads & Housing	Public Installations	All Sectors
Baden-							
Württemberg	.67	.87	.66	.85	.85	.59	.44
Bavaria	.61	.22	.94	.93	.64	.80	.53
Hesse	.80	.75	.87	.97	.68	.16	.65
Lower							
Saxony	−.05	.64	.29	.72	.13	.30	.10
NRW	.74	.56	.46	.64	.68	.66	.55
Rhineland-							
Palatinate	.84	.90	.79	.71	.84	.55	.49
Schleswig-							
Holstein	.78	.42	.76	.88	.40	.38	.14
All							
cities	.47	.57	.62	.74	.65	.56	.45

Notes: Author's calculations from unpublished financial records of 255 cities, as described in
footnotes 1 and 2 of the present chapter. An identical analysis has been carried out by Schäfer
et al. (1977a) on the basis of a smaller sample of cities. Grant-investment relationships tend
to be somewhat closer in our analysis, but there are no remarkable differences between both
analyses.
    Correlations are Pearson correlations. Grant and investment data are those described in
footnote 2, above.

vary among states or among investment sectors. City per capita investment expenditures have been aggregated over time and correlated with
the corresponding per capita investment grants within different states and
different investment sectors. High correlations thus indicate that cities
with higher per capita grants also spend more than other cities; low correlations indicate that this is not the case. Table 7-4 shows that there are
remarkable differences among states and among investment sectors.
Hesse, Bavaria, North Rhine-Westphalia, and Rhineland-Palatinate have
the highest correlations, and correlations are lowest for Lower Saxony,
where city spending levels seem to be almost unrelated to the amounts of
grants received. The state pattern looks quite similar to the state rankings
for grant-investment ratios presented in table 7-2. This indicates that city
expenditure levels within the different states are highly influenced by the
share of investment costs financed out of grants within the states. In states
where cities can expect only a small share of their investment costs to be
covered by grants, cities that receive large grants are not likely also to
invest more than other cities. In these states cities seem to carry out their
investment decisions without regard to the amounts of grants received.
The same pattern holds with respect to investment sectors. The relationship between grants and investment is higher in those sectors where a
relatively high share of investment costs is covered by grants (health,

roads, social affairs) and lower in sectors where the grant-investment ratio is considerably lower (cultural affairs, public installations). Only with school investments is the grant-investment relationship low and the grant-investment ratio high.

How grants and investments are linked over time is especially relevant for long-term grant policy. Intergovernmental grants will be able to counteract business cycle swings in local public investments only if grants and investments are closely linked over time. In an analysis based on the present aggregate data, Knott (1977, p. 63) has shown that in the 1966–67 recession and in the 1969–71 boom phase only four states pursued a clearly anticyclical policy with respect to their grants-in-aid for local government investment: North Rhine-Westphalia, Schleswig-Holstein, Lower Saxony, and Bavaria. The others pursued a clearly procyclical grant policy. While neither wealth, population size, nor party-political orientation explain these differences, these four states experienced the most severe unemployment rates during the recession and therefore received large shares of the 1967 federal stabilization program (Knott 1977, pp. 106–7). Within the four states that carried out an almost uniform anticyclical grant policy, local government investment still shows a high degree of variation. During the 1966–67 recession, local investments in North Rhine-Westphalia followed a less procyclical pattern than elsewhere. Still within the same group of states, local investments in Schleswig-Holstein and Bavaria show a slightly more procyclical pattern, and local investments in Lower Saxony have the most procyclical pattern (Knott 1977, p. 68).

The variation of local investment patterns within this group of states confirms the importance already attributed here to different grant-investment ratios among the states. The state rank order with respect to anticyclical influence is the same as that regarding grant-investments ratios. The extreme cases are North Rhine-Westphalia and Lower Saxony. The local investment fall-off in Lower Saxony during the 1966–67 recession is about twice as high as that in North Rhine-Westphalia, while the share of grants that account for local investments in North Rhine-Westphalia more than doubles that in Lower Saxony. The analysis presented by Knott (1977) provides insight into state differences with respect to grant-investment relationships over time, but the data base can also provide more disaggregated results. An indicator is the Pearson correlations of the yearly variations of grants and investments (see Russett 1971). This indicator will be high if grants and investments follow the same pattern over time and it will be low if this is not the case.

Computing these indicators for each city and each of the six investment sectors[4] shows a great deal of variance. The state rank orders with

<hr>

[4] The present method of measuring grant-investment relationships over time is based on the assumption that grants for specific investment projects are registered in the same year as investment expenditures for the same project. This is normally the case. (For larger projects,

Table 7-5   State Rank Orders of Average Grant-Investment Correlations over Time

State	Schools	Cultural Affairs	Social Affairs	Health	Roads & Housing	Public Install.
Baden-Württemberg	5	5	4	5	7	5
Bavaria	6	2	2	3	1	4
Hesse	2	7	5	2	5	2
Lower Saxony	7	4	6	6	6	7
NRW	3	3	1	4	2	3
Rhineland-Palatinate	1	5	3	7	4	1
Schleswig-Holstein	4	1	7	1	3	6

Note: Author's calculations from unpublished financial records of 255 cities, as described in footnotes 1, 2, and 4 of the present chapter.

respect to average grant-investment correlations within sectors are presented in table 7-5. It shows that the relation over time between grants and investments is above average in cities within North Rhine-Westphalia, Bavaria, Rhineland-Palatinate, Schleswig-Holstein, and Hesse and below average in Baden-Württemberg and Lower Saxony. The pattern looks quite similar to the state rankings for grant-investment ratios presented in table 7-2, especially for school and health investments. The main difference between the tables is Bavaria, which ranks much higher than its grant-investment ratio ranking. The grant-investment relationships—i.e., parallel developments of grants and investments over time—tend to be higher in those states in which a higher share of investments is financed out of grants. Only in Bavaria does a relatively low grant-investment ratio seem to exist with a relatively high grant-investment relationship.

On the other hand, investment sector rank orders with respect to grant-investment correlations over time (see table 7-6) indicate that control effects are higher in the social infrastructure sectors (cultural and social affairs, health, schools) than in the sectors of roads and housing and public installations. This suggests that among different investment sectors the extent to which investments are financed out of grants does not play

which are not carried out in just one year, grants are normally allocated in yearly portions that correspond to portions of expenditures.) The possibility of registration of grants and corresponding investments in different years (maximum difference is about one year) cannot, however, be totally excluded. Not only therefore have simultaneous grant-investment relationships been computed, but also two different types of lagged correlations, one lagging investments behind grants and the other vice versa (see Russett 1971, pp. 35–38). In cases (there were relatively few) where one of these lagged correlations was higher than simultaneous correlations, these lagged correlations were used for further analysis.

Table 7-6   *Investment Sector Rank Orders of Average Grant-Investment Correlations over Time*

State	Schools	Cultural Affairs	Social Affairs	Health	Roads & Housing	Public Install.
Baden-Württemberg	3	2	1	4	5	6
Bavaria	5	1	2	3	4	6
Hesse	3	5	2	1	6	4
Lower Saxony	6	1	2	3	4	5
NRW	3	2	1	5	4	6
Rhineland-Palatinate	1	3	2	6	5	4
Schleswig-Holstein	4	2	5	1	3	6
All cities	4	1	2	3	5	6

Data Source: Russett 1971, pp. 35–38, and Deutscher Städtetag, annual. See, particlarly, idem 1954; 1971, vol. 58.
Note: Author's calculations from unpublished financial records of 255 cities, as described in footnotes 1, 2, and 4 of the present chapter.

a predominant role in determining the relation between grants and investments over time. Cultural and social affairs are sectors in which grant-investment ratios tend to be relatively low and yet correlations tend to be above average. Thus more elaborate hypotheses are needed to explain control effects among different investment sectors. For the moment, it appears that correlations tend to be higher for social infrastructure because these investments tend to have uncompensated positive external effects, whereas other public installations and roads accrue more exclusively to individual cities or offer possibilities for refinancing from users' contributions. It seems therefore plausible that social infrastructure investment expenditures are more closely related to grants than other local investment expenditures, but this proposition must await elaboration in future research.

CONCLUSION

The quantitative analysis has shown that the effects of grants upon local investment expenditures vary according to program, state, and community characteristics. Thus the degree to which a city relies (or has to rely) on intergovernmental grants in order to finance a specific investment project tends to be higher in states and in investment sectors in which a relatively high share of investment costs is covered by grants; and in smaller and "poorer" cities. Additionally, grants and investments are more likely to follow the same fluctuations over time in states in which a higher share of investment costs is covered by grants; in social infrastructure investment sectors; and in smaller and "poorer" cities and cities in which a higher share of investment costs is covered by grants. The results of the quantitative analyses thus generally confirm the hypotheses listed above.

Categorical grants in the Federal Republic of Germany thus seem to be far from completely determining local government investment decisions. Control effects of grants upon investments vary widely among states, sectors, and cities. According to these variances, local investments in rural areas, and smaller and "poorer" communities, are more likely to be controlled by grants than local investments in highly industrialized urban agglomerations. Investment grants as a control instrument for regional policy may be able to increase local investments in poorer areas but may also fail to decrease investments in areas where they are no longer desirable. With respect to grants being used for stabilization policy purposes, the findings imply that grant programs will have to cover a large share of investment costs in order to counteract business cycle swings in local investment.

The relatively low correlations shown in tables 7-3 and 7-4, however, indicate that quantitative analyses fall far short of fully explaining which factors control effects of grants upon investments. The factors tend to vary. State policies with respect to grant-investment ratios, externality characteristics, city size, and wealth influence control effects, but there are still many differences in grant-investment relationships that cannot be explained by these structural and socioeconomic variables. One would therefore suppose that these differences would have to be explained by political and administrative variables (Hofferbert 1974) that describe the decision-making structures and processes in and between granting and spending institutions. Further case studies should be undertaken to identify these political and administrative factors that seem to play important roles in the relationship between grants-in-aid and local investment expenditures.

REFERENCES

Baestlein, A., et al. 1978. State grants and local development in the Federal Republic of Germany. In K. Hanf and F. W. Scharpf, eds. *Interorganizational policy making,* pp. 115–42. London: Sage.

Barbarino, O. 1969. Die Beziehungen zwischen Finanzausgleich und Raumordnung, dargelegt an der Finanzpolitik des Landes Bayern (The relations between financial equalization and regional policy, the case of fiscal policy in the state of Bavaria). In *Finanzpolitik als Gegenstand der Regionalpolitik* (Fiscal policy as the subject of regional policy), pp. 13–55. Hannover: Jänecke.

———. 1972. Raumordnungsaspekte in der kommunalen Finanzreform und im Finanzausgleich (Regional policy aspects in local financial reform and financial equalization). In

Finanzpolitik und Landesentwicklung (Fiscal policy and regional development), pp. 33–47. Hannover: Jänecke.

Bertram, J. 1967. *Staatspolitik und Kommunalpolitik* (National and local politics). Stuttgart: Kohlhammer.

Biehl, D.; Jüttemeier, K. H.; and Legler, H. 1974. Zu den konjunkturellen Effekten der Länder- und Gemeindehaushalte in der Bundesrepublik Deutschland, 1960–1974 (The effects of state and local budgetary policy on the development of the business cycle in the Federal Republic of Germany, 1960–1974). *Die Weltwirtschaft*, pp. 29–51.

Boldt, H. 1975. Kommunale Finanzen im Rahmen der Finanzverfassung der Bundesrepublik (Local finance within the financial constitution of the Federal Republic). In H. G. Wehling, ed. *Kommunalpolitik* (Local politics), pp. 131–53. Hamburg: Hoffmann & Campe.

Break, G. F. 1967. *Intergovernmental fiscal relations in the United States*. Washington, D.C.: Brookings Institution.

Demny, I. 1966. Die Gefahr der Einschränkung der Autonomie der Gemeinden durch die Zweckzuweisungen, erläutert am Beispiel Nordrhein-Westfalen (The danger of restricting the municipal autonomy through specific purpose grants, explained through the example of North Rhine-Westphalia). Ph.D. dissertation, University of Cologne.

Deutscher Städtetag. Annual. *Statistisches Jahrbuch deutscher Gemeinden* (Statistical yearbook of the German municipalities). Cologne: Deutscher Städtetag.

———. 1973a. *Kommunaler Finanzausgleich in den Bundesländern* (Local financial equalization in the states of the federation). Cologne: Deutscher Städtetag.

Ehrlicher, W. 1967. *Kommunaler Finanzausgleich und Raumordnung* (Local financial equalization and regional policy). Hannover: Jänecke.

Evers, A., and Lehmann, M. 1972. *Politisch-ökonomische Determinanten für Planung und Politik in den Kommunen der Bundesrepublik* (Political/economic determinants for planning and politics in the communities of the Federal Republic). Offenbach: Sozialistisches Büro.

Ewringmann, D. 1971. *Zur Voraussage kommunaler Investitionsbedarfe: Ein Beitrag zur positiven Theorie öffentlicher Bedarfe* (Forecasting needs of local investments: A contribution to a positive theory of public needs). Opladen: Westdeutscher Verlag.

Fuchs, M. 1969. Zweckgebundene Zuweisungen—Hilfe oder Last für die Gemeinden? (Specific purpose grants—Aid or burden for the municipalities?). *Der Gemeindehaushalt* 70 (July/August): 145–48; 169–72.

Gellen, H. M. 1971. *Zweckzuweisungen und kommunale Selbstverwaltung: Eine verfassungsrechtliche Untersuchung* (Specific purpose grants and community self-administration: A constitutional inquiry). Cologne: Deutscher Gemeindeverlag.

Gerhardt, K. 1976. *Der kommunale Finanzausgleich in Baden-Württemberg* (Local financial equalization in Baden-Württemberg). Stuttgart: Kohlhammer.

Grüner, F. 1976. Handlungsspielräume kommunaler Planung, dargestellt am Beispiel des kommunalen Finanzausgleichs und des Schulhausbaus (Elbowroom for community planning, shown through the example of local financial equalization and the building of schools). Lic. dissertation, University of Karlsruhe.

Haller, H. 1960. Probleme einer konjunkturpolitisch orientierten Finanzpolitik unter besonderer Berücksichtigung des Finanzausgleichs (Problems of a business-cycle-oriented fiscal policy, especially financial equalization). *Zeitschrift für die gesamte Staatswissenschaft* 116: 47–65.

Hansmeyer, K. H. 1970. Zweckzuweisungen an Gemeinden als Mittel der Wirtschaftspolitik? (Specific purpose grants to municipalities as a means of economic policy?). In H. Haller et al., eds. *Theorie und Praxis des finanzpolitischen Interventionismus* (Theory and practice of state interventionism in industry via the budget), pp. 431–50. Festschrift für Fritz Neumark. Tübingen: Mohr/Siebeck.

Hesse, J. J. 1974. Politische Planung im Kommunalbereich (Political planning in the community sphere). *Die Verwaltung* 7, no. 3: 273–304.

Hesse, W. 1973. Die finanzpolitische Abhängigkeit der Gemeinden von Bund und Land und ihre politischen Folgen—Versuch einer Operationalisierung am Beispiel von Konstanz und Singen (The fiscal dependence of the municipalities on the federation and state and its political consequences—An attempt of operationalization in the example of Konstanz and Singen). Dipl. thesis, University of Konstanz.

Hofferbert, R. I. 1974. *The study of public policy.* Indianapolis, Ind.: Bobbs-Merrill.

Knott, J. H. 1977. Accommodating purposes: Fiscal and budgetary policy in West Germany. Ph.D. dissertation, University of California, Berkeley.

Kock, H. 1975. *Stabilitätspolitik im föderalistischen System der Bundesrepublik Deutschland* (Business-cycle policy in the federal system of the Federal Republic of Germany). Cologne: Bund-Verlag.

Krämer, H., et al. 1966. *Gemeindehaushalt und Konjunktur* (Municipal budgets and the business cycle). Cologne: Westdeutscher Verlag.

Krumsiek, R. 1969. Die Gemeinden und das Dotationswesen (The municipalities and the grant system). *Der Städtetag* 22: 590–92.

Littmann, K. 1968. *Die Gestaltung des kommunalen Finanzsystems unter raumpolitischen Gesichtspunkten* (The shaping of the local financial system under regional policy aspects). Hannover: Jänecke.

Maxwell, J. A. 1975. *Specific purpose grants in the United States: Recent developments.* Canberra: Australian National University.

Meyer, H. 1969. *Die Finanzverfassung der Gemeinden: Ein Beitrag zur Stellung der Gemeinden in der Finanzverfassung des Bundes* (The financial constitution of the municipalities: A contribution to the position of the municipalities in the financial constitution of the federation). Stuttgart: Kohlhammer.

Oates, W. E. 1972. *Fiscal federalism.* New York: Harcourt, Brace.

Petri, W. 1977. *Die staatlichen Zweckzuweisungen im kommunalen Finanzsystem, dargestellt am Beispiel des Landes Niedersachsen* (Specific purpose grants in the local fiscal system, the case of the state of Lower Saxony). Berlin: Duncker & Humblot.

Porter, D. O. 1973. *The politics of budgeting federal aid: Resource mobilization by local school districts.* Beverly Hills, Calif.: Sage.

Reissert, B. 1978. Federal and state grants to local governments: Some descriptive material on the West German case. Berlin: IIM papers 78-1, publication series of the International Institute of Management.

Reissert, B., and Hesse, B. 1976. The impact of federal and state grants on local government investment expenditures in the Federal Republic of Germany: A research design. Berlin: Preprint Series of the International Institute of Management.

Russett, B. M. 1971. Some decisions in the regression analysis of time-series data. In J. F. Herndon and J. L. Bernd, eds. *Mathematical applications in political science.* Vol. 5, pp. 29–50. Charlottesville: University Press of Virginia.

Schäfer, G. F.; Georgieff, P.; and Klaczko, S. 1977a. Staatliche Zuweisungen: Welche Spielräume bleiben den Gemeinden? (State grants: What elbowroom remains to the municipalities?). *Transfer* 3 (March): 21–38.

———. 1977b. Analyse kommunaler Finanzpolitik im sozialen Infrastrukturbereich—Ansatz und erste Ergebnisse (Analysis of local budgetary policy in the social infrastructure sphere—Conceptualization and first results). In F. X. Kaufmann, ed. *Bürgernahe Gestaltung der sozialen Umwelt* (Citizen-oriented formation of the social environment), pp. 45–79. Kronberg/Meisenheim: Hain.

Scharpf, F. W., et al. 1974. Strukturelle Ineffizienz in der Politikverflechtung zwischen Land und Kommunen (Structural inefficiency in joint policy making by state and communities). *Stadtbauwelt* 44: 292–98.

Scharpf, F. W.; Reissert, B.; and Schnabel, F. 1976. *Politikverflechtung: Theorie und Empirie des kooperativen Föderalismus in der Bundesrepublik* (Intergovernmental policy making: Theory and practice of cooperative federalism in the Federal Republic). Kronberg: Scriptor.

———. 1978. Policy effectiveness and conflict avoidance in intergovernmental policy formation. In K. Hanf and F. W. Scharpf, eds. *Interorganizational policy making,* pp. 57–112. London: Sage.

Statistisches Bundesamt. Annual. *Finanzen und Steuern: Haushaltswirtschaft von Bund, Ländern und Gemeinden. Jahresabschlüsse. Öffentliche Finanzwirtschaft, Kommunalfinanzen* (Finances and taxes: Budgetary data of nation, states, and municipalities. State finances, local finances). Stuttgart/Mainz: Kohlhammer.

Statistisches Bundesamt, ed. 1954a. *Richtlinien zur Aufstellung der Gemeindefinanzstatistik* (Directives for the setting-up of the fiscal statistics of the municipalities). Wiesbaden: Statistisches Bundesamt.

Tillmann, B. 1976. Politikverflechtung zwischen Zentralinstanz und lokaler Ebene (Intergovernmental policy making between central and local levels). In R. Frey, ed. *Kommunale Demokratie* (Local democracy), pp. 66–96. Bonn-Bad Godesberg: Neue Gesellschaft.

Timm. H. 1969. Gemeindefinanzpolitik in den Wachstumszyklen (Local fiscal policy in the business cycle). *Finanzarchiv* 28: 441–58.

Voigtländer, H. 1969. Die speziellen Finanzzuweisungen im Rahmen des kommunalen Finanzausgleichs als Instrument zur Finanzierung der Gemeinschaftsaufgaben von Land und Gemeinden (Specific purpose grants within the system of local financial equalization as an instrument to finance the common responsibilities of the state and municipalities). *Informationen dem Institut für Raumordnung* 19, no. 12: 345–76.

————. 1970. Die Finanzzuweisungen an die Gemeinden und Gemeindeverbände in konjunkturpolitischer Sicht (Business cycle aspects of financial grants to the communities and counties). *Archiv für Kommunalwissenschaften* 9: 303–13.

Wilms, E. H. 1968. Probleme einer konjunkturgerechten Gestaltung der Gemeindefinanzen (Problems of an accurate handling of the municipal finances in the business cycle). Ph.D. dissertation, University of Freiburg.

Wright, D. S. 1973. *Federal grants-in-aid: Perspectives and alternatives.* Reprint ed. Washington, D.C.: American Enterprise Institute.

Zeitel, G. 1970. Kommunale Finanzstruktur und gemeindliche Selbstverwaltung (Local finance structure and municipal self-administration). *Archiv für Kommunalwissenschaften* 9: 1–20.

Zielinski, H. 1975. *Diskrepanz zwischen Aufgabenentwicklung und Finanzierung in den Gemeinden* (Discrepancy between development of responsibilities and financial resources in the municipalities). Göttingen: Schwartz.

CHAPTER 8

JAPAN CONFRONTS ITS CITIES: CENTRAL-LOCAL RELATIONS IN A CHANGING POLITICAL CONTEXT

Michio Muramatsu
Ronald Aqua

FORCES OF CHANGE

Japanese society is usually regarded as consensual in nature, but in recent years a variety of conflicts have surfaced to mar that image. A frequently cited example is the conflict that has erupted between citizens and the administrative/business world concerning environmental problems. One implication of conflict in the public policy arena is evident in central-local governmental relations, particularly as they affect central-local financial relations. In the past, such relationships have been conducted harmoniously within a framework of mutual understanding, but recently local authorities have raised frequent objections to directives issued from Tokyo as well as to the basic policies behind them. Furthermore, as the number of local governments whose chief executives are affiliated with the opposition parties (the so-called "progressive municipalities") has increased (MacDougall 1975), local officials have increasingly resorted to confrontation tactics in their dealings with the central government.

The early functionalists in political sociology might have treated central-local governmental relations in Japan up until the 1960s in terms of exchange or reciprocity between actors of equal rank (Gouldner 1960). The central government, by channeling large subsidies into local public works projects, won approval for its economic growth policies and, significantly, for the introduction of industry locally. Local governments believed that through industrialization they would be able to achieve regional economic prosperity while acquiring a variety of infrastructural improvements. Throughout the postwar period, the prefectures rather than the cities were the active partners of the central government in regional development programs.

Even up to the present time, the functional divisions within the prefectural governments are often regarded as little home ministries. The Ministry of Home Affairs in Tokyo and the corresponding local affairs divisions in the prefectural governments have served as buffers between the central and local (particularly municipal) governments, responding to the needs and complaints of local authorities. Despite the existence of such buffers, however, fissures have recently surfaced in intergovernmental relations. The basis for conflict stems from central efforts to impose standardized policies on localities that have resisted those policies; and because problems vary so much from area to area, local authorities have gradually begun to exercise their right to local autonomy as guaranteed in article 92 of the Japanese constitution. The tactics employed by local officials of an earlier era to resist central standardization were narrow and circumscribed, consisting mainly of petitioning; but once the decision was made to exercise local prerogatives in the broader sense, the range of confrontation tactics expanded accordingly. At present, openly hostile actions have become quite common.

Open conflict erupted in central-local relations after the rapid urbanization accompanying economic growth in the 1960s produced a host of new problems. Throughout the sixties, the population of the greater Tokyo and Osaka metropolitan regions increased at a frantic pace, and problems such as traffic congestion and environmental pollution intensified. The population of rural villages and outlying islands correspondingly decreased due to the outmigration of younger inhabitants, and the elderly and children were left behind in what have come to be known as areas of "excessive depopulation." The negative effects of both over-congestion and excessive depopulation are being corrected little by little, but political solutions to the two problems differ considerably. In the depopulated regions, local residents and local governments have often been content to wait for tutelary assistance from the central government. To some extent they could place their expectations in the pork barrel politicking of parliamentary representatives from their districts, who are, largely speaking, members of the Liberal Democratic party (LDP), and in the paternalistic attitude of the Ministry of Home Affairs and other central administrative agencies. In contrast to this rural passivity, the response of the overcongested areas has been more positive. The problems of Japanese urbanization manifested themselves not in inner city slums, as in urban America, but in a shortage of basic public services such as housing and schools in the rapidly growing suburban peripheries. In the suburbs, residents organized for the purpose of making demands on their local governments. These in turn engaged in extensive lobbying on behalf of their residents and pleaded with central administrators for more money for their regions.

In the present chapter this new dimension of intergovernmental relations in Japan will be analyzed and discussed in some detail. Discussion will focus on how local authorities have attempted to cope with problems engendered by large-scale shifts in settlement patterns during the period of high economic growth.

SETTSU FIGHTS BACK

Until quite recently, local governmental litigation against the central government had been unthinkable. In Japan, litigation is thought of less as a means of resolving conflict than as a last resort to be used only when all other means of negotiation have been exhausted. It was almost never used in the context of intergovernmental relations. The Ministry of Home Affairs and the local affairs divisions of prefectural governments served as intermediary agents in precisely those difficult instances in which strong differences of interpretation or interest seemed to be involved. A lawsuit finally arose in 1973, however, and the present paper will treat this case in some detail, since it marked a turning point in Japanese intergovernmental relations.

The plaintiff in this particular suit was the city of Settsu, which claimed that the central government had illegally withheld payment of a subsidy to the city for day care center construction. Settsu is located in Osaka prefecture. Its population in 1965 was 41,153; but by 1975 the population had risen to 73,287, an increase of 76 percent in only ten years.

The claim made by Settsu against the central government was not a complicated one. The city had built four day care centers between 1969 and 1972 at a cost of ¥92,729,990. According to article 52 of the Child Welfare Act, the central government should have provided at least half of the funds necessary for the construction of these schools, namely, ¥46,364,995. In fact, Settsu had received only ¥2,500,000 and wished to press its claim for the remaining ¥43,864,995.

The issue raised in the Settsu case echoed the plight of many suburban cities facing similarly dramatic increases in their population, whether under conservative or progressive local administrations; and the question at hand was the central government's method of calculating subsidies for certain types of municipal services.

For its part, the central government (notably the Ministry of Health and Welfare) took the position that subsidies for day care center construction are not calculated strictly and automatically in accordance with the provisions of article 52 of the Child Welfare Act but are determined in accordance with the provisions of the Subsidy Rationalization Act. Local governments apply for subsidies and the appropriate ministry then decides on the concrete amount. According to the central government,

> ... this [Subsidy Rationalization Act] should be interpreted as providing that a concrete right to claim a subsidy is established for the first

time by the decision to grant the subsidy applied for, which is an administrative act of the head of the respective ministries and of other administrative agencies (*Collected Decisions in Administrative Litigations*, vol. 27, II-12, p. 1790).

In 1977, four years after Settsu initiated its suit, the Tokyo District Court ruled in favor of the central government's position, asserting that the right of a local government to claim a subsidy from the central government does not arise directly from the provisions of a particular act (such as the Child Welfare Act) governing that locality's operations; rather, the right comes into effect only after an executive agency makes a concrete administrative disposition in accord with the provisions of the Subsidy Rationalization Act. The court went on to state that if the right to claim a subsidy stemmed directly from the Child Welfare Act, by passing the procedures mandated in the Subsidy Rationalization Act, it would be difficult for the central government accurately to forecast the scope and nature of its fiscal obligations. Consequently, it would be difficult to compile the national budget and maintain the discreteness of each fiscal year, rendering the efficient utilization of the nation's revenues impossible. In this particular instance, furthermore, the central government would conceivably confront the prospect of unlimited claims on its resources for day care center construction, a demand that would be both unreasonable and infeasible in the court's view.

One might agree with the court that the claim advanced by Settsu was unreasonable in legal terms. Still, most local officials felt that Settsu had not received sufficient funds from the state for the construction of its day care centers. The provision of supplementary child care is a task delegated to municipalities by the Diet according to law. Local officials would argue that the state thereupon assumes the responsibility for providing adequate subsidies to support this delegated responsibility. Yet when the state evaluates applications for subsidies, it frequently decides on amounts much smaller than the amounts actually needed or requested. This results in what has become known as the "excess burden" problem.

In recent years, confrontation tactics have come to characterize relations between the state and "progressive" municipalities, and these municipalities have accumulated a rich storehouse of wisdom concerning the possible outcomes of such tactics. The divergence of viewpoints between the central government and localities over the allowable extent of air pollution is well known, and many localities have adopted social welfare programs—such as medical care for the elderly—toward which the center reacted negatively at first. In such cases, however, confrontation was not especially dangerous or risky, and the center ultimately yielded to demands for change from lower levels. Litigation is one area, though, in which local governments are still inexperienced. The central administrative agency that is the object of a lawsuit might retaliate in some fashion. Still, the city of Settsu believed that public opinion was on its side. Other municipalities furthermore were well aware of the fact that Settsu had brought suit despite the obvious risks involved because its administration had made "excess payments" in connection with day care center construction; and they basically agreed with Settsu officials that, for rapidly growing suburban municipalities, larger state subsidies offer the only real hope for solving their financial problems.

In discussing Settsu's decision to initiate litigation against the central government, it is important to consider Settsu's action from the perspective of the reciprocal relationships that bind central and local governments together in a system. To say that the central and local governments are "bound together" means that while the central government has the right to supervise local governments, it also has the duty to consider their special needs and problems and to provide them with adequate financial and information resources. Local governments, on the other hand, are obliged to carry out tasks and functions delegated to them by the center, but they also have the right to present their needs and problems to the state. Should one party fail to fulfill its responsibilities to the other, the mutual ties begin to erode. Formal relations between the two levels of government will not break down completely, however; rather, each side will strive to discover the shortcomings of the other's policies, and both will compete in an effort to win public support for their positions.

Many analysts in Japan interpret the Settsu initiative as an effort to appeal to public opinion rather than to win the particular case at hand. From this perspective, at least two conditions had to exist before Settsu could initiate its suit. The first was that Settsu had to have a Socialist mayor. In contrast to conservative mayors, who are supposedly able to obtain large state subsidies that they can then use to win popular support, progressive mayors must rely more on policy positions that emphasize issue areas previously neglected by the state in order to appeal to local voters. Political opposition to the state would then seem to strengthen the position of local progressive leaders rather than weaken it. The second condition is linked to changing social values in Japan. Almost seventy years ago, the governor of Tokyo, Yoshikawa Kensho, made a statement reflecting policy priorities that was apparently heeded by central planners until quite recently: ". . . roads, bridges, and riparian works are basic; water, housing, and sewage come last" (Ogura 1963). In fact, up through the 1960s, this line was consistently followed and infrastructural development took precedent over social overhead development. This situation changed dramatically beginning in the late 1960s, however, and the point was eventually reached where national goals were openly criticized and the devolution of power was sought.

The Settsu case was able to attract such wide attention because it was the first case in Japan of a local government suing the state. As this paper has already pointed out, the Japanese generally do not regard litigation as the most rational way of resolving conflict, and the number of lawsuits overall is still very small compared to that in the advanced Western nations. Litigation in the area of public law is notably rare. The central government for its part has never been content to allow popular discontent to take its own course; rather, it makes efforts to anticipate problems and needs and to react to them in a tutelary and timely manner. Government authorities have communicated with citizens in the past through organizations such as the *chōnaikai* (neighborhood associations) and continue to show concern over newer forms of citizen participation.

In earlier times, local governments were not as concerned with "autonomy" as they are now, and there was greater trust of the central government. Before, as now, the various central executive agencies held hearings during the budget-drafting season to determine the needs of local authorities. Because most of the state's programs were implemented by local governments, the views of local officials were of great importance to central officials; and as long as this atmosphere of mutual respect persisted, there was no apparent necessity for local governments openly to confront the state or to challenge central government policies. Obviously, much has changed over the years, and in the following section the evolving relationship between the central and local governments will be examined in more detail.

CENTRAL-LOCAL RELATIONS

From a legal perspective, the Japanese administrative system is highly centralized, and intergovernmental relations are dominated by bureaucratic and political actors at the center (Steiner 1965). It is significant, however, that there has never been a case of removal of a local executive for failure to implement an order or law emanating from the center, nor is there the slightest possibility that this will occur in the future. The tutelary powers of the state over local governments have been exercised in the context of the buffering influence of the Home Ministry and the local affairs divisions of the prefectural offices. By tradition the central government has furthermore always listened in detail to the needs and problems of local governments prior to compiling the national budget. Seen in this light, the "centralized" Japanese system begins to appear much more flexible and balanced.

The operations of local governments focus on services desired by local residents. Although the central government ostensibly exercises control over local policy making through the assignment of certain tasks and functions to the localities, in fact the degree to which central laws are implemented is determined largely by the localities themselves. In the case of child care, for example, the determination of how many children are in need of care is usually left to local officials. The same holds true in matters relating to public assistance, road and park construction and maintenance, sewerage service, and other essential local services. Intergovernmental relations may thus be likened to shopping: the state determines what goods are to be placed on the shelf, but local governments select and buy only those goods for which a local need seems to exist.

Problems arise, however, when the central government recognizes only a limited need for certain services to which local governments have assigned a high priority. In those instances localities cannot hope to obtain all the financial assistance they seek, and petitions and other pressure activities directed toward the center become necessary. Fortunately for the local governments involved, there is flexibility built into the overall system through the nurturing and manipulation of various political channels of influence.

In Japan, as elsewhere, political appearances can be deceiving. The city of Kyoto, for example, long known as a bastion of progressive opposition to the center, maintains extensive bureaucratic contracts with the central government (Miyake, Muramatsu & Fukushima 1977). In a recent survey, eighteen of the top twenty-one officials in the city reported considerable contact with central executive agencies. The only officials reporting little contact were those concerned with internal liaison and routine matters (Muramatsu 1975b). Although the formulation and execution of policies in Japan are carried out by administrative officials, not by legislators, city assemblymen can participate to a considerable extent in pressure activities directed at the center. In the survey cited above, 70 percent of the city assemblymen interviewed reported frequent or occasional contact with officials of central government agencies. In contrast, only 44 percent reported frequent or occasional contact with prefectural officials.

It should be noted that this contact with central administrative agencies is suprapartisan. The mayor of Kyoto is considered to be oriented toward the Japan Socialist party. Members of the other four parties nevertheless carry out on behalf of the city government even *more* extensive pressure activities vis-à-vis the state, indicating that such activities rise above partisan considerations. The more important of these lobbying efforts center around financial matters. At the time the above-mentioned survey was conducted Kyoto was involved in a major program of subway construction for which an enormous amount of state aid was necessary. City officials placed high expectations on the lobbying efforts of LDP assemblymen, who had an effective pipeline to the central government. In response to those expectations, 52 percent of the LDP assemblymen reported contacts with central governmental agencies concerning transportation matters. When incumbent Mayor Funabashi had been elected for the first time, he had had the backing of the Socialist and Communist parties, defeating a candidate backed by the LDP and Democratic Socialists. When he stood for reelection, however, he was supported by all the parties, including the LDP. One may speculate that Funabashi sought cooperation even from the LDP because he anticipated the necessity of seeking very large subsidies from the Transportation Ministry for subway construction.

In the case of suburban governments, it would be difficult to say that assemblymen have much influence vis-à-vis the central government; their level of activity simply does not match the activities of Kyoto city assemblymen. Suburban bureaucrats, on the other hand, spend a great deal of time trying to wrest subsidies from the central government through pressure activities and petitions to the center offered with suprapartisan backing. In the Settsu case, for example, the litigation was endorsed at a meeting of all members of the city assembly. After losing the suit in the first instance, the assembly quickly agreed to appeal the decision. Not to agree might have spelled defeat in the next local assembly election.

Many observers regard the modern Japanese state as incomplete, and one incomplete aspect of the Japanese system that has carried over from the prewar period is the allocation of financial burdens among the various tiers of government. This very old debate has taken on new life in recent years, as government revenues plummeted in the wake of continuing economic "stagflation," leaving central and local officials groping for new solutions to fiscal problems that seem inexorably linked to the overall performance of the economy. Local officials realize that their precarious financial situation has made them vulnerable to central intervention in local affairs and that the growth in revenue accompanying the economic boom of the 1960s obscured underlying deficiencies in the local finance system, deficiencies that were to become highly visible in the new era of low economic growth.

The structure of local finance binds local and central actors together in a manner that promotes strong feelings of interdependence, and an action taken at one level of the system almost invariably provokes a response at another level. The next section will focus on the financial aspects of intergovernmental relations in order to examine in greater detail the structural concomitants of central-local conflict.

SPENDING IS A LOCAL DECISION

Most students of Japanese local finance point to three facts of administrative life with which local officials must contend every working day. The first is the central government's domination and control over the collection and allocation of public sector revenues. Local officials frequently speak of "30-percent local autonomy," referring to the fact that about one-third of local revenue needs are met through the system of local taxation. The remainder must come from other sources, principally from various types of central government grants and subsidies. This situation is generally thought to restrict the autonomous policy-making capabilities of local authorities.

In discussing the "one-third" problem, local officials will often imply that local autonomy is weaker in Japan than in countries such as England and the United States. When considering certain types of aggregate data that are used to measure the degree of economic concentration in capitalist systems, however, one is led to far different conclusions. Among six industrial nations—Japan, the United States, England, West Germany, France, and Italy—for example, only Italy's percentage (21.3) of its gross national income aggregated as public sector revenues in 1973 was lower than Japan's (22.4 percent). In the same year Japan furthermore ranked second of the six (after the United States) in the percentage of gross national income aggregated as local taxes (7.1 percent for Japan, 11.9 percent for the United States) (see Japan 1975a, pp. 208–9). Based on such data, it is clear that the catch phrase "30-percent local autonomy" belies a comparatively low degree of financial centralization.

The second fact of administrative life in Japan is a tendency for the central government to delegate specific functional tasks to lower administrative tiers while retaining a supervisory capacity with respect to the implementation of those tasks. At present it is possible to enumerate more than 700 of these tasks, and the practice itself is a continuation of the prewar administrative system.

Here again one can refer to data from the other advanced capitalist systems. Comparative data do show, however, that the delegation of tasks is most pronounced in Japan,[1] where there are few program areas in which the preponderance of administrative responsibility does not rest with local authorities. Only national defense, agricultural development, and the pension system fall largely within the central government's sphere. Programs such as social welfare, public housing, or employment assistance, which tend centrally to be administered in other political systems, fall within the purview of local government in Japan.

The implications of this state of affairs for local policy making—when considered along with the fact of central government dominance over the collection of public sector revenues—are enormous. Local authorities must obviously depend on the center to finance many of their most important programs. The central government must also rely to a considerable extent on local cooperation in implementing these programs. Localities thus find themselves in a position to trade off receptiveness toward central initiatives with demands for central acquiescence in local attempts to

---

[1] National accounts statistics published annually by the United Nations and the Organization for Economic Cooperation and Development (OECD) show that the central government in Japan tends to transfer larger proportions of its revenues to local authorities for ultimate disbursement than do most of the other advanced industrial countries.

expand or otherwise restructure programs. Central officials, for their part, understand that an overly rigid set of guidelines and procedures can cripple the effectiveness of the most well-intentioned program, but the degree of flexibility that would seem to be required poses a serious dilemma. The expansion of services in one prefecture can easily lead to new demands for similar services in neighboring prefectures regardless of the economic factors that must be taken into consideration by central agencies, which eventually pay the larger share of new services. If irreconcilable positions emerge, the way is cleared for a political solution that may not be deemed in the best interests of either side.

The third feature of administrative life derives from the first two, involving as it does the failure of the central ministries to provide adequate levels of support for programs that have been delegated "downward." This is the "excess burden" problem illustrated in the Settsu case. *Excess burden* refers to a situation in which central agencies provide subsidies for local services at one level while municipalities offer those services at a higher level or spend more to provide services at the legally required level, paying the difference in cost themselves. The extent of this problem is illustrated in data collected by the Ministry of Home Affairs. According to its own survey, the rate of "excess burden" for day care centers in 1971 was 259; for public educational facilities, 44; and for police, 59 (Japan 1975b, p. 359). *Excess burden* is that portion of local spending not matched by central grants-in-aid for a "subsidized" program. An *excess burden rate* of 100 means that a local government is actually spending at a level twice that of the subsidized portion of a centrally mandated program. The excess burden problem reveals much about the degree of interdependence between the central and local authorities. Local officials sometimes claim that the center's reluctance adequately to finance important local programs is purposive and obstructive of local policy goals. Central officials counter that deliberate obstruction is not involved and that local authorities create excess burdens by engaging in reckless and expansionary spending practices. Charges and countercharges by local and central officials reflect strongly held views about principles of local autonomy and public finance practices, but they do not necessarily tell the whole story. What often remains unsaid is that when local officials are unable to provide promised levels of services to their citizens, the cry of "excess burden" shifts the blame to the center. The very fact, however, that local governments raise the level of services beyond their ability to finance them poses questions about the central government's capability to control local spending. Thus, just as local officials would not readily admit that they are unable to deliver promised services, central officials would not wish to admit that they cannot regulate unsound local spending practices. In the face of this ironic intertwining of roles, an easy or equitable solution will continue to elude officials at all levels.

One could search in vain for a set of clear or consistent principles

guiding the allocation of functional tasks and the control of public resources in Japan's local government system. Steiner (1965) aptly described
this situation as a "muddle of functions" (pp. 231–62 and ch. 11). For the
foreseeable future, the lines of mutual interest and points of divergent
interests seem clearly drawn. It would be therefore useful to examine in
more detail the structural components of local finance to learn just how
intricate the web of mutuality really is.

Not unlike their counterparts in other countries, local officials in Japan
rely upon four types of revenue sources to meet their current and capital
expenditure requirements. Data from the Ministry of Home Affairs indicate that the single most important source of local revenues over the years
has consistently been local taxation. Revenues derived from local taxes,
which comprise up to 40 percent of all local revenues, are generally
earmarked to cover the operational expenses of ongoing programs (Japan
1975a, pp. 349–50).

The central government has also instituted a program of equalization
grants (sometimes referred to as "local allocation tax") to help assure that
localities unable to meet their current expenses from local taxes can
achieve a minimum standard of performance for basic municipal services.
Equalization grants now comprise more than a fifth of local revenues. The
allocation of equalization grants by the central government is determined
according to a complicated formula that computes each local authority's
"basic financial need" and compares it to that locality's revenue base. The
equalization grant then makes up the difference between financial capability and financial need after adjustments are made to account for factors
such as climatic conditions, changes in the population base, or the occur-
rence of a natural disaster. Generally speaking, poorer prefectures receive
considerable supplemental support through the equalization grant system, while wealthier prefectures receive proportionally smaller grants.
Funds transferred to localities under this system are not project-specific
in nature, and their ultimate disposition by localities is difficult to trace.
So long as such funds are used to meet legitimate expenses, there is little
apparent effort by central agencies to monitor their impact on local spending patterns.

The third source of local revenue is central treasury disbursements, or
grants-in-aid, whose effect on local spending patterns can be more easily
measured. Treasury disbursements comprise roughly a quarter of all local
revenues, and much of this money is designated for capital construction
projects.

A final source of local revenues is borrowing, usually through the issuance and sale of bonds. Bond revenues generally account for less than a
tenth of local revenues. Local officials often complain that the central
government, which must approve the issuance of local bonds, exercises
influence over local borrowing practices in a manner not always consistent
with demonstrated local needs. This accusation is difficult to verify, how-

ever, and there is little direct evidence that the bond approval procedure is capricious or discriminatory.[2]

In addition to local taxes, equalization grants, categorical grants-in-aid, and bonds, local authorities also generate revenues through the operation of local enterprises such as gambling facilities, hospitals, or electric utilities. There is an enormous range of variation in the ability of local governments to supplement revenues in this manner, and the systemic impact of revenues from local public enterprise on local finance is not thought to be significant, though such revenues may be an important income source for a particular locality.

In general, the central government is able to exert influence over two quite different aspects of local policy making through the system of local revenues. On the one hand, central agencies hope to attain minimum standards of performance through the equalization grant formula. Whether the formula has this intended effect is uncertain, but it is clear that these grants do go a long way toward equalizing the availability of revenues for basic local projects. For example, in 1973 six "rich" prefectures (Tokyo, Kanagawa, Aichi, Osaka, Shizuoka, and Kyoto), containing 34 percent of the population, collected more than half of total local tax revenues in Japan; while six "poor" prefectures (Saga, Tottori, Iwate, Akita, Kagoshima, and Shimane), containing 5.9 percent of the population, collected less than 3 percent of total local tax revenues. When the equalization grant has been factored in, however, the "rich six" received revenues in rough proportion (38.3 percent) to their share of the total population; the outcome is also similar for the "poor six" (see Japan 1975a, pp. 268; 323–24).

The second aspect of local policy making that is subject to central government influence through the local revenue system is local investment in capital construction or capital equipment. Local investment decisions of this type are closely tied to the center's "counter-cyclical" policies for regulating the rate of growth of the economy, and the most important control mechanism available to the central government is embedded in its distribution of treasury disbursements (categorical grants-in-aid) to localities.

In general, central officials are more likely to be concerned with ways of regulating economic growth through investment in public works than with assuring minimum levels of public service. These officials perceive that a failure to achieve "civil minima" can easily become a political liability for local leaders who promise more than they are able to deliver; capital projects, on the other hand, provide tangible evidence of central

---

[2]In personal interviews conducted by Aqua in 1975–76, local officials repeatedly stressed that while the bond approval mechanism was cumbersome and potentially constraining, in fact local governments exercised considerable control over their own borrowing and spending practices. Few local officials stated that they sensed ministerial discrimination against their locality for political or other reasons.

(i.e., LDP) generosity and can thus be viewed as a political asset. Such perceptions are not necessarily as accurate as they are logical, but most central officials subscribe to them, nonetheless.

The four "pillars" of local finance described above would seem to be more than accidents of history or the result of equivocation over the proper division of roles and tasks. Rather, they reflect a conscious and deliberate effort to assure a preeminent position for central elites. Whether in fact the structure sustains and protects central dominance will be the focus of attention in the following section.

CAPITAL NEEDS VARY

Capital investment is generally regarded as crucial for economic develop-ment, and the issue of who controls capital resources can be expected to generate conflict in any system. In Japan, central control over the alloca-tion of public sector capital brings local officials to Tokyo annually to compete for funds for their regions. During the petitioning season, one can expect to find several sets of actors formulating and reformulating strategies; organizing and dissolving coalitions; and, in the process, con-suming large amounts of public funds for lobbying. The goals and assump-tions of each group are:

1. Most central government bureaucrats tend to be interested in eco-nomic development and the continued expansion of the economy. They attempt to make investment decisions derived from the norms of effi-ciency and equity. *Efficiency* implies a maximum return on the invest-ment based on local resource endowments, an adequate physical infra-structure to support industrial growth, a skilled and plentiful labor pool, and, not insignificantly, a relatively passive citizenry that turns the other way if and when environmental destruction occurs. *Equity* implies the distribution of resources in a manner that serves to redress imbalances among regions in terms of living standards and access to social advance-ment. In any trade-off between efficiency and equity, considerations of economic performance are likely to override regional imbalances in the minds of most central bureaucrats.

2. Local government bureaucrats are also interested in economic de-velopment, of course, but the nature of their concern and their underlying motivations frequently contrast with those of their central government colleagues. Whereas central planners envisage economic growth as the key to advancing Japan's standing in the community of industrial democ-racies, thereby assuring a voice for Japan in various international eco-nomic circles, local planners are more likely to be interested in expanding the local revenue base so as to enlarge the purview of local policy preroga-tives. If national officials strive for "autonomy" in the international mar-ketplace, local officials seek "autonomy" within a much more limited

sphere. Local planners seek to bring capital investment and economic growth to their region despite poor factor endowments in the hope that this will help to enlarge the local revenue base. The best way to accomplish this with minimum political cost is to attract investment capital from outside the region (and, in particular, from the central government). Existing local revenues can then be used to meet current expenses, allowing "service" and "growth" policies to be pursued simultaneously.

3. Members of the national Diet and other groups active in national political affairs are also deeply concerned with regional development and with the allocation of central treasury funds. Political influence over economic policy making is difficult to gauge, but it is clear that the central bureaucracy's regional development program became highly politicized when Japan entered the peak years of economic expansion in the late 1950s and early 1960s (Muramatsu 1975a). At that time, the "equity-vs-efficiency" debate emerged with dramatic intensity as localities, through their Diet representatives, engaged in a "war of petitions" that had the effect of turning the government away from "rational" and carefully considered investment criteria. Diet representatives and national bureaucrats did not always share a common perspective on the question of national development: Dietmen were required to make extremely difficult calculations with respect to the impact of their actions both on their electoral supporters and on the major business and labor groups on whom they depended for financial support.

4. Local politicians share with national politicians a concern for being reelected, but the composition of their constituency is vastly different from that of Dietmen. Diet representatives are required to form electoral support groups within multiple-member election districts and frequently find themselves standing for election against other candidates from their own party. This has the effect of forcing candidates to appeal to voters on the basis of personality or kinship rather than on the merit of the issues. Candidates for local election, on the other hand, compete in a political environment that has traditionally put local concerns ahead of national issues. Mayoral and gubernatorial elections furthermore produce only one winner, and candidates must amass hundreds of thousands or even millions of votes to be elected.

Because voter interest in local issues and local candidates is so intense, candidates for local office must be prepared to defend local interests even against "higher" national interests. Candidates for the Diet must also defend local interests, of course, but the definition of *local* varies with the composition and size of the constituency. For a mayoral or gubernatorial candidate facing a large electorate, it may be necessary to show support for the interests of a wide array of groups with conflicting programmatic or ideological goals, whereas the vote-getting ability of Diet candidates can be enhanced primarily by supporting narrower, instrumentally based interests.

Local politicians frequently clash with local bureaucrats over the allocation of development funds. A mayor may demand more investment in "unprofitable" social overhead than planners deem desirable; and, not infrequently, mayors must respond to the demands of civic action groups, whose motives are perceived as obstructionist by civil servants. It is furthermore not at all uncommon to find conservative mayors rallying to local causes against the better judgment of their conservative colleagues in the Diet. Local politicians of any political stripe, it seems, do not hesitate to place local interests ahead of partisan ties if they feel they have community opinion behind them.

Local and central politicians and bureaucrats do not, of course, structure their decisions solely according to the norms prescribed here. Still, if one can accept, for the moment, the notion that four distinctive groups of actors pursue goals according to separate sets of criteria, it would be useful to determine which forces, local or central, political or administrative, seem to prevail in deciding ultimate performance. Conventional wisdom might show that central bureaucrats seem to dominate overall; but is this really so?

An examination of changes over time in the rate of spending for certain types of programs may help to pin down this issue. Local spending data for the period 1968–73, for example, reveals that capital spending for roads and bridges; waterways; city planning; and administration, sanitation increased at rates slightly above or below total capital spending during this period, while spending for construction in the education and social services fields increased at a considerably faster rate during the same period (Japan 1975a, p. 74). There had thus been a marked shift in priorities toward the social overhead sector, suggesting a rise to prominence of local political over bureaucratic forces.

A further analysis suggests that localities have been utilizing *central subsidies* to increase their social overhead capital in recent years. In table 8-1 are the results of a correlation analysis between rates of change in central treasury disbursements and in certain local expenditure items over a recent ten-year period, using equalization grants as a "control" to monitor the effect of noncategorical grants on spending changes. Changes in spending for roads and bridges, which consumes about a fifth of the local capital budget, were not significantly correlated with changes in central treasury disbursements for capital construction. In fact, the expenditure item showing the strongest association with central construction was middle school construction; elementary school construction and the other categories of services followed closely behind. The effect of equalization grants on any of the spending items seemed to be negligible.

These findings indicate that the redirection of local priorities away from economic development and toward social services represented the assertion of a new and powerful *local political* will. And in this context of a growing local opposition to the state's economic policies, the priorities

Table 8-1   *Simple Correlation Coefficients Between Percentage Rates of Increase for Three Revenue Items and Nine Expenditure Categories in Eighty-eight Medium-sized Municipalities, 1964–1973*

Expenditure Items	Revenue Items		
	Total Central Treasury Disbursements	Central Treasury Disbursements for Capital Construction	Total Equalization Grant
Social welfare for the indigent, handicapped, & retarded	.29	.36	−.05
Social services for the elderly	.54	.40	.04
Social services for children, including day care	.56	.28	.03
Sanitation	.58	.33	−.04
Roads & bridges	.05	.03	−.13
Preparation of land for housing construction	.34	.30	−.07
Elementary schools	.56	.38	.08
Middle schools	.47	.57	.02
Equalization grant	.18	.02	

Notes: Financial data taken from settled accounts in Japan, Ministry of Home Affairs, 1964–75. Rates of increase calculated on the basis of total for each item in yen.

The eighty-eight medium-sized cities included all cities having a population of 100,000–500,000 in their "densely-inhabited-districts," according to the 1970 census published by the Office of the Prime Minister. Refer to that census for the definition of *densely-inhabited-district*.

of the LDP itself began to move away from economic growth and toward the social sphere in response to its rapidly deteriorating electoral base (MacDougall 1975).

On the basis of these findings, it would seem that the structure of the local finance system may actually have contributed to the politicization of local policy making in an ironic and unintended manner: as local governments shifted from policies emphasizing economic development to policies stressing social issues, central officials found themselves being pulled along reluctantly. This situation posed a dilemma to the central state, for to resist the flow of local policy making might be reflected not only in a loss of credibility on the part of localities over the reciprocal nature of central-local relations but also in a de facto denial of the constitutional guarantee of local autonomy. At this particular juncture in Japan's political development, both issues raised unsettling questions that rendered resistance virtually impossible.

THE FUTURE

What can be said about the future of intergovernmental relationships in Japan from these observations on the Settsu case and on the question of central-local financial relationships? First, an evaluation of the litigation is needed.

The Settsu lawsuit was ostensibly a failure for the city of Settsu; but were the confrontation tactics a failure? The answer is both yes and no. The objective of the Settsu suit was to make the state revise its method of determining subsidies. In that this objective was not achieved, the confrontation tactics were a failure. The number and amount of subsidies for day care centers available to local governments from the state increased, however, following the Settsu case. Local officials generally feel that this increase was due to the impact of the Settsu litigation on the policies of the central government. In this sense, the tactics were successful.

The means for solving the local financial crisis are not limited to the resolution of the excess burden problem. Both central and local governments are groping after a better method of allocating financial resources. One response has been the establishment of a supplemental local finance program in 1977 that yielded approximately ¥517 billion in the 1977 budget. This measure was an interim solution, the compromise result of a bitter dispute between the Ministry of Home Affairs and the Ministry of Finance during the compilation of the 1977 national budget. The Home Ministry insisted that, due to the pauperization of local governments, the share of total revenues from liquor, income, and corporate taxes allocated to equalization grants should be increased from the present 32 percent to 37 percent and, in addition, a local finance public corporation should be established as a drastic reform. The Finance Ministry's position was that, since 1977 was a hard year for the national budget, as well, no special measures should be taken for the benefit of local finance. The supplementary local finance program mentioned above was a result of compromise between the two contending ministries. For years to come, the reallocation of financial resources will remain the biggest problem in intergovernmental relations.

As discussed above, the excess burden reveals many things about Japanese central-local relationships. On the one hand, it tells us about the concept of protest from the localities when the center does not meet their needs. Here the principle of mutuality or reciprocity does not work. On the other hand, it shows the attitude of dependence on the part of localities. Local governments tend to spend more than they can afford, expecting the center to take care of their deficits by some means or other.

The central and local governments share so much responsibility in executing national laws that they tend to influence each other to a great degree. Thus in the case of welfare programs, localities have contributed to an increase of expenditure in many items of welfare, as discussed above. The litigation by Settsu would be understood as local government persuasion directed at the center.

If local governments are to be strong, they must be autonomous; but how are they to become so amid a worldwide trend toward a new centralization? The total expenditures of local governments in 1975 constituted 72 percent of all public sector expenditures. It is practically impossible however for local government to finance that much without the work, help, and direction of the center. If some portion of this work were returned to the state and a few additional revenue sources were put under the jurisdiction of localities, they could broaden their scope of autonomy and assume broader political responsibility, while the state could lighten its burden and use this respite to place greater emphasis on urban planning and other basic areas.

To the extent that local governments become more powerful and autonomous, some might predict that it will become impossible to maintain as in the past the functions of the Home Ministry and the local affairs divisions of prefectural governments. Various central executive agencies might then begin to feel that the Home Ministry and the local affairs divisions are useless as specialists in exercising central control over localities, and local governments might begin to see them as unnecessary foes. This prediction cannot be realized in the near future—the role of intermediary will continue. One can see already, however, the changing attitudes of both central and local governments. When Settsu was preparing its suit, for example, the Local Affairs Division of the Osaka prefectural government was in a very delicate position. The Welfare Department of the Osaka government tried to persuade the mayor of Settsu not to sue, but the Local Affairs Division tried to remain formally neutral in the matter, and some administrators even helped advise Settsu informally.

A sentiment similar to that of these Osaka administrators can be seen even in the Home Ministry itself. In one instance, for example, a former permanent vice-minister of the Home Ministry ran successfully for governor in Okayama prefecture with the backing of the Socialist, Clean Government (Kōmei), and Democratic-Socialist parties. In another instance, a high-ranking Home Ministry official accepted an appointment as lieutenant governor of Osaka prefecture, which at the time had a governor backed by the Socialist and Communist parties. Both of these cases suggest that former Home Ministry officials were now prepared to work with, if not actually coopt, various progressive party organizations. One could thus conclude that if the Settsu litigation is symptomatic of changes in attitudes toward the central government among municipal administrators, the attitudes revealed by certain Home Ministry officials are symptomatic of changes on the part of persons who occupied high-ranking positions within central ministries. Both types of change would seem to hold profound implications for the course of national political life in contemporary Japan.

REFERENCES

Collected Decisions in Administrative Litigations. Vol. 27, II-12.

Gouldner, A. 1960. The norm of reciprocity: A preliminary statement. *American Sociological Review* 25 (April).

Japan. Ministry of Home Affairs. 1975a. *Chihō zaisei no jokyō* (Local finance white paper: The state of local finance, 1975). Tokyo.

———. 1975b. *Chihō zaisei no shikumi to sono unei no jittai* (The structure of local finance and the state of its management, 1975). Tokyo.

MacDougall, T. E. 1975. Political opposition and local government in Japan: The significance of emerging progressive local leadership. Ph.D. dissertation, Yale University.

Miyake, I.; Muramatsu, M.; and Fukushima, T. 1977. *Toshi seiji-ka no kōdō to iken* (The views and behavior of urban politicians). Kyoto: Kyoto University, Institute of Humanistic Studies.

Muramatsu, M. 1975a. The impact of economic growth policies on local politics in Japan. *Asian Survey* 15 (September): 799–816.

———. 1975b. Survey research on public administrators in the city of Kyoto. Unpublished.

Ogura, K. 1963. City planning and public utilities in Tokyo. Tokyo Bureau of Municipal Research. Mimeographed.

Steiner, K. 1965. *Local government in Japan.* Stanford: Stanford University Press.

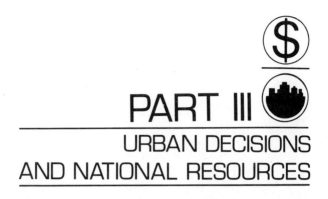

PART III

URBAN DECISIONS
AND NATIONAL RESOURCES

At the urban level, decisions are the result of irrational pressures, limitations of time and information, and immediate political advantage, as well as the result of more pervasive influence of how transfers are indeed made available by higher levels of government. Case studies remain the best device to plumb the realities of policy decisions. They also provide evidence about misleading generalizations, particularly where one assumes that intentions and motives are easily harnessed by political and social forces in order to achieve policy objectives or to serve political self-interest. If resource allocation among levels of government has neither the harmony of interest nor the degree of conflict that might be supposed, then it is important to see how actors indeed respond within the urban setting as financial decisions are made. The New York fiscal crisis shows remarkable continuity between the powers of municipal unions a century ago and those of today. The construction of airports reveals how varied cities are in mobilizing their political and financial influence. The case of housing in London shows how the suburban-central city tension may influence, possibly undermine, major urban programs. The more theoretical final essay wrestles with the problem that public goods often do not correspond to major political differences in the society, in this case American racial conflict.

CHAPTER 9

NATIONAL-LOCAL INTERACTION AND THE NEW YORK CITY FISCAL CRISIS

Martin Shefter

Three of the major themes in the political and economic history of Europe and the Americas over the past century have been the extension of the elective franchise, the growth in the functions and expenditures of the state, and the inflation of national currencies. These themes are related in a rather straightforward way. As new groups enter the political system they are able to get governments to accede to their economic demands; and if, for reasons indicated below, tax revenues do not rise as rapidly as public expenditures, then public deficits will grow and inflation will follow.

Although American cities have operated under a system of universal (or almost universal) white manhood suffrage for more than 150 years, their political and economic histories have followed a broadly comparable course. As new ethnic groups have been mobilized into urban politics, municipal expenditures have grown; and if political conditions are such that tax revenues have not risen commensurably, cities have accumulated large debts. New York City experienced just such a combination of political circumstances over the past fifteen years; and it is this combination that lies behind and explains the current New York fiscal crisis.

There are, however, some novel elements in New York's recent political history. The national government and national bureaucracies played a much larger role in the city's politics during the period 1965-75 than they had in earlier episodes of political expansion and budgetary inflation,

This chapter is a revised and expanded version of an article entitled "New York City's Fiscal Crisis: The Politics of Inflation and Retrenchment," *The Public Interest*, no. 48, summer 1977, pp. 98–127. Copyright 1977 by National Affairs, Inc. The revised article appears here by permission of National Affairs, Inc.

The author would like to thank Martha Derthick, Stephen Elkin, Nathan Glazer, and Irving Kristol for their comments.

while political parties played a much smaller role. These differences, as argued in the present essay, have had important consequences for the way the current New York City fiscal crisis unfolded and for how it is likely to be resolved.

THE POLITICS OF BUDGETARY INFLATION AND RETRENCHMENT

Municipal indebtedness, as the above remarks indicate, can be viewed as the functional equivalent of national inflation. The political conditions that lead city governments to increase municipal expenditures at a rapid rate and to accumulate large deficits are similar to those that encourage national governments to pursue highly inflationary fiscal and monetary policies. Such policies are likely to be adopted in the following combination of circumstances: (1) a social group that has recently gained political power begins to assert claims upon the government for greater public benefits or for a larger slice of the national income; (2) the government responds to these claims either because it is allied with the group in question or because it cannot survive its opposition; and (3) the government is too weak politically to finance these new claims by reducing the flow of benefits to other groups or by raising taxes. To cover the differences between expenditures and revenues, both municipal and national governments can borrow money. In addition, national governments are able to print money —in large quantities, if need be—to finance their deficits; and hence on the national level, deficit financing can generate rampant price inflation.

These political conditions have prevailed, as the historian Charles Maier (1974) has noted, during the major episodes of national inflation in this century. The hyperinflations in Central Europe in 1919–22, for example, followed upon the creation in Germany and Austria of democratic regimes that for the first time granted representation in the government to working class parties. These regimes, however, were threatened by antidemocratic forces on the Right and dared not alienate the nation's industrialists. The only economic policies compatible with the maintenance of this tacit coalition between labor and industry were highly inflationary: industrialists would not tolerate any new taxes on corporate or personal incomes, and hence the government increasingly financed its operations by resorting to the printing presses (Maier 1975, p. 358). Similarly, in Latin America periods of severe inflation characteristically occur after the accession to power of regimes that speak for the urban or rural lower classes but that, by virtue of political weakness, administrative incapacity, or corruption, are incapable of collecting taxes from the middle and upper classes, of preventing the wealthy from sending their money abroad, or of fostering economic development. The Peronist regime in Argentina, for example, sponsored the organization and political incorporation of labor; but its inefficient efforts to industrialize the nation failed to generate the wealth necessary to pay for the benefits it provided its supporters. Consequently, claims the government granted to the national income exceeded the national income, and inflation followed (Scobie 1971, pp. 223–41).

The European nations that are experiencing the highest levels of inflation today—Portugal and Italy—are the ones whose politics most closely approximate the pattern outlined above. The Italian case is too complex to be outlined here,[1] but the Portuguese situation is quite straightforward. Following the revolution of 1974, which granted the Portuguese political rights they had been unable to exercise freely for fifty years, a succession of weak governments (six in two years) either encouraged or found it impossible to resist the demands (1) of the army for an immediate withdrawal from Portugal's colonies, (2) of agricultural laborers for land, (3) of workers and civil servants for wage increases, and (4) of unions for greater control over factories and offices. The result was a rise in the nation's wage bill, a decline of labor and military discipline, the influx of more than half a million refugees from Angola who had to be housed and fed by the government, a rise in government deficits, and consequently an inflation rate in 1975 of 46 percent.

The conditions that foster very high levels of inflation are inherently unstable. Double- or triple-digit inflation can lead to a credit or liquidity crisis, to balance-of-payments difficulties, and ultimately to a recession. As this occurs, industrialists become less willing to acquiesce in inflationary policies. Middle-class rentiers—who generally are the most seriously injured by inflation and who under normal circumstances find it difficult to assert themselves politically against groups that are better organized—can erupt into an angry political force when inflation threatens to wipe out the fruits of a lifetime of thrift. Finally, the banks, which are in a position to extend the loans that are necessary to stabilize the nation's currency and to refinance its international debt, gain enormous political leverage by virtue of their ability to attach conditions to these loans. If these interests coalesce, they can overturn the government that fostered inflation and install a government that will implement a program of retrenchment.

Retrenchment involves the elimination of nonessential public expenditures. This commonly boils down to eliminating expenditures for novel purposes; and what this means in practice is that those groups having only recently gained a measure of power will be deprived of the benefits they achieved by virtue of their incorporation into the political system. If this is to be accomplished, these groups must either be driven off the political stage or compelled to accept a more modest role on it.

---

[1] Italy's high inflation rate is a result not only of the response of its government to the economic demands of an increasingly turbulent working class but also of the patronage practices that a succession of weak Christian Democratic governments have pursued in a desperate effort to remain in power wihout making political concessions to the nation's major working class party, the Communists (PCI). See Tarrow (1977).

Historically, the first of these alternatives probably is the more common one: retrenchment often occurs at the expense of democracy. The Austrian government in 1922, for example, received a stabilization loan from the League of Nations by agreeing in the Geneva protocols of that year to abrogate parliamentary authority over all financial matters for a period of two years; and the enactment of the package of agreements that brought stabilization to Germany involved the overthrow of the last coalition government in Weimar in which a working class party had representation. In Latin America typically only military governments are capable of carrying out the retrenchment policies that international lending agencies insist be implemented by the nations whose economies they bail out. Argentina—and Chile—provide stark examples of what the implementation of a retrenchment program can entail.

The second route to retrenchment involves the imposition of a system of discipline upon the new political force, not by domestic conservatives in tacit alliance with foreign bankers but rather by the leadership of the group in question; and this system of discipline can be a harsh one. The drift to the left of Portugal's revolution was halted in 1975, and the moderate Socialist government of Mario Soares came to power only after many offices of the Portuguese Communist party were firebombed, leftist groups in the military were smashed, and the army was purged by a stern disciplinarian, General Antonio Ramalho Eanes; and the Socialists finally allied themselves with the nation's two most conservative parties behind the presidential candidacy of General Eanes. In similar fashion, the success of Italy's current retrenchment program depends, ironically, on the ability of a Leninist party—namely, the Italian Communist party—to impose its new line (the "historic compromise") on restive party militants and to compel the unions affiliated with the Communist labor federation to limit their wage demands.

BUDGETARY INFLATION AND RETRENCHMENT UNDER TAMMANY HALL

New York City's budget rises and falls in response to a political logic that is similar to the one outlined above. Periods of rising public expenditures and indebtedness follow upon the coming to power of new but loosely organized political coalitions, and periods of retrenchment are associated with either the expulsion of these new forces from the political arena or their subjugation to a tighter system of political discipline.

In New York City these new political forces have generally been coalitions between elements of the city's business community and members of ethnic groups that previously had been politically weak. Traditionally, these political coalitions have been pieced together by machine politicians who placed the members of new ethnic groups on the public payroll to win their votes and at the same time sponsored the public projects favored by their allies in the business community. This method of purchasing political support can be costly. On three occasions in the city's history— in 1871, 1933, and 1975—it led to a fiscal crisis that enabled the banks owning the city's debt to insist that municipal expenditures be drastically reduced as part of any bail-out plan. The politicians who were in office when the city amassed its debt were discredited by their responsibility for the city's difficulties and weakened by the retrenchment program, permitting the political agents of the bankers to label themselves "reformers" and to win the next election. This experience chastens the defeated political forces and enables a more sober leadership to emerge among them. It also provides these leaders with an incentive to organize their followers more tightly, so that when they return to power they are able to be less generous when dealing with their rank and file supporters and more accommodating in dealing with their erstwhile opponents.

The rise and fall of the Tweed Ring illustrates this process quite clearly. Tweed was allied with businessmen who operated chiefly in local markets, an element of the New York business community that had long played second fiddle to the city's mercantile and financial elite. These building contractors, real estate men, street railway promoters, savings bank owners, and manufacturers benefited from Tweed's ambitious program of opening up new streets and transit lines in the northern sections of the city (Mandelbaum 1965, ch. 7). Uptown development had proceeded slowly prior to Tweed's day, when city officials had been most responsive to the merchants and bankers who operated in national and international markets, interests that were oriented to the downtown district and the port and that regarded uptown development on the scale that Tweed sponsored as utterly profligate.

Tweed also sponsored the political incorporation of the immigrant Irish. In the three weeks prior to the election of 1868, for example, the judges allied with the Tweed Ring naturalized several thousand new citizens and expanded the number of registered voters in the city by more than 30 percent (Davenport 1894). The attachment of these new voters to Tammany was reinforced by placement of many on the public payroll and by a public welfare program that bore some marked similarities to the poverty program of the 1960s. Just as the poverty program of that decade was to funnel public monies into community groups and influential churches in black neighborhoods, Boss Tweed's public welfare program channeled public funds into charitable institutions and Catholic churches in Irish neighborhoods (Pratt 1961).

The cost of bringing these two new groups into the political system was high. The budget of the Streets Department, for example, quadrupled in Tweed's first year as deputy commissioner. It was especially high because the Ring was structurally weak (Shefter 1976). Tweed was unable to command the obedience of other politicians; rather, he was compelled to purchase with cash bribes the support of state legislators, county supervisors, and even of his immediate associates. To finance its operations, the Ring levied a surcharge on all city contracts; moreover, because the Ring was weak, Tweed hesitated to raise taxes sufficiently to meet the city's current expenses, let alone to cover the costs of the capital improvements he sponsored. Just as Mayors Lindsay and Beame were to do a century later, Tweed financed short-term expenditures with long-term bonds. In the last four years of Ring rule in New York, the city's outstanding indebtedness tripled.

The Ring was brought down by the city's creditors, who were driven to act by two events that destroyed their tolerance for a regime based upon the groups from which Tweed drew his support (Montgomery 1967, ch. 9). The first was the Orange Riot of July 1871, sparked by a parade of Protestant Irish celebrating the Catholic defeat at the Battle of Boyne. Catholic spectators threw stones at the troops protecting the marchers, and the troops responded with a volley of gunfire that killed thirty-seven spectators. The press blamed the city government for provoking the disturbance, and respectable elements in New York concluded from the incident that a municipal government dependent upon the political support of the Irish could not preserve public order.

The second event that led the city's financial elite to move against the Ring was the suspension of trading in New York City bonds on the Berlin Stock Exchange and the refusal of bankers in London, Paris, and Frankfurt to extend any more loans to the city after a series of exposes in the press revealed the extent of municipal corruption and the size of the city's debt. The collapse of the city's credit threatened the solvency of all the New York banks that owned municipal securities. To protect itself, the city's financial community felt it imperative that the Ring be overthrown, and it accomplished this, in the words of a contemporary pamphlet, through an "insurrection of the capitalists" (Montgomery 1967). A group of prominent businessmen, the Committee of Seventy, organized a tax strike: 1,000 of the city's largest property owners refused to pay their municipal taxes until the city's accounts were audited. In addition, the city's bankers refused to lend to the municipal government money that was needed to meet the city payroll and cover debt service payments until a reformer, Andrew Haswell Green, was appointed as deputy comptroller, with absolute authority over the city's finances. The coup de grace was given to the Tweed Ring when the Committee of Seventy entered a slate of candidates in the 1871 municipal elections and won control of the city government.

The collapse of the Tweed Ring enabled John Kelly, in alliance with a group of wealthy, nationally oriented Democrats, to seize control of Tammany Hall. Kelly inferred from the Tweed episode that Tammany could not survive if all elements of the business community united against it and that to avoid such opposition it must shed its reputation for corruption and profligacy. This he accomplished by purging Tammany of its more disreputable elements and by centralizing and strengthening the party organization. (Kelly, it has been said, "found Tammany a horde [and] left it a political army." See Werner 1928, p. 276.) Kelly then used this organization to elect to the mayoralty a succession of respectable merchants, to discipline any lower level Tammany officials who engaged in the grosser forms of corruption, and to make himself comptroller, in which position he pursued an extremely tightfisted policy of retrenchment (Shefter 1976).

By creating the modern Tammany machine, Kelly and his successors, Richard Croker and Charles Murphy, established a mechanism for incorporating immigrants into the city's political system in a way that was tolerable to, if not entirely to the liking of, the city's propertied elite. This reconciliation involved the extrusion from the political system of competing contenders for control over the city's immigrant masses. Kelly's victory represented the triumph of a respectable lower middle class leadership group among the Irish (Kelly himself was married to a niece of Cardinal McCloskey), and the maintenance of this group's control entailed the defeat of both the lower class gangs, which formerly had played an important role within Tammany, and of the trade union and socialist movements, which at various times (most notably in the 1880s and the 1910s) attempted to assume political leadership of the working classes (Shefter 1978c).

The preservation of Tammany's hegemony, however, required that the machine's subordinate functionaries be tightly disciplined and that new ethnic groups be given a share of the spoils. When the hold of the machine's central leadership weakened, as it did increasingly after Murphy's death in 1925, Tammany officials were free to enrich themselves without limit and to freeze out newcomers. The bacchanalia of corruption during the administration of Jimmy Walker and the inability of Tammany's fragmented leadership to face up to, or to impose upon their subordinates, the stringencies that the Great Depression required set the stage for both the New York fiscal crisis of 1933 and also the triumph in the municipal election that year of a coalition of reformers, businessmen, Italians, and Jews under the leadership of Fiorello LaGuardia.

THE 1960S: POLITICAL MOBILIZATION AND BUDGETARY INFLATION

The last political leaders in New York who successfully pursued Kelly's strategy were Carmine DeSapio, Alex Rose, and Robert Wagner. These won a secure position for the Italians and Jews in New York politics by participating in the expulsion from the political system of those elements of their ethnic constituency who were least acceptable to other groups in the city. DeSapio consolidated his hold over the Democratic party by purging Tammany of its gangster element, one that was primarily Italian but that included some Jewish district leaders (Moscow 1971, ch. 5). Rose established the influence of the Liberal party by destroying the Communist-dominated American Labor party, one that was heavily Jewish but whose most prominent leader was the Italian-American congressman, Vito Marcantonio. Both DeSapio and Rose created tightly centralized party organizations; and, when they united behind the same candidates, elections in New York involved as little competition as they had during the heyday of machine rule in the 1920s. In the mayoral election of 1957 Robert Wagner, who had the support of both parties, won 72 percent of the vote and defeated his Republican opponent by almost one million votes.

The politicians who governed New York during the 1950s defused opposition by accommodating the major organized interests in the city.[2] The downtown business community was satisfied because control over the development programs that were of prime interest to them was placed in the hands of Robert Moses and/or various public authorities responsible only to their bondholders. Municipal civil servants and the city's prestigious civic associations were granted substantial influence over the city's major service-delivery agencies; and in making revenue and expenditure decisions, elected officials paid special heed to the views of the city's tax-conscious lower middle class home owners. Consequently during Mayor Wagner's first two terms the city government did little that aroused controversy, and its expense budget increased at an average rate of only 6.6 percent a year between 1953 and 1960.

This political calm was shattered in the 1960s by the emergence of three new political movements in New York: the Democratic reform movement, the school integration movement, and the movement to unionize city employees. The effort of politicians to gain power in the city by allying with these movements destroyed the regime that had been constructed by DeSapio, Rose, and Wagner and initiated the present era of budgetary inflation.

The first to gather force was the reform movement in the Democratic party. In the face of its threat, Mayor Wagner in 1961 undertook to salvage his career by turning on his political mentor, DeSapio, and by seeking renomination with the support of the reformers and the municipal civil service (Lowi 1967). The steps Wagner took to win the backing of the reform movement and the civil service unions—especially his sponsorship of a new city charter—weakened the regular party organizations, loosened some of the restraints upon budgetary inflation in New York, and made him more dependent politically upon service-demanding groups. Consequently municipal expenditures during Wagner's third term increased at an average annual rate of 8.9 percent.

---

[2]This analysis of New York City politics in the 1950s is substantially similar to Stephen Elkin's more general analysis of postwar urban politics in his essay in the present volume (chapter 12). See also Shefter (1978b).

In 1965 the reformers and liberals abandoned their former allies in the municipal labor movement and supported the mayoral candidacy of John Lindsay. The political forces that rallied behind Lindsay sought to drive the civil service unions from power and to seize control of the municipal bureaucracy themselves. Lindsay centered his 1965 election campaign around an attack on the "power brokers" (i.e., civil service union leaders and party politicians); he undertook to reorganize the municipal bureaucracy into ten superagencies that would be responsive to his leadership; and he regularly contracted with outside institutions (such as the RAND Corporation, the Ford Foundation, and various universities) to perform tasks that formerly had been conducted by municipal civil servants.

To gain political support for this endeavor, the Lindsay administration allied itself with the third new political movement of the 1960s, the black civil rights movement. Blacks were useful allies because they could be used to legitimize the administration's efforts to seize control of the bureaucracy, which was criticized for its failure to adopt "innovative" programs that were "responsive" to the needs of the black community. In addition, the alliance Lindsay cultivated with blacks provided the administration with shock troops who could attack the autonomy of the bureaucracy from below. This was the function served by the mechanisms of community participation that the administration established.

The Lindsay administration had very good ties to the national government and to other national institutions. Lindsay himself was appointed vice-chairman of the National Commission on Civil Disorders by President Johnson, and there was a substantial flow of personnel between his administration and the federal government. J. Lee Rankin, the Lindsay administration's corporation counsel, for example, had previously served as solicitor general of the United States and as the chief counsel of the Warren Commission. John Doar, whom Lindsay had appointed as chairman of the New York City Board of Education, had previously served as the assistant attorney general in charge of the civil rights division of the U.S. Department of Justice; and he went on to serve as chief counsel for the House Judiciary Committee's impeachment investigation. McGeorge Bundy, whom Lindsay appointed to chair a panel that studied the decentralization of the New York City school system, had previously served as national security advisor in the Kennedy and Johnson administrations and was president of the Ford Foundation. Mitchell Sviridoff, Lindsay's first human resources administrator, went on to become vice-president for national affairs of the Ford Foundation. Ralph Tyler, who ran the urban renewal program in the early years of the Lindsay administration, went on to head the program nationally as an assistant secretary in the Department of Housing and Urban Development.

The Lindsay administration used these ties to national institutions in its campaign to enhance its influence over the agencies of municipal government. By applying for federal grants-in-aid, which were subject, of course, to federal guidelines, the administration was able to provide municipal bureaucracies with a greater incentive than they otherwise would have had, to embark upon new programs, hire new personnel (chiefly, upper middle class professionals who spoke the language of federal grant-giving agencies), and to serve new clienteles (namely, blacks and Puerto Ricans). The lure of federal money also provided elected officials who were not allied with the Lindsay coalition—i.e., members of the Board of Estimate and the city council—with an incentive to appropriate municipal funds for purposes that the administration favored, for a small expenditure of the city's own revenues could bring in a large infusion of federal matching funds.

The alliance the Lindsay administration cultivated with federal grant-giving agencies enabled it to reshape the city's budget far more rapidly and with less difficulty than otherwise would have been possible. In the absence of federal grants-in-aid the administration's ability to increase the flow of benefits to its constituency would have been more closely tied to, and constrained by, its ability to raise local taxes or to reduce expenditures on other programs—to its ability, that is, to impose costs upon other groups. The administration would have found it possible to do this only were it backed by a far broader electoral base than, in fact, it commanded. The availability of federal aid, then, meant that the administration did not have as strong an incentive to mobilize mass electoral support as it would have had in the absence of such aid; it did not have a particularly compelling reason to bring larger numbers of blacks and Puerto Ricans into the active electorate.

New York City's budget during the early Lindsay years reflected the political strategy and political constituency of the administration. The three major municipal programs for which expenditures rose the most rapidly during the period 1966–71 were higher education (251 percent), welfare (225 percent), and hospitals (123 percent).[3] The clientele of two of these programs (welfare and public hospitals) is predominantly black, and the explosion in expenditures for the third program (higher education) occurred after the enactment of an open admissions program that tripled black enrollments at the city university. In each of these programs, moreover, the staff that provides services to this clientele (and whose salaries account for much of this increase in expenditures) is composed of large numbers of highly educated and well-paid professionals. The availability of federal and state aid under the Aid to Families with Dependent Children (AFDC) and Medicaid programs helped the city finance a large proportion of these new expenditures. The city, however, was required to match every $3 of this aid with $1 of its own revenues; and hence, even if one confines one's attention to the city's own funds (so-called tax levy expenditures), welfare and higher education remain by far the budgetary

---

[3]The budgetary figures in this and the following paragraphs are drawn from the Temporary Commission on City Finances (1976).

categories that grew the most rapidly during the Lindsay administration's first five years.

The Lindsay administration was not in a position to finance the benefits it provided to its constituency by reducing, or even holding the line on, expenditures for other municipal programs, for Lindsay's victory in the mayoral election of 1965 did not destroy the influence of the unions that represented the employees of the more traditional municipal agencies. After Lindsay's election, the city employee unions may no longer have had an ally in the mayor's office, but they retained their capacity to strike, to lobby before the state legislature, and to support or oppose candidates in future municipal elections. By the end of his first term, the mayor discovered how vulnerable he was to each of these influence techniques. Initially he attempted to break the power of the unions by refusing to enter into the give-and-take of labor negotiations—inviting strikes—and then by seeking to mobilize public opinion (and, in one instance, the national guard) against the unions. These efforts failed repeatedly and the mayor eventually learned that he could not govern the city without the cooperation of the unions.

In addition to the wage increases they obtained by striking, the unions were able to secure very lucrative retirement benefits from the state legislature during the Lindsay years because as the regular party organizations in New York grew weaker, many state assembly members and senators from the city found the civil service unions to be their most effective source of campaign assistance (Shefter 1978a). Finally, Mayor Lindsay himself was desperately in need of such assistance in his campaign for reelection in 1969. To win union support for the campaign and to pay off his campaign debt, Mayor Lindsay gave the unions everything they demanded during the 1969–70 round of contract negotiations. In these ways the civil service unions were able to secure substantial salary and benefit increases for city employees during the Lindsay years, and they thereby compelled the mayor to increase expenditures for the agencies that employed their members. During the period 1966–71 the budgets of the traditional municipal departments—police, fire, and sanitation departments and the Board of Education—may not have doubled or tripled, as did expenditures for welfare, hospitals, and higher education; but they nonetheless did increase on the average by 66 percent.

The administration did not find it possible to obtain enough additional federal or state aid or enough additional taxing authority to finance all these expenditure increases. As for the first of these sources of revenue, the administration sought to increase the flow of federal dollars to the city as much as possible; but participating in federal programs almost always resulted in the expenditure of additional local monies. The most immediate way in which this occurred already has been mentioned: the requirement that federal aid be matched in varying ratios by local contributions. In addition, federal monies financed neighborhood groups that then would pressure the city to provide additional locally financed services in their neighborhood or to its residents. As Marris and Rein (1973) note, this form of leverage is precisely what the framers of the New Frontier and Great Society urban programs had intended to achieve with federal grants-in-aid to cities; and as Piven and Cloward (1971) observe, this was precisely the effect these programs did achieve.

The flow of state aid to New York City, like the flow of federal aid, did increase substantially during the Lindsay years, but there were limits to the willingness of upstate and suburban legislators to tax their constituents for the benefit of New York City. The state legislature furthermore followed a set of informal procedures when it considered New York City financial legislation that enabled political forces unfriendly to Lindsay to block some of the mayor's proposals for tax increases and favored the passage of legislation authorizing the city to borrow money to close its annual budget gap. The Republican and Democratic leaders of the state assembly and senate would round up the votes necessary to pass New York City financial legislation only if every assembly member and senator from the city voted in favor of the bills in question. This informal requirement for unanimous consent meant in practice that these bills had to meet with the approval of each of the major interests that enjoyed access to the city's legislative delegation, the legislative leaders, and the governor. One such group was the lower middle income home owners, who may not have been able to defeat Lindsay in mayoral elections but who did send Republican assembly members and senators to Albany to defend their interests. These legislators found it politically difficult to vote for tax increases; and to avoid losing their votes the mayor and governor found it necessary to substitute bond and note issues for those tax increases that were most noxious to these legislators.

The city's major banks were quite happy to endorse such deficit financing because bond and note issues provided them with healthy commissions and good investment opportunities. Moreover, so long as the office boom of the 1960s continued—a boom that was assisted by capital projects the city and state constructed with borrowed funds—it appeared that rising municipal tax receipts would enable the city to cover its debt service payments (Fitch 1977).

Ultimately, the Lindsay administration was compelled to abandon its efforts to break the power of the public employee unions, to seize control of the municipal bureaucracy, and to use the authority of the city government for new purposes. These efforts suffered a number of serious setbacks at the end of the mayor's first term and the beginning of his second. The mayor's efforts to decentralize the city school system precipitated a bitter controversy and a teachers' strike—the Ocean Hill-Brownsville strike of 1968—and the settlement that resolved the controversy was a defeat for the most militant advocates of community control (Ravitch 1974, ch. 34). The upper middle class liberals and blacks who comprised the core of the

Lindsay coalition were unable on their own to provide him with the votes he needed to win reelection in 1969, and consequently Lindsay was compelled to come to terms with the civil service unions. Finally, the administration's plans in 1971 to place a large, low-income housing project in the middle-class neighborhood of Forest Hills generated intense local opposition and had drastically to be scaled down.

The defeat at Forest Hills broke the mobilizing thrust of the Lindsay administration, and the growth rate of the city's budget slowed considerably after Lindsay had been chastened. From 1966 through 1971 the city's operating expenditures had increased at an average rate of 16.5 percent a year. In 1972 the growth rate of the city's budget declined to 8.6 percent; in 1973 it was 9.3 percent. Much of this budgetary growth moreover resulted from rising prices; and thus the deceleration of the city's budget after the Lindsay administration had received its political chastening is particularly dramatic when measured in constant dollars. Annual expenditure increases in constant dollars average 11.5 percent in 1966–71; they averaged 3.7 percent in the next two years. Abe Beame's election as mayor in 1973 was simply a confirmation that a new political and fiscal plateau had been reached. Mayor Beame's budgets, measured again in constant dollars, grew at an average annual rate of only 2.8 percent.

This new political and fiscal plateau did not involve a return to the situation that had existed prior to 1965. The new players in the political game, who had been ushered onto the field by John Lindsay, were not expelled, apart from a few unruly ones who had attempted to drive some of the older players from it; and the claims of these new players to a share of the gate were recognized. Consequently, as Mayor Lindsay left office and Mayor Beame came in, the city's budget was more than three times as large as it had been at the close of the Wagner administration.

In the mid-1970s, however, it was far more difficult than it had been in the late 1960s for New York City to honor the claims upon its budget granted during the Lindsay administration. Inflation drove up the cost of providing a fixed bundle of municipal services, and the failure of the city's economy to recover from the recession of the early 1970s made it increasingly difficult for New York to cover these rising costs. By the mid-1970s, moreover, there was an explosion in the costs of the retirement benefits that the municipal government and the state legislature had granted to city employees during the previous decade, and in the costs of continually rolling over the city's debt. In 1965 the city's retirement costs had been $364 million; by 1974 they had risen to $1.121 billion and in 1976 they were $1.480 billion. In 1965 the city's annual debt service payments had been $470 million; by 1974 they had risen to $1.269 billion and in two more years they reached $2.304 billion. In order to close the gap between current expenditures and current revenues and to refinance its short-term debt as it fell due, the city resorted ever more heavily to borrowing. By 1975 the city's cumulative short-term debt had risen to $5.3 billion. The budget Mayor Beame presented to the state legislature early in 1975 anticipated a further deficit of $1 billion; and it was predicted that the city's short-term debt might soon amount to as much as 33 percent of the entire outstanding short-term municipal debt in the United States (Congressional Budget Office 1975). The city's request for huge grants and additional taxing authority from the state legislature and its enormous demands upon the municipal securities market for additional loans set the stage for the New York fiscal crisis of 1975.

THE FISCAL CRISIS AND POLITICAL DEMOBILIZATION

The New York fiscal crisis of 1975 was precipitated by a combination of events that resembled the taxpayers' strike and the bondholders' coup that had brought down Tweed a century earlier. The Republican state senators from New York City banded together in May 1975 and agreed to present a common front against pressure from their party leaders and colleagues to vote for legislation granting additional taxing authority to the city. The refusal of these spokesmen for the city's taxpayers to consent to any new taxes increased the city's demand for credit, thereby weakening the market for New York City securities. Later that month the major New York banks refused to underwrite or purchase any more New York City notes and bonds, and thereby drove the city to the verge of bankruptcy.

There is little reason to believe either that the Republican legislators or the New York bankers foresaw the enormous consequences their actions would have or that in precipitating the crisis they were motivated by anything beyond the desire to protect both the short-run economic interests of the groups for which they spoke and their own short-run political and institutional interests. As for the Republican state legislators, they were heavily dependent upon the support of small property owners, who were being squeezed by the combination of inflation, recession, high levels of taxation, and rent control in New York City and who were voting increasingly on the Conservative party line. In 1975 moreover the governor's office was, for the first time in sixteen years, occupied by a Democrat; hence Republican legislators no longer had a compelling reason to support a tax package hammered out in negotiations between the governor and the mayor.

As for the major New York banks, there were a number of strictly economic reasons why they were becoming increasingly reluctant to purchase the city's securities. Other, more lucrative investment opportunities (foreign loans, leasing, consumer financing) had recently been developed by the banks or had been made available to them by amendments to the Bank Holding Company Act; and the failure of the real estate investment trusts had created liquidity problems for many of them (Alcaly & Bodian

1977). Most importantly, however, as the city's short-term debt began to skyrocket, it was becoming increasingly clear to outsiders as well as insiders that the city was engaged in a great Ponzi game: it was financing current expenditures by borrowing and paying off old debt by issuing new debt. So long as dealing in New York municipal securities had been a high-profit, low-risk venture for the city's banks, they had been quite happy to participate in these practices without asking too many embarrassing questions of city officials; but when in the spring of 1975 the eleven major New York banks discerned that the outside world would shortly be able to figure out what the municipal government had been doing, they unloaded some $500 million in New York City securities that they owned. With the banks flooding the market with old New York bonds from their portfolios at the same time that the city was seeking to sell additional hundreds of millions in new New York notes and bonds, the market in the city's securities collapsed, confronting the banks with dangers that were immediate and grave.

Unless the city could borrow additional money, it could not redeem its old notes and bonds as they fell due; and if the city defaulted on these obligations, the New York securities that remained in the banks' portfolios would plummet in value. If this occurred, not only would the banks suffer a direct loss, but they also could be sued by their clients, whose money they had invested in the city's paper. Thus the major New York banks sought desperately to keep the city from defaulting: they pleaded with out-of-town banks to purchase New York securities; and, when that attempt failed, they pleaded with the federal government to guarantee the city's bonds. The very desperation of the banks, indeed, made it possible for the architects of the plan that bailed out New York to squeeze additional loans out of the banks to shore up the city's finances.

In addition to these short-run economic dangers, the fiscal crisis has presented the banks with long-run political opportunities. It has enabled the banks (and, more generally, the city's corporate elite) to gain a dominant voice in municipal affairs. Some of this influence rests upon the ability of the banks to extract concessions from the city government in return for lending it money. The banks, however, actually have lent the city less money than either the municipal employee pension funds or the federal government. The major reason that the banks have become so influential, rather, lies in the following combination of circumstances. First, the city must be able to regain access to the municipal credit market unless some other means of managing its cash flow, financing capital projects, and discharging its outstanding debts becomes available. Second, the city has no chance whatever of regaining access to the market unless its most prominent bankers and business leaders are prepared to assert that they are satisfied that the city is managing its affairs in a prudent and economical fashion. Third, public officials at the municipal, state, and national levels have accepted the banks' claim that if the business community's retrenchment program is adopted, the market will reopen to the city; in other words, that enactment of the retrenchment program is sufficient, as well as necessary, for the city to regain access to the market. This claim, to say the least, is highly conjectural.

In the name of making New York bonds marketable, the banks have managed to extract enormous concessions from the city. In the process, the New York business elite has come to play a larger and larger role in governing the city; and the conduct of public policy in New York has come increasingly to reflect the priorities of the business community. Initially the state created a Stabilization Reserve Corporation (SRC) to market a new series of bonds for the city, and it specifically set aside the proceeds of certain city taxes to cover the debt service payments on these bonds. When the bonds failed to sell, a new state-appointed board, the Municipal Assistance Corporation (MAC), was created to replace the SRC. In addition to being granted the authority to issue bonds and to use New York City tax revenues for debt service on these securities, the MAC was granted the power to revamp New York City's accounting system. When the bonds issued by the MAC also failed to sell, the state passed a statute requiring the city to balance its budget in three years' time and to limit its expenditure increases to not more than 2 percent a year during that period. The statute also created an Emergency Financial Control Board (EFCB) empowered to freeze the wages of city employees, to approve all city contracts, and generally to supervise city finances. The EFCB is composed of two state officials (the governor and state comptroller), two city officials (the mayor and city comptroller), and three governor-appointed private citizens. The governor resisted pressure to appoint a labor and a minority representative to the EFCB and selected instead the top executives of the New York Telephone Company, American Airlines, and Colt Industries. When investors still refused to purchase New York City or MAC securities, the federal government did step in and agreed to extend short-term loans to the city. Federal intervention has not, however, reduced the influence of the city's corporate elite. Although the New York City Seasonal Financing Act requires the U.S. Treasury to certify that the city is pursuing sound financial policies and will be able to repay the money it borrows, before each loan is extended, the Treasury essentially has interpreted this to require simply that the city continue to obey the dictates of the EFCB.

There are a number of channels in addition to the MAC and the EFCB through which the executives of the city's major corporations now exercise influence over municipal affairs. Mayor Beame, at the urging of the business community, established the Mayor's Committee on Management Survey, chaired by the president of the Metropolitan Life Insurance Company, to reorganize the municipal bureaucracy along business lines. Also, in response to pressure from the banks, the mayor fired from the position of first deputy mayor one of his oldest associates and appointed prominent business executives to three of the more important financial and managerial positions in the city government: deputy mayor for city finances, budget director, and director of operations. Just as the New York banks in 1871 were able to install their man, Andrew H. Green, as deputy comptroller and thereby gain control of the city's finances, so too have the leaders of the New York financial and business community been able, since the fiscal crisis, to install their representatives in key positions and thereby gain effective control over the city government today.

These spokesmen for the city's business community have argued that New York has little alternative but to close the gap between its expenditures and revenues by reducing its expenditures. Tax increases, they assert, would encourage more employers and taxpayers to leave the city, thus exacerbating New York's economic and fiscal problems. Among the city's expenditures, however, two categories have been the particular targets of New York's fiscal overseers. The first is labor costs. In response to pressure from the MAC and the EFCB the city instituted a wage freeze and eliminated 56,000 employees from its payroll. This represents a 19-percent reduction in the city's work force. Second, programs whose clienteles are predominantly black—youth services, addiction services, compensatory higher education—have suffered disproportionately severe budget and personnel cutbacks. Personnel moreover have been fired in disproportionate numbers from job categories—clerical, paraprofessional, and maintenance—occupied heavily by blacks and Puerto Ricans. Consequently, between July 1974 and February 1976, the number of Hispanics employed by mayoral agencies declined by 51 percent, and the number of black males declined by 40 percent. In other words, what *retrenchment* has meant in practice is that the city has curtailed the benefits it provides to two of the groups—civil servants and blacks—that had gained a measure of political power in the 1960s.

Squeezing out the blacks has been a rather simple matter. Black leaders had mobilized their constituency in the 1960s by relying upon the resources provided by federal and local agencies and by drawing upon the publicity and support of the press, national foundations, and universities. In the early 1970s, however, the Nixon administration turned sharply to the Right, and federal expenditures for community organization were cut drastically. At about the same time, the Lindsay administration abandoned its mobilization strategy; and the various institutions in the not-for-profit sector that had committed themselves wholeheartedly to social activism in the 1960s felt the pinch of a declining stock market and of reduced federal social expenditures and became far less aggressive politically. Finally, upper middle class youths, who had provided much of the manpower for community organization drives in the 1960s, turned in the following decade to other causes such as environmentalism, consumerism, feminism, or simply careerism. The New York fiscal crisis represents the culmination of this trend: blacks simply have been abandoned by their erstwhile supporters. It appears that the upper middle classes, who in the flush 1960s saw blacks as useful allies in a drive to extend their influence over municipal government, have concluded that in the harsher climate of the 1970s their political interests can best be served by entering into an alliance with the banks. The *New York Times,* for example, has accepted uncritically the most questionable assumption that underlies the retrenchment program advocated by the city's business leadership (that retrenchment will restore the city's access to the capital market), and it now attacks the civil service not in the name of responsiveness and innovation but rather in the name of economy and productivity.

It has been a far more troublesome problem to deprive the city employees of the gains they achieved in the late 1960s and early 1970s than it has been to cut out the blacks because city employees are far better organized than blacks and their power is less dependent upon the steadfastness of their allies. The proponents of retrenchment nonetheless have been quite successful in dealing with the civil service unions, which have been compelled to accept a wage freeze, layoffs, longer hours, and heavier work loads. In addition, they have been induced to invest (or to commit themselves to invest) some $3.7 billion of their pension fund assets in New York City and MAC bonds. Indeed, since the onset of the fiscal crisis the tables have been entirely turned in municipal labor relations. No longer do the unions and the city bargain to determine which of the unions' demands the city will accede to; now the question has become, Which of the city's demands will be acceded to by the unions?

How has this been accomplished? In an immediate sense the tables in municipal labor relations were turned by the state's Financial Emergency Act, which granted the EFCB the power to review—and to reject—municipal labor contracts. One must ask, however, why the unions have agreed to play by these new rules instead of striking to obtain higher wages. The most immediate explanation for the unions' meekness is that such strikes would almost certainly fail. New York City's creditors and potential creditors regard the wage freeze as the acid test of whether public officials in New York are prepared to mend their ways. Were city and state officials to bow to the demands of a striking union, the city's present and future sources of credit would dry up. Were the unions to strike nonetheless in an effort to compel the mayor and governor to choose between the Scylla of losing its access to credit once the city's current cash balance was depleted and the Charybdis of an immediate and total disruption of municipal services, the mayor and governor would probably take the strike. The success of a strike depends ultimately upon public tolerance or, more concretely, upon whether the public will countenance the use of the national guard to perform essential municipal functions of striking workers. Mayor Lindsay floated the idea of using the national guard for this purpose during the 1968 sanitation strike and quickly discovered that it was totally outside the realm of political possibility in New

York at that time. It is a measure of how dramatically New York politics have been transformed since the fiscal crisis that the municipal unions dare not tempt the mayor to make such a proposal today.

Another reason for the remarkable restraint of the unions during the crisis is that they have an enormous stake in the city's fiscal viability. Bankruptcy would cause the New York City and MAC bonds owned by the union pension funds to plummet in value. More importantly still, bankruptcy would throw the city into the hands of a receiver who would have the authority unilaterally to abrogate union contracts, slash wages, order wholesale firings, and reduce pension benefits. This would mean the end of collective bargaining and would threaten the very existence of the unions. To avoid these dangers, municipal union leaders have undertaken the task of selling the retrenchment program to their members, convincing them that they have no alternative but to bear with it. By doing this, they have made it unnecessary for the bankers and business leaders to rely upon harsher measures to implement their program. In this respect since the fiscal crisis the municipal labor leaders have played a role in New York politics similar to the one played by John Kelly after the overthrow of Tweed. They have assumed the job of disciplining the municipal labor force, just as Kelly imposed a system of discipline upon the ward heelers in Tammany. Furthermore, in praising Victor Gottbaum for being "responsible" in urging his members to bear with the wage freeze, the editorial writers for the *New York Times* in 1975 were saying precisely what the editor of the *Commercial Advertiser* a century ago had said of Kelly in somewhat more forthright terms: "Kelly has ruled the fierce Democracy in such a manner that life and property are comparatively safe. . . . It requires a great man to stand between the City Treasury and this most dangerous mass. . . . Dethrone Kelly and where is the man to succeed him?" (Townsend 1901, p. 154).

SOURCES OF INSTABILITY

There are, then, some striking parallels between the political and fiscal developments that have occurred in New York over the past two decades and those that occurred in the city one hundred years earlier. In both periods new groups had been brought into the city's politics under the auspices of weak regimes with the consequence that municipal expenditures and indebtedness skyrocketed and the city was confronted with the prospect of fiscal collapse. To avoid that danger the city, under pressure from its creditors, has embarked upon a retrenchment program, one that has entailed a reduction in the flow of benefits to the groups that had only recently acquired political power. This process of contraction has been accomplished with the cooperation of at least some leaders of the very groups that are being compelled to accept the harsher discipline of the

new fiscal and political order. In particular, in the process of retrenchment, municipal labor leaders are today playing a role that resembles the
one played by John Kelly a century ago.

The parallel between the New York City of Lindsay and Beame, on the
one hand, and the New York City of Tweed and Kelly, on the other, is not,
however, perfect. In the first place, the federal government has played a
far more active role in the city's affairs during the 1960s and 1970s than
it did during the 1860s and 1870s. In particular, in the last decade federal
grant-in-aid programs played an important role in bringing blacks into the
city's political system and in providing public benefits to them. This difference between the way in which blacks, on the one hand, and the Irish and
the city employee organizations, on the other, have obtained benefits from
the government has had important consequences both for the rates at
which the members of these various groups have participated in politics
and for the ability of these groups to defend their prior economic and
political gains in the face of pressures for retrenchment. In the second
place, the regime that currently governs New York City is less highly
centralized and less broadly based than was the Tammany of Kelly,
Croker, and Murphy; consequently, no single organization today is capable of subjecting both the electorate and public officials to its discipline.
For these two reasons, the modus vivendi that has emerged among the
major actors in New York politics during the present crisis and sustained
the retrenchment program so far is not entirely stable.

One potential threat to the success of the current retrenchment program arises from the weakness and indiscipline of some of the city's public
employee unions. If the leaders of a union are to dare to negotiate a
contract that reduces their members' benefits, they must be politically
secure; and if they are to get their members to approve such a contract
the union must be organizationally strong. Victor Gottbaum and the union
organization that he leads (District Council 37 of the American Federation
of State, County, and Municipal Employees) may well be strong enough
to impose discipline upon their rank-and-file, but some of Gottbaum's
colleagues in the municipal labor movement are not so well situated. The
leadership of the Patrolman's Benevolent Association (PBA), in particular,
is very insecure, and the union itself is highly factionalized and quite weak.
It is not surprising, therefore, that two successive presidents of the PBA,
Ken McFeely and Douglas Weaving, refused to agree to the wage freeze
and were reluctant to negotiate a contract that—in the city's judgment,
at least—stayed within the EFCB's guidelines. When Weaving did finally
hammer out an agreement with the city's negotiators it was rejected by
the union's delegate assembly, and bands of policemen, encouraged by
Weaving's political opponents within the union, staged a series of protests
and demonstrations. Unable to mediate successfully between his members
and the EFCB, Weaving resigned, as had McFeely before him. The refusal
or inability of any one union to accept wage restraints, of course, makes
it more difficult for the other unions to do so.

The very fact that New York City employees are represented by a number of independent unions is another potential source of instability in New York today. In such a situation each union can attempt to exploit its peculiar advantages and pass the burdens of moderation on to the other unions. On a number of occasions the United Federation of Teachers (UFT) has sought to do this. The UFT is one of the most politically powerful of the city employee unions because it can both draw upon its own resources and also count on other groups to rally to the cause of education. Thus the UFT relied on its strength in the state legislature to secure passage in the spring of 1976 of the Stavisky-Goodman bill, which directed the mayor to restore $150 million of the funds he had cut from the Board of Education's budget; and the UFT has been the only civil service union to stage a strike during the first two years of the financial crisis. The contract settlement that ended the brief teachers' strike of September 1975 provided salary increases for senior teachers, which the Board of Education financed by reducing the length of the school day and by failing to rehire any of the teachers whom it had earlier laid off. In all probability when the UFT and the board agreed to this contract they anticipated that they would be able, in conjunction with aroused parents' groups, to pressure the mayor to give the schools enough money to rehire teachers and to restore the full school day.

The examples of the Stavisky-Goodman bill and the 1975 UFT contract point to another set of tensions that can undermine the retrenchment program: those between the handful of officials in New York who are directly responsible for the city's finances and the hundreds of officials in legislative and administrative positions who do not have this responsibility. The overriding concern of the mayor and comptroller of New York City and of the governor and comptroller of New York State is what might be termed the *cash flow imperative*. The city simply must have cash on hand to pay its bills as they fall due—especially to meet its payroll and debt service obligations—if the government of the city is not to grind to a halt. The cash flow imperative is the central preoccupation of these four officials because they bear the ultimate responsibility for the day-to-day administration of the city's affairs and for obtaining the loans the city needs if it is to continue to operate. It is of less-immediate concern to city and state legislators and to administrative officials who are responsible only for spending money but not for raising it. Because politicians in New York today (in contrast to the situation that existed during the heyday of Tammany rule), are independent political operators not subject to the discipline of a common party organization, the mayor and governor have found it difficult to compel other officials to heed the imperatives imposed upon the city by the capital market.

The inability of the mayor and the governor to control other politicians provides service-demanding groups with the opportunity to get their way by mobilizing other public officials against the mayor and governor. The Stavisky-Goodman bill, for example, was strenuously opposed in the name of fiscal responsibility by Mayor Beame and Governor Carey, both of whom, it should be noted, are moderately liberal Democrats. Nonetheless the UFT and its allies were able to secure overwhelming majorities in the state assembly and senate to pass the bill, even though the governor had vetoed it, the legislature had not overridden a gubernatorial veto in more than one hundred years, and one house of the legislature was controlled by moderately conservative Republicans. The UFT was also able to pressure the EFCB into approving its labor contract—although questions had been raised by the EFCB staff about whether the contract was consistent with the wage freeze—by getting the two U.S. senators from New York to urge ratification in public testimony before the board. In a similar vein, the New York City Board of Higher Education and its Health and Hospitals Corporation, which as quasi-independent agencies have somewhat more leeway to maneuver politically than regular city departments, have attempted to resist budget cuts by getting various elected officials to support their cause. In this way they hope to isolate and to put pressure upon the mayor and governor.

The final difference between the regime that governs New York today and the regime Kelly and his successors constructed presents what is perhaps the most serious threat to the retrenchment program. The Tammany machine in the days of Kelly, Croker, and Murphy rested on a very broad and tightly controlled electoral base. The structure of electoral politics in New York today is quite different. A substantial proportion of the city's electorate—particularly its potential black and Puerto Rican electorate—does not vote; and many of the groups that do vote but that have acquiesced in the retrenchment process so far, are capable of acting independently in the electoral arena and of seeking through such activity to protect themselves from the full rigors of retrenchment. The potential thus exists for elections to disrupt the retrenchment process. If black leaders were to mobilize a broader electoral base than they have in the past—and they now have a stronger incentive to do so than they formerly had—public officials would not find it so easy to slash expenditures on programs that have a black clientele. Furthermore, if various groups that thus far have acquiesced in retrenchment were to adopt a new stance and enter into a new set of alliances in the electoral arena, public officials might find it politically impossible to heed the imperatives imposed upon the city by the capital market.

In short, the structure of electoral politics in New York today is such that political campaigns can generate serious strains within the retrenchment coalition and can result in the election of public officials who are committed to oppose aspects of the retrenchment program. Just how real this possibility is can be seen by examining the potential electoral resources commanded by blacks, home owners, liberals, and city employees and by considering the various ways candidates might construct coalitions among these groups in their efforts to win citywide elections.

Blacks and Puerto Ricans participate in elections in far smaller proportions than other major groups in the city. (During the first round of the 1973 Democratic mayoral primary election, for example, a total of 3,828 votes were cast in the predominantly black 54th Assembly District in Brooklyn, while 23,080 votes were cast in the predominantly Jewish 45th Assembly District a few miles to the south.) This is a consequence, in part at least, of the peculiar role blacks and Puerto Ricans played in the city's politics in the 1960s, a role that contrasts sharply with the one the Irish played in New York politics a century before. While the political leaders of the Irish were rewarded in direct proportion to the number of votes they commanded, black leaders in the 1960s for the most part were not rewarded on this basis because their support was valued less for the number of votes they could swing in municipal elections than it was for the legitimacy they were able to confer upon public officials or public programs in the eyes of federal grant givers, national opinion leaders and the most ardent local supporters of these officials and programs (cf., Wilson 1969). To the extent that black leaders were able to obtain federal grants, administrative appointments, influence over policy making, access to the mass media, or election to public office in predominantly black constituencies—all without mobilizing a large popular following—they had no compelling incentive to undertake the difficult tasks such an undertaking would involve.

The legitimacy that black leaders can confer on the programs and politicians they support has been a far less valuable commodity in the political climate of the mid-1970s than it was in the late 1960s, and consequently blacks have suffered heavily from retrenchment. As noted above, for example, blacks (and Puerto Ricans) have been fired from city jobs in grossly disproportionate numbers. The immediate reason why blacks have borne the brunt of the recent wave of firings, of course, is that the city removes workers from the municipal payroll in reverse order of their seniority. Black leaders, predictably, have denounced this practice as "racist" and "anti-black." The city has adhered to it, nonetheless, because any alternative would be denounced with equal vehemence by the civil service unions; and the mayor is less willing to arouse their ire than that of the black leadership. If it were the case, however, that blacks and Puerto Ricans were to cast as large a proportion of the vote in the Democratic primary as their proportion of the city's population (roughly one-third) rather than voting at less than half that rate,[4] it is likely that the mayor would have taken greater pains to protect blacks from the full force of the "last-hired-first-fired" rule. He might, for example, have cut more deeply into job categories occupied predominantly by whites rather than those held chiefly by blacks.

The lessons of retrenchment are not likely to be lost on black politi-

---

[4]In the 1976 Democratic senatorial primary less than 15 percent of the total vote in New York City was cast by blacks and Puerto Ricans. The author is grateful to Gary Orren for providing this datum from the New York Times-Yankelovitch survey.

cians. To the extent that black leaders in the future will be rewarded only in proportion to the help they are able to give their friends at the polls or the harm they are able to inflict on their enemies, they will have a stronger incentive than they had in the 1960s to mobilize the enormous pool of black nonvoters. At the same time retrenchment will provide black politicians with the incentive to adopt a new leadership style, and it may well spark leadership struggles within the black community. The skills involved in organizing large blocs of voters and in forging coalitions in the electoral arena are not the same as those that were rewarded and hence encouraged by the city's political system in the 1960s. In this way the current fiscal crisis may well foster leadership changes within the black community akin to those that occurred among the Irish a century ago, changes favoring the respectable and taciturn John Kelly over both the fiery Irish nationalist, O'Donovan Rossa, and the disreputable gambler, John Morrissey. There are some indications that such a transformation may in fact be taking place today. In announcing his candidacy for the 1977 Democratic mayoral nomination, for example, Percy Sutton ignored racial issues and focused his remarks solely on the problem of crime, an issue around which he hoped he could mobilize a biracial electoral majority. Over the long run, then, the fiscal crisis of 1975 may have consequences for blacks similar to those that the overthrow of Tweed had for the Irish: it may facilitate their incorporation into the political system under a chastened and more sober political leadership.

Whatever its long-run consequences may be, however, in the short run the mobilization of the enormous reserve army of black nonvoters into the electoral arena cannot but upset the current retrenchment program, whose success is contingent upon the political feasibility of firing a large fraction of the city's minority group employees and cutting heavily into the budgets of municipal agencies that provide services to blacks and Puerto Ricans. No black leader could hold onto his following while tolerating a retrenchment program whose burdens fall so disproportionately on his constituency. (Though his general strategy entailed avoiding racially divisive issues as much as possible, Percy Sutton was constrained to rise to the defense of John L. S. Holloman, the black director of the Health and Hospitals Corporation, whose removal from office was engineered by the EFCB and Mayor Beame because Holloman resisted cutting the budget of a public hospital system most of whose patients and nonprofessional personnel are black and Puerto Rican.) The entry of thousands of blacks into the electorate would give black politicians the bargaining power to back up their demand that the burdens of retrenchment be reallocated. Any such reallocation, of course, would be resisted by the groups that would be disadvantaged by it; and elected officials might well find it impossible, within the constraints imposed upon the city by the municipal bond market, to arrange a new set of fiscal and political accommodations that the city's unions, taxpayers, business interests, liberals, and blacks are prepared to accept.

The civil service unions comprise another interest that is in a position to use its influence in the electoral arena to improve its bargaining power in the retrenchment process. The unions can deploy manpower and money in political campaigns, and public employees together with their spouses constitute a substantial voting bloc, one especially influential in primary elections. A natural strategy for a candidate to pursue would be to court the organizational support of the unions together with the votes of middle-class Jews (the group whose turnout rate is the highest in the city's electorate) by casting himself in the role of defender of the city's traditional public programs, especially its public schools and colleges, and its subsidized middle-income housing program and rent control program. The two chief sponsors of the Stavisky-Goodman bill—one of whom had his eye on the presidency of the city council and the other, on the mayoralty—appear to have been laying the groundwork for such a campaign appeal when they introduced their bill in the state legislature.

Elections and political campaigns can also lead to changes in the relative influence of the two groups most strongly committed to budgetary cutbacks—the city's downtown business elite and its home-owning population—and might thereby disrupt the retrenchment coalition. Since the eruption of the fiscal crisis bankers and corporate executives have enjoyed enormous influence in the governmental arena by virtue of the position they occupy as mediators between the city and the capital market. They are able to exercise far less leverage in electoral politics, however, because apart from the Republican organization in Manhattan they have no organizational presence in the electoral arena. On the other hand, representatives of the city's home owners have played little direct role in governmental affairs since the onset of the fiscal crisis (no spokesman for this group sits on the EFCB or the MAC); but they are an important force in the city's electorate, and their representatives play a considerable role in municipal elections both through the Conservative party and through the regular Democratic and Republican organizations in Brooklyn, Queens, and the Bronx. The question of who speaks for retrenchment in the governmental and electoral arenas is quite significant because the politicians who represent the city's home owners are likely to cultivate alliances that differ considerably from the ones that the bankers have struck. It would be natural for a candidate who seeks the votes of the home owners (who are chiefly lower middle class Catholics) to advocate (1) that the municipal bureaucracies that employ and serve the members of this group (the police and fire departments) be spared drastic budget cuts and (2) that compensating reductions be made in programs (especially welfare) that have a black clientele and that employ upper middle or middle-class personnel. Nothing could be calculated more to alienate the reformers and liberals, who have been happy to join a retrenchment coalition led by men of their own or a higher social class (such as Felix Rohayton) and who would find it difficult enough in any event to overcome cultural and ethnic antipathies in order to collaborate with politicians who speak for the Irish and Italian lower middle classes.

Finally, as these last remarks indicate, reformers and liberals may come to play a different role in the city's politics during and after an election campaign than they have played since the eruption of the fiscal crisis. Since 1975 reformers and liberals have followed the political leadership of the banks. In electoral politics, however, they have the capacity to act independently; and they command a number of important resources: organization skills, money, talent, energy, and a committed mass following. During an election campaign these resources could be deployed in one (or both) of two ways. One alternative, which might be called the "West Side option," would be for liberals to recultivate an alliance with blacks; oppose budgetary cutbacks; attack the banks; and, apart from calling for increased federal aid, ignore the issue of how the city is to pay its bills. The second alternative, the "East Side option," would see liberals maintain their current alliance with the banks; insist that the city has no choice but to cut its budget; attack the politicians and union leaders (the power brokers?) who were responsible for getting the city into its present mess; and, apart from opposing appeals to racism, ignore the blacks.

The dynamics of electoral politics in New York, then, are potentially centrifugal. Campaigns can open the question of who should bear the burden of retrenchment, and elections can compel public officials to commit themselves to protect various municipal programs from budgetary cutbacks. When this source of strain is considered along with the other tensions that beset the retrenchment coalition, it is little wonder that New York City's creditors and potential creditors are reluctant to trust their fate to democratic politics.

THE LOGIC OF POLITICAL CONTRACTION

There are, as noted above, two fundamental routes to retrenchment. One, the path of political organization and internally imposed discipline, preserves at least the forms of democracy. The other, the path of political contraction and externally imposed discipline, does not. Any particular retrenchment program, of course, may involve elements of both self-discipline and political contraction. Thus, though New York recovered from the fiscal crisis of 1871 for the most part by pursuing the path of self-discipline, there were aspects of the post-Tweed regime that scarcely can be considered democratic. The reform charter under which the city operated from 1873 through 1897, for example, included provisions for "minority representation" that guaranteed the anti-Tammany forces at least one-third of the seats on the Board of Aldermen; and Tammany relied, in part at least, upon its control of the police to deal with opponents who challenged its hegemony over the working classes: the police commonly intervened against unions in labor disputes and they dealt rather harshly with socialists and anarchists.

These qualifications aside, New York City recovered from its 1871 fiscal crisis without abandoning the forms of democracy, and it was able to do so because John Kelly and his successors discovered a way, in a city where the ownership of property was not widespread, to reconcile mass political participation with the security of private property. They accomplished this by constructing a political machine that exchanged patronage for votes and that had both a broad base and a centralized structure and was therefore able to subject voters, public officials, and public employees to its discipline.

No such political organization exists in New York today. This is why the process of retrenchment in New York is currently beset by so many tensions and why political campaigns and elections could so easily upset the retrenchment program. It is for this reason that legal and institutional reforms that would sharply limit the scope of local democracy are being seriously considered in New York today.

New York City's creditors are well aware of the dangers that threaten the retrenchment process. This explains the character of the proposals that the banks have advanced and that public officials themselves have supported in an effort to make the city's bonds marketable. At the insistance of the banks, for example, the statute that created the MAC diverted the revenues of the stock transfer tax and sales tax from the city's general fund and earmarked them for debt service payments on the MAC bonds. Then in February 1977 Mayor Beame proposed that revenues from the city's property tax be set aside in a fund under the state comptroller for the purpose of meeting debt service payments on New York City bonds and notes. Together these reforms would deprive locally elected officials in New York City of the authority to determine how the monies raised by the city's most productive taxes are to be spent.

In a similar vein, Governor Carey proposed that a "health czar" be appointed jointly by the mayor and governor to exercise all the authority of the city and state governments over hospitals and health care in New York City. Such a mode of appointment would permit both the mayor and governor to disclaim responsibility for the health czar's actions and thus would give him enough autonomy from popular pressures to accomplish what officials who are subject to such pressures find impossible to do: order the closing of hospitals.

Finally, in March 1977, the banks proposed that a state-appointed budget review board be established as a long-term successor to the EFCB. The board would have the power to review the city's budget before it was adopted, to reject it if in the board's judgment it was not legitimately balanced, and to approve or disapprove all subsequent budgetary changes and all city borrowing. If city officials refused to obey the orders of the board, it would have the authority to assume total control over the city's finances and even to prefer criminal charges against municipal officials. Finally, the banks proposed that restrictions be placed upon the city's ability to issue short-term debt, that a fund be created to cover revenue shortfalls and expenditure overruns, and that city officials be required to observe various reporting requirements and internal budgetary controls.

As these proposals indicate, a process of political contraction is well under way in New York, and the logic behind that process seems to be inexorable. If New York City is to manage its cash flow, finance capital projects, and pay off its accumulated deficit, it must enjoy access to credit. It will obtain such access only if its creditors—including the federal government—are convinced that the city is able to repay the money it borrows.[5] The city can pay its debts only if its current expenditures do not (as they presently do) exceed its revenues. Since the city's ability to increase its revenues through additional taxation is approaching the point of diminishing returns, it has little alternative but to reduce its expenditures. If elected officials find it politically impossible to reduce municipal expenditures, then the city can obtain the loans it requires only if outsiders are empowered to do the job for them or if their authority to do otherwise is restricted by law.

In the absence of a political leadership having the power that John Kelly did to impose restraints upon public officials, New York City's creditors, then, have searched for other means to insure that their loans will be repaid. In an effort to provide such guarantees, the city has been driven down the second route to retrenchment: that of political contraction. New York City, to be sure, is not the Weimar Republic or Argentina. David Rockefeller is not in a position to organize bands of black-shirted thugs to beat up municipal union leaders and break up meetings of West Side reformers, nor is Felix Rohayton likely to propose that welfare recipients be disqualified from voting in municipal elections. The process of political contraction, however, can proceed not only through direct assaults upon the rights of newly powerful groups but also by removing authority from the hands of elected officials who are amenable to the influence of these groups and transferring it to officials who are insulated from popular pressures. Statutes moreover can be enacted and standards can be placed in the covenants of twenty-year municipal bonds that limit the freedom of action of elected officials within the domain where they do retain some authority. Also, as Boss Tweed learned, the criminal law can be used to

---

[5]The federal government almost certainly would intervene as creditor-of-last-resort in the event of an imminent New York City default. Experience thus far, however, suggests it would do so on terms that do not differ substantially from those that private bankers would extract from the city.

keep profligate politicians in line. Just such reforms have been enacted or are being proposed in New York in an effort to make the city's bonds marketable. Whatever the long-run consequences of the city's fiscal crisis may be, as a result of these reforms the citizens of New York over the next decade may be left with very little control over how they are governed.

REFERENCES

Alcaly, R., and Bodian, H. 1977. New York City's fiscal crisis and the economy. In R. Alcaly and D. Mermelstein, eds. *The fiscal crisis of American cities.* New York: Vintage.
Congressional Budget Office. 1975. New York City's fiscal problem: Its origin, potential, repercussions, and some alternative policy responses. Background Paper no. 1.
Davenport, J. 1894. *The election and naturalization frauds in New York City, 1860–1879.* New York: Author.
Fitch, R. 1977. Planning New York. In R. Alcaly and D. Mermelstein, eds. *The fiscal crisis of American cities.* New York: Vintage.
Lowi, T. 1967. Machine politics—Old and new. *The Public Interest,* no. 48, fall, pp. 83–92.
Maier, Charles. 1974. The political contexts of inflation: Some tentative considerations. Paper delivered at the Conference on Twentieth-century Capitalism, September 10–13, 1974. Cambridge, Mass. Under the auspices of the Council for European Studies.
———. 1975. *Recasting bourgeois Europe.* Princeton: Princeton University Press.
Mandelbaum, S. 1965. *Boss Tweed's New York.* New York: Wiley.
Marris, P., and Rein, M. 1973. *Dilemmas of social reform.* 2d ed. Chicago: Aldine.
Montgomery, D. 1967. *Beyond equality.* New York: Knopf.
Moscow, W. 1971. *The last of the big time bosses.* New York: Stein & Day.
Piven, F., and Cloward, R. 1971. *Regulating the poor.* New York: Vintage.
Pratt, J. 1961. Boss Tweed's public welfare program. *New York Historical Society Quarterly* 45 (October): 396–411.
Ravitch, D. 1974. *The great school wars.* New York: Basic Books.
Scobie, J. 1971. *Argentina: A city and a nation.* 2d ed. New York: Oxford University Press.
Shefter, M. 1976. The emergence of the political machine: An alternative view. In W. Hawley and M. Lipsky, eds. *Theoretical perspectives in urban politics.* Englewood Cliffs, N.J.: Prentice-Hall.
———. 1978a. Local politics, state legislatures, and the urban fiscal crisis: New York City and Boston. In S. Tarrow et al., eds. *Territorial politics in industrial nations.* New York: Praeger.
———. 1978b. Party, bureaucracy, and political change in the United States. In Louis Maisel and Joseph Cooper, eds. *The development of political parties: Patterns of evolution and decay.* Sage Electoral Studies Yearbook. Vol. 4. Beverly Hills, Calif.: Sage.
———. 1978c. The electoral foundations of the political machine: New York City, 1884–1897. In J. Sibley et al., eds. *The history of American electoral behavior.* Princeton: Princeton University Press.
Tarrow, S. 1977. The Italian party system between crisis and transition. *American Journal of Political Science* 21 (May): 193–224.
Temporary Commission on City Finances. 1976. *An historical and comparative analysis of expenditures in the city of New York.* 8th report. New York: Temporary Commission on City Finance.
Townsend, J. 1901. *New York in bondage.* New York: Author.
Werner, M. R. 1928. *Tammany Hall.* Garden City, N.Y.: Doubleday, Doran.
Wilson, J. Q. 1969. The mayors vs. the cities. *The Public Interest,* no. 16, summer, pp. 25–40.

CHAPTER 10
OPTIONS ON THE METROPOLITAN FRINGE: STRATEGIES OF AIRPORT DEVELOPMENT

Elliot J. Feldman
Jerome Milch

Urban studies over the past two decades have focused primarily on the city center, where the more varied activities are concentrated and the more dramatic problems have emerged. These studies have advanced the understanding of the dynamics of urban life as well as the sources of decay and social unrest; but, with a few notable exceptions, they have ignored the process of urbanization on the periphery. The future of advanced industrial societies depends, to a large extent, on the future of their cities; and that, in turn, increasingly depends on decisions about growth and development on the periphery; for those who exercise the options on the metropolitan fringe decide what is possible—and in which directions—in the next generation.

Metropolitan growth is a matter of land use. Large land-using facilities, which cannot find homes in built-up urban areas, are inevitably destined for the metropolitan fringe. How large they may be permitted to be, how far beyond the fringe they may locate, and in which direction from the center (i.e., where along the fringe they will go) are all matters of public policy. Yet the largest land-using facilities are generally technological, and they often generate technological imperatives: nuclear power plants, for example, need large quantities of cooling water; atomic accelerators require earthquake-proof bedrock; and storage depots require major access routes. The conflict over site location—over the options on the metropolitan fringe—often becomes a contest between technological imperatives

Support for the research for the present essay was provided by the German Marshall Fund of the United States, the Societa Esercizi Aeroportuali (SEA), the American Philosophical Society, the Centre for Transportation Studies of the University of British Columbia, the Western Societies Program of Cornell University, and the Cornell Program on Science, Technology, and Society.

and democratic preferences; that is, the debates over site location on the urban periphery are debates over the relationship between technology and democracy.

The largest land-using facilities on the urban periphery today are airports. They have dictated, to a remarkable degree, the future of cities and of societies. Sheer scale is indicative: Charles de Gaulle Airport, only sixteen miles from Notre Dame Cathedral, is one-third the size of Paris. The surface area of Dallas/Fort Worth Regional Airport is as great as the city of Dallas, and more than 150 square miles (96,000 acres) of Quebec were purchased by the Canadian government for the development of Mirabel Airport. The concept of the major airport on a small parcel of land (such as LaGuardia, which occupies 550 acres) seems obsolete.

Land on the urban periphery is scarce and competition for it is intense. Residential developments, the growing tendency of industry to move to the suburbs, and the continued importance of good agricultural land (as well as "green belt") near the metropolitan area compete with airport projects. The extent of the problem may vary, of course, from place to place. The Dallas/Fort Worth Regional Airport, despite its 18,000 acres, placed fewer constraints on land use in the North Texas region than the proposed jetport in Morris County, New Jersey, would have placed on the New York metropolitan area. The Morris County site, which involved only 10,000 acres, constituted the last remaining tract of land of this size within twenty-five miles of Manhattan.

The impact of airports moreover is not confined to the facilities' physical borders. The British Airports Authority estimates that Heathrow Airport is an important nuisance for people living within ten miles in almost every direction from the airport boundaries. Paris authorities fear that if obliged to apply present rules associated with Charles de Gaulle Airport to relieve residents near Orly, they would have to compensate 70,000 persons.[1] Also, the International Air Transport Association, the organization representing most of the world's international airlines, believes that the ideally safe airport has no nearby construction and is surrounded by sterilized fields that keep birds from interfering with aircraft (Durante 1976). The swathe the airport cuts is ever larger, and its impact on cities,

---

[1] A special noise tax is levied on all passengers utilizing the Paris airports, and the income is devoted to soundproofing or purchasing homes in the vicinity of the airport. In the most exposed areas (zone A), both private and public buildings are eligible for compensation. Further away (zone B), only public buildings are eligible; and in zone C there are strict limitations on further construction, but there is no compensation for inhabitants. These procedures, when applied to Charles de Gaulle, became the focal point of fierce controversy; Orly neighbors demanded comparable arrangements, but the government was reluctant to accede, for there are far more people in the vicinity of that airport. There also has been a strict noise code in West Germany since 1974, with government responsibility for replacing schools, hospitals, and other public buildings that fall within high-noise areas. The British Airports Authority offers funds to airport neighbors who request assistance for soundproofing, but there have been few requests so far.

ever greater. The location of airports is one of the urgent matters of public policy in the advanced industrial world.

Airports are, of course, but one example of technological challenge to democratic institutions; but the example is particularly compelling because of its scale and because, as part of a system necessarily linking two distant places, the problems posed are constantly replicable in different settings. Ordinary citizens, moreover, have understood the gravity of site location decisions, for no more virulent domestic conflicts have arisen in the 1970s in the advanced industrial world than those over airport construction (Milch 1976a). The controversy over the development of Narita Airport outside Tokyo was perhaps the most dramatic example of citizen opposition, but it was by no means unique (Bowen 1975). The international airport poses similar technical and environmental problems everywhere, and public reaction has proved consistently similar.

The analysis that follows is derived from more than 300 elite, in-depth interviews and from hundreds of documents. Research was conducted over a three-year period in Rome, Milan, Paris, London, Montreal, Ottawa, Toronto, Vancouver, Washington, New York, and Dallas/Fort Worth. The presidents or directors of nine major airlines, the directors of airports in eight cities, aviation specialists, government ministers, and civil servants in five countries were interviewed, as well as citizens whose land has been taken for airport development and citizens who have protested airport development in eight cities. Similarity is the overwhelming impression given by the data (Feldman 1977). Everywhere the airport poses similar technical problems and similar challenges for the urban as well as the national environment (de Neufville 1976). Despite great differences in each city, the problems for the policy maker are sufficiently similar to make the lessons from one setting to some degree applicable in another.

THE IMPACT OF AIRPORTS ON THE METROPOLIS

Transportation planners and government authorities responsible for aviation view the airport primarily as an indispensable component of a national, or international, system of air transportation. Its function is essentially to facilitate the transfer of travelers and cargo between one mode of transport—aviation—and another—surface transit. The airport is inevitably a national facility, a communications and transportation link insuring the mobility of people, goods, and, since its earliest days, mail. It is important for international trade. A community without an airport—in an era of decline in rail transportation, particularly in North America—may lose contact with its nation and with the world. The limited capacity of an airport may reduce the contact between a community and all other communities; and airport policy in any single community necessarily affects policy in all communities that share routes. The cohesion of a nation is related to the mobility of goods, services, and people; and airports are vital to such mobility.

The case for the national interest in airport development and operation may be obvious, but it tends to obscure the more local consequences of airports. Land use is perhaps the most dramatic metropolitan impact of airports, but there are many other consequences that are highly visible when national lenses are exchanged for local ones. Urban dwellers and their designated authorities do not necessarily share the national perspective. For them, the airport is a public utility with a broader range of impact than is perceived at the national level, where the airport is, above all, a single element in the aviation infrastructure.

Traditionally, the airport has been seen by urban officials as a necessary ingredient for the enhancement of commerce and for the continued viability of local business and industry. Since the dawn of the air age, aviation enthusiasts have extracted local investment in airports through warnings of the consequences of exclusion from the "air map." Local chambers of commerce own and operate most of the airports in France and Italy, and business interests in the United States often have played a major role in planning, developing, and operating air facilities. More recently, local authorities have supported airport development on the basis of direct economic benefits to the metropolitan area. A consultant with the Port of New York Authority estimated in 1961, for example, that a fourth jetport in the New York metropolitan area would generate 134,000 new jobs and more than $700 million in new regional income (Hammer 1961). Similarly, the Special Task Force of the Intergovernmental Committee for the Montreal International Airport concluded that construction of a new facility would add $1.5 billion to national income, and the operation of the completed airport would generate 75,000 new jobs and an annual income of $750 million (Higgins 1971). Decision-making structures have prevented consideration of economic advantage that might be associated with alternative development (Feldman & Milch 1979), and the airport has been perceived, therefore, as a particularly valuable investment.

If airports involve high levels of employment at or near the facilities, they must also involve housing for employees; but here the airport has at least three associated consequences. First, the airport occupies so much land that employees must live some distance from their work. Nearby housing may be scarce, especially with the implantation of a major facility, obliging large numbers of workers to travel considerable distances between their homes and the work place. The concentration of many jobs in a location where there is insufficient housing strains the entire surface transportation system, for more people must travel greater distances than is necessary to reach more typically deconcentrated employment. Pressure builds to increase the housing stock near the airport at the same time that adjacent communities become less-desirable residential areas because of the airport's negative environmental impact.

Second, airport development not only reduces the land base for construction of new homes and apartments but frequently requires the purchase and demolition of existing buildings. New residences must be found for those expropriated, a task that is often difficult, if not impossible, in the overcrowded cities of the industrial world.

Third, airports invariably alter the character of adjacent communities, largely because of the unwanted costs that they impose. The problems stem from aircraft noise, concerns over safety, and increased traffic flow on neighborhood streets. One measure of these costs is the change in real estate values that accompanies major airport development projects. According to one recent study, ". . . the evidence suggests that residential land values fall during periods of substantial change . . . [as] noise-avoiders sell their residential property driving down the price." Eventually, real estate values near airports will increase as land shifts to industrial use and as "noise-indifferent" people (often airport workers) move into the neighborhood. Nonetheless, "the important difference is that the type of resident and the pattern of land use change substantially" (Crowley 1972). Some residents, then, lose out in the process of development. Since they are not compensated for their losses, they have an important incentive to resist the planned development project.

Thus airports reduce the quantity of available land and may reduce the housing stock at the same time and in the same places that they increase the demand for housing. The inability of the dense urban environment to reconcile this contradiction taxes other urban systems.

Not only must airport employees have access to their work, but a functional air facility also requires adequate access to and from the center city for passengers. New highways and mass transit facilities are necessary to meet these requirements, and subnational authorities are expected, in most countries, to assume at least some financial and managerial responsibility for them. The costs of construction are high; and mass transit systems, in particular, cannot hope to recover these expenses, since the potential market is inherently limited (de Neufville 1976). In Paris, for example, construction of rapid transit linking Orly and Charles de Gaulle airports is presently estimated to cost more than $200 million; by 1985, no more than 600 transfer passengers per day will use this system (RATP 1976; Commissariat Général du Plan 1976). In addition to these direct outlays, the construction of new modes of access to airport sites disrupts communities along the route, further reduces housing stock and undeveloped land, damages the environment, and frequently conflicts with existing transportation and development plans within the metropolitan area.

THE ROLE OF URBAN AUTHORITIES IN AIRPORT DECISIONS

Urban officials are usually responsible for managing the impact of aviation facilities and providing access, surface transport, and housing; but they rarely exercise a substantial role in formulating and implementing programs for airport development. The extent to which city authorities have been excluded from the decision-making process varies somewhat from country to country and even, within some countries, from city to city. The Canadian system is the most centralized of the five countries studied here. All major international airports as well as the overwhelming majority of domestic air facilities that cater to airline passengers are owned and operated by the federal government through the Ministry of Transport (MOT). The decision-making structures for airport development provide no opportunity for municipalities to express their interests and concerns. In practice, of course, federal authorities must consult with, and obtain the cooperation of, critical local actors in order to facilitate the comprehensive planning that modern airports require. In Canada, however, those local actors have been on the provincial, not the metropolitan, level. Thus the planning of air facilities in Montreal, Toronto, and Vancouver was conducted with virtually no participation from local government officials; only in mid-1973, after the intensity of local protest threatened the execution of federal plans in Vancouver, was an institutional framework, the Airport Planning Committee, established in order to incorporate metropolitan participation.

Airport development in Britain and France is not as centralized as in Canada, but major cities have little more influence over the decision process than their Canadian counterparts. For a short period during the 1950s and early 1960s, a policy of decentralization of air facilities was pursued in the United Kingdom. Several airports acquired by the state during the 1940s were turned back to local authorities by Conservative governments; by 1961, only twenty-two airports remained under the ownership and control of the minister of aviation (Sealy 1976). After 1966, however, the trend toward decentralization of airport development in the United Kingdom was reversed. The British Airports Authority, created by Parliament as a national industry, began with three London airports and Prestwick in Scotland and now owns and operates seven of the nine most important airports in the country. Only two major air facilities, Manchester and Luton, are not in state hands. Final decision-making responsibility for airports in London, Edinburgh, and Glasgow lies with the national authority, out of the reach of local officials.

The French airport system is, in many respects, similar to that of the United Kingdom. France has both state and local air facilities, the latter operated by chambers of commerce, which often provide subsidies to the semiprivate domestic airline, Air Inter, in order to insure local service. Decisions about airport construction are made in Paris, but local authorities can exercise considerable influence over the process. The 1969 decision to construct an international airport in Lyons was largely the result of local pressure; in an effort to please the Lyonnais, particularly a powerful mayor, government authorities ignored the competition of high-speed rail service on the Paris-Lyons axis and constructed an oversized and underutilized airport.[2]

Air transportation decisions for the capital region, however, are strictly national. The Aéroport de Paris (AdP), a public corporation established by Parliament in 1946, owns and operates all the civil airports serving Paris. The AdP is an autonomous creation of the state, so powerful that ministry officials, who theoretically can veto airport projects, never in fact have rejected an AdP proposal; and, whereas the central ministry has legal authority to control the AdP, local governments, including Paris, have no legal authority at all. Local input is entirely a matter of AdP discretion.

Theoretically, the Italian airport system is more centralized than that of the British or French because authority to operate any airport rests ultimately with the central government. Major cities in Italy, however, have an explicit opportunity to participate in the formulation and implementation of airport policies. Airport concessionnaires designated with city approval operate in every major city except Rome; and the Milanese airports—Malpensa and Linate—are operated by a private company, Societa Esercizi Aeroportuali (SEA), whose principal stockholder is the commune of Milan. Although at each stage in the development of the Milanese airport system the SEA is required to obtain authorization from the state, the SEA consistently has been the initiating agent for changes in infrastructure. The commune of Milan has been able, therefore, to exert great influence in the decisions affecting the urban community.

The structures and procedures through which the United States' system of airports has been developed are by far the most decentralized of these five nations. The Department of Transportation (DOT) in Washington supervises the development and operation of the system and provides financial and technical assistance for construction projects; with the exception of the District of Columbia, however, the DOT neither constructs nor operates any metropolitan air facility. In a number of instances, city governments have total responsibility for air facilities; Chicago's O'Hare Airport, for example, is operated by an agency of the city government; and the Dallas/Fort Worth Regional Airport was built and is managed by a board of representatives from the two cities. In such cases, the urban entities retain considerable influence over the decision process.

Even in the United States the direct participation of local officials in airport issues nevertheless has declined in the years since World War II.

---

[2]The new airport, Lyons-Satolas, was designed as a major air facility but was exposed to severe competition from the beginning. For one thing, the decision to construct a new airport in Lyons infuriated the Société Nationale des Chemins de Fer (SNCF), the state rail agency. In an effort to pacify the SNCF, the government promised to proceed with the development of the Train de Grand Vitesse (TGV) on the Paris-Lyons axis; but the new airport did not even have a monopoly on air traffic in the Lyons region. Shortly before the airport was completed, the government decided to permit the existing air facility in the city to remain open. Thus the Lyonnais are blessed with rapid train service and with two airports, both of which are underutilized.

Financial difficulties stemming, in part, from technological developments in aviation and the growth of a "managerial ethos" that has elevated the prestige of "unbiased, apolitical experts" have encouraged many municipalities to abdicate their responsibilities in this area to public authorities over which they exercise relatively little control. Boston's Logan International Airport, operated by the city government until the mid-1950s, was turned over to an independent agency, the Massachusetts Port Authority (Massport), established by, and responsible to, the state government; subsequently, city officials were able to exercise virtually no influence over Massport's choices, and even the state has experienced constant difficulty in its effort to exercise control (Nelkin 1974). Similarly, New York City leased its air facilities to a bistate agency, the Port Authority of New York and New Jersey, in 1948, when it encountered financial difficulties in the construction of Idlewild (now Kennedy) Airport (Kaufman 1952). The lease agreement stipulated that the city would neither undertake any competitive efforts in airport construction nor interfere in any way with the activities of the port authority. These developments, of course, did not enhance central control over the airport system in the United States, but they deprived elected urban officials of a substantial voice in the decision-making process.

Elected local authorities have had relatively little voice in airport development. Of the cities considered in the present study, only Milan, Chicago, and Dallas/Fort Worth have succeeded in maintaining significant influence over decisions. Despite the impact of modern air facilities on the metropolis, critical choices have been made elsewhere.

TECHNOCRACY AND THE IDEOLOGY OF BUSINESS

There is no guarantee that the decisions of elected metropolitan officials would necessarily reflect the city's best interests, nor is it possible to assume that the metropolis is necessarily harmed because nonurban interests control decisions. The character of airport operation and development decisions, however, suggests that the public corporation thinks above all in terms of the corporation and that the state thinks above all in terms of the state. Neither thinks in terms of the city. The public corporation and the state, moreover, when dealing with airports, think the same way everywhere.

The primary objective of authorities responsible for airport services is to meet traffic demand by functioning as a well-managed business (Feldman 1977). Canada's MOT operates a "revolving fund" for four major international airports (Dorval and Mirabel in Montreal, Malton in Toronto, and Vancouver) in which cost recovery is a matter of policy.[3] The British

---

[3]Transportation facilities in Canada have operated at a deficit throughout the history of the country (Glazebrook 1938), and airports have constituted no exception to this general rule.

Airports Authority was organized in 1966 to put airports on a profitable business footing; and civil aviation, never governed by a ministry of transport, is currently overseen by the Department of Trade (formerly the Board of Trade). The charter of the AdP requires the exploitation of airport facilities for commercial profit; and at least 25 percent of the land acquired for Charles de Gaulle Airport is being committed to a commercial complex of hotels, restaurants, cinemas, banks, and laundromats. The SEA is a private share-holding company that diversified to operate buses, handle cargo, and serve as a travel agency; and the Port Authority of New York and New Jersey, like other revenue bond authorities in the United States, is organized to satisfy investors and to encourage development.

Businesses promote growth, which generates increased revenue. As businesses, airport authorities have not been willing to interfere with airline (customer) choices in scheduling, even though schedules are the chief source of pressure on infrastructure. Airports are underutilized during many hours every day and many days every year. Saturation of terminal or runway facilities is confined to "peaks." The alternative to leveling peaks—i.e., to spreading traffic more evenly by day and by season—has been to build additional infrastructure.

The high cost of infrastructure is often beyond the financial capabilities of airport authorities. Whereas a strictly private enterprise, faced with investment costs exceeding available revenue, may search out alternatives to construction, public authorities turn to the public treasury. In order to secure public subsidy, they promote their activities as public services and they couch their needs in technical terms. The layman and the politician are expected to accept two premises: that expansion of service is necessary in the public interest and that construction is the best technical alternative available. The mixture of the business ideology and the technocratic impulse yields demand for public support.

THE PERCEIVED OPTIONS

Forecasts in the 1960s projected the saturation of international airports in the 1970s (Milch 1976b). Airport authorities defined two solutions to the problem posed by a potential limitation on revenue-producing traffic. One approach was to expand existing airports. This solution was often limited by urban encroachment. The possibility of finding space for one additional

A major reason for confederation in 1867 was to provide viable transportation services in a large country whose population is widely distributed. According to Canadian transportation officials, geographic considerations foreclose the option of unsubsidized transport. Thus the "cost-recovery" policy instituted several years ago by the MOT is something of a misnomer. MOT officials hope to recover a fixed percentage of expenses on aviation infrastructure at some future date and have moved very cautiously in raising landing fees and other sources of income; they do not expect to recover all their costs in the foreseeable future. Even these small efforts to increase income from the airlines apparently have generated considerable tension within the ministry (McLeish 1976).

parallel runway at Orly did not appear sufficient to meet the long-term requirements of Paris; neighbors of New York's LaGuardia and Kennedy airports were not prepared to sanction expanded infrastructure, which would guarantee increased nuisance; and design error in the construction of London's Heathrow, closing the terminal area inside crisscrossing runways with sole access through a tunnel under a runway, made major expansion impossible. Still, in a number of cities expansion of existing facilities did become policy: in Vancouver because geography foreclosed the option of an alternative site and in Milan because poor access and great distance from the center left quantities of adjacent land for development.

The second perceived solution, often expressed as the alternative to expansion, was the construction of a new airport. When this choice was exercised, a common lesson was perceived in the experiences that had made the choice necessary; encroaching development and protesting neighbors had required grandiose projects, so future conflict would be avoided through the construction of the "environmental airport." Enough land would be taken—sufficiently far from populated areas—to guarantee future development without interference. This strategy was adopted in Paris, Dallas/Fort Worth, and Montreal and was pursued vigorously in Toronto and London until political circumstances required the suspension of planning.

Authorities everywhere were committed to build. Not to build was to fail. Only when public opposition mobilized to cajole, embarrass, and sometimes overwhelm officials did a third solution reach the agenda of airport authorities and planners. Although contrary to the tenets of business and technocracy, the idea of seeking a solution to airport saturation that did not require the construction of additional infrastructure (the "no-build" solution) was accepted eventually by airport planners and developers in New York and London.

Option 1: Expand

Vancouver International Airport occupies most of Sea Island between the lower mainland and Lulu Island (the municipality of Richmond) in the southwestern corner of Canada, seven miles from downtown Vancouver. The airport is the third busiest commercial air center in the country. When the MOT decided to increase the aviation infrastructure in the Vancouver metropolitan area, political and geographic considerations apparently foreclosed the selection of alternative locations for a new airport. The United States border is less than thirty-five miles south; and between Sea Island and the border, residential development has occupied much of the fine agricultural land. A new airport south of Vancouver would impose dependence on United States air space and would remove some of the last agricultural land that the province of British Columbia, as a matter both of law and of policy, is trying to preserve. Immediately north of Sea Island are soaring mountains; the sea lies to the west of the city. The principal development of the Vancouver metropolitan area has been eastward, through the Fraser River Valley. Abbotsford, sixty-five miles east, is the site of Vancouver's backup airport; a mountain just beyond its single runway restricts its use.

As a result of these geopolitical limitations, most parties to the debate in Vancouver concur that expansion of the existing site is the only option if increased traffic is to be accommodated through increased infrastructure. In 1970 the MOT announced plans to build a parallel runway and to expand the passenger terminal and parking facilities on Sea Island. Southwest Marine Drive, the road that faces Sea Island from the lower mainland, is known as "millionaires' row." The new runway would be built on the lower mainland side of the island within earshot of Southwest Marine Drive. Once the ministry's plans became public, battle ensued. Although the ministry now possesses the land necessary to execute its plans, the project as of June 1977 is five years behind schedule and apparently suspended.

Malpensa was Milan's first civil airport, developed after World War II around a runway paved by the German military. It began as a venture of local businessmen in the province of Varese; and when civil aviation began to boom in northern Italy in the late 1950s, a second airport, Linate, only four miles from Milan's central cathedral, opened to commercial traffic. This airport absorbed all the traffic growth of the 1960s; the number of aircraft movements at Malpensa actually declined in the decade after 1962.

In the late 1960s the neighbors of Linate challenged the airport's operations and expansion. Sustained citizen action groups—unique in Italy, where protest tends to be dramatic but sporadic—organized in the neighboring communes to demonstrate, petition officials, and even to meet with air traffic authorities in Rome. Although they rarely accomplished their objectives,[4] they put the SEA on notice that major development of infrastructure would not be tolerated (Mansson 1974). With a single runway, no available land adjacent for a second runway, and chronic problems of fog, Linate's future operations inevitably were limited.

Malpensa already possessed parallel runways, a large cargo area, a new terminal building, considerable vacant land, and few neighbors. By 1970 it was also the most underutilized international facility in western Europe. Wide-bodied jet aircraft rendered the passenger terminal obsolete; and access to the airport, located forty miles north of Milan, was inconvenient with no rail or scheduled bus service and no direct highway. In every other respect, Malpensa appeared to be the best possible site for major airport development, not only to serve Milan but all of northern Italy.

---

[4]A lawsuit based on a disturbing-the-peace ordinance did find the Director-General of Civil Aviation guilty of violating the rights of airport neighbors.

The SEA planned an extension of the second runway and the construction of a new runway, passenger terminal, and cargo area. By 1968 the project had become so grand that it was christened the *"nuova Malpensa."* The SEA officials simultaneously promoted the total quality of the project to audiences enthusiastic about development and understated the "expansion" concept to skeptics. It would be difficult, however, in light of utilization of the airport in the 1960s, to consider the plans as much less than the construction of a whole new facility.

Conflicts with Rome, opposition from landowners bitter over expropriation, intense opposition from neighbors conscious of what a major expansion of traffic may mean for them, lack of cooperation from the region of Lombardy, the province of Varese, and the railroads (Ferrovie dello Stato) concerning the provision of improved access, and the near-bankruptcy of the commune of Milan—all stopped the development. The SEA completed land acquisition in 1973 but as of August 1977 nothing was built. In the interim, the SEA had expanded its corporate headquarters at Linate and developed the passenger terminal there.

Throughout the 1950s and 1960s airport authorities everywhere developed facilities through expansion within existing sites. In the late 1960s and early 1970s, however, neighbors acquainted with the damaging implications of civil aviation growth made expansion difficult and often impossible. Familiarity with jet aircraft bred more than contempt. Many neighbors vowed to take any action, regardless of legality, to force growth into other backyards. It was often easier, if not cheaper, to plan whole new airports than to expand old ones.

Option 2: The Environmental Airport

Planners have justified the construction of large, new "environmental" airports on the grounds that zoning regulations have failed to protect noise-sensitive land adjacent to existing facilities. The level of coordination and control required to implement sophisticated land use policies is too high to overcome the incentives to promote urban development that confront local and, occasionally, national actors. Airport builders have argued that protection is possible only through direct control over the disposition of the adjacent real estate, a policy that has required the purchase of immense tracts of land. Thus builders propose a dual protection: the airport is to be protected from urban development, and the airport neighbor's environment is to be protected by eliminating the possibility of many neighbors.

The growth associated with vast land packages beyond the urban fringe tends to spread toward other cities. Consequently, the environmental airport has been touted as the logical solution to the problem of metropolitan air facilities, for it circumvents the problems of incompatible land use through distance from populated areas, assures multiple markets for the facilities, and provides the regional population with high-quality air services. In many instances, however, the environmental airport has been criticized both by aviation interests and by urban authorities.

Mirabel Airport, originally conceived as a single facility to serve both Montreal and Ottawa, is, despite a less central location, in many ways the ultimate air facility.[5] Located thirty-five miles northwest of Montreal, Mirabel occupies 17,000 acres and is surrounded by a 79,000-acre buffer zone. The entire land mass, considerably larger than the city of Montreal, was expropriated by the federal government; nearly 10,000 inhabitants were evicted or became tenants on their own land. With virtually unlimited room for expansion and with no obstacles posed by incompatible land use, federal authorities expected aviation interests to be ecstatic about Mirabel. Yet reaction has been muted and even hostile. To some extent, the controversy between the airlines and the MOT, the airport builder, concerned the design of terminal facilities, an issue with considerable financial implication for both parties. The central complaint, however, concerns the strategy itself. Airline companies generally have been uneasy because sites are so far from their markets (or "catchment areas"). Passengers have not always been willing to accept the extra burden involved in traveling to a distant airport. When the Dallas/Fort Worth Regional Airport opened in January 1974, for example, passenger traffic declined, as many Dallas residents using convenient Love Field preferred other modes of transportation to intrastate destinations to commuting the extra distance (approximately seventeen miles) to the new airport (Macrady 1975). The plans for a London jetport in Maplin Sands, some sixty-five miles from the central business district, were abandoned when planners conceded that it was too far to build economical access and to attract a sufficient number of passengers. The air carriers servicing Montreal, consequently, have been wary of the impact on their local market of the new airport location.

Other airport users also have been unhappy with Mirabel. The International Federation of Air Line Pilots Associations awarded Mirabel a "black star," its lowest rating, partly because there are no emergency medical services nearby.[6] Distant airports are inherently difficult to service, precisely because they have been isolated. Government authorities, conscious of the enormous cost of development, prefer to delay expenditures for ancillary services as long as possible.

One major exception to the pattern of environmental airports far from

---

[5]The site preferred by the MOT planners and consultants was due west of the island of Montreal, along the major roadway to Ottawa. The Quebec government objected to the location, and a special economic task force established to review the decision persuaded the federal government to choose a site northwest of the city (Higgins 1971). At one point in the debate, a consultant firm hired by the ministry proposed a single air facility in the Kingston area to serve Montreal, Ottawa, and Toronto. For both political and technical reasons, the proposal was not taken seriously by the cabinet (Beinhaker 1977).

[6]Ironically, Paris authorities have been chastised for building a hospital near Charles de Gaulle Airport, creating an unnecessary noise victim.

urban centers is Charles de Gaulle Airport, sixteen miles from the center of Paris. The availability of a huge, vacant site on the urban fringe (one farm with three buildings) was a fortuitous accident of history that motivated French planners in 1957 to develop a new airport (Delouvrier 1976). Aviation interests are uniformly pleased with the location but have been critical of the airport's design and operation. Airlines were excluded from the planning process for a decade; twenty years after the airport was conceived, Air France and the AdP, the airport authority, are still fighting over management of the flag carrier's terminal. Perhaps the major difficulty for the airlines, however, is a dilemma of their own making. They wanted the new airport but they did not want to leave the existing international airport at Orly because of capital investments there. They have been free to consolidate or split their services. Some have perceived the need to operate from different locations within the same metropolitan area, and others with transfer passengers have been troubled by which airport would maximize their market. The costs of operating independent facilities at two different airports are so substantial that Air France secured a special subsidy, approved by the cabinet, to defray moving and operating costs in 1976; the loss of transfers has led Air Inter to operate from both airports as a long-term investment that courts substantial short-term losses. Most airlines moreover object to the AdP's division of traffic between the two airfields. Air France claims many passengers, unwilling to tackle the hazards of commuting for connecting flights, have sought to avoid Paris entirely. Air France has lodged an identical complaint, along with other major airlines (especially Canadian Pacific), over the split of operations between Mirabel and Dorval.

Mirabel and Charles de Gaulle have been mixed blessings for aviation interests, but they have been no blessing at all for the metropolitan areas they were designed to serve. The key problem has been access to the airport from the urban center. Special highways were planned to link Mirabel to the center of Montreal and to Dorval; the costs were to be borne formally by the provincial government, but with generous assistance from Ottawa. Nearly two years after the opening of the airport, however, these roads are not yet completed and the existing links are congested, particularly during rush hours. Ironically, the access problem is even worse at Charles de Gaulle, despite its proximity to the center of Paris. The Autoroute du Nord, which serves the new airport, was congested before the facility was opened; during peak hours, it has become known in France as the world's largest parking lot.

Congested highways, of course, do not affect only air travelers. They also complicate the problems of urban transportation for everyone else. Transit by rail to the airport has proved unfeasible in Montreal and uneconomic in Paris. A rail link to Mirabel was on the drawing boards in the early 1970s, but the costs were prohibitive and the project eventually was shelved. French authorities abandoned original plans for an *aérotrain* along the Paris periphery, and the new rail system will cross the center of Paris underground with no special provision for airline passengers and their baggage. The Régie Autonome des Transports (RATP) (Métro) officials, on the basis of a cost/benefit analysis, opposed construction of the rail link; but the cabinet gave airport service priority and demanded RATP cooperation.

Charles de Gaulle also has encountered many of the problems of incompatible land use, which its planners promised to avoid. Citizen action groups complaining about noise and safety have formed in the rural communities surrounding the airport. Part of the difficulty stems from the inability of central authorities to control the behavior of municipal officials; local mayors continued to issue building permits for obviously incompatible development well after plans for the new airport were announced. The central government, however, also failed to plan comprehensively, approving the 1969 construction of a hospital in Tremblay along the airport's perimeter (Lapautre 1976; Becker 1975). The AdP positioned runways along the edges of the airport rather than in the center in order to maximize land available for airport-related commercial development, thereby contradicting the noncommercial designations for land use of the Fifth, Sixth, and Seventh National Plans. The village of Roissy-en-France, which gave the airport its original name, is undergoing systematic, government-sponsored demolition because it is now adjacent to the engine-testing zone, the noisiest area of any airport.[7] The location of this zone was determined by airline pressures[8]; the village was not consulted. Little concern was given to the comfort of neighbors as aviation interests, the central government, and even municipal officials prevailed.

The enormous scale of Mirabel has enabled Canadian authorities to avoid some problems that beset the French at Charles de Gaulle, and residents of the Montreal region will not have to suffer from airport noise and pollution once the existing facility at Dorval is ultimately closed. The price, however, has been high, for local residents have surrendered control over urban development to the federal government. Provincial and local authorities may have some influence over specific choices, but the crucial decisions that will determine the character of the Montreal region will henceforth be made in Ottawa. Urban policies, according to the British North America Act, are formally the responsibility of the provincial government; by expropriating this enormous tract of land, ostensibly to protect the airport, the federal government has succeeded in circumventing the constitutional division of power.

In both Montreal and Paris, the construction of new "environmental"

---

[7] As of October 1976, 225 homes had been demolished. With only 1,500 inhabitants originally in the village, Roissy-en-France is disappearing.

[8] Air France objected to the distance, under the original plans, that its planes would be required to taxi between the main runway and the service area. Subsequent changes required the expropriation of an additional area under separate proceedings. But when terminal 2 is completed, Air France will be further from the testing area than it would have been under the original plans. Air France denies this explanation offered by AdP informants.

airports has fenced in the metropolis. The "Plains of France," north of Paris, had been the last remaining undeveloped area of more than 1,000 acres within the Paris region; the development of Charles de Gaulle Airport has foreclosed most options for urban development on the fringe of the metropolis. The situation is not as serious in Montreal, where there is more undeveloped land; but the land mass expropriated for the development of Mirabel has transferred most remaining options from local to federal hands.

Option 3: The No-Build Solution

Authorities responsible for aviation infrastructure have, in a number of instances, concluded that current facilities must suffice for the foreseeable future. This no-build solution, eventually adopted in both New York and London, came only after exhaustive site searches spanning more than a decade. Authorities remain persuaded that the economic consequences of the failure to act decisively are long term and serious, but they were forced by overwhelming political opposition to give up the quest for additional infrastructure as a solution to the problem of providing high-quality airport services.

The search for a fourth jetport in New York began in the mid-1950s and centered on a 10,000-acre tract in Morris County, New Jersey. The opposition of well-to-do local residents and their extensive support in the New Jersey legislature doomed the project almost from the start (Gladfelter 1961). The Port Authority of New York and New Jersey, however, the agency responsible for airport development, stubbornly refused to seek other sites, even after federal agencies committed to environmental protection joined forces with Morris County opponents. An alternative, the expansion of Kennedy International Airport, was proposed in 1969 amid dire warnings against inaction, but a National Academy of Sciences (NAS) report condemning the project guaranteed its cancellation (NAS 1971).

The early efforts of the British Ministry of Aviation to find a suitable location for a third jetport for London centered on Stansted, where a small World War II airport could be expanded to meet future requirements and where Britain's longest paved runway was located. Local opposition brought on a series of commissioned studies and public hearings (Cook 1967), leading to a government-sponsored independent review chaired by Lord Justice Roskill and costing more than £2 million sterling over three years. The Roskill Commission selected a site near Cublington, but again local opponents persuaded the government to reconsider (Commission on Third London Airport 1971). The third official choice of planners in the Department of Trade, the governing agency for airports in the United Kingdom since 1965, was Maplin Sands, an isolated spot in the Thames estuary sixty-five miles from London. The Department of

Environment made common cause with powerful opponents in Essex and Kent and with former members of the Roskill Commission who had opposed a coastal site. British Airways threatened not to use the airport, and a new Labour government decided the entire project was economically and environmentally unjustifiable (Feldman forthcoming; McKie 1973; Perman 1973).

Major new construction in London and New York was politically, economically, and socially impossible, but the problem of congestion remained. The first new solution was designed to discourage general aviation—i.e. noncarrier operations—from utilizing congested international airports. The port authority, in August 1968, increased the minimum landing fee for small aircraft operating at New York's three major airports during peak hours. General aviation traffic declined 30 percent over the next few months as the policy effectively discouraged peak-hour operations (Levine 1969; Eckert 1972). The following summer the Federal Aviation Administration (FAA) imposed hourly quotas on air traffic at five metropolitan airports in the United States, including all three in New York. Although general aviation was allotted a number of slots in the quota, the new system's regulations further discouraged nonscheduled traffic (Eckert 1972).

The British Airports Authority took even more decisive steps to reduce congestion at Heathrow. A pricing scheme, introduced in 1971 to generate additional revenue by penalizing peak use, was altered substantially in 1976, following final cancellation of the Maplin Sands project; it became a mechanism designed to reduce congestion. The sliding scale of airport fees at Heathrow, far more complex and detailed than the measures taken by the Port Authority of New York and New Jersey, immediately began to drive out general aviation. Nontechnological solutions that discourage traffic violate the basic operating premises of airport technocrats; and the British, like the Americans, conceded the possibility of alternatives to the "one best way" only when ingenuity appeared to be a last resort.

Municipal governments in New York and London had little influence on the abandonment of development schemes, but the no-build option is not free of consequences for them. The least significant implications are undoubtedly the exaggerated fears of increased safety hazards for neighboring communities as a result of the stacking of aircraft in the vicinity of congested air facilities. That these problems have not materialized in New York or London in the 1970s is, in part, only the result of the specific measures taken by airport authorities. The quotas imposed in New York by the FAA in 1969 were lifted in subsequent years as demand slackened: the product of recession, the soaring costs of fuel, and erroneous forecasts of future growth. Pressure on runway capacity was also alleviated at predominantly international airports through what the chairman of the British Civil Aviation Authority calls the "Boeing equilibrium"; increased loads in wide-bodied aircraft succeeded in keeping pace with the growth in passenger demand (Lord Boyd-Carpenter 1977).

The absence of congestion in the air, however, has not resolved all the problems facing metropolitan airports. Despite the decline in aircraft operations, the number of passengers utilizing existing air facilities has continued to increase through the introduction of wide-bodied jets and increased load factors on scheduled flights. Airport operators must now process more passengers, urban authorities must still provide access to the airport for more people, and neighboring communities suffer from increased surface traffic. Thus the failure to expand airports or to build new ones does not guarantee the perpetuation of existing conditions at tolerable levels.

The most significant impact of the no-build option on the urban community is associated with estimated costs and benefits. Airport construction is, from the perspective of metropolitan authorities, a "free good," for the costs are usually borne by the state or the private market. Airports can mean the infusion of substantial monies: Charles de Gaulle's construction costs, for example, have brought $500 million into the Paris economy so far. Airports can also provide employment: Heathrow Airport is one of London's leading employers, with 50,000 jobs. On the other hand, the no-build option relieves urban authorities of fiscal and administrative responsibility for surface transport and services. At least to some extent, the chance to exercise the options on the metropolitan fringe and, hence, to determine the future of the city is thus retained by the local authorities.

The analysis of the relative costs and benefits of this approach to the airport problem depends, in part, on the economic conditions of the community and the political values of urban authorities. In communities where unemployment is a major problem and resources are unavailable, the constraints imposed by airport development projects are usually perceived as a small price to pay for the benefits of growth. Where political leaders favor private or nonurban investment, airport projects are generally welcome, as in the construction of Dallas/Fort Worth and Berlin's Tegel. The attitudes of urban officials, however, also depend on the size of their constituency. Projects generating employment and new income are sought frequently by local authorities, who are responsible for the welfare of the entire metropolitan area. While they may disagree with the choice of site or the design of the facilities, they are generally enthusiastic about urban growth and development. On the other hand, local officials who govern only portions of the metropolis, particularly the suburbs, may regard airport projects with disfavor, since their particular constituencies may suffer disproportionately from development.[9]

---

[9]Vancouver constitutes an exception to this general pattern. The suburban municipality of Richmond draws substantial direct economic benefit from the airport and favors development, in opposition to the Greater Vancouver Regional District and the municipality of Vancouver.

GIVING THE CITY A VOICE

How can the diverse interests of the urban population be defended against the narrow market orientation of airport builders? One possible solution involves proxies, other government agencies or citizen groups who represent urban interests in the decision process. Despite consensus on the national significance of airports, central governments are increasingly divided over specific proposals for construction. Agencies representing the interests of the aviation community have been opposed, in a number of instances, by other government agencies that respond to different, sometimes urban, clienteles.

A number of different agencies may oppose development. In the United States, environmental agencies have constituted the chief opponent for airport builders within the federal government. As early as 1968, the Department of the Interior intervened to thwart the Port Authority of New York and New Jersey on behalf of an environmental clientele by agreeing to accept a gift of land for a wildlife refuge in the center of the proposed Morris County site. The passage of the National Environmental Protection Act and the establishment of the Council on Environmental Quality within the executive office of the president have increased the influence of national environmental interests (Milch 1976a). By forcing strict compliance with the procedures of the environmental impact statement, the Council on Environmental Quality has obstructed airport development plans in several United States cities.

In Canada, both environmental and urban-oriented agencies have helped block the development plans of the MOT. Representatives of the Ministry of the Environment in Vancouver challenged the proposed runway project because it threatened the delicate ecology of the Fraser River Estuary. They were supported, although for different reasons, by the local representatives of the federal Ministry of State for Urban Affairs (MSUA). Similarly, the MSUA supported the Ontario government's concerns for the impact of a new air facility on regional development patterns and challenged the MOT's proposed site for a second international airport in Toronto. Airport development plans in both Toronto and Vancouver began with discussions between one federal ministry and local spokesmen, but the Toronto dispute had to be settled in the end by the federal cabinet, and the Vancouver dispute still awaits cabinet resolution.

Active opposition to airport development plans within the central government is also present in Europe. The British Airports Authority's plan for a new London Airport at Stansted, for example, was opposed by Labour back-benchers; eventually, the Department of Environment, concerned chiefly about impact on local neighbors, reversed Department of Trade plans. In Italy, the Ministries of Finance, Defense, and Industry obstructed the SEA plans, which were originally supported by the Ministry of Transport and Civil Aviation. Only in France did all ministries concur in the development of Charles de Gaulle Airport.

Voluntary associations of local residents and their sympathizers, which have emerged in each of the five countries, have fought airport-related expropriation in order to protect their property and tranquility. Concerned with urban sprawl, congestion, environmental degradation, and the quality of life, these groups often have claimed to speak on behalf of the urban community as a second possible proxy in their opposition to airport development.

The extent to which citizen action groups have elicited the support of the local community varies considerably from place to place. In Toronto and in Vancouver, local government provided financial and technical assistance to local airport opponents in the struggle against federal construction plans. The Toronto City Council actually perceived an identity of interests with local airport opponents. In the communes surrounding Malpensa Airport, citizen action groups emerged through the *quartieri* (neighborhood government) of the municipalities; and in some instances activists and communal officials were identical. In most places, however, government leaders on the metropolitan level have refrained from direct contact with local citizen action groups.

Without a direct voice in the decision process, the metropolitan community cannot protect vital interests; the activities of third parties, whether other government agencies or citizen action groups, would seem to offer some opportunity for urban officials to participate vicariously in determining the city's future. In one respect, of course, the conflict between airport builders and opponents is always in the interests of the urban community because disputes delay the decision process and force it into the open. Secret planning, characteristic of airport projects in the past, almost always excluded the participation of diverse urban interests; opening the process gives urban interests a chance.

In the final analysis, however, no proxy can represent adequately the diverse interests of the urban community. For one thing, opposition within the central government does not necessarily promote urban interests. The intervention of several Italian ministries into the SEA's plans for airport development in Milan effectively thwarted the local initiative of the principal city. Environmental agencies and citizen groups moreover may defend the city's interests in preserving the environment from the negative impact of technology, but they do not share concerns for employment and tax relief. Urban-oriented agencies like the MSUA in Canada are better candidates for representation; their mandate, as a spokesman for urban clients, is virtually unique among central government agencies (Feldman & Milch 1978). MSUA intervention in airport development decisions, however, may exacerbate existing divisions among urban clients. In Vancouver, tacit MSUA support for one set of urban interests, committed to principles of "slow growth" (Lash 1976) has denied the interests of other municipalities, particularly Richmond, Delta, and Surrey, committed to further rapid industrial development. The Vancouver case suggests that a national agency cannot fulfill a local mission unless there is local and even regional consensus. The clash between Vancouver and Richmond forced the MSUA, contrary to its mandate, to take sides in a local dispute.

Public discord and exposure, which are the only outcomes guaranteed by citizen action groups and bickering national agencies, do not assure compromises aiding urban interests. National and local constituencies are not identical and active opposition may, in any event, be too weak to force compromise. National agencies and local activists do not often work in harmony or even pursue the same interests. Environmental agencies in Canada and the United States, for example, are interested in protecting fragile ecological systems, while citizen groups are concerned to protect their own neighborhoods. The neighborhoods of citizen groups, moreover, are not necessarily consistent with the concerns of the metropolis, and they have no formal claim to represent anyone but themselves (Altshuler & Curry 1975).

STRATEGIES FOR THE FUTURE

Until the 1970s, the international elite responsible for civil aviation solved the problem of increased passenger demand by building new infrastructure. Construction often brought great financial benefits to metropolitan areas; but as available land disappeared and the contributions of aviation interests concentrated on the airports proper, the costs in lost opportunity for land use and in demands on associated infrastructure awakened urban authorities to risks as well as benefits. They were usually unable, however, to break into the decision-making circle to control their own future.

Even as the first alternatives to construction are tested, formal decision-making arrangements make little or no provision for urban or local participation. The strategy of the environmental airport remains alive in many places, including Toronto and Munich; and price-mechanism alternatives to level peaks are still rare exceptions to the strategies of construction. The options on the metropolitan fringe continue to close with little participation of metropolitan authorities.

Airport development merits careful appreciation of social, economic, and political trade-offs. One of the more fashionable techniques is cost/benefit analysis; but the most comprehensive effort to employ this technique, the Roskill Commission report, merely assumed the benefits of an international airport while comparing the costs of competing sites (Mishan 1970). More rigorous measurement of benefits could offer clearer choices for the makers of public policy.

The central question posed by airport development probably concerns equity and constituency. The airport that serves a widespread population is a nuisance for a localized community. To guarantee the benefit of available air transport for the community at large, in the future it will probably prove necessary in some way to compensate airport neighbors.

Perception of the airport as a community and national service may alter substantially the policies that have derived from the business premises of the past. Obstacles to construction have obliged planners, who are often civil servants, to examine the assumptions that have governed development strategies. The city may have a much greater place in debates over a community service than it has enjoyed in discussions over transportation business.

The many competing constituencies, both locally and nationally, have created boundless confusion in the quest for structures devoted to equitable solutions for problems of air traffic. The two possible schemes suggested in this essay to provide representation for the diverse interests of the metropolis—the proxies of citizen action groups and national agencies —appear inadequate. There is no third scheme. Various short-term solutions, including curfews to reduce nighttime disturbance, pricing mechanisms to level peaks, flight path adjustments to avoid populated areas, compensation for soundproofing, and encouragement of alternative transportation modes, may all relieve some of the pressures affecting airports and urban populations; but growth economies will generate more traffic, and present infrastructure, even with solutions of this kind, is likely to prove inadequate for quality air service again in the future.

The overwhelming problem is institutional: structures do not exist, in any of the countries studied here, that guarantee that the voice of the most affected will be heard. In most cases, structures guarantee that those most affected will not be heard. The federal court ruling in New York in May 1977, permitting the federal government to lower the environmental protection standards in the New York area by authorizing the operation of the Concorde at Kennedy Airport, proves that the challenge to the exclusive control of central authority that developed in the 1960s and 1970s has not yet prevailed. So long as civil aviation is treated as a business, constituencies will contend, not cooperate; and so long as there is no institutional framework to guarantee the participation of the multiple values and perspectives, options on the metropolitan fringe will be exercised by narrow interests.

Hence in the end the institutional failure is also an ideological one. Institutional change, recognition of diverse local claims on control of the local environment, depends on ideological change and alteration in the perception of civil aviation as the domain of experts and businessmen. Both kinds of changes may materialize with the shortage of resources and land, and technology may ease some of the pain in political choices. Change may never come, however, outside the framework of national dominance; and the city may not acquire a voice until there is nothing left to shout about.

REFERENCES

Altshuler, Alan, and Curry, R. 1975. The changing environment of urban development policy: Shared power or shared impotence. *Urban Law Annual* 10: 1–43.

Becker. 1975. Personal interview, former Chief Engineer, Air France.

Beinhaker, Philip. 1977. Personal interview, consultant for the Canadian Ministry of Transport.

Bowen, Roger Wilson. 1975. The Narita conflict. *Asian Survey* 15 (July): 598–615.

Commissariat Général du Plan. 1976. *Rapport de la commission de transports et des communications—Préparation de VIIe Plan.* Paris: Documentation Française.

Commission on the Third London Airport (Roskill Commission). 1971. *Report.* London: HMSO.

Cook, Olive. 1967. *The Stansted Affair: A case for the people.* London: Pan Books.

Crowley, Roland W. 1972. The effects of an airport on land values. Ottawa: Ministry of State for Urban Affairs.

Delouvrier, Paul. 1976. Personal interview, former director of the Paris District.

de Neufville, Richard. 1976. *Airport systems planning.* Cambridge, Mass.: MIT Press.

Durante, Jeffrey. 1976. Personal interview, senior airports advisor, IATA.

Eckert, Ross D. 1972. *Airports and congestion: A problem of misplaced subsidies.* Washington, D.C.: American Enterprise Institute for Public Policy Research.

Feldman, Elliot. 1977. Air transportation infrastructure as a problem of public policy. *Policy Studies Journal* 6, no. 1: 20–29.

———. *White elephants and the albatross: Civil aviation in the supersonic age.* Cambridge: Harvard University Center for International Affairs, forthcoming.

Feldman, Elliot J., and Milch, Jerome. 1978. Coordination or control? Federal initiatives in Canadian cities. Paper presented at the 1978 Annual Meeting of the American Political Science Association, New York, September 1, 1978.

———. 1979. *Canadian federalism and airport development.*

Gladfelter, David. 1961. Jets for the Great Swamp? In Richard T. Frost, ed. *Cases in state and local government,* pp. 302–18. Englewood Cliffs, N.J.: Prentice-Hall.

Glazebrook, G. P. de T. 1938. *A history of transportation in Canada.* Toronto: Ryerson Press.

Hammer and Company Associates. 1961. Economic effects of a new major airport. New York: Port of New York Authority.

Higgins, Benjamin. 1971. The Montreal airport site. *Growth and Change* 2 (January): 14–22.

Kaufman, Herbert. 1952. Gotham in the Air Age. In Harold Stein, ed. *Public administration and policy development: A case book.* New York: Harcourt, Brace.

Lapautre, René. 1976. Personal interview, Director-General, Air Inter.

Lash, Harry. 1976. Personal interview, former director of planning, Greater Vancouver Regional District.

Levine, Michael E. 1969. Landing fees and the airport congestion problem. *Journal of Law and Economics* 12 (April): 79–108.

Lord Boyd-Carpenter. 1977. Airport planning in the United Kingdom: Past, present and future. Paper presented at the Fifth Annual World Airports Conference, London.

McKie, David. 1973. *A sadly mismanaged affair: A political history of the Third London Airport.* London: Croom Helm.

McLeish, Walter. 1976. Personal interview, chief of the Air Administration of the Canadian Ministry of Transport.

Macrady, Howard. 1975. Personal interview, aviation director, city of Dallas.

Mansson, Per-Henrik. 1974. *La Guerra dei Decibel:* Citizen protest at Milan's Linate Airport. Manuscript, Johns Hopkins University, Bologna Center.

Milch, Jerome. 1976a. Feasible and prudent alternatives: Airport development in the age of public protest. *Public Policy* 24 (winter): 81–109.

———. 1976b. Inverted pyramids: The use and misuse of aviation forecasting. *Social Studies of Science* 6: 5–31.

Mishan, E. J. 1970. What is wrong with Roskill? *Journal of Transport Economics and Policy* 4 (September): 221–34.

National Academy of Sciences (NAS). 1971. *Jamaica Bay and Kennedy Airport: A multidisciplinary environmental study.* Washington, D.C.: National Academy of Sciences.

Nelkin, Dorothy. 1974. *Jetport: The Boston Airport controversy.* New Brunswick, N.J.: Transaction Books.

Perman, David. 1973. *Cublington: A blueprint for resistance.* London: Bodley Head.

Régie Autonome des Transports Parisiens (RATP). 1976. *Plan d'Entreprise, 1977–1981.* Paris: RATP.

Sealy, Kenneth. 1976. *Airport strategy and planning.* London: Oxford University Press.

CHAPTER 11

IMPLEMENTING AN URBAN STRATEGY: THE CASE OF PUBLIC HOUSING IN METROPOLITAN LONDON

Ken Young

London, as most major cities in the Western world, has experienced a continuing and substantial metropolitan housing shortage. Besides the aggregate shortage and misallocation of homes, London's housing stock is also characterized by vivid contrasts between the overcrowded urban core and the pleasant and spacious outer suburbs. At the same time London possesses the somewhat mixed blessing of the classic panacea for metropolitan problems: integrated local government. The favored nostrum of reformers since the turn of the century, metropolitan governmental integration[1] was and is thought to be a precondition of any solution to the territorial inequities of the city, in this case via a policy of decanting the ill-housed urban poor into suburban locations. This paper will argue that London has, despite metropolitan government, achieved no marked success in the redistribution of housing opportunities; "opening up the suburbs" seems as fraught with difficulties under London's metropolitan structure as in the "fragmented" cities of North America.

Each generation of London policy makers has characteristically seen the solution to the housing crisis as being just ten years away. By that token, the history of London housing policy is a history of failure; but neither the magnitude of the problem nor the policy measures that might relieve it are central to this essay. Rather, the concern here is with the political constraints on such an achievement; that is, with the inescapable

While the present paper bears a single authorship, it reports on work carried out during a fruitful collaboration with Professor John Kramer of the Department of Sociology, State University of New York, Brockport, during 1974–75. The research was funded by the Social Science Research Council and the Centre for Environmental Studies, London.

limits to the success of any redistributive housing strategy for metropolitan London.[2]

The first section reviews the twists and turns in metropolitan housing policy during the first decade of the new metropolitan system's life, 1965–75. The second section discusses the degree to which the attempt to formulate a workable "strategy" was hampered by the uncertainties surrounding the very meaning of that term; it describes the effects of political discontinuity in a field where the time horizons of policy greatly exceed the life of any single regime; and then it argues that even a metropolitan authority with a clear strategic purpose and medium-run political stability may lack the resources to implement a housing strategy. Finally, some observations are offered on alternative forms of metropolitan governance, and posed is the question of whether the concept of "strategy" is itself appropriate to the problems of urban policy in a complex society.

"OPENING UP THE SUBURBS": AN URBAN STRATEGY FOR LONDON?

The suburbs, argues Downs (1973), hold the key to the solution of the cities' housing problems.[3] The same view commands wide support among London politicians and is widely, but by no means exclusively, held by members of the Labour party. Equally significant, it has been consistently supported by the leading salaried officials of London's own powerful governmental bodies: the London County Council (LCC) and, since 1965, the more widely drawn Greater London Council (GLC).[4] Devoting their professional careers to the acquisition of land, the construction of low-cost rented housing, and the supervision of the families who occupy them, County Hall's permanent officials have for fifty years drawn invidious comparisons between the overcrowding and decay of the central areas, and the space and amenity of the outer suburbs.[5] Policies to "export" the inner city population to suburban sites have thus featured prominently in their plans to alleviate housing stress by rebuilding the inner area at more tolerable densities.[6]

Suburban governments and populations have likewise resisted these efforts in order to protect their local amenity, their social distance, and, in the case of the officials, their organizational boundaries. They have also consistently resisted proposals for metropolitan or areawide government, seeing a close connection between the maintenance of governmental fragmentation and a guaranteed social exclusivity.[7] Thus the imposition of a metropolitan structure by the national government under the Local Government Act of 1963 was strenuously resisted by the suburbs. Important concessions to suburban separatism were made in response: while they did not escape being encompassed by a new and directly elected GLC, suburban governments nevertheless retained very considerable local autonomy under the new act. Significantly, the powers of the GLC in the field of housing were drastically trimmed so as to diminish the threat of planned overspill of the inner city poor into the leafy gardens of Kentish or Surrey suburbs.[8]

Such powers as were vested in the GLC were ambiguous, temporary, and unworkable. Yet the broad presumption that the new authority had a definite areawide responsibility remained; it was to be a *strategic authority* in a "two-tier" governmental system wherein the local authorities remained as "the primary units of local government."[9] So ill-defined a situation contained unlimited potential for rival interpretations. Would the GLC operate so as to threaten or preserve suburban amenity? Clearly much would depend on its overall political control, for the Labour party was committed to a strong redistributive line.

The initial optimism of the suburban leaders on this score turned to dismay as they saw first the election of a Labour majority on the new GLC in April 1964, and then the election of a Labour government at the national level six months later.[10] Suburban fears that metropolitan and national authorities might combine against them were rearoused by the new government's commitment to give any support necessary to the GLC's Labour leaders against the London boroughs. The government also gave high priority to a massive public housing drive centered on the larger cities, and under ministerial pressure local governments were required to make substantial increases in their public housing programs.[11]

The new GLC's aspiration to the role of areawide reallocator of housing opportunities was also fortuitously endorsed by a committee of inquiry into the conditions of London housing. The Milner-Holland Committee report both revealed the magnitude of the London housing crisis and identified the GLC as the appropriate authority to aid the decaying inner areas by redistribution.[12] Overcrowding in the decayed inner area of London demanded that some out-migration be sponsored if the slums were to be redeveloped at tolerable densities. New sites for new development had therefore to be sought. In this way the striking disparities in the allocation of space to the various "housing classes"—and in particular the continued low-density development of "luxury homes" in the outer suburbs—emerged as major issues for public policy.[13]

With ex-LCC housing expert Evelyn Denington in the housing chair, the Labour GLC's first response to the situation was to emulate the LCC and attempt to acquire suburban sites for its own very substantial housing construction program. These intentions were immediately frustrated. The suburbs promised a determined resistance. The precise executive powers of the GLC were not clear.[14] The political costs of a direct confrontation with the suburbs were high, for such action would be predictably unpopular. Moreover, the outcome of such a confrontation, being subject to appeals for ministerial adjudication, was by no means certain.[15] Faced with pressure to produce quick results, the GLC policy was switched from site acquisition to the less-threatening strategy of negotiating access via "nomination rights" to a share of the small but recently augmented public housing programs of the independent and individual suburbs.[16]

The tactics of conciliation produced fewer returns than had been expected. By the time the Conservatives deposed Labour in the GLC election of 1967 the policy of negotiated access to the suburbs' own housing stocks had made only minimal and temporary headway. For the next three years the suburbs enjoyed their expected hegemony in London politics. Their autonomy was explicitly guaranteed by housing committee chairman Horace Cutler, a fervent and flamboyant advocate of market solutions. No attempts were made to open up the suburbs to the inner city working class, for the main thrust of Conservative GLC housing policy under Cutler was to promote privatization and social diversity.

By 1970 the very extent of the suburbs' success in maintaining their exclusivity began to count against them. The GLC housing officials, fretting under unaccustomed Conservative control, succeeded in sponsoring a study of the pattern of metropolitan housing needs.[17] The study was carried out by an intergovernmental body chaired by a senior civil servant from the Ministry of Housing and Local Government; and the study drew heavily upon data collated by the GLC itself.[18] The evidence was conclusive. The disparities in the housing conditions between the suburbs and the central city were *widening,* for suburban conditions were improving more rapidly than those of the inner area.[19]

The completion of the "housing needs" report early in 1970 coincided with another unexpected development, the election of a Conservative national government. While Conservative regimes at London's County Hall and in the suburbs had maintained exclusionary policies that favored the middle-class owner-occupier, the new Conservative housing ministers were reformist and interventionist in outlook. The new secretary of state, Peter Walker, adopted and published the housing needs report. County Hall's Conservative leadership, in tune with developments in the national party and aware of the explosive potential of the report, had meanwhile anticipated the changing political climate. Following the Conservatives' second successive GLC election victory, housing committee chairman Cutler was unexpectedly fired. His successor, Geoffrey Chase-Gardener, was more easily persuaded of the political and moral necessity of a major campaign to acquire suburban space.[20]

The next two years saw a critical struggle with the suburbs as the GLC, with strong backing from the central government, sought to acquire suburban land for working class housing. By 1972 the issue was resolved in the suburbs' favor. The Conservative suburban leaders had worked within their own party to defuse the threat. In a series of stormy meetings at Conservative Central Office they totally repudiated the policies of their national and GLC colleagues. Recognizing defeat, the ministers withdrew from the "political mine field" of London politics having achieved little. The GLC leadership, shaken by the display of suburban *force majeure,* reverted to the previous policies and dismissed the interventionist housing chairman, Chase-Gardener, in favor of a hastily promoted conciliator, Bernard Perkins. Once again the suburbs successfully maintained their exclusivity, and their intransigence was vindicated by a series of secretly negotiated "nonagression pacts" in which Perkins renounced the GLC's future rights to bid for suburban space. These guarantees—legally worthless but morally advantageous to the suburbs—were barely ratified by the local and metropolitan leaders before the 1973 GLC election, when control of the council once again fell into the hands of the Labour party.

With a Labour majority at County Hall, the recurrent threat to suburban amenity was once again renewed. The London Labour organization had moved toward a more interventionist stance during its six years of opposition. The new housing chairman was Gladys Dimson, an intellectual on the center-right of her party. She immediately advocated a strong areawide drive to open the suburbs. Her campaign was however unexpectedly delayed by internal political wrangles within the new Labour administration. Not until eighteen months had passed and Labour had returned to power nationally was it announced that the GLC had formulated a Strategic Housing Plan for the metropolis.

The plan took the form of a thoroughly researched analysis of the London housing situation and a package of proposals to remedy its deficiencies within ten to fifteen years.[21] For the suburbs the most threatening aspect was the promulgation of building targets for each sector of London; the outer suburbs were faced with a demand for massive increases in building. As London's *Evening Standard* commented:

> ... the implication is that leafy suburban boroughs with relatively few problems must build homes to rent for the families trapped in the overcrowded twilight areas of inner London.[22]

But the advertised confrontation between the GLC planners and the defended suburbs never materialized. Economic crisis overtook the hopes of the plan's supporters. A political upheaval within the ruling GLC Labour party in March 1975 led to massive cuts in the GLC housing program, the apparent renunciation of the plan, and the dismissal of the housing chairman who had sponsored it.[23] These developments insured that for the third time in ten years the threat of large-scale public housing in the suburbs was lifted.

Neither Labour nor Conservative administrations at County Hall succeeded in their sporadic attempts at a strategy of opening up the suburbs. Their failure was not, except in the most obvious sense, a failure of will; rather, the interventionist spirit encountered formidable obstacles: conceptual, temporal, and political. London's metropolitan government suffered during its first decade from multiple handicaps that may be broadly summarized under three heads: ambiguities of the strategic role; imperatives of political management; and deficiencies of implementation resources.

THE LIMITS OF STRATEGY

Role Uncertainties

The problems of operating a strategic authority on the metropolitan scale were entirely novel in 1965. There were no prototypes whose examples could be followed, nor was it easy initially to vest the concept of "strategy" with much substance. When eventually these difficulties were overcome and strategy, concretized in particular policies, it was discovered that other important actors in the metropolitan network dissented from those policies. With that discovery furthermore came the simultaneous realization that in the absence of firm line (or command) relationships, dissent could paralyze the new-found metropolitan purpose.

One problem in operationalizing a strategic role lies in the characteristics of the term itself. *Strategy* is difficult to conceptualize. The *Shorter Oxford Dictionary* defines the term unhelpfully as "the art of projecting and directing the larger military movements and operations of a campaign." At best a metaphor, *strategy* belongs to that vocabulary of politics wherein a maximum of appeal is combined with a minimum of substance, and in political life it tends to manifest itself in rhetoric or incantation.[24] That metropolitan strategy initially took a rhetorical form and was largely devoid of substance is attributable to the initial commission report on London government and its subsequent consideration.[25] It was seen as axiomatic that a distinction between strategic and nonstrategic functions could be made and that the metropolitan policy vacuum could be filled simply by the attribution of a "strategic responsibility" to the new GLC. When the crucial decisions were taken—between 1960 and 1965—few dissented from the proposition that "strategy" needed to be "done." There was little grasp even within academic circles, however, of *what strategy might look like.* So, with a convenient and glib circularity, strategy became "what the strategic authority will do" in an unconscious echo of Herbert Morrison's dictum, "Socialism is what the Labour government does."

The lacunae of "strategy" were most apparent and most troublesome in the case of the GLC's land use planning role.[26] The new authority was distinguished from its predecessors and from the existing higher and lower levels of government by its possession of an areawide remit. While there was no clarity as to *what* the GLC should do, few disputed that it should do *something* at the level of Greater London "as a whole." This image of a *strategic arena* derived its strength from the very structure of the metropolis. The fundamentals of London's urban form—its pronounced monocentricity and its physical discontinuity—had a deceptively direct impact upon the imagination and lent itself to simple diagrammatic representation; but the problems that remained were twofold. In the first place, the image gave no guidance, in concrete terms, as to how the management of metropolitan structure would be carried out. In the second place, the image was founded upon a myth of metropolitan containment.

By 1970, and arguably by as early as 1963, the claim that London was functionally separate from the rest of the South-East region was no longer plausible.[27] The attention of planners had already drifted from the metropolitan to the wider regional level, and the concept of a discrete conurbation land use and transportation "strategy" was discredited almost before the new system began to operate. The imperatives of regional planning dictated that choices at a high level of generality had to be made under conditions of uncertainty. The geographic scale and pattern of regional interdependencies, however, rendered the GLC a singularly inappropriate body to make them. Three successive regional plans compounded the initial role uncertainties of the metropolitan planners, uncertainties that were further heightened by the delayed preparation of London's own plan and its referral to lengthy, public, acrimonious, and inconclusive examination by an independent panel of inquiry.[28]

These role uncertainties were equally apparent, though perhaps less acute, in the field of housing. Here the GLC was to operate *both* in an executive capacity *and* as a "strategic housing planner." Nobody quite understood, however, what the second role entailed. With no agreed explicit and properly elaborated definition of *strategic purposes,* the initial leaders and officers of the GLC lacked any signposts as to how they should operate. There were no prototypes or precedents to guide them. Their confusion was enhanced by the nature of the transition from the old system to the new, in which a plethora of unresolved issues and temporary powers awaited them on April 1, 1965.

Both levels of London government had to work out their roles from scratch, and neither the statute nor the subsequent stream of circulars and circular letters that issued from Whitehall did much to help them. Intergovernmental relations are in any event a matter of informal rules and accepted procedures. To begin with, these rules and procedures had to be forged in experience. In the meantime, County Hall's policy makers, who retained the old housing powers of the LCC in Inner London, grasped at the one familiar role available to them and became the LCC "writ large." The housing department was necessarily dominated by ex-LCC officers, and their understanding of their role was echoed by the first housing chairman: "I was part of County government before. I continued to be part of County government. The problem was the same."[29]

Unhappily for County Hall policy makers the problem turned out to be very different, and their initial role regression generated embarrassment and conflict. For more than a century, London's borough politicians had sought radically enhanced status.[30] The new act gave them it and added real political muscle. County Hall officials and politicians (reflecting a possible tendency for organizational actors in situations of role uncertainty to revert to past, known patterns of conduct) soon discovered that the days of County Hall tutelage were over. A series of initial disputes established new precedents that favored the boroughs and led to new procedures to routinize future conflict episodes. Perhaps the most important by-product of this painful experiential role learning, however, was a sharpening of the mutual perceptions of government officials at both levels. As the unknowns in their relationship were filled in, the politics of breezy assertiveness gave way to the politics of wariness.

The wariness on the boroughs' part was well justified, for the GLC, backed by the political support of the Labour government and the moral authority of the Milner-Holland report, was finding a plausible strategic role in the much-publicized "London housing problem." The term *strategy* in common usage denotes an appropriate approach to a problem of unusual magnitude, complexity, and intractability; the qualitative and quantitative deficits in the London housing stock exhibited all of these characteristics. Largely concentrated in Inner London, it seemed an appropriate subject for GLC activity; but what the GLC officials knew, and what the suburban politicians soon discovered, was that the redevelopment of the decayed parts of the inner area would reduce densities there by as much as 50 percent on any site, creating an irresistible demand for "overspill" land. If housing stress was to be relieved, Inner London's population needed *Lebensraum.* The GLC, as prime actor in Inner London housing, demanded access to suburban space. In these circumstances, the emerging definition of housing "strategy" was inescapably *redistributive.* [31]

By 1967 the GLC Labour group felt able to declare that "the role of the GLC as the strategic planner and distributor of resources begins to become clear."[32] They failed to mention the marked incongruity between the role and the means available to its performance, for under this emerging concept of strategy, the GLC's sphere of intervention would have to be considerably wider than that granted under the statute. But Labour had missed its opportunity to seize such powers. The ministry civil servants who had drafted a memorandum on the GLC's proposed housing powers in 1962 had a clear and specific view of the need for the GLC to build "for the purpose of facilitating a proper distribution of population throughout Greater London" and "generally for the purpose of supplementing the housing efforts of the boroughs in the interests of Greater London as a whole."[33] They had accordingly proposed a system of building consents that vested enormous power in the GLC and in the minister of housing only to find it fatally repudiated by the defensive and influential suburbs and ignored by inner city Labour councils.

The problem for the Labour GLC in 1967 was *either* to seek the powers to carry out the role that the civil servants had earlier proposed and that they themselves had recognized too late in the day *or,* alternatively, to find yet another notion of strategy that was roughly commensurate with their powers. The first Labour council was however defeated before it could resolve the issue.

The election of a Conservative council enabled the problem to be shelved for three years. Horace Cutler's notion of "strategy" was not one of areawide redistribution but one of promoting movement among the existing tenure categories and so to diminish the social and fiscal significance of public housing. With his departure in 1970 the GLC housing officials resurrected the nascent concept of the GLC as an urban space reallocator, but the role was abandoned again two years later. In the Strategic Housing Plan of 1975 Gladys Dimson proclaimed a generalized *indicative planning* role for the GLC, a "strategy" possibly achievable within the framework of its existing powers.[34] Whether these powers were indeed adequate, however, was not put to the test. As before, a redistributive strategic consciousness had flowered late, and it was briefly admired before being fatally pruned. It could hardly have been otherwise, for the sine qua non of an effective reallocative purpose—continual and long-term political commitment—was never available.

Policy Discontinuity and the Imperatives of Political Management

One obvious reason why no past GLC housing chairman can look back with satisfaction on his/her period of office lies in its brief duration. Each chairman had his/her own distinctive interpretation of the GLC's "strategic" function. None was in office long enough to carry it through. Those interpretations embodied long-term ends and gradualist means. They were moreover discontinuous, indeed contradictory. A change of chairmanship signified a *reversal* of policy and the supersession of one concept of "strategy" by another incompatible commitment that simply happened to be dignified by the same term. The time horizons of any "strategy" were necessarily distant, but political discontinuity insured that those horizons were in no case approached. This was not a common experience in English local government. Very often the "permanent" salaried professionals and administrators provide the element of continuity during a time of changing political leadership. The first decade of the GLC's operation, however, saw departmental chiefs repeatedly overruled by their political masters. That was a new experience for County Hall officials.

The LCC, which had experienced only two changes of political control in seventy-six years and undisturbed Labour control from 1934 to 1965, had been able to pursue long-term objectives. In contrast, the GLC changed control twice in its first nine years. The six years of Conservative control served to almost halve the impetus of the Labour GLC's housing program; but it took years to lose momentum and even longer to build it up again. The life span of a single project could be anything up to ten years or more. Major changes in the direction of policy in what had become the largest public sector house-building machine in Britain (outside Northern Ireland) would take a decade to carry through. Such long-term goals as were envisaged by the GLC housing department officials crumbled in the face of the time horizons of the GLC's comparatively temporary regimes. Policies moreover were evolved, adopted, abandoned, and dismissed within the lifespan of a single regime, almost of a single chairmanship. No one chairman could count upon being reelected or reappointed; two of them were dismissed during the lifetime of their council, and one was moved from housing on reelection. Two were victims of a change of political control and would certainly have remained in their posts but for electoral reversals.

In 1965 Evelyn Denington, unable to make progress with suburban land acquisition, had opted instead for the immediate gains promised by rights to nominate tenants to the boroughs' own housing stocks. As the negotiations evolved, the policy acquired a longer term potential. The GLC sought to gain "a foot in the door," accept token concessions, and renegotiate later to a higher level of assistance. Recurrent negotiations to build a vast pool of nomination rights thus became the basis of Denington's latter-day "strategy." Ironically, there is little likelihood that nominations would have proved a successful strategic tool, even if GLC control had not changed before the negotiations were renewed. Nominations were for the boroughs a mere expedient, a short-term concession prudently to be made at a time of political vulnerability. The nominations policy moreover demanded continual and increasing pressure, for the initial apparent willingness of the boroughs to concede units to the GLC was dependent upon the supply surpluses of a short-term building boom.[35]

Horace Cutler's own aims were similarly foiled, despite his being the only chairman to run a full three-year term of office. The time horizons of his policies were very long term, for his overriding "strategy" was to bring about substantial shifts in the pattern of housing tenure. The cornerstones of his 1967–70 policies were a shift of emphasis from "council housing" to the quasi-public housing associations, and a program to sell thousands of council-owned homes to their occupiers. Cutler had insufficient time for his policies to have much impact. It was simple enough to get political agreement on expanded aid to housing associations, but it would take time for the housing association sector to mature sufficiently to cope with the task of implementing a program on that scale; nor could the sale of council houses be put into immediate full-scale operation, despite the extraordinary degree of preplanning that it enjoyed. The GLC, with its massive operations, could not move rapidly in the direction of expansion or contraction, and the sluggish pick-up of the sales program owed more to the administrative diseconomies of large-scale operation and to unforeseen technical problems than to any intrinsic lack of appeal.

Geoffrey Chase-Gardener, whose appointment in 1970 marked a cautious reversion to the Denington policies, was forced to operate on a short time horizon, for he was looking to the next GLC election as the deadline by which the housing program land bank and the nominations pool should have been restored. He was however frustrated in even this modest endeavor; he needed more time to persuade the recalcitrant suburbs to help County Hall. Once again the substance of strategy was changed before any results came forth. The abrupt abandonment of the redistributive policy commitment in 1972 left the incoming chairman Bernard Perkins with only a year in which to achieve *his* purposes. Perkins' policy aims were, in the long run, to encourage a multisectoral numerical increase in housing provision and, in the short run, to ease the pressure on the suburbs for land assembly. In some areas—the stepping-up of overspill to new and expanded towns, for example—Perkins was able to bring about sudden and significant changes in policy and to show early results. The 1973 election intervened, however, before Perkins was able to carry his policy redefinitions very far.

The fate of Gladys Dimson's Strategic Housing Plan provides the latest demonstration of time horizon disparities. For the first time London had, in concise and comprehensive form, a substantial, long-term, and area-wide housing policy covering most aspects of the housing system and providing for the participation of the major public and private interests. The time horizon of policy, at ten to fifteen years, was, however, incomparably greater than the life span of any incumbent of the housing chair. No previous policy had been maintained for more than three years. Interventionist commitments (and the plan was more radically interventionist than any earlier, less-formalized policy) had lasted no more than two years. To have any relevance as a set of guidelines or aspirations, the Strategic Housing Plan needed long-term political commitment. It could not afford to be the victim of partisan conflict or intraparty feud. Yet the plan, like its predecessors, was a victim of the imperatives of political management.

The major actors in what Holden has termed the "diplomatic system" of the metropolis are governmental bodies.[36] Yet any attempt to understand intergovernmental relations that treats these bodies in isolation from their political environments is doomed to failure. While governmental leaders have a statutory responsibility in fields such as public housing, they also have a responsibility for insuring that the electoral fortunes of their parties are properly considered and that their vital constituencies are attended to. In the politics of London housing, the imperatives of political management insured that the party activist, the loyalist voter, and the "floating" voter played an invisible, surrogate role in the wrangles over "strategy."

So it was that a coherent and consistent policy of shifting the public housing role to the private sector, to housing associations, and to would-be home owners was nervously abandoned in 1970 for fear that it provided the Labour party with powerful political ammunition. Similarly, long-term electoral calculations torpedoed attempts to agree to a mildly redistributive housing strategy within the coordinative and policy-making bodies of the Greater London Area of the Conservative party during 1972. Had they succeeded, the more disruptive effects of policy continuity could have been avoided and some degree of bipartisan policy could have been achieved. County Hall officials would have been enabled thereby to work within policy time horizons that permitted a sustained attack on London's housing problems. The great rift in the party from 1970 to 1972—the most severe policy crisis London Conservatives had experienced in this century —ended however in the triumph of the "localists," the suburban leaders and their County Hall allies, and was later consolidated by the election of Horace Cutler as Conservative leader at County Hall. From 1970 to 1972 the imperatives of political management had been thought to dictate an interventionist policy; this posture was designed to protect the Conservative party—liable as it is to charges of social indifference—from the electoral consequences of laissez-faire. The belief that the party needed to demonstrate its prowess in the public housing field or lose the uncommitted voter was however eventually swamped by the contrary view. This was that any attempt to open up the suburbs, even at the socially minimal but symbolically potent levels proposed, would put marginal seats at risk through the alienation of the party workers, would export a fecund proletariat to currently safe areas, and in the very long run would put their political control in jeopardy.

Whatever the real predictive merits of these several arguments, the Conservative Central Office managers needed party unity, and the dismissal of Chase-Gardener in 1972 was a precondition of its attainment. Incoming chairman Perkins' urgent remit was twofold: to restore party morale through conciliation and to devise a politically defensible housing policy that would simultaneously reassure both the socially concerned (but politically uncommitted) voter and the anxious suburban Conservative activist. Both were tasks for which Perkins, with his distinguished reputation in the housing field, was well equipped.[37] Party unity was impressively restored, though it made little difference in the 1973 election result; but the price of the restoration was the abdication, for some years to come, of any Conservative attempt to operate the GLC as an areawide redistributive agency.

The fate that befell Labour's Gladys Dimson was, in its essentials, not dissimilar to that of Chase-Gardener. Her party colleagues were acutely sensitive to London's marginality and were unwilling for that reason to support the costly and, in their view, electorally dangerous programs of acquisition, rehabilitation, and construction envisaged in the Strategic Housing Plan. A controversial and complicated scheme for the "coordinated allocation" of the housing stock on a London-wide basis was the sole and sickly survivor of the Labour party's internal feud. This however remained—as did the nominations scheme it was intended to replace—at best a complement to the substantial redistribution of urban space. The plan had been suppressed and much of its momentum and currency, sacrificed in the belief that it would harm Labour in the uncertain political environment of 1974. With London borough elections and two general elections taking place, the plan's opponents feared that it would cost Labour votes in marginal areas; and the publication and half-hearted adoption of the plan did little to extinguish those fears, which finally prevailed in the housing program cuts of spring 1975.

The perceived need to vacate a politically exposed position led Labour, like the Conservatives before, to give priority to political management. The electoral sensitivities of both parties' leaderships in London's delicately balanced political structure insured that the more vociferous suburbs, not themselves politically marginal, carried the day repeatedly and enabled them effectively to dictate the limits of metropolitan "strategy." Different leaders might of course have been more prepared to carry the inherently incalculable political risks of a policy to open up the suburbs, but the necessary conditions for such success are genuinely formidable and should not be underestimated. First, the leaders must be able to conceptualize a plausible sense of strategic purpose. Second, they must be confident of sufficient political continuity to carry through a program that would outlast several councils and probably outlive many of their own political careers. Third and ultimately, however, they must be sure that they possess the resources to implement their intentions. This last, the problem of implementation, transcends questions of political will; it is founded in the very structure of the metropolitan government, itself.

Deficiencies in Implementation Resources

The fervor with which the suburbs would resist attempts to implement a continual and concerted redistributive housing strategy may be gauged from the obstacles that County Hall interventionists encountered in trying to effect their modest policies. Even the nominations policy, which entailed the very minimum trespass upon local territory and maintained the symbolism of borough autonomy, was notoriously difficult to operate. That the GLC lacks the power that it needs to carry out its purposes is to radical critics self-evident, for it seems to them to be axiomatic that if the GLC had more power it would be more effective. This is a misunderstanding. While it is true that the GLC lacks statutory powers that would enable it to enforce policies rather than negotiate them, the notion of County Hall violating the normal diplomatic procedures and acting unilaterally in land use issues is farfetched. It overlooks the necessity for the GLC actually to bargain, negotiate, and manipulate the diplomatic network, if only in order to attain many of its secondary objectives.

Greater formal powers, perhaps along the lines of the 1962 memorandum, might have been granted to the GLC and still could be. Formal power is not however the crux of the issue of metropolitan effectiveness. The resource deficiencies of the GLC are not statutory but arise from a lack of *information* on local housing and land use situations, combined with a lack of *appreciation* of local political conditions.

County Hall's information deficiencies were particularly acute in the early years, and during 1965–66 the council's housing officials were called upon to justify specific local proposals—themselves derived from very general assessments of housing supply and demand in London as a whole —in terms of dangerously vague and challengeable data on local housing situations. During the period of the initial negotiations with the suburbs, the GLC housing policy makers were operating in the dark and explicitly relying upon an element of bluff in their negotiations.

A major function of the GLC was to build a data bank, and the land use surveys of 1966 and 1971 and the House Condition Survey of 1967 went a long way to remedying the data deficiencies. These were comprehensive surveys, taking nine months to a year to complete, and they provided a range of information never before available. They were augmented by the research work carried out for the Greater London Development Plan (GLDP), the GLC's major statutory responsibility.

The impact of these data nevertheless was minimized by the organizational context in which they were generated. In the first place, they became available for use only during the years of Conservative control from 1967 to 1973. Only briefly during this period were the housing department officials able to act as policy initiators and take advantage of the political confusion and dissension among the ruling Conservative group.

Far more important were the interdepartmental stresses within County Hall. Required under the statute to establish a research and intelligence unit, the GLC leaders had placed this unit within the powerful Planning and Transportation Department.[38] Vital data on housing conditions were thus available only within a department that rivaled housing in weight and authority. The top housing officials jealously guarded their organizational autonomy. Attempts by junior planning researchers to define policy options for housing were briskly rebuffed by the assertion that the director of housing alone had the statutory duty to advise the council on housing matters. In maintaining this role, the housing department distanced itself from the data generators, while the latter lacked the resources within the organization to bypass or circumvent what they saw as their formalistic, limited, and traditional housing colleagues.

In 1974 an important decision was taken, one that laid the foundations of the Strategic Housing Plan. The research function was moved from the allegedly roads-oriented planning and transportation department, recast as the policy studies and intelligence branch, and placed at the center of the council's structure, responsible to the director general, the GLC's chief executive. With complementary changes in the housing department's own top management, the GLC was by 1974 equipped to analyze and *use* the existing housing and land use data. The outcome was a linear programing exercise to analyze population, density, household size, distribution, housing stock, and occupancy rate data in the light of a range of exogenously determined constraints. From that exercise grew the Strategic Housing Plan, a formidable analytic and policy document.

The plan itself was not unchallengeable. It was based upon certain assumptions about local capacity that could be checked or verified only against local data provided by the boroughs themselves. In a series of joint meetings, the Conservative-led boroughs overturned many of the assumptions in the plan and demonstrated their own monopoly of the information necessary to produce a revised version; and the Conservatives were determined to withhold that data.

The GLC, then, was dependent upon the boroughs for much of its data collection and provision and lacked the political muscle to demand it. In some cases moreover the boroughs themselves failed to maintain a data base for their own domestic policies. An intergovernmental working group set up by the Conservative ministers in 1971 gave particular attention to this problem, but the group was at a loss to discover a means of persuading suburban boroughs to provide for GLC use data, which they themselves had no interest in collecting.[39]

In their negotiations with the boroughs, County Hall chairmen and officers were also handicapped by a sheer lack of appreciation of local values and interests. Often failing to understand, except in very general terms, what the present author elsewhere terms the "assumptive world"[40] of the local policy makers, they were unable to predict just what demands were unrealistic, just what incentives could usefully be offered, and just what issues could be negotiated, given skill and sympathy. The appreciative gaps between metropolitan policy makers and the local leaders who could block the implementation of policy denied to the former the opportunity of trading with the latter.

The metropolitan politicians operated within a set of their own assumptions, which amounted to a crude model of the forces that swayed suburban leaders. Conservative chairmen Cutler and Perkins, themselves former local council leaders, had an accurate grasp of the localist impulses that moved the suburbanites; but *they* were not attempting to impinge upon suburban territories. Those who were pursuing interventionist policies—in particular Denington and Chase-Gardener—had the greatest need to understand their opponents' positions. As pure "metropoliticians" their careers had provided them with the least opportunity to have gained that understanding. Their relations with the borough leaders were distant, and their characterizations of the local political situations in which they were attempting to intervene were often colored by the myth of the monolithic opponent. They could neither see the divisions within suburban councils where they existed nor appreciate the ideological congruity between suburban leaders and their followers. The policy of opening up the suburbs resembled in this respect the abortive federal land release program in the United States, where failure to grasp the realities of local politics in a number of diverse settings led to the formulation of idealized policies that were easily deflected.[41]

From the metropolitan leaders' inability to appreciate the texture of suburban politics arose the suburban politicians' major tactical asset. A reliance upon procrastination, disguised as protocol, could enable local leaders to outwit and outmaneuver most of their intergovernmental opponents. They could delay and protract the bargaining process while operating quickly and flexibly on the home policy front, for example by placing compulsory purchase orders on sites for which the GLC was negotiating or by making rapid policy decisions on specific site use.

In some suburbs, the decision system had undergone a process of modernization and change, leading to a considerable centralization of policy making. Here the local leaders, confident of political support, could introduce new policies at short notice, channel resources toward them, and develop them rapidly. In the case of domestic policies that impeded the metropolitan policy makers—accelerated land assembly for use by private developers, for example—this flexibility gave the local leaders a distinct edge on the GLC and national government.

At the same time the unwelcomed pressure from higher level agencies could be treated with excessive and unreal formality. A local leader, conscious of his real local power, could pretend a show of deference to his council and initiate a lengthy process of formal committee and council consideration and reconsideration, a process that would move *yet more slowly* where management reforms had extended the cycle of committee and council meetings.[42] The niceties of protocol—indispensable when, as in this case, the protagonists were independent and constitutionally established governmental bodies—were not lightly violated by either partner, and this formalism operated as a distinct disadvantage to the demanding body. Any direct and personal appeal could be brushed aside with reference to the protocols of policy making, and metropolitan or national policy makers had no way of penetrating this ponderous process. When the metropoliticians moreover tried to break the deadlock by unilateral action, the local leaders proved themselves to be capable of swift and decisive response.

THE PROBLEM OF METROPOLITAN GOVERNANCE

Uncertainties, partisan conflicts, political change, and policy discontinuities insured that no serious and sustained attempt to open up the suburbs was made during the first decade of London's metropolitan experiment. The suburban leaders moreover showed great tactical resourcefulness in deflecting challenges to their exclusivity and in wresting concessions from fatigued national and metropolitan leaders. The years 1965 to 1975 were a decade of frustration for London's metropolitan policy makers. The alternations in London housing policy and the recurrent offensives against the suburbs served both to heighten the awareness of the basic conflicts of interest between the differing social areas of the conurbation and to increase the sensitivities as well as the abilities of the defended suburbs. There is no reason to suppose that another decade of those alternating policies would bring about a reallocation of suburban space. Indeed, while the inner city dwellers are denied access to the outermost areas, the process of private sector development and redevelopment continues there, consuming the shrinking land supply and enhancing the opportunities for the longer distance commuter to move inward and settle his home and family in London's pleasant fringe.

On the other hand, suburbia's trump card—that the planned redeployment of working class homes *and jobs* to the new and expanding towns makes better sense—is no longer the ace it once seemed. With the retreat from overspill in recent British government policy, the spotlight shifts once again to the role of the suburbs in London's future; but it should not be assumed that policies to open up the suburbs will enjoy increased support thereby. The pace and scale of employment and population loss in the inner city is already shifting attention from housing conditions to more broadly based measures to maintain the vitality of the urban core.[43] The previous panacea for the inner city population—relocation—is now seen as more deleterious than the ills it sought to cure. Some pressure to open the suburbs will nevertheless remain.

What then might be done to increase the effectiveness of metropolitan housing policy? Leaving aside the question of the desirability of reallocating power or even that of the desirability of changing the social composition of the suburbs, there exists a range of options. The ability of any of them to facilitate the opening up of the suburbs, however, is at least doubtful. First among them is the reinforcement of the GLC's powers. This does not address the question of effectiveness, for the GLC's resource deficiencies are political. Its relation with the other governmental bodies is diplomatic; that relation will not be fundamentally altered by adding *powers* (as distinct from *power*) to County Hall. If the reinforcement of the GLC's powers is ruled out as irrelevant to the deficiency of political resources, the more radical option of the abolition of the boroughs as independent entities remains. A revival of this old Edwardian radical policy would transform the local authorities into the creatures of the metropolitan council.[44] While it certainly addresses the question of implementation, it can hardly be considered feasible. As the history of London government has shown, a certain threshold of bipartisan tolerance has to be reached if any institution is to survive in the long term. It cannot be doubted that both the Conservative party as a whole and very substantial numbers of

Labour members currently active in local political life would be totally opposed to such a change. Political acceptability apart, there is no convincing reason to believe that even a "Gargantuan" authority would enjoy unimpeded progress toward the reallocation of urban space. Rather, it would in all probability encounter fierce resistance from local communities where ordinary residents, deprived of their protective suburban councils, would find themselves necessarily engaged in direct action to preserve the amenities of their areas. The reverberations of such encounters between Gargantua and the grass roots are unknown but almost certainly unwelcome.

If a revival of old centralist policies provides no solutions they may yet be found in sweeping structural change along localist lines. Under the much-discussed "Powell plan" of the early 1950s, areawide planning in the London region (a wider entity than the existing conurbation) would be carried out by a representative body drawn from all the local authorities in the region, operating much as the contemporary Standing Conference on London and South-East Regional Planning does today.[45] Beneath this intergovernmental umbrella would exist just a single tier of local government, large and powerful London boroughs. The novelty of that proposal (and the feature that led to its rejection by anxious local leaders in 1954) was that borough boundaries would be arranged so as to provide approximate balance of needs and resources among the boroughs with a fair chance of political control accruing to either political party.

The Powell plan was drawn up as a response to Conservative dilemmas in the old LCC area, but its logic is perhaps even more applicable in Greater London as a whole. Under a resurrected "Powellite" scheme the role of the areawide planning body would be recognized as no more than advisory (or at best indicative). With the virtual abolition of the GLC, decision power would be formally placed where it is indeed ultimately exercised, in the Department of the Environment, or perhaps, as has been proposed by the London Conservatives, in the hands of a minister for London.[46] The metropolis, with the exception of the crucial and functionally unique central area, might then be redivided into perhaps a dozen large boroughs radiating from the central area boundary to the suburban fringe, great wedges incorporating the entire range of social areas from decaying urban core to spacious residential suburb. With such a population balance, the radial boroughs would enjoy rough political balance and periodic alternation in political control. Each would have the unequivocal and independent responsibility for housing its own population. Each might have a Labour group in office periodically with a power base in the inner part of the "wedge" and a strong incentive to relieve housing conditions there by rippling out population to the less-dense areas. The style of local politics would certainly be far more acrimonious than is the case in most of the thirty-two separate areas at present; but the reallocation of space among the diverse housing classes would be high on the agenda of local politics.[47]

The remaining options have the advantage of requiring little change in the existing governmental structure. First among them is the creation, alongside the GLC, of a specialist areawide housing authority, modeled on the Northern Ireland Housing Executive.[48] This proposal is widely, if covertly, discussed among London politicians. This does not mean, however, that a consensus might emerge on such an agency. Its supporters on the Right see it as a means of insulating public housing from partisan control, as permitting an eventual shift of emphasis in housing policy toward other forms of tenure, even as reviving the moribund private rental sector. On the other hand its supporters on the Left see the possibilities of a unifunctional agency, throwing off the County Hall heritage and relentlessly confronting London's housing deficits and inequities. What this latter expectation overlooks is that effective housing powers entail some control over land use decisions; in the London case (in contrast with the Ulster case) these would remain a local prerogative.

That a single housing executive for London would be hamstrung by its isolation from key local land use decisions prompts the conclusion that any areawide housing plan is doomed to failure unless it brings the implementation agencies—the local boroughs—into the planning process, itself. If *strategy* denotes "direction," then the very concept should be allowed to wither away. In its place might be sought the long-term collective, cooperative, collaborative agreement—necessarily bipartisan—that is a precondition of effective action in the housing policy field. This final option might be best termed *concertation.* [49]

Concertation recognizes that the metropolis is composed of major interests that must be directly involved in the policy process, not merely for the purpose of consultation but as *collaborators in decision.* The range of actors included in this network would include the governmental and quasi-governmental as well as the nongovernmental and would be determined by the potential of an agency to aid or block any policy otherwise made by a metropolitan elite. Thus concertative policy would contrast with the system wherein areawide "strategy" is decided by regional officeholders and imposed upon—or deflected by—the local authorities. Rather, decisions would be bargained with them and a consensus, established that, in its reflection of existing interests, would fall far short of idealized strategic aims but that would enjoy a high probability of implementation.

The possibilities of such an approach to housing strategy are not new, and there is a growing awareness that housing planning in Greater London's second decade will have to be a more cooperative activity than was the case before 1975. The recent and rising hopes of concertation may, however, in turn prove hollow. Bargaining is carried out most successfully when the distribution of resources between the contestants is roughly equal. In the case of metropolitan housing policy a large number of bargaining partners may reach agreement on a plan that a very small number can effectively veto. London's outermost suburbs, which have a virtual oligopoly in relation to land supply, are the least likely to cooperate in any strategy that threatens their territorial integrity. Their "votes" are thus heavily weighted, and they are certain to be negative. Any collective housing plan agency, furthermore, that attempts simply to proceed on a majoritarian basis will, of course, find itself in the GLC's position, subject to the same resource deficiencies, outmaneuvered and deflected by nimble suburban politicians with very high stakes to fight for.

Is there then any case for retaining the present, and much-criticized, governmental arrangements for Greater London? As the present author has argued elsewhere (Young 1975a) the metropolitan future is likely to alternate between unitary and federalist solutions, and the move now seems to be one toward a loosening of London's "federal" structure. More generally, as London's experience demonstrates, governmental forms do not necessarily produce desired or expected outcomes. Alternative structures, however, do embody or define alternative *feasibilities*. The radical reallocation of space, whether desirable or not, is probably not feasible, for it cannot be achieved by intergovernmental bargaining.

The experience of metropolitan housing policy points to a gloomy verdict on the efficacy of metropolitan government. Jurisdictional integration is not a sufficient condition for the solution of metropolitan problems. Rather, it may be an impediment to successful action by national governments. Ministers are loath to intervene in metropolitan affairs when a nationally appropriate authority already exists. Yet it is arguable that they could deal more effectively with local resistance, since they are less politically dependent upon local support. Their legitimacy moreover is less likely directly to be challenged. With three tiers of government operating upon the urban scene, the much-vaunted metropolitan level is caught between local interests and national policies. Inevitably, it is the former that prosper in the political vacuum arising from metropolitan integration.

NOTES

1. For the support for "metro" in the United States, see particularly Sayre and Polsby (1967). The London parallels are explored in Young (1975b), and some more general reflections are offered in idem (1975a).

2. A fuller account of the material presented here is given in Young and Kramer (1978).

3. The title of this section is deliberately intended to evoke Downs' polemic against the U.S. suburbs. The problems of suburban land use are discussed also by Rubinowitz (1974), Bergman (1974), and Danielson (1976), among others. One of the few important works on London's housing is Harloe, Minns, and Isacharoff (1974).

4. For the institutional arrangements of London government see Rhodes (1970; 1972). A thorough and penetrating discussion of the legal and administrative aspects of the division of power in metropolitan London is given by Gelfand (1975).

5. The continuing theme of city-suburb relations in metropolitan London is central to a full-length history of London's governmental politics, *The Politics of Metropolitan Governance: London, 1855–1965* (London: Edward Arnold, forthcoming).
6. This issue achieved prominence following the war damage of 1914–18 and 1939–45. The regional planning initiatives of 1946–47 deflected the threat of large-scale out-migration to the suburbs by adopting a strategy of urban containment. See Hall (1973).
7. This argument is developed further in Young and Kramer (1978; 1977).
8. The proposals for metropolitan integration were contained in the Report of the Royal Commission on London Government. They were initially modified by the government to minimize opposition to the plan, and further attenuation of the powers of the proposed GLC proved necessary to mollify the suburbs. Thus while the boroughs are the "primary" authorities with the responsibility for meeting local housing needs, the GLC has powers to build only for its own purposes (rehousing the displacees of highways developments, for example), for certain comprehensive redevelopment purposes, for "overspill" to relatively distant towns. In addition, the GLC possesses some ill-defined "temporary" powers to meet general needs within greater London.
9. This phrase was formulated in the Royal Commission's report and has since proved a rallying cry for the defense of local—and especially suburban—autonomy. See Herbert (1960).
10. The GLC was elected in April 1964 but did not begin formal operation until April 1965. The "transitional year" was one of careful sparring between the would-be adversaries.
11. In London as a whole, public housing programs increased on an average over 80 percent. Some councils had their plans cut back by ministry civil servants; others were persuaded to aim for higher targets. The program was announced with a flourish in autumn 1965 but fell far short of realization.
12. The committee was established in the wake of a major scandal concerning slum landlordism in London. See Holland (1965).
13. The Holland report drew eloquent comparisons between the inner and outer areas, juxtaposing aerial photographs of localities with residential densities of 200 persons per acre and 20 persons per acre.
14. The GLC retained the powers of the former LCC in inner London for an unspecified temporary period. Plans for a transfer of housing to the boroughs were to be made and submitted by 1970.
15. Under sec. 21(5) of the London Government Act of 1963 the GLC could acquire sites for building within the area of a London borough with the permission of that borough or, failing that, of the minister of housing and local government.
16. The essence of this scheme was that the GLC bid for the right to nominate families to vacancies created both by new building and by relets in the local housing stocks. A percentage of vacancies, varying from 10 to 15 percent, was chosen as a reasonable initial target, and comparable proportionate help was sought from each of the independent suburbs. The local governments of the inner area were thus to obtain relief from their own local housing stress by drawing, via the GLC, on this central housing pool. The "nominations scheme" proved a source of considerable initial conflict between the GLC and the suburbs. Strenuous diplomatic efforts resulted in the establishment of a very modest pool of vacancies, which thereafter declined over a seven-year period to an inconsequential level. See Young and Kramer (1978, chs. 3–6).
17. The chief salaried officials of the LCC housing department had long records of service with the council in its era of Labour control. Only J. P. Macey, the director of housing, had any experience of the policy reversals that normally follow changes in partisan control in English local government. In addition, these officials were committed by their professional ideology to a major role for public housing in a program of social reform. Although constitutionally nonpartisan, several of them have privately expressed an allegiance to the Labour party. While they were not—at least at the higher levels—disloyal to their new political masters, they were distressed by some of the new policies and sought a reversion to the traditional objectives of their organization.
18. The study was nominally carried out by the Standing Joint Working Party on London Housing, a body composed of salaried public officials from Whitehall, the GLC, and the London borough councils.
19. The report revealed that the level of housing deficiency—that is, the excess of potential

households over available accommodation—ran at 12 percent for Greater London as a whole in 1966. The degree of deficiency varied from 7 percent in the southern suburbs to 20 percent in Inner North London. The pattern of generally substandard housing reinforced the pattern of numerical deficiency. Current trends revealed a faster rate of improvement in the suburbs than in the inner area. The projections to 1974 indicated that some outer suburbs would be in a notional surplus situation by that year, while shortfalls and vast tracts of inadequate housing would remain in the inner area. The report called for "a new initiative" to tackle these growing inequities. See Ministry of Housing and Local Government (1970).

20. Chase-Gardener had very little political experience but had served as vice-chairman of housing under Cutler. Emotional, and with a strong social conscience, he found himself in close accord with the housing department officials, who saw him as their most valuable "lever" with the leadership.

21. The plan was published as a "discussion document" and accompanied by a substantial Report of Studies describing the research base of the proposals. See GLC (1974). For a critical analysis of these proposals see Nevitt (1975).

22. The plan's appearance was delayed for some months following its completion; the reasons for this are discussed below. The *Evening Standard* comments followed the "leak" of the plan to the *Standard* in an attempt to force the GLC leadership's hand. Until that moment, the plan's existence had been publicly denied. Following the *Standard's* revelations the plan's existence was conceded and arrangements were made to publish it in autumn 1974.

23. The leadership group were anxious neither to make the financial commitments that the plan demanded nor to upset suburban voters. Huge expenditure cuts were forced upon Gladys Dimson, the housing chairman, who was dismissed for failing to accept them. Taking the issue to the majority Labour party group she challenged the leaders and narrowly missed victory on the crucial vote of confidence.

24. *Strategy* may of course have a clear and accepted meaning in a particular context. Analytic writing often identifies a strategic dimension in policy making. Friend and Jessop (1969), for example, understand strategy as inherent in certain public choice situations, specifically, those in which there is uncertainty in related fields of choice. Hence purposive planning is a process of *strategic choice.* This sense they see as being bound up with contingency expectations and as being akin to "strategy" in chess and military campaigns.

25. For contemporary comment on the Herbert report, see Self (1962) and McIntosh (1961).

26. For a searching critique of the land use planning system in metropolitan London, see Self (1971). An analysis of the significance of the urban motorway proposals, centerpiece of the Greater London Development Plan (GLDP), is given by Hart (1975). A basic discussion of metropolitan structure is given in Ash (1972).

27. From the early 1960s academic planning theory came to abandon the very concept of metropolis for the "urban field" and "megalopolitan" notions. See, for four very different statements of the same disavowal of metropolitan containment, Goheen (1971), Dyos (1968), Friedman and Miller (1965), and Hall (1973).

28. The three regional plans were the *South-East Study*, carried out by the Ministry of Housing and Local Government and published in 1964; A *Strategy for the South-East*, the first report from the South-East Economic Planning Council published in 1967; and, published in 1970, the *Strategic Plan for the South-East,* a report of the South-East Joint Planning Team established by the ministry, the planning council, and the Standing Conference on London and South-East Regional Planning. These reports were based on contrasting assumptions and bore varying implications for regional policy. The GLC's GLDP was published in 1969; the following year the secretary of state announced that it would be referred to a special tribunal of inquiry chaired by Mr. Frank Layfield Q.C. The Layfield report was published in 1973 and went to the Department of the Environment for decision. In October 1975 the secretary of state announced his verdict on the several aspects of the GLDP and Layfield's appraisal.

29. Dame Evelyn Denington, in an interview with the author. For the numerical and positional dominance of ex-LCC officers and councillors in the new GLC, see Rhodes and Hastings (1972).

30. For the history of this consistent and eventually successful demand see Young (1973; 1975b).

31. The changing orientation of the GLC housing policy makers is discussed in Young and Kramer (1978).

32. In anticipation of the 1967 GLC election campaign, this statement was made by the

Labour leaders in their annual report to the London Labour party conference in 1966.

33. For the story of this surprising Whitehall bid to equip the GLC with sweeping powers, see Young and Kramer (1978).

34. For the classic discussion between "indicative" and "directive" planning in economic policy, see Schonfield (1965). The experience of French planning influenced the conception of the British Department of Economic Affairs National Plan of 1965, which in turn served as a mode prototype for London's Strategic Housing Plan in 1974–75.

35. The limited concessions made to the GLC normally represented 10 percent of relets and new lettings in the local housing stock. This was not too costly in terms of local resistance, as the ministry-inspired new building programs had just been approved; but to maintain even this modest numerical help would have required pressure for increasing proportionate help in subsequent years. The powerful London Boroughs Association advised that all agreements be made for two years only.

36. This proposition of Holden (1964) and the related attempts to discuss metropolitan intergovernmental relations in terms of models of international integration are discussed further in Young (1975a).

37. As leader of the Lambeth Borough Council (from 1968 to 1971), Perkins had gained widespread admiration for his dynamic and innovative housing policies. As a "borough man" and an ideological localist, he was also well liked in the outer suburbs.

38. For the proposals to establish a research and intelligence unit for the GLC, see Rhodes (1970, pp. 71–72) and Sharpe (1965). The fate of the unit is described in Griffin (1975).

39. The "Action Group" established by the Conservative ministers was intended to resolve the disputes between the GLC and the suburbs by reinforcing the GLC/ministry line. Borough representatives were also appointed to the group, which remains in existence and over time has issued a number of reports.

40. For elaborations of this concept see Young (1977a) and Young and Kramer (1977).

41. For this comparable case, see Derthick (1972).

42. Since 1967 local governments in England have been exhorted to reorganize, streamline, and centralize their decision-making systems. For a general review of these developments see Richards (1975).

43. Growing pressure from inner city Labour politicians led in 1976–77 to a reversal of the thirty-year-old policies of planned overspill. During the previous decade, manufacturing employment in Greater London had fallen by more than a third. A new wave of concern for "the inner city" is marked by a redeployment of public funds, new interventions by local authorities in their local economies, and a rapid reorientation of intellectual interest. For an excellent review see Inner City Working Group (1977). Some general points concerning the economic management role of local government are made in Young (1977b).

44. Work is continuing on the larger scale history of the politics of metropolitan reform. A short review of the Victorian, Edwardian, and contemporary debates is given in Young (1975b).

45. For a brief discussion of the Powell plan and subsequent Conservative schemes see Young (1975b) and Young (1975c).

46. The Conservatives' response to the Labour victory at the 1973 GLC election and to the long-term threat to the political control of London presaged by Labour's housing policies, was to reconsider their stance on London government. For Geoffrey Finsberg's plan to redistribute decision powers among the three levels of government, see Young and Kramer (1978).

47. This has occurred in those outer suburbs where socially disparate areas have been merged. In Hillingdon, where Labour and Conservatives have alternated control, plans for public housing in middle-class areas aroused bitter controversy, despite which Labour held narrowly on to control in 1974. In Croydon a growing Labour vote, concentrated in the inner parts of this borough, was accompanied by demands that the low-density outer parts be used for the relief of housing stress. The Labour party has not managed to take control of Croydon at the time of the present writing. Should it do so, a Hillingdon-type situation is likely to emerge. See Saunders (1975).

48. The Northern Ireland Housing Executive, established in 1971, is "the United Kingdom's first comprehensive regional housing authority. It has powers and responsibilities covering the whole field of housing and is not merely a body which manages publicly owned property. Its duty is to assess housing need, to study the entire housing stock with a view to preventing neglect and decay, and to produce a programme for new building and rehabilitation and improvement, so that in due course good housing will be available to all." The executive

assumed the housing functions of sixty-one local authorities, three development commissions, and the Northern Ireland Housing Trust. It has a stock of more than 140,000 houses. The nine-man executive is the authority, but there is also a large housing council on which each of the superseded local authorities has a representative. The chairman, vice-chairman, and the majority of the executive members are appointed by the minister but are obliged to consult with the Housing Council not less than once a year about its housing program. Certain local authority land use powers are exercised by the Northern Ireland Office to facilitate the executive's work. The appeal of this body to London Labour politicians is obvious; moreover, the first director general of the executive was Harry G. Simpson, subsequently comptroller of housing, GLC.

49. For a discussion of "concertation" in economic planning, see Ionescu (1975) and Coombes (1974). Arguably, the concertative policy mode rests upon a particular vision of society as neither conflictual nor consensual but as *consociational.* Consociational leadership is provided by an accommodating elite, and its expectations of problem solving are low. For a discussion of the concept (which originates with Robert Dahl), see Lijphart (1969).

REFERENCES

Ash, M. 1972. *A guide to the structure of London.* Bath: Adams & Dart.

Bergman, E. M. 1974. *Eliminating exclusionary zoning.* Boston: Ballinger.

Coombes, D. 1974. "Concertation" in the nation-state and the European community. In Ghita Ionescu, ed. *Between sovereignty and integration.* London: Croom Helm.

Danielson, M. M. 1976. *The politics of exclusion.* New York: Columbia University Press.

Derthick, M. 1972. *New Towns in-town: Why a federal program failed.* Washington, D.C.: Urban Institute.

Downs, A. 1973. *Opening up the suburbs: An urban strategy for America.* New Haven: Yale University Press.

Dyos, H. J. 1968. Agenda for urban historians. In H. J. Dyos, ed. *The study of urban history.* London: Edward Arnold.

Friedman, J., and Miller, J. 1965. The urban field. *Journal of the American Institute of Planners.*

Friend, J. K., and Jessop, W. N. 1969. *Local government and strategic choice.* London: Tavistock.

Gelfand, D. 1975. Conflict and resolution in politically decentralized local government. *Columbia Journal of Law and Social Problems* (summer).

Goheen, P. 1971. Metropolitan area definition: A re-evaluation of concept and structural practice. In Larry S. Bourne, ed. *The internal structure of the city.* New York: Oxford University Press.

Greater London Council (GLC). 1974. *A strategic housing plan for Greater London.* London: Greater London Council.

Griffin, A. 1975. *Research and intelligence in the Greater London Council.* Master's thesis, Kent University.

Hall, P. 1973. *The containment of urban England.* London: Allen & Unwin.

Harloe, M.; Minns, R.; and Isacharoff, R. 1974. *The organization of housing: Public and private enterprise in London.* London: Heinemann.

Hart, D. A. 1975. *Strategic planning in London: The rise and fall of the primary road network.* Oxford: Pergamon Press.

Herbert, Sir E. 1960. *Report of the Royal Commission on Local Government in Greater London, 1957–60.* London: HMSO.

Holden, M. 1964. The governance of the metropolis as a problem in diplomacy. *Journal of Politics* (August).

Holland, Sir M. 1965. *Report of the Committee on Housing in Greater London.* London: HMSO.

Inner City Working Group. 1977. *Inner area studies: A contribution to the debate.* Birmingham: At the University.

Ionescu, G. 1975. *Centripetal politics: Government and the new centres of power.* London: Hart Davis, MacGibbon.

Lewis, J., and Weiner, S. 1975. The view from the districts. *British Medical Journal* (5 July).

Lijphart, A. 1969. Consociational democracy. *World Politics* (January).

McIntosh, M. 1961. The Report of the Royal Commission on Local Government in Greater London. *British Journal of Sociology* (September).

Ministry of Housing and Local Government. 1970. *London's housing needs up to 1974: Report no. 3 of the Standing Working Party on London Housing.* London: The Ministry.

Nevitt, D. A. 1975. Towards a Greater London Housing Strategy. *London Journal* 1, no. 1 (May).

Rhodes, G. 1970. *The government of London: The struggle for reform.* London: Weidenfeld & Nicolson.

————. 1972. *The new government of London: The first five years.* London: Weidenfeld & Nicolson.

Rhodes, G., and Hastings, S. 1972. The Greater London Council. In G. Rhodes, ed. *The new government of London: The first five years.* London: Weidenfeld & Nicolson.

Richards, P. G. 1975. *The reformed local government system.* London: Allen & Unwin.

Rubinowitz, L. 1974. *Low income housing.* Boston: Ballinger.

Saunders, P. 1975. They make the rules: Political routines and the generation of political bias. *Policy and Politics* (September).

Sayre, W., and Polsby, N. 1967. American political science and the study of urbanization. In P. Hauser and L. Schnore, eds. *The study of urbanization.* New York: Wiley.

Schonfield, A. 1965. *Modern capitalism: The changing balance of public and private power.* London: Oxford University Press.

Self, P. J. O. 1962. The Herbert report and the values of local government. *Political Studies* 10.

————. 1971. *Metropolitan planning.* London: Weidenfeld & Nicolson.

Sharpe, L. J. 1965. *Research in local government.* Greater London Paper no. 10, London School of Economics.

Young, K. 1973. The politics of London government, 1880–1899. *Public Administration* (spring).

————. 1975a. "Metropology" revisited: On the political integration of metropolitan areas. In Ken Young, ed. *Essays on the study of urban politics.* London: Macmillan.

————. 1975b. The Conservative strategy for London. *London Journal* 1, no. 1 (May).

————. 1975c. *Local politics and the rise of party.* Leicester: At the University Press.

————. 1977a. Values in the policy process. *Policy and Politics* 5, no. 3 (March).

————. 1977b. Environmental management in local politics. In Richard Rose and Dennis Kavanagh, eds. *New trends in British politics.* London & Beverly Hills, Calif.: Sage.

Young, K., and Kramer, J. 1977. Local exclusionary policies in Britain: The case of suburban defense in a metropolitan system. In Kevin R. Cox, ed. *Urbanization and Conflict in Market Societies.* Chicago: Maaroufa Press.

————. 1978. *Strategy and conflict in metropolitan housing.* London: Heinemann.

CHAPTER 12

CITIES WITHOUT POWER: THE TRANSFORMATION OF AMERICAN URBAN REGIMES

Stephen L. Elkin

A striking feature of the politics of large American cities over the past twenty-five years is the number of changes in style and substance that they have in common. Also striking are the similarities in the pattern of urban politics that emerged in the post–World War II period. A real understanding of contemporary American urban politics must rest on analysis of the origin of these common features and the sources and dimensions of changes in them.[1] In any explanation of these changes and commonalities, aspects of the national political economy will play a central role. A conception of urban politics is required that allows for the impact of national changes affecting cities in common as these changes operate over time. This paper, then, will focus on the concept of urban regimes and will analyze the pressures making for stability and change within these regimes. A case is presented for the decisive importance of national developments in explaining the major shift of urban political patterns that took place in the last half of the 1960s, as the "pluralist" regimes of the postwar period came under attack. Two major changes in the national political economy—an alteration in social structure and a change in the economic functions of the city—are related to conflicts over land use and the character of the public bureaucracy. These changes converged, producing coalitions of hitherto poorly or totally unmobilized elements whose claims concerning the control of land use and the public bureaucracy threatened the pluralist regimes. Also, some attention is given to regimes other than pluralist ones, and variation in the impact of national forces is briefly noted.

URBAN REGIMES

An urban regime is principally defined by the pattern of interests included and excluded from the exercise of governmental authority. Among those included, some will be more politically active than others. Those included need not be equals; regime members with interests in a given policy area may be able to influence events outside their focal interests and others may not.[2] The more active and influential members (senior members) may be organized in a variety of ways, ranging from a small, tightly knit elite to an inclusive coalition operating through a complex accommodation process. In addition to the establishment of such a pattern of leadership, an enduring regime also requires: a stable electoral base[3]; functionaries who help implement any policies adopted and who work to maintain its electoral foundations[4]; the ability to draw on widely shared values that legitimate its position and confirm the worthiness of its purposes[5]; and the continuing acquiescence of those excluded from the regime and/or those who play an extremely limited role.[6] To the degree that all of this is accomplished, the pattern of inclusion will be relatively stable, and one may speak of a fully realized regime.

It should be emphasized that the composition of leadership elements need not coincide with the strata and classes from which the regime draws its principal electoral support. Indeed, those who provide a substantial portion of the votes may play little or no part in governing. Conversely, leading regime members may not speak for any visible group, and their value thus will clearly depend on something other than command over votes.[7]

The sources of stability and change in urban regimes may be classified by their major constituent elements. They may be considered under factors that enhance or retard: cohesion of leadership; the acquiescence of those excluded; the loyalty of functionaries; a shift in electoral allegiance or diminished participation of classes and strata providing the principal base of the coalition's support; and the potency of the symbols from which the regime draws its legitimacy. Each of these regime elements may be affected not only by local actors and processes, but also by actors whose aim is national political power and by national processes. The impact of national actors and forces on regime decline is the principal concern of this essay.

A general urban analysis would require consideration of regime creation and maintenance and a definition and explanation of periods of regime dominance, their decline, and interregnums—in short, an explanation of regime transformation. Significant moments in urban politics would then be seen as those in which there are conflicts over the principal elements of existing regimes and in which there are struggles to create new ones.[8]

THE PLURALIST REGIMES

In the larger American cities, particularly those in the Northeast and Midwest, what may be termed *pluralist regimes* were substantially realized during the 1950s and the first half of the 1960s. These regimes were created in older industrial cities with ethnically and racially heterogeneous populations whose politicians had sufficient organizational resources to be independent figures. The newer cities of the South and Southwest evidenced regimes with some similar characteristics, but the differences were substantial enough that these cities need separate treatment.[9]

The primary feature of the pluralist regimes was an inclusive coalition that dominated land use questions, particularly those linked to the economic vitality of the downtown area.[10] These regimes are enshrined in the period's urban politics literature, from whose pluralist emphases comes the name "pluralist regimes" (Dahl 1961; Banfield 1961; Banfield & Wilson 1963; Wolfinger 1974; Sayre & Kaufman 1960). There are important differences from such accounts, as will be evident below.

The senior partners in these regimes, the coalitions concerned with land use matters, derived their "seniority" from influence they brought to bear in other policy areas while persons in the latter were largely unable to return the favor (Mollenkopf 1975; Lowi 1967). The coalitions were by no means able to determine decisions in domains other than land use, however; and indeed a principal feature of the regimes was the relative autonomy of the functional bureaucracies and their associated interest groups (Lowi 1967; Sayre & Kaufman 1960, chs. 8, 11). This pattern was reflected in the budgetary process: incremental adjustments were made to departmental budgets for the previous year, with the departments and their group allies having a principal voice. There was little attempt to redistribute resources from one department or policy to another (Crecine 1969; Meltsner & Wildavsky 1970).

The pluralist regimes were made possible because the land use coalitions did not need to dominate all domains in order for their members to serve their central interests. Had the coalitions not been able to define focal and peripheral concerns, it is possible that the regimes would have foundered. If decisions in areas such as education, police, fire, or health care were seen to have been fundamental to economic growth, particularly that of the downtown area, the political difficulties of promoting central core expansion might have been insurmountable.[11] The regimes' pluralism revolved, then, around such functional autonomy; it did not center on vigorous bargaining and debate over policy questions with easy access for affected interests and a shifting cast of characters. The principals in each domain were a more stable set, and the decision-making process was less visible and permeable than at least a crude pluralism suggests.

The coalitions' focal concerns were to reshape the land use patterns of the city, particularly downtown, and to improve transportation into the business district. Implementation of both concerns was needed to promote economic growth, secure investments already made, and insure the tax base of the city. The context of these interests was a widely shared sense that the economic foundations of the city were starting to shift away from an industrial base (Mollenkopf 1975; Hoover & Vernon 1959) and that any substantial outflow of jobs, commerce, and high-status/high-income taxpayers was bound to be pernicious to those who had substantial economic and political interests in the city. An indicator of the general problem was limited tax bases built on slowly growing (and occasionally falling) land assessments in the postwar period. Adding to the dilemma were the rising costs of capital investment and service provision (Mollenkopf 1975). Reshaping land patterns would provide more efficient movement of workers and goods, eliminate blight and poor housing, make for more attractive physical surroundings for business, provide housing for higher income taxpayers, and generally strengthen the tax base of the city. Overall the concern was to manage a shift from the industrial city to a city in which business headquarters and related service functions as well as high levels of private consumption might flourish (Harvey 1975; Mollenkopf 1975).

The inclusive nature of the coalition is indicated by a list of the major partners. In addition to the principal elected officials, spokesmen for organized interests were an important component, with businessmen's organizations being the most active of the latter (Salisbury 1964; Mollenkopf 1975). The elected officials included reformers who had recently taken over city halls (e.g., in Philadelphia, St. Louis, and Detroit)[12] and regular party politicians (e.g., in Chicago and Pittsburgh). In spite of their differences, they shared an uneasiness over fiscal difficulties and the loss of middle-class citizens.[13] They had three other things in common:

1. If the mayors were not reformers, they were persuaded that good government is good politics; and thus at least a show of concern over the use of expertise, efficiency, and honesty was of substantial electoral importance—the image of a corrupt machine politics required refurbishing (Banfield & Wilson 1963, ch. 9).

2. Mayors, sometimes with the help of officials adept at land assembly and gaining federal funds (in New York, Moses was likely the central official actor), played the key broker role, performing such services as getting principals together, inducing compromises, and arranging implementation of agreements.

3. Both reformers and party politicians had independent electoral standing; businessmen and other interests that wished changes in land use patterns needed to gain their cooperation. They could not be easily captured and in some cases took the lead in setting the agenda (Dahl 1961; Wolfinger 1974; Banfield 1961; Salisbury 1964). In general, the mayors were either elected on a platform of revitalization and reform or they realized the soundness of being a leading party to such efforts as a means of insuring success at the polls.

Land use professionals played some role in the coalition in all cities as their expertise in design, land assembly, the intricacies of burgeoning federal assistance, and other areas was required. It is important to distinguish between those—like Moses and Logue—who were as much brokers as experts (Mollenkopf 1975) and the less-important and visible officials, who were executive functionaries. The importance of both types varied among cities. Each type was less important in strong party cities, where party heads could handle the brokering role and suspicion of professionals was likely to be high; while in cities where there were either reform mayors or weaker parties (or both), they had a larger role.

A variety of businessmen were involved in the coalition: typically, those in real estate and the major investors in the downtown, including department stores, banks, insurance companies, and industries with central city headquarters.[14] Organizations specifically devoted to renewal were formed (e.g., in Pittsburgh and Philadelphia), and public committees were created in which businessmen and government officials could reach agreement (Dahl 1961; Wolfinger 1974). In some cities, businessmen were more-or-less-equal partners with mayors and their lieutenants (notably in Pittsburgh and Philadelphia); whereas in others, elected officials were more powerful (notably in Chicago). (See Lubove 1969; Petshek 1973; Banfield 1961.) In no case does it appear that businessmen determined the agenda or the substance of decisions. (This situation is unlike that which existed in the cities of the Southwest, for example; and the difference, as will be indicated below, weakens the value of the comparison.) Given, however, a large degree of agreement on ends, the substantial legitimacy accorded to economic growth, and the general prestige of businessmen at the time (see below), major conflicts did not develop with enough frequency to enable any judgment to be made over who would prevail. The variation in relationships between businessmen and elected officials probably depended a good deal on the relative cohesion of the former and the strength of the electoral organization of the latter (Banfield & Wilson 1963, ch. 18).

Party leaders comprised another important element of the coalition, both in cities where there were reform mayors and in those with regular party mayors. In the former, this element represented the leadership of the party that the reformers for the moment had displaced (Reichley 1959); and in the latter, it represented party figures other than the mayor. In both cases of particular importance were those on the city council, whose consent would be needed at various junctures in the renewal process.[15] In cities where the party still controlled the mayoralty, joining the coalition would help forestall electoral challenge as the incentive for downtown businessmen to finance challengers was reduced. In cities where there was reform, so long as party leaders were not cut off from patronage, the long-term prospects of regaining control of the city hall were reasonable and the short-term costs bearable. Reform typically did not reach far into the bureaucracy, and reform mayors were likely to devote a substantial portion of their attention to land use matters, giving less time to areas of the city administration that were of greater interest to party officials (Petshek 1973). In addition, in all types of cities, councilors and party officials with ties to particular neighborhoods were not excluded from land use decision making (see below).

While there was substantial agreement about the general need to re-shape land use and revitalize the downtown, project decisions were also required. These were largely made through bargaining and negotiation among coalition partners; disagreements typically did not become social-ized, mobilizing other actors and drawing in the larger public. As noted, where residential neighborhoods were involved, city councilors and party officials concerned with the areas were bargained with, and the expecta-tion was that the agreements reached would be implemented without substantial neighborhood resistance (Gans 1963; Banfield 1961). One of the important emollients of the bargaining was a politics of ethnic recogni-tion in which slating procedures provided symbolic satisfactions for the many and material rewards for the few. Ethnicity here operated as a conservative force, making it less likely that citizens would give extensive attention to substantive issues, particularly redistributive questions (Wolfinger 1974, ch. 3). Arriving at agreements was also made noticeably easier by the availability of federal urban renewal (especially after 1960) and highway funds (Mollenkopf 1975). The impact of renewal on local budgets was thus reduced, particularly as local contributions could be "in kind."

The electoral and administrative functionaries of the regimes pre-sented few problems. The relevant bureaucracies might be expected to implement bargains struck among coalition partners, while the adminis-trative functionaries working in peripheral areas were operating in rela-tive autonomy and providing at least minimally acceptable service with-out intense conflict. Even among those functionaries who were party regulars operating under reform control, most were not under great pres-sure. In the parts of the bureaucracy that were of principal concern to the coalition, any disaffection by party regulars could be compensated for by the allegiance of land use professionals, whose employment opportunities had greatly expanded and who were now in a position to exercise skills that had been developed over many years (Hardin 1971, ch. 1). An in-crease in professionalization of at least the parts of the civil service con-cerned with land use would also increase the loyalty of bureaucrats con-cerned with upgrading their status. Overall, the sense of expansion and movement, especially as compared to the thirties, must have promoted allegiance. As for electoral functionaries, the central point is already ap-parent. So long as no serious attempts were made by reformers to weaken parties, party regulars might be expected to work in tandem with them. Where there were regular party mayors, clearly the loyalty of electoral functionaries was less of a problem.

The electoral base of the regime, and particularly the support for downtown revitalization, was comparatively broad and stable. Positive support came from upper and middle-income home owners, for whom increases in the tax base held the promise of steady or even reduced property taxes and a halt to what was perceived as the deterioration of the city. The same applies also to businessmen, even smaller ones who were not partners in the coalition. (The principal exceptions were those in renewal areas, particularly if they did not receive adequate compensation.) Liberally inclined voters—especially in the earlier years of the regime, before it was clear that the principal burden of renewal was being borne by the less well off (Gans 1966)—also were a major source of support, as renewal promised an improved housing stock. Those who suffered the principal costs of reshaping land use (largely lower income minorities living at the edge of the central core) provided substantial passive support —often in exchange for the favors and friendship traditionally provided by big city parties—by continuing to vote for party candidates or reformers bent on renewal. Others were excluded from even the minimum participation of voting and thus from the regime. Such exclusion did not depend only on the vicissitudes of poverty, but it was helped along in some cases by the limited interest displayed by party organizations, particularly with regard to black supporters (Piven & Cloward 1971).

Legitimizing the major lineaments of the regime were two sets of values, one emphasizing the prestige of businessmen and a conception of the good city as growing larger and wealthier (boosterism is the extreme version) and the other focusing on the virtues of expertise and professional autonomy.[16] In comparison to the present, for example, in the 1950s and early 1960s the value of preserving "life's amenities" (Williams & Adrian 1963, ch. 10) and the virtues of more equality apparently were held in lower esteem than business activity, with its promise of increased affluence. In many ways related to the high regard for business activity and its fruits, was the value accorded to experts who were supposed to improve the functioning of the city. Altering land use merely in the service of increasing the tax base would be unlikely to garner as much approval as if this was part of an overall set of expert recommendations on reshaping the city. Expertise also carried with it the implication of autonomy; and while this might not be realized in land use areas, it could be served by relatively autonomous functional bureaucracies headed by persons of substantial repute.

Origins and Antecedents of Pluralist Regimes

The pluralist regimes, and particularly the land use coalitions at their center, emerged to deal with the fiscal and economic difficulties of the older, industrial cities. But if the only things the cities of the Northeast and Midwest had in common were their fiscal and economic characteristics, a good deal more variations in political patterns would be expected. A complete analysis of the common characteristics of the pluralist regimes requires an examination of the political material from which they were formed and particularly of how they arose from the urban politics of the 1930s.

A list of the major elements of city politics in the 1930s would include: the strengthening of industrial unions, which was attended by intense conflict with owners and managers and which was associated with visible class conflict (Elkin 1978); the struggle, sometimes violent, over relief payments for the unemployed (Piven & Cloward 1971); the heightened role of banks in local affairs as financial stringency increased (Gelfand 1975); the shift in party control in some cities from Republicans to a combination of machine and New Deal Democrats and, where Democrats were already in control, an addition of New Dealers (Kilson 1971); and the uneasiness of many local businessmen over shifts in party control of city halls, which may have prompted withdrawal from local politics by some, while fiscal crisis and class conflict activated others. The general picture one gets is of an unsettled politics, of struggle, with relief payments and class concerns being important and new major groups being mobilized. Perhaps the best formulation would be of an interregnum between the earlier urban regimes—which reached back into the late nineteenth century—and their pluralist successors.

That the urban politics of the thirties is not to be considered under the heading of the earlier regimes can easily be seen by noting a few of the latter's main features. The appropriate adjectives for these earlier regimes and their politics would seem to be *conservative* and *particularistic* (Wolfinger 1974; Katznelson 1976; Elkin 1978). The urban working class was tied to local politics through divisible rewards, often of a material kind, thereby making collective action aimed at class ends more difficult. In much the same way ethnic conflict was diminished. The most important political formations were machines, originally built up from territorial alliances, which often worked in close connection with local businessmen (Shefter 1976). The machines emphasized personal advancement, mostly through corrupt practices, neighborhood rewards, and ethnic recognition. A politics was created in which (1) the conflicts surrounding intensive industrialization, extensive immigration, and migration from the South did not dominate the public agenda and (2) mass democracy did not seriously shake the foundations of industrial capitalism (Shefter 1976; Katznelson 1976; and Elkin forthcoming).

The close of the depression, the blunting of the New Deal, the return of high levels of domestic investment, and the wealth and prestige accruing to businessmen from World War II—all were important in allowing a major assertion of the latter's interests in local politics. On the other hand, industrial unions as they became more secure found local politics less important and left the field to craft unions tied to local economies (Banfield & Wilson 1963, ch. 19). And, contrary to what is often asserted, it is probably the case that in some cities local parties were strengthened and machines even created with the help of New Deal largesse. This allowed local politicians to contemplate vigorous action to repair their economies[17] and made them more attractive allies for businessmen. It was out of such elements that the pluralist regimes were created; and, as the brief description suggests, the crucial transition was from a politics in which conflict over relief payments, class divisions, and economic decline were important factors to one in which such antagonisms were muted and economic growth was seen as possible.

Entrepreneurial Regimes

As noted above, in cities of the South and Southwest the political pattern differed from that in the cities of the North. Most importantly businessmen played a far larger part and politicians a smaller one. Altogether the features differed enough so that the big city politics in these regions cannot be counted as pluralist. A brief description of the political character of Dallas will suggest the outlines of the more general phenomena.[18] Dallas and other large cities, at least in the Southwest, may be said to have had "entrepreneurial" regimes.

The most revealing beginning point is an examination of the interests of the major business figures of Dallas. In contrast to their counterparts in the North, investors in the city were not concerned with using governmental authority to reshape land use patterns. Private capital was plentiful, as was space to build, and relatively easy annexation of outlying land could keep tax revenues within the city boundaries (Nathan & Dommel 1977). If the private sector could remain unfettered—with occasional exercise of zoning controls to facilitate or protect investments—and if a climate conducive to substantial investment—particularly honest, efficient government with low tax rates—was produced, then the important goals of businessmen would be served. Starting in the early 1930s, major business figures in Dallas, in fact, joined to form the Citizens Charter Association (CCA) to serve just such aims.

From the early 1950s to the mid-1960s (and indeed somewhat before and after), the CCA was able to dominate the electoral process. By offers of financial support and other types of assistance, the organization was able to select a slate of candidates for the city council who, given the need to run at-large and without party organization, had few if any organizational and financial alternatives. The same applied to the mayoralty, which, although essentially a full-time job, paid $50 a week, more or less assuring that only persons with some other source of income could run. The CCA was also able to enforce a rule denying a candidate for council support more than twice, thus helping to prevent any councilman from building up much expertise or personal organization. The result was a city council and mayor acceptable to business leaders.

Given its success in recruiting appropriate public officials, the CCA felt little need to intervene directly and consistently in local decision making and was more or less invisible between elections. Where matters of direct concern to businessmen were at issue, a business organization, the Citizen's Council, or other ad hoc alliances carried on the negotiations and raised the funds. For the most part, the day-to-day affairs of the city were left to the professional manager and his staff. The loyalty of executive functionaries was largely achieved through a professionalized local government service. Had local businessmen felt they needed more than an attractive business climate (for example, had they wanted substantial use of governmental authority and resources), the importance of elected officials and the loyalty of executive functionaries would have risen.

The electoral support for the regime probably came largely from upper and middle-income home owners financially secure enough to absorb the costs of economic growth. The costs in any case were likely to be small, and these groups had much to gain from low property taxes and efficient services. The participation of Mexican Americans (and blacks) was sufficiently limited that they could be considered as excluded from the regime. Economic dependence—and, for Mexican-Americans, scattered residence and unfamiliarity with English—all contributed to this state of affairs.

The prestige accorded to businessmen, the high value set on economic growth, and the use of businesslike management in local affairs—all undergirded the regime. Spokesmen for the interests of workingmen and the values of trade unionism would, in comparison to their northern counterparts, have found stony ground. Altogether, the success of the regime in Dallas depended not on conspiracy and manipulation by businessmen but on sufficient control of the electoral process to insure a local government conducive to business aims.[19] One important consequence illustrated in the Dallas regime was that politicians were protectors of professional managers rather than brokers putting coalitions together. Another was that entrepreneurial efforts proceeded more or less unimpeded.

PRESSURES ON THE PLURALIST REGIMES

The decisive political phenomena for an analysis of the stability of the pluralist regimes are what may be called the "struggles" for control of land use and of the public bureaucracy. The consequences of these struggles, where they became intense (typically starting in the late sixties), were a substantial weakening or destruction of the regimes and an ushering in of an interregnum. In other cities, the struggles were either less intense or were deflected. In these cases, the regimes continued with some alteration or they were effectively reconstituted. The urban riots by themselves did not markedly weaken the regimes: that required mobilization of previously unorganized or weakly organized interests.[20] The struggles themselves with their attendant mobilization need in turn to be explained. Particularly, the sources of the mobilization in developments taking place in the national political economy need examination, as well as how the various strata and interests became active political formations. The study will turn to these topics after a description of the conflicts over bureaucracy and land use.

The struggle for control of the public bureaucracy typically involved burgeoning disagreement over criteria of recruitment and, thus, what population groups would be favored and what standards used for promotion. Also at issue was the manner in which groups would be served (Bellush & David 1971; Fainstein & Fainstein 1974; Piven & Cloward 1971). The urban bureaucracy had long been a focus of conflict, largely over matters of patronage, professionalism, and civil service reform as well as political advantage for the groups associated with various stands on these matters (Shefter 1978). In the late 1960s however not only had new issues been introduced (particularly the treatment of clienteles), but the struggle was more intense and public, involving a larger number of actors and engaging the attention of a much larger portion of the citizenry.

The principals in the struggle were civil rights organizations devoted to black interests. Particularly when agitating for better treatment for minorities, they were assisted by welfare rights and educational associations and, in general, by what may be called "adversary professionals." Prominent among the latter were lawyers working for community legal services programs. Also important were planners and health care professionals. The defense of bureaucratic practice was most often taken up by street-level bureaucrats, organized through municipal unions (Lipsky 1976), who comprised the principal subject of attack. Organizations serving municipal employees of particular ethnic and racial backgrounds were also involved, as were heads of bureaucracies who were worried about meeting their responsibilities and maintaining professional standards, and organizations with established relationships worried about competition for bureaucratic access. Also concerned were mayors and chief administrative officers, who were anxious about the political consequences of a struggle between clients and bureaucrats. Foundations, state officials, and legislators also became involved in extreme cases such as New York's, where the conflict spilled out into the streets and produced deep bitterness. It was in the course of these struggles that proposals for decentralization were advanced, partly as a way of diffusing conflict and stemming the decline in legitimacy of city institutions and partly out of despair of improving the situation (Altshuler 1970).

By the later 1960s, the struggle for control over land use made it increasingly difficult for any significant capital investments to be made in cities. Major downtown building as well as building in the residential neighborhoods were called into question. Urban renewal projects (Mollenkopf 1975) as well as highways (Lupo, Colcord & Fowler 1971) came under attack. Sites ended up lying fallow and cross-town and commuter routes were abandoned. Major urban institutions such as hospitals and universities found it increasingly difficult to expand, and their actions were often interpreted through a rhetoric of white racism and the need for black defense. Conflict over land use was not a new phenomenon; and, indeed, when racial questions were central, the conflict could be intense. If public housing controversies are laid aside, however, in contrast to the postwar period in particular and perhaps going well back into the century, the conflicts in the 1960s mobilized a higher percentage of the population and were of greater intensity.

In addition to those persons and organizations previously noted in the discussion of land use coalitions, the other major participants in the land use conflicts were a wide array of neighborhood groups. In black neighborhoods, organizations in part stimulated by antipoverty programs and requirements of citizen participation were created or strengthened. Working class white neighborhoods also evidenced increased organization, often with an ethnic cast (Lupo, Colcord & Fowler 1971). Recently renovated, middle-class neighborhoods, many heavily weighted with younger professionals, became activated as highways and other civic projects threatened the immediate environment, promising a halt in expansion and a deterioration of what had been recently won. Once again, adversary professionals were important in bringing court cases, preparing alternate plans, and helping to organize. Even projects that did not threaten neighborhoods (for example, those in the central district), became the subject of controversy, often with a coalition of neighborhood associations and public interest lawyers arguing that public funds should not be used downtown when there were more pressing needs.

THE IMPORTANCE OF THE NATIONAL POLITICAL ECONOMY

What has just been described may be called "mobilization": strata and interests previously inactive politically become active and engage in struggle over public policy and the division of public benefits. The role of organizations—both newly created and existing ones—was central. In addition, alliances were formed and new tactics, particularly protest-related ones, employed. In all this, the assistance of professionals employed by public agencies or subsidized by public money was prominent, and a new set of leaders was thus introduced.

The central theoretical question in the analysis of mobilization is captured by the observation that new strata may arise and interests may be formulated, but political action of any consequence may not follow. This suggests that analysis must be of an historical kind[21] and particularly that major attention should be given to organizational formation, which is clearly a prerequisite for understanding coalitions, leadership, and tactics.

There is also the need to consider the intimately related question of how the broad claims of the strata were sharpened into the demands and programs that were the ostensible purpose of political action.

The particular story to be told here concerns the consequences of the combination of a vulnerable urban population with social strata in the process of making extensive political claims. The rise of young, well-educated professional strata and their black allies constituted a shift in the national class structure. The presence of a deprived population was in part at least a consequence of a general shift in industrial location and attendant economic activity that had its principal impact on older cities. Thus the roots of the mobilization are to be found outside the city in developments over time in the national political economy.

Flowing from these national developments, two streams of mobilization can be identified: one primary and of major consequence, the other at least partly derivative of the first and of somewhat lesser impact. A substantial part of the organization, coalitions, leadership, and new tactics evidenced in cities flowed from an alliance between blacks and the new professional strata; and the progeny of this alliance range across both the struggles for control of land use and bureaucracy. The second stream—a heterogeneous grouping involving neighborhood ethnic groups and young, middle-class types as well as public employees—was the partial offspring of the first. It made defensive responses to the protests of black organizations and their allies, emulated tactics, and made use of new rules created in response to black-new class activity. Its efforts were modest, as they did not involve an attempt by a strata to invest itself in the political order. In contrast to the first stream of mobilization the primary but not exclusive focus of the organizations involved was the struggle over land use. No more will be said here about this second stream, but its importance should not be underestimated. The intensity of the struggles over land use and the bureaucracy would have been noticeably lower without the involvement of these groups.

The New Class and the Blacks

The mobilization of blacks and the new professional strata and its relationship to changes in the national political economy require further attention, particularly the development of common interests and consciousness and the process through which claims of each strata were sharpened and developed. It is also necessary to understand how organizations that pressed these claims and programs were created and the necessary alliances, consumated. The conjunction of the rise of this "new class" and its black allies (Bazelon 1964; Shefter 1978) with the large, economically weak populations in the cities provided one crucial step in the transformation of the two strata into important political claimants. The development of mutual understanding among leaders was another important step, which led to mutual assistance and finally to the achievement of support from national Democratic politicians and other elites that was necessary in order for adequate public funds to be available. The public treasury would be used to join local activists and adversary professionals of both colors and the organizations they could create, to an alliance at the center built around new class professionals and liberal Democratic leaders.

Little can be said here on a topic as complex as the coming to political consciousness of blacks except to note that the highpoint of its expression is associated with an increase in economic independence for at least some sectors, making political action possible and various kinds of remaining restrictions intolerable. The new class as a strata, however, requires more discussion, if only because it has been less often analyzed.

The rise of the new class encompasses a mixture of ideology, a need for employment, a desire for power, and a concern for electoral advantage. The leading elements of the class were liberal professionals who, starting with the Kennedy administration and flowering under Johnson, saw the opportunity to make a significant impact on national domestic (and foreign) policy.[22] The late 1950s, when many of them were on university faculties, was a barren time for departures in social welfare policy, and one can imagine the exhilaration of the Kennedy task forces as the new agenda was formulated. If, for these people, the concern was access to power (Shefter 1978), for their somewhat younger counterparts employment was as important. The expansion of higher education and, particularly, the emergence of a large, well-educated, liberally inclined group, often of urban origins, meant the need for an increase in intellectually based jobs. It would be implausible to say that the increase in government social services at all levels and, for example, of satellite jobs in universities and research firms was planned in order to accommodate these strata. The conjunction of circumstances being discussed here made it possible. Without the expansion, a quite different kind of political conflict might have ensued than in fact did, and it would likely have been of a less-productive character. The kind of employment that did transpire moreover fit the inclinations of these young professionals, and they provided part of the constituency to support its continued expansion. The younger members of the new class staffed the organizations, on the top of which their elders passed into the seats of power. It need be added only that a significant portion of all these were Democrats, an alteration in the composition of the party allegiance of the professional strata (Ladd & Hadley 1975, ch. 5).

As noted, the major economic consequences of the movement out of the city's industrial activity provided an important link in the mobilization of the two strata just described. As the attempt was made to transform the city from a center of production to a consumption unit and service center, that portion of the urban population for whom public services were an essential part of their real income and for whom public jobs became increasingly valuable (if they could be obtained) remained at least constant and was perhaps enlarged. On the one hand, the continuing and accelerating mechanization and (dare one say) the collectivization of southern agriculture meant an influx of persons who could have benefited from industrial employment. On the other hand, what they increasingly found was an economy in which many of the available jobs were in the competitive low-wage sector (O'Connor 1973). Part-time work, unemployment, below-poverty-line wages, and discouragement were often the lot of those who came and for those already there.[23] Equally important, the economic shift of the city prompted the changes in land use patterns discussed above, eventually affecting a wide variety of the city's population, particularly neighborhoods composed of blacks, ethnic groups, and young, middle-class types, the first of which groups is of concern here. Central city blacks, then, were not only economically vulnerable but subject to being moved about as a consequence of redevelopment. A population was created (1) for whom the urban public sector had become and was likely to continue to be a major source of costs and possible benefits and (2) for whom political action aimed at an expansion of public services and government jobs might be made to seem compelling.

This aggrieved, insecure, and politically receptive population provided the basis for a program, a specification of interests, for strata that might otherwise have floundered and had inchoate notions about what they desired and how to get it. A potential clientele was at hand and a set of programs to serve them could be designed, the achievement of which would also provide benefits to the new class, blacks able to staff them and some measure of political power.[24] The coincidence of a shift in the economic functions of major cities—and the attendant deprivation—with bids by two major groups for greater political power was thus central for mobilization.

For black leaders and blacks, generally, having interests was one thing: having organizations to promote them was quite another.[25] Common interests did not guarantee collective action. To understand the manner in which the dilemmas of collective action were overcome, a brief statement of its requirements is necessary. Once this is done, the nature and significance of the black-new class alliance becomes apparent, as does the need for cooperation between the latter and national Democratic politicians.

The problem of collective action is to discover when rational individuals will contribute to the provision of a public good. The centerpiece of the existing theoretical work is that in many circumstances these individuals will not realize a return for their contribution that will exceed its cost and that will be over and above what they otherwise would receive; and they will thus not contribute (Olson 1965). What requires explanation here, then, is why, contrary to much argument, the provision of public goods— ranging from stopping road and urban renewal projects to more equitable treatment of clients and more public jobs for blacks—elicits contributions. These may be given in return for *private* goods such as money and jobs as well as to assuage guilt or to satisfy a sense of duty.[26] All of these were at work, but it does not seem reasonable to explain the creation and maintenance of the organizations at issue largely on this basis.

Collective action for the provision of public goods involves consideration of the following: factors associated with the perception of the desirability of cooperation for collective purposes; factors that affect the value individuals attach to public goods as well as the cost of achieving them; and factors that affect the sharing of costs to achieve the goods.[27] Under each of these headings considerations can be adduced that enhance (or retard) the possibility that a subset of a larger group will undertake to provide a public good from which the others will benefit.[28] In other terms, a variety of factors may be listed that will make it rational for enough individuals to contribute so that the good will be provided and the whole group will benefit.

With these broad considerations in mind, three points are of particular importance in fashioning an explanation of the heightened organization of blacks: (1) a credible ideology explaining the present and future position of urban blacks (and blacks, generally) was required not only to promote a sense of collective identity but also to increase the value of marginal returns to those who contributed; (2) the costs of organization needed to be reduced and the ease of cost sharing, increased; (3) divisible benefits needed to be found for those unwilling to contribute to the provision of a public good.

All of these were forthcoming with the assistance of the new class, providing one essential link in the black-new class alliance. Black leaders elaborated an ideology arguing that the fate of blacks was a collective one from which individuals would find it difficult or impossible to escape. Either collective action directed at government should be taken or the community's well-being would decline. The alternatives to employment in the public sector were poor or nonexistent; there were few if any alternatives to adequate public services; and alternative neighborhoods were significantly worse. In such circumstances, where individual alternatives are severely circumscribed and collective decline is imminent, even small gains in the direction of preventing deterioration are deemed valuable. Just as important, in terms of creating the alliance as the elaboration of an ideology, was the support provided by new class spokesmen; i.e., by experts and others of comparatively high status. Their statements substantially enhanced the credibility of the analysis offered by black leaders. Also with the major assistance of the new class, new federal rules were instituted (and old ones expanded) that provided requirements for participation of the minority poor and that called for greater receptivity to citizen views among local bureaucracies. These changes reduced the cost of organization. Similarly, with new class help, federal programs to support emerging and existing leaders and to provide jobs, other material benefits, and prestige for the minority poor were created (Greenstone & Peterson 1973).

Another major link in the black-new class alliance was the assistance provided by black leaders to the new class in the latter's efforts to stake out significant political territory. An alliance with growing black organizations that aimed at aiding victims of social injustice provided the cloak of legitimacy. It also provided a potentially large complement of votes that might be put in the service of national politicians as well as a ready-made coterie of local leaders who could help carry out any programmatic or policy tasks.

The Importance of National Democratic Politicians

The crucial link in the entire central-local alliance built around black-new class cooperation was the assistance provided by national Democratic politicians. Public money was required to support the programs that would provide the basis for the new class rise to political power, the resources for local black leaders and their white allies, and programmatic assistance to the poor. The definition of interests for both blacks and the new class provided by the consequences of the changing economic status of the city, and the aid each could provide the other would count for little without support from the center.

Foremost, professional politicians needed to be convinced of the electoral advantage of subscribing to the institutionalization of the new class. In part, Kennedy and Johnson saw the advantages in terms of continuing New Deal programs and solidifying that coalition (Bazelon 1964); but more was at issue, since the principal focus of the proposed social welfare programs was urban blacks who, while they voted strongly Democratic, were not singled out for any particularly substantial attention by previous Democratic candidates or officeholders. Piven and Cloward (1971, ch. 9) suggest that members of the Kennedy and Johnson administrations wished to insure that the blacks, who continued to arrive in the large northern cities, voted Democratic in national elections.[29] (Most would not have previously voted, although their sympathies would be Democratic.) The combination of the disappearance of the Solid South and the limited interest displayed by local parties in recruiting and promoting blacks made the problem of some consequence and the solidification of their support through programs promoted by the new class, particularly as blacks were already mobilizing, an attractive proposition.

If there is added to this amalgam the support of some major corporate leaders for at least some social welfare departures (Bazelon 1964; Piven & Cloward 1971), the general outlines of the coalition at the national level and its manifestations in the cities are complete. The new class-black alliance operating in the context of a Johnson administration able to tolerate the objections of party regulars in the cities proved decisive in helping to raise the intensity of urban conflict. The resources for such a departure were easily acquired in an era of economic expansion. Extra revenues were forthcoming and banks and state legislatures were more inclined to contribute. Furthermore, even as federal support for mobilization and adversary politics waned, the riots and the attendant worries of corporate leaders helped to support a continuation of high levels of federal contributions. At least initially, leaders in both the public and private sectors financed a major act of political inclusion, particularly for blacks but also to some degree for the new class. Reactionary elites might have responded quite differently and with results that were a good deal more violent.

To all of the preceding must be added something that often is lost in the details of analysis; i.e., that it was possible and necessary for a central-local alliance to be created to support a major domestic departure. The particularistic nature and the relative independence of American urban politics meant that it was possible for those at the center to cast around for local allies. Consider by contrast a system in which central-local relations revolve around well-disciplined, nationally organized parties and/or a national bureaucracy. Departures in urban policy might be impossible if they cut deeply into the resources or domains of these organizations.

To summarize, the attempts by two strata to invest themselves in the state coincided with the changing economic status of the city to produce two interrelated streams of mobilization that were particularly manifested in the struggle for control of land use and the bureaucracy. The cumulative effect was to challenge the pluralist regimes, and the analysis now turns to a consideration of the precise nature of the difficulties posed for them.

CONSEQUENCES OF THE STRUGGLES

The struggles over land use and the public bureaucracy threatened major elements of the pluralist regimes.

1. The ability of the leadership coalitions to dominate land use questions was challenged in at least two ways. Mobilization of neighborhoods made quiet bargaining less likely. Councilmen and neighborhood party leaders found it increasingly difficult to speak for neighborhood interests, and this affected projects both in these areas and in the central core, perceived as diverting resources from residential areas. In addition, policy matters that had been treated as peripheral no longer could be treated in this manner, and disagreements arose over whether and on what terms the coalitions should become involved in problems such as the organization of schools. Where efforts were made, the comparative lack of knowledge of the terrain (particularly on the part of businessmen) also led to strains.

2. The ability of functional bureaucracies and their traditional allies to dominate the remaining governmental domains was called into question. The increase in the number of actors concerned with the behavior of the public bureaucracy, the intensity of their convictions, and the variety of their resources made it increasingly difficult. For the coalition, electoral difficulties loomed as new organizations and issues of a divisive kind arising out of conflict over the bureaucracy were at hand and the costs of going to the aid of functional bureaucracies rose perceptibly. Social peace was also threatened and, thus, the economic attractiveness of the city.

3. The loyalty of party leaders and workers was threatened as they became anxious about the new claimants for public jobs and the increase in neighborhood groups that might act as competitors toward local parties.

4. The loyalty of executive functionaries, particularly land use professionals, was similarly at issue, especially if the land use struggle became intense. Less conflictual pastures might beckon.

5. The possibilities of political action by those excluded from the regime were broadened by the turmoil that threatened arrangements at all levels.

What actually transpired varied across cities and reflected the intensity of land use and bureaucratic struggles. Some regimes in fact disintegrated, ushering in an interregnum; others managed to maintain themselves more or less intact—Chicago, for example; and, in still others such as Philadelphia, there was a reconstituted pluralist regime with a somewhat more conservative cast than its predecessor.

Where the regimes collapsed, one of the proximate causes was that businessmen withdrew from the coalitions. The incentive to do so, engendered by conflict and disagreement, was abetted by a number of other factors: a continued decline in local ownership of industry; suburban residence of many businessmen; and the protection of much of the most important downtown investment by the mid- to late sixties. The defection of businessmen was added to the previous departure of liberals and the built-in disagreements between reformers and party leaders over how to divide up the bureaucracy. In addition, as a corollary to the breakdown of the domination of the functional bureaucracies and their allies, the separation of land use from other domains disappeared. Many organizations now no longer confined their attention to particular policy areas, and others were created that had wide-ranging concerns. A weakened or disintegrating coalition now had to share the field with actors such as teachers unions. Less important—because the regimes probably could have withstood it—was the defection of some executive and electoral functionaries.

An analysis of how the regime remained intact in Chicago would certainly focus on the Democratic party's political acumen and organizational strength. As Wilson (1973, ch. 5) points out, mobilization of all kinds of groups is made more difficult in such circumstances. In addition, adversary professionals can expect to find fewer allies outside government and fewer receptive ears inside. In Philadelphia, on the other hand, the striking thing is the way in which the land use coalition was put back together after a brief period of instability, this time with a mayor, Frank Rizzo, who was unsympathetic to the aspirations of working class and poor blacks, as the dominant partner and businessmen as secondary figures. The original more-or-less-equal partnership between liberal reformist mayors and businessmen has been substantially altered.

Rizzo's 1971 victory depended heavily on the support of both Italian neighborhoods and uniformed city employees and also on the ability of at least some ward organizations to deliver traditional Democratic voters. It took place in the face of substantial black defections from the Democratic party. The initial governing coalition, insofar as one existed, rested on some regular party leaders, newspapermen recruited into the administration, and the heads of the uniformed city employees. Many businessmen were suspicious, even hostile; and the civil service, which under Tate had retained much of the professional cast built up under reform mayors, was quite apprehensive.

Within five years, the land use coalition was recreated around what must be the largest block of downtown construction in the country.[30] Downtown businessmen, who are substantially less cohesive than in the late 1950s, have gotten two other bonuses: a fiscally astute and conservative finance director and a concentration of police in the city center that guarantees at least three squad cars within minutes of any call. The allegiance of a corps of electoral functionaries[31] has been gained by a takeover of the party organization fueled by increased income opportunities, while executive functionaries unsympathetic to the new order have been induced to leave to be replaced by loyalists. In the process, at least the spirit of the civil service rules has been violated. The electoral side of the regime has been bolstered by public pledges not to build publicly assisted housing in any neighborhood that does not wish it and by rewards for some black ward leaders who have managed to deliver 20 to 30 percent of the total black vote in the face of such statements. The uniformed services have not gone unloved, as attempts to increase the number of blacks and women have been fought through the courts and charges (and indeed extensive eye-witness evidence) of police brutality have gone unattended.[32] Federal public safety money has also helped.

In the example of Dallas, the differences between cities of the Southwest (and South) and the North will again be apparent. In the latter part of the 1960s, the struggle for control over land use and the public bureaucracy was not as intense as was the case in northern counterparts. Consistent with our analysis of the older cities of the Northeast and Midwest, a considerable part of the explanation turns on differences in the economic bases of southwestern cities and the relevance of the rise of the new class. Dallas (and cities like it) did not suffer from a shift away from the industrial metropolis, nor was it nearly as much unsettled by new class attempts to find local allies in their quest for national power. Dallas did not offer a fertile ground for new class efforts, as its minority poor were not ready to be organized (an ideology denying the viability of individualist alternatives being less compelling in a growing economy), nor were there many local leaders who might be encouraged to make a serious organizing effort or much in the way of neighborhood political consciousness.[33] By the early seventies, however, the cohesion of the business elite had waned as its composition altered from a group dominated by men who had worked together for long periods to one where there were many outsiders. Whether this presages a change in regime to a politics in which businessmen play a less dominant role is not clear, however, nor is the extent to which similar changes are taking place in other cities of the Sunbelt.

CONCLUSION: THE AFTERMATH OF THE SIXTIES

The changes in social structure and urban economies were not associated only with threats to pluralist regimes but also with a major alteration in the public sector of cities. The two consequences are of course related: one result of the struggles over land use and the bureaucracy was to enlarge the size and importance of the public sector as insurgents pushed for greater benefits and regime members offered those benefits to quell the unrest (Katznelson 1976). By the mid-1960s the public treasury was no longer simply a source of income for a variety of local businessmen and the more corrupt politicians, of modest services for the general population, or of rewards for the faithful. With some simplification, the change might be characterized as a shift from a politics where governmental authority was a handmaiden to private economic activity to one where it was increasingly a substitute for and/or the most significant influence on it. Central cities, then, were a principal locus for the working out of significant changes in the national political economy, and the alteration in the cities' public sectors ushered in a politics of collective consumption. The pluralist regimes were created in more modest governmental circumstances; but events over which they had little control and, to some degree, their attempts to direct the changes, particularly with regard to land use, created a new situation, the politics of which were difficult to manage. Many regimes faltered.

By the mid-1970s this politics of collective consumption was no longer occurring in an expanding economy and, indeed, was being carried on in a stagnating or declining one. A changing national political economy combined with budgets pushing against local revenue sources soon transformed conflicts between, say, neighborhood groups and mayors or between organizations representing blacks and municipal workers from conflicts that sometimes could be settled by liberal distribution of public largesse to ones for which this type of solution was increasingly less possible. Some cities have been slower getting to this point either because the conflicts of the sixties were less intense and budget increases, therefore, less pronounced (Katznelson 1976) or because their economies were more buoyant. As noted, cities of the Southwest (and South) are in the last category and have not in fact entered into the politics of collective consumption in any serious way. Consumption of privately produced goods still dominates.

A more detailed consideration of the conjunction of the politics of collective consumption with continued and even heightened economic weakness in the cities will point to major features of urban politics in the seventies. The politics of collective consumption in its extreme version, especially in the context of fiscal strain, looks like nothing so much as the politics of an underdeveloped country (Long 1971). A list of the major, interrelated characteristics of this pattern of politics would start with a public sector that is a major source of income for a substantial portion of the population. Even without complications introduced by economic decline or stagnation, the distribution of the social product is a collective choice involving conflict and bargaining. Put another way, the disaggregation into individual contracts created by market choice is not available, nor is the ideology that avoids the issue of fair distribution by focusing on productivity as the measuring rod for reward. If, in addition, many of the claimants are at the bottom of the economic pile and there are few serious private alternatives for them, then political conflict can be a deeply serious matter for the participants. For the more self-seeking suburbanites and other non–city dwellers, it may be a gratifying spectacle watching the have-nots fighting it out among themselves. Public employees, whose position allows them to raise their wages, increasingly come into conflict with the larger body of the citizenry, who find it more difficult to raise theirs. Municipal workers become the focus for relative deprivation, while the incomes of those who work in the leading economic sectors remain out of view.

A second feature revolves around the centrality of vertical relationships to higher orders of government. A weakening export sector creates increased dependency on outsiders. This in turn is associated with the creation in the local polity of powerful figures whose position depends on their reputation with outside providers and on the receipt of funds from that source. A limited or declining export sector means little or no economic growth (Thompson 1965), increasing the power of what major private investors there are. If these investors (for example, banks and corporate headquarters) have most of their capital elsewhere, they can afford to act quite independently in local politics in ways that maximize their economic self-interest. They may resort to creating various kinds of walls—physical, political, and legal—around their investments, and in this they may be aided by central authorities who see them as the leading sector of the local economy, the only hope for future growth, and the possessors of the only tangible assets worth protecting. The division of the urban economy into two sectors, one with the high benefits and security attendant on large-scale organization, the other with none of these, may become increasingly visible.

Third, continued economic weakness magnifies what social weaknesses exist, and social disorganization becomes a more significant problem. Outside authorities with the encouragement of leading local sectors provide funds for social control, and some portion of the local administrative and political apparatus becomes in effect an arm of the central authorities, although the latter may recognize that day-to-day supervision is impossible. So long as local conditions suggest that social control will be moderately effective, decisions may be left in local hands. The staff of the local apparatus will come increasingly from the same strata where disorganization is concentrated, and they will find themselves increasingly allied both with those at the center who are anxious about the safety of local investment and also with the local investors, themselves.

Finally, equality becomes the principal local concern. Since a significant portion of economic well-being is subject to collective choice, it will at least seem realistic to talk about equalizing the cost of housing through rent control, distributing public jobs along egalitarian criteria, and giving out credentials to all above a certain (low) minimum of ability. Continuing economic weakness will intensify egalitarian concerns.

In the most general way, the politics of such cities will revolve around two concerns and the political forces associated with them: (1) the use of the public budget for social control and the priorities implied by that and (2) the use of it as a way of promoting equality of condition. Now the major question is what circumstances will in fact produce this outcome. More precisely put, given that economics, demography, and political history are already pushing at least the larger cities of the Northeast and Midwest in this direction, will developments continue along the same lines? The ability of particular cities to resist such trends varies greatly. For the politics of underdevelopment actually to transpire, at least the vertical relationships noted and the apparatus of social control must be constructed or enhanced and maintained.

The whole question is perhaps best understood in the general context of future developments in the welfare state. The politics of underdevelopment is one aspect of what might be termed the *rationalization* of the welfare state; no major departures are entertained, efficiency and control become the motifs, and major private interests are propped up or left in peace to prosper. Alternatively, political alignments might produce a new thrust that would at least retard a politics of underdevelopment. The evidence indicates this latter course is unlikely. An apt general description of these events would be the exhaustion of the rising political forces concerned about the welfare of the cities. The first major wave of the new class is securely set at the top of major bureaucracies or near them, leading black elements are similarly (albeit more likely at a local and lower level) administering the apparatus created, and the willingness of the private sector to support and finance major efforts at political inclusion has been dissipated. The heart of the matter may well be that the interests of the new class were never securely tied to "saving the cities" but rather to achieving national power. The achievement of that power has meant that new class talents are now directed at administering the liberal corporate state, not battering it from without. There does not seem to be any substantial coalition standing in the way of efforts to save what is deemed savable and to administer substantial doses of efficiency and control to the rest. Indeed, the present Democratic administration indicates that these latter views are strong enough to overcome party differences in the executive branch.

The corollary of a flowering of the vertical coalition and the apparatus of control in the context of rationalization will be a weak, disorganized local politics. Those elements who are left to *play* city politics will do so without strong national allies in the struggle to pay for large public sectors that can be financed only by substantial infusions of federal money. They will increasingly have to deal with other local individuals who have established strong vertical alliances, and they will confront deep disagreements on demands for greater equality versus more control. There will be arguments over the interpretation of more equality, especially in the context of weak economies. And the elements remaining may be without the organizations that provide the strong mass following necessary to secure their demands at the polls.

The prospects for the creation of new urban regimes are thus not good (although some of the existing ones may hang on for quite some time), and the heart of urban politics may well cease to be local at all. The local polity has diminished in significance. In a politics of collective consumption, local actors carry less weight, unlike the time when city governments were largely the handmaidens of private wealth accumulation. In the latter instance, the politically active were local people, and their concerns localistic. The choice, however, between two types of city politics—one whose vital center is private choice, the other where the real substance is elsewhere—is not easy to make. Localism in this context may breed just as much homogeneity of dominant interests and lack of widespread participation as does the nationalization of urban politics. The prospects for a vital local democracy in either case are not great, but localism at least invited the comforting illusion that a meaningful urban civic life could be created without attending to the larger systemic questions.

NOTES

1. Cf. Katznelson's (1976) comment, quoting Lévi-Strauss, that the literature on urban America treats cities as if they had been "spared the agitations of history."

2. A more elaborate and theoretical characterization of the focal interests of regime members may be employed. Instead of talking about policy areas, we may employ formulations of the kind suggested by Lowi (1972) and Froman (1965), who attempt to construct a policy typology.

3. Analytically, the possible methods by which this might be achieved may be discussed along dimensions such as the divisibility of inducements and whether they are material or non-material. See, for example, Wilson (1973) and Ostrom (n.d.).

4. The means by which the coalition receives reliable services from its functionaries, both executive and electoral, may vary considerably. Regarding the former, the coalition may be the beneficiary of bureaucrats who conceive of their role requirements as establishing that they must carry out authoritatively rendered decisions. Or, the coalition may need to use various kinds of material inducements and threats of dismissals. Or, it may have to bargain over the substance of policy. Much the same means apply to producing a reliable core of electoral functionaries: they may be hired; on the basis of party loyalty, they may accept directives; or they may have to be given policy concessions. To the degree that major policy concessions are made to either kind of functionary, they become members of the governing coalition. Functionaries who are particularly influential with others of their kind are likely regularly to receive such concessions.

5. Examples of such values prominent in the history of urban politics are fiscal integrity, economic growth, and professionalism.

6. Among the possibilities for insuring this are shared conceptions of political rules, material rewards, and violence. Historically, in American cities the mix has changed substantially.

7. A particular complexity in the analysis of urban regimes, as against national ones, needs to be mentioned. Among those exerting substantial influence may be actors who are not members of the city's polity in the sense of being voters but who hold legal authority from other levels of government or other sources of power that allow them to pursue what interests they have in city affairs. (Clientelist states, however, or states penetrated by foreign intelligence services may be in much the same situation as cities.) In the American context, obvious examples would be state-level political figures and managers of large corporations having substantial holdings in the city but whose headquarters are elsewhere. At various points in the history of American cities, the former have in fact been members of senior coalitions in some cities. Similarly, functionaries can be drawn from outside, as, for example, consulting and public relations firms. *Urban* then should be interpreted as "focused on the city" rather than "being of the city." See Elkin (1974). For different views see Williams (1971) and Castells (1975).

8. See Bachrach and Baratz (1970); Pickvance (1974); Katznelson (1973); and Elkin (forthcoming). Schumpeter, in discussing capitalist business firms and their study by economists, makes a similar point: "In other words, the problem that is usually being visualized is how capitalism administers existing structures, whereas the relevant problem is how it creates and destroys them" (1950, p. 84).

9. As noted below, Atlanta politics is in many ways closer in character to Philadelphia's than to Dallas'. Some cities of the Pacific Coast can be treated under the heading of "pluralist regimes"; e.g., San Francisco. Others (for example, Los Angeles) are closer in character to southwestern cities, given the relative weakness of politicians, although the situation in this regard does not seem to have been as extreme as in Dallas (see below). On Los Angeles, see Banfield and Wilson (1963) and Fogelson (1967); on Atlanta, see Stone (1976); and on San Francisco, see Wirt (1974).

10. The principal land use question of any importance that the coalitions preferred to avoid, and which they could not control even if they wished to, was the siting of public housing. This touched racial antagonisms too deeply, and mobilization could be substantial.

11. Mass transit may more closely have touched the coalition's focal concerns. Where separate boards or authorities governed a particular policy area, the autonomy was reinforced by legal barriers.

12. It is likely that reformers' principal image of the city was the downtown, rather than its neighborhoods; in addition many either had had careers in firms operating in the central core or had money invested there.

13. Comparative study of the incidence of reform in the postwar period might reveal that it was in cities where regular party politicians showed little interest in the economic vitality of the city and/or where they were too engrossed in personal advancement, particularly of a monetary type, that businessmen worked for reform. So, one has Philadelphia; but there is also Pittsburgh, and this suggests businessmen were quite happy to ally them-

selves with regular party types able to look beyond their immediate material interests.
14. This is not meant to imply that there was a complete homogeneity of interests among businessmen. Clearly this was not and is not so, if only because they operate different types of establishments and will differentially benefit from almost any important public decision. One ought not be too impressed with the diversity, however, as some are more powerful than others and the degree of homogeneity among the powerful is crucial. There are in fact broadly shared and important concerns among them. Businessmen operating in the downtown core in *general* benefited, even at the expense of others, from downtown renewal.
15. Again, the siting of public housing and projects where large numbers of blacks were involved was the most volatile, and it is on such matters that city councilmen were most likely to balk. The regime could remain intact as long as agreements could be negotiated without a high degree of citizen mobilization and, during the period under discussion, this was largely possible.
16. As it stands now, this is the rankest kind of impressionistic statement, as is much of what follows in the paragraph. For the point to take on any real weight, a careful search of case study material, elite statements, and mass attitude surveys would be required.
17. Cf. Stave (1970). After all, a good deal of the largesse was either directly or indirectly distributed by local parties. Also one has only to note that the present Democratic machine in Chicago was created in the 1930s. For a contrary view see Katznelson (1976).
18. As indicated, Atlanta politics is closer to that in northern cities, at least in the sense that politicians are more independent than they are, say, in Dallas. There are however also a number of important differences and the combination of characteristics may not only differentiate Atlanta from its northern counterparts but also from other large southern cities. Any inventory of major features would include the following, in addition to the relative independence of politicians. Coalition building and maintenance was at the center of politics with racial antagonisms *not* producing a ready-made alliance among white interests. In fact, blacks played a major role in the electoral coalition and were junior partners in the land use coalition for the period under consideration. Blacks also were major electoral functionaries. In all, blacks of varying statuses played a somewhat similar role to working class whites in northern cities but were unable at any time to dominate the electoral apparatus. It is interesting to note that when black mobilization rose to full pitch in the 1960s, the Atlanta regime was battered from within, while both northern cities and other cities of the Deep South were battered from without. In general, see Stone (1976).

The description of Dallas politics is drawn from open-ended interviews conducted in 1977 with major civic figures and is part of a larger study of southwestern cities.
19. Lukes (1974, ch. 3) speaks of this as the "second dimension of power."
20. The succeeding discussion does not explicitly deal with this point. It is best to set out the argument advanced here in some detail and save for future work a consideration of how it compares with ones in which the riots command a central place.
21. For a largely ahistorical analytical treatment of organizational formation, see Olson (1965). An analysis that emphasizes the importance of historical changes is Stinchcombe (1965).
22. More accurately, we are talking about the liberal, public-oriented (as against business-oriented) sector of the new class, many of whom are in fact second generation "members." The whole class itself is described by Bazelon (1964, p. 308) as "people gaining status and income through organizational position." Shefter (1978) argues that the new class is based in the "grants economy": universities, foundations, consulting firms, government agencies, for example.
23. Spring, Harrison, and Vietoriz (1972) point out that in seven sample areas in New York, neighborhoods between 39.7 percent and 66.6 percent of the potential working population were unemployed, too discouraged to look, working part-time, or earning less than the Bureau of Labor Statistics lower level budget.
24. This description makes what was undoubtedly a complex process of trial and error, compromise, and negotiation between and among groups seem positively straightforward and calculating. It is meant merely as a summary description. The whole process requires more attention than is possible here.
25. The same point applies to the new class; but, as may be already apparent, circumstances did not require formation of organizations. Allies to provide much of the organizational

resources were available, and other means of access to the public treasury were possible.
26. Wilson (1973) provides a comprehensive treatment of contributions to organizations in return for private goods, although this is not how he presents his work. He is largely concerned with what kinds of returns individuals get from joining organizations where such benefits are only available by doing so. All motives therefore are transformed into private goods, since the benefit is withheld from the individual unless *he* joins. Public goods, if they are provided, are available to individuals whether or not they join.
27. What follows is most pertinent for explaining what Hardin (1975) calls "non-monitizeable goods," which, in fact, are the object of a large portion of political action. The following owes a good deal to discussions with Hardin, and readers requiring a general statement of the perspective adopted here should consult his paper where it first appeared.
28. Hardin (1975) convincingly argues that contrary to Olson, at least for the kinds of public goods at issue here, the size of the group is not the key variable affecting whether the good will be provided. Even in large groups, a subgroup may form.
29. See also the party identification and voting figures, which show a decline in black support for the Democratic party during the Eisenhower years. Cf. Nie, Verba, and Petrocik (1976, p. 228) and Ladd and Hadley (1975, pp. 142; 158).
30. The projects include a new department store (!) plus shopping mall, rebuilding part of the river front, several major office buildings, a hotel, several high-rise apartment buildings, a pedestrian mall on a main shopping street, a recently approved commuter railroad tunnel, and an office-residential complex spread over several acres. All of this is concentrated in an area roughly two miles square. Not included in the list is a new hotel and science center right at the edge of downtown and a substantial amount of private rehabilitation.
31. Recent primary votes for comptroller and district attorney, in which Rizzo-backed candidates lost decisively, suggest either that his takeover of the party is incomplete or that the party is now no longer well enough organized to bring out votes for unpopular candidates. In any case, Rizzo's electoral standing has had, from the beginning, a strong element of a personal following. How pertinent this is for understanding elements of the regime other than its electoral aspects is not clear. At the least, the electoral coalition appears unstable beyond electing Rizzo himself. If other aspects of the regime are similarly tied to his skills and talents, an analysis built around a reconstituted regime would be wrong. Substantially complicating all this is that the mayor is limited to two terms, and Rizzo is well into the second one. The problem of succession is presently highlighting the manner in which a personal following is a poor substitute for organization.
32. See, for example, the Philadelphia *Inquirer,* 12 June 1977, "Rizzo Tries to Thwart Police Probes."
33. The lack of political parties may be crucial here.

REFERENCES

Altshuler, Alan. 1970. *Community control.* New York.
Bachrach, Peter, and Baratz, Morton. 1970. *Power and poverty.* New York.
Banfield, Edward C. 1961. *Political influence.* New York.
Banfield, Edward C., and Wilson, James Q. 1963. *City politics.* Cambridge.
Bazelon, David. 1964. *Power in America.* New York.
Bellush, Jewell, and David, Stephen. 1971. *Race and politics in New York.* New York.
Castells, Manuel. 1975. Urban sociology and urban politics: From a critique to new trends in research. *Comparative Urban Research* 3, no. 1: 7–13.
Crecine, J. P. 1969. *Governmental problem solving: A computer simulation of municipal budgeting.* Chicago: Rand McNally.
Dahl, Robert. 1961. *Who governs?* New Haven.
Elkin, Stephen L. 1974. Comparative urban politics and interorganizational behavior. *Policy and Politics* 2, no. 4: 288–309.
———. 1974. *Politics and land use planning.* London & New York.
———. 1978. Urban regimes in the twentieth century. Paper presented to the Conference Group on the Political Economy of Advanced Industrial States, American Political Science Association.

————. Political structure, political organization and race: English-American comparisons. *Politics and Society.* Forthcoming.

Fainstein, Norman, and Fainstein, Susan. 1974. *Urban political movements.* New York.

Fogelson, Robert. 1967. *The fragmented metropolis.* Cambridge, Mass.

Froman, Lewis A. 1965. The categorization of policy contents. In Austin Ranney, ed. *Political science and public policy.* Chicago.

Gans, Herbert. 1963. *The urban villagers.* New York.

———— 1966. The failure of urban renewal. In James Q. Wilson, ed. *Urban renewal: The record and the controversy.* Cambridge.

Gelfand, Mark. 1975. *A nation of cities: The federal government in urban America, 1933–1965.* New York: Oxford University Press.

Greenstone, J. David, and Peterson, Paul E. 1973. *Race and authority in urban politics.* New York.

Hardin, Russell. 1971. Emigration, occupational mobility and institutionalization: The German Democratic Republic. Ph.D. dissertation, MIT.

———— 1975. The politics and economics of collective action. Fels Discussion Paper no. 66. University of Pennsylvania, Fels Center.

Harvey, David. 1975. The political economy of urbanization in advanced capitalist societies: The case of the United States. In Gary Gappert and Harold M. Rose, eds. *The social economy of cities.* Beverly Hills, Calif.

Hoover, Edgar M., and Vernon, Raymond. 1959. *Anatomy of a metropolis.* Cambridge.

Katznelson, Ira. 1973. *Black men, white cities.* London.

———— 1976. The crisis of the capitalist city: Urban politics and social control. In Willis Hawley et al., eds. *Theoretical perspectives in urban politics.* Englewood Cliffs, N.J.

Kilson, Martin. 1971. Political change in the Negro ghetto, 1900–40's. In Nathan Huggins et al., eds. *Key issues in the Afro-American experience.* New York.

Ladd, Everett Carll, and Hadley, Charles D. 1975. *Transformations of the American party systems.* New York.

Lipsky, Michael. 1976. Toward a theory of street level bureaucracy. In Willis D. Hawley et al., eds. *Theoretical perspectives on urban politics.* Englewood Cliffs, N.J.

Long, Norton. The city as reservation. *The Public Interest,* no. 25, fall, pp. 22–38.

Lowi, Theodore. 1967. Machine politics: Old and new. *The Public Interest,* no. 9, fall, pp. 83–91.

———— 1972. Four systems of policy, politics and choice. *Public Administration Review* 32, no. 4: 298–310.

Lubove, Roy. 1969. *Twentieth century Pittsburgh.* New York.

Lukes, Steven. 1974. *Power: A radical view.* London.

Lupo, Alan; Colcord, Frank; and Fowler, Edmund P. 1971. *Rites of way.* Boston.

Meltsner, A. J., and Wildavsky, Aaron. 1970. Leave city budgeting alone! A survey, case study, and recommendations for reform. In J. P. Crecine, ed. *Financing the metropolis,* pp. 311–58. Beverly Hills, Calif.: Sage.

Mollenkopf, J. H. 1975. The post-war politics of urban development. *Politics and Society* 5: 257–85.

Nathan, R. P., and Dommel, P. R. 1977. The strong Sunbelt and the weak Coldbelt cities. In Subcommittee on the City of the House Banking, Finance and Urban Affairs Committee. *Towards a national urban policy.* April.

Nie, Norman; Verba, Sydney; and Petrocik, John. 1976. *The changing American voter.* Cambridge.

O'Connor, James. 1973. *The fiscal crisis of the state.* New York.

Olson, Mancur, Jr. 1965. *The logic of collective action.* Cambridge: Harvard University Press.

Ostrom, Elinor. N.d. On the variety of potential public goods. Manuscript.

Petshek, Kirk. 1973. *The challenge of urban reform.* Philadelphia.

Pickvance, C. G. 1974. On a materialist critique of urban sociology. *Sociological Review* 22, no. 2: 213–20.

Piven, Francis Fox, and Cloward, Richard. 1971. *Regulating the poor.* New York.

Reichley, James. 1959. *The art of government.* New York.

Salisbury, Robert. 1964. Urban politics: The new convergence of power. *Journal of Politics* 26 (November): 775–97.

Sayre, Wallace, and Kaufman, Herbert. 1960. *Governing New York City.* New York.

Schumpeter, Joseph. 1950. *Capitalism, socialism, and democracy.* New York: Harper & Row.

Shefter, Martin. 1976. The emergence of the political machine: An alternative view. In Willis Hawley and Michael Lipsky et al., eds. *Theoretical perspectives on urban politics.* Englewood Cliffs, N.J.

————. 1978. Party, bureaucracy, and political change in the United States. In Louis Maisel and Joseph Cooper, eds. *The development of political parties: Patterns in evolutional decay.* Sage Electoral Studies Yearbook. Vol 4. Beverly Hills, Calif.: Sage.

Spring, William; Harrison, Bennett, and Vietoriz, Thomas. 1972. In much of the inner city 60% don't earn enough for a decent standard of living. *New York Times Magazine,* 5 November.

Stave, Bruce. 1970. *The New Deal and the last hurrah.* Pittsburgh, Pa.

Stinchcombe, Arthur. 1965. Social structure and organization. In James March, ed. *A handbook of organization.* Chicago.

Stone, Clarence. 1976. *Economic growth and neighborhood discontent.* Chapel Hill, N.C.

Suttles, Gerald. 1972. *The social construction of communities.* Chicago.

Thompson, W. R. 1965. *A preface to urban economics.* Baltimore: Johns Hopkins Press.

Williams, Oliver P. 1971. *Metropolitan political analysis.* New York.

Williams, Oliver P., and Adrian, Charles. 1963. *Four cities.* Philadelphia, Pa.

Wilson, James Q. 1973. *Political organizations.* New York.

Wirt, Fredrick. 1974. *Power in the city.* Berkeley, Calif.

Wolfinger, Raymond. 1974. *The politics of progress.* Englewood Cliffs, N.J.

CHAPTER 13

CONCLUSION: RESTRUCTURING THE RESOURCE FLOW

Douglas E. Ashford

Extracting capital and operating funds from the national economy is the lifeblood of the modern city. It is not unrelated to major social conflicts in each society, nor is it immune to short-term, partisan political manipulation. But it is also a structural feature of the decision process that is recognized by individuals and groups at all levels of government. National governments are not about to let major cities go bankrupt, for they are too closely linked to the social and economic fabric of the society; nor do cities in the final analysis have any place to go. One of the important ways of examining the nature of national and urban interdependence is resource allocation, which has been long recognized by economists (for example, Netzer 1966) but which has been neglected in political analysis. Building on earlier analyses of spending patterns and accepting cities simply as the providers of services, politics entered into the issue by concentrating on short-term fluctuations that seemed to be related to political differences. Little research was done—outside the mainstream of politics—on the structural differences within city governments in relation to policy (Hawley 1973). It is perhaps a reflection on the social sciences that, not until the fiscal and financial problems of cities became fairly obvious with the serious economic dislocations of the 1970s, did attention move to the external constraints exercised on urban government by higher levels of government. Though New York is in many ways an exception among cities of the world, Caro's fine study (1975) left no doubt that external forces on urban development had for many years virtually escaped the notice of the disciplines.

Until more is known about how lower levels of government react to external constraints, theory building is a precarious enterprise. The aggregate figures alone raise important doubts about there being a simple cause-

and-effect relationship. As Reissert and Ashford argue, in France and Germany the institutional links affecting the transfers among levels of government have not changed much over the past decade, though the plight of the cities has become more evident. The major restructuring of British local government did not alter the fiscal base of city revenues, nor, as Ball observes, are there any signs that Whitehall will relax the tight controls on local capital spending. Japan unfortunately is less explored, but the work included in the present volume shows that, next to the most advanced welfare states, Sweden and the Netherlands, it provides the largest transfer. The continuity of the resource relationship, therefore, seems to be in the institutional links among levels of government, their flexibility and their responsiveness.

If one looks more closely at the institutional structures affecting resource transfers, a basic distinction is noted: (1) specific controls, often exercised in conditional form (project by project) or (2) general, unconditional support for cities. An intriguing possibility is to regard the fiscal and financial link not as the product of certain social or political conditions at each level of government but as an institutional relationship which itself affects choices at both levels. Instead of the resource link being a dependent variable, it can also be conceived of as an independent variable to explain how fiscal and financial choices are indeed distributed to levels of government. The countries examined in this volume differ considerably, for example, in the extent to which the institutions governing the transfer are geared to micro- or macro-level decisions. The French system of subsidies for loans *(subventions)* gives the Caisse des Dépôts and its financial affiliates remarkable control over actual projects. The United States' preference for programmatic forms of transferring funds has played into the hands of local politics and supports the tradition of logrolling politics at the center. Each system is congruent with the political needs of local mayors and is generally accepted, but the systems also provide very different kinds of control for national government.

Another major distinction in the resource transfer problem is how the institutions distinguish between operating and capital spending. This is heavily influenced, of course, by the level of spending of localities. In Britain, where local governments spend nearly a third of the public budget and more than a tenth of the gross national product, controls are relatively strict on both kinds of spending. Since 1971 there has been central determination of "key" and "locally determined" capital spending, with roughly five-sixths falling in the key sector (Great Britain 1976, pp. 128–29). More surprising, the central government did not experience effective resistance to the imposition of cash limits on current spending in 1975. In France, in contrast, local governments account for only about a sixth of current spending of government but nearly two-thirds of public capital investment. The complexity of the institutional arrangements to influence local choices about capital spending are, thus, a product of the

overall importance of communes and departments in building the infrastructure for urban services and industrial development. A fundamental
question is, then, whether these institutionalized controls should be seen
as the product of more general patterns of public expenditure (dependent
variable) or as a way of organizing the decision process around the key
decisions that are indeed shared by central and local governments (independent variable).

The same formulation can be used in the analysis of financing urban
debt and loans. In the United States (see Boast), Japan, and Germany, the
central contribution to local credit is fairly small, no more than about a
fourth of the financing need. Though policy has varied over the years, in
Britain the Public Works Loan Board provides about half the volume of
local credit (see Ball). In France, the lower interest rates offered by the
state's financial institutions have resulted in public banks providing nearly
90 percent of local investment loans. The readiness of public banking
facilities to respond is to a large extent institutionally determined. French
state banks and financial institutions have been closely involved with government since Napoleon (Priouret 1966). Like the United States, British
and German cities have been long accustomed to working with the private
capital market. If the sectoral distinction is taken seriously, then capital
finance becomes a product of market forces, most clearly in the United
States (see Boast). If the link between national and local finance is looked
upon as influencing how credit is made available in the larger institutional
sense, then the way decisions are influenced is part of the financial machinery of the state.

LOCAL DECISIONS AND NATIONAL RESOURCES

How cities have placed their claim on national resources over the past
decade varies greatly among countries, but in each case aspects of the
fiscal and financial relationship among levels of government are crucial to
understanding the future of cities. Whether cities have received what they
need is disputable; but, at least for the United States, it is clear that the
growth of transfers is attributable to new federal programs (Wright 1972).
Anton (chapter 2) has described the programmatic character of American
assistance to cities, which is made easier by the inability of cities to form
coalitions to influence the terms of lending and credit. In France the
system of capital grants is an essential element in the web of dependency,
forcing mayors to work within the administrative framework of the state
(Grémion 1976). In England the effectiveness of central controls on capital
spending contributes to the intense concentration on the biennial reformulation of the current spending transfers, now about 40 percent of total
local revenues, but, as Young shows, London's government can still affect
outcomes. Although overall levels have not changed much in Germany,

Bonn and the states overcame their mutual suspicions in 1969 to place the local fiscal system on a more flexible tax base that more rapidly adjusts to inflation. Of the cases in this volume, Japan (chapter 8) appears to be the only system where the central government has not adjusted to urban fiscal and financial needs; and it is perhaps indicative of the risk that in Japan we find cities breaking out of the "rules of the game" in bargaining with the center.

Thus, the politics of resources helps define the situation from which mayors bargain for resources. There are important differences among countries and within countries (Mollenkopf 1975). While it may be true that half or more of the increased federal support for states in the United States can be attributed to political intervention (ACIR 1968), this tells us little about how mayors actually get more resources. While it is certainly true, as Meltsner (1970, p. 116) reminds us, that no one can tell mayors how to build a winning coalition, this process continues and must be better understood. Both the Bacharach and Shefter essays (chapters 3 and 9) provide a grip on this issue. Bacharach's work extends the established methods of community studies to examine transfers in New York State and shows how levels of government have fared in the complex game of "distributive localism" (Beer 1976). Shefter uses historical analysis to show how the power structure within a city managed to reassert itself under conditions of crisis. Consistent with much of the recent urban literature, he argues that a winning coalition is partly defined by the allocation of resources.

American and French mayors seem relatively adept in exercising influence over resources, though each system places difficult constraints on local intervention. French mayors form complex alliances with administrative officials (Thoenig 1973), and American mayors become part of the intergovernmental lobby (Haider 1974). Where the odds become overwhelmingly unfavorable, urban governments find ways to resist national demands. Two of the most important ways of doing so are described in the essays of Feldman and Milch (chapter 10) and Muramatsu and Aqua (chapter 8). Major investment decisions, such as airports, require huge amounts of land and capital. Local control of land use becomes a lever against external manipulation of urban resources. As Feldman and Milch show, the ways in which airport development is connected to urban government become crucial factors in determining whether airports will be built. New York's financial plight did not prevent it from blocking airport construction, nor were the fragmented British local governments helpless in fighting a number of airport proposals. In two cities, Montreal and Paris, "environmental" airports were constructed.

A second alternative is provided by democratic politics. Rather like the socialist and communist mayors of France during the period of Gaullist hegemony, Japanese mayors are learning how to protest directly and how to use the courts to stall external threats to the quality of life in cities.

Direct resistance is becoming more common in France, England and the United States (here particularly for major capital projects affecting the environment). In England a group of town councillors recently went to jail rather than implement centrally mandated increases in public housing rents (Mitchell 1974). Important as protest may be as another form of inertia on central designs, it does not seem likely that it can affect the major institutional links of resource allocation.

DISTINCTIONS WITHIN THE TRANSFER

Although relatively little research has yet tried to relate the different kinds of grants to the level of support nations give local governments, the overall figures display considerable variation and provide evidence for a preliminary analysis of how transfers in total relate to the institutional organization of center-local relationships. The distinction is particularly important, for it reverses many of the more obvious inferences that might be drawn from an examination of the aggregate figures. Although the French communal budgets are a very small part of public expenditure, the communes are heavily dependent on a national spending subsidy (*versement représentatif de la taxe sur les salaires,* or VRST). More important, the relief for localities must be assessed within the framework of the French administrative system, which places very specific requirements on the communes. Sweden and Germany provide roughly the same overall level of local support through transfers, but Germany does so in a remarkably strong federal structure where the states can transform general grants into specific—and therefore more restrictive—grants for municipalities. Japan provides a curious contradiction. A single-party regime since the war and a government with conservative national economic policy have in fact provided a large proportion of urban spending from national revenues. The qualification is that more than half this transfer is linked to subsidies for specific urban services.

The general figures in table 13-1 offer several intriguing hypotheses. It appears, for example, that regardless of the overall fiscal importance of local government, general transfers are favored where more highly developed administrative systems can guide local choices. For many years both European and North American local governments have associated increased, unrestricted revenues with more autonomy. If the French prefectoral system and the intricate Swedish budgetary procedures are taken seriously, this is not necessarily the case. Much the same kind of theorizing can be done about specific forms of support, often taken as the most restrictive or coercive form of transfer. The most elaborate system is the United States, which has over 1,000 specific grant programs for state and local governments. By sheer multiplication of the grants the United States has devised a transfer system equal to most European systems, but one

Table 13-1   Transfers as Percentages of Local Revenue

Nation	Total %	General	Specific
Japan (1975)	47	21	26
France (1974)	40	40	
Britain (1974)	40	32	8
Sweden (1976)	25	6	19
United States (1973)	24	3	21
West Germany (1973)	23	10	13

which permits all kinds of combinations of local needs and preferences to be joined with federal budgets. Thus, the first general conclusion must be that there is no simple, linear relationship to be found in the size or the form of transfer. A higher proportion of specific grants does not necessarily bring more central control, nor does a higher proportion of unrestricted income assure local autonomy. Historical and institutional circumstances also affect the transfer process, so that moving in the same direction (more general or more specific) does not necessarily have the same outcome in one country as it may in another.

REORGANIZING TRANSFERS

An aggregate examination of the growth of transfers to local governments cloaks the important policy changes. Perhaps the clearest illustration is West Germany, where the aggregate figures on federal transfers to states and cities from 1956 to 1973 show that total grants have made only a modest increase from slightly under 19 percent of local revenues to just under 23 percent. These cross-sectional figures, in fact, represent huge sums of money. An increase of 1 percent in 1973 would be almost 250 million deutsche marks, and the annual rate of increase has been about 10 percent. More important, the apparent stability of the transfer hides the major reorganization of the transfers in 1969, when the local government system traded 40 percent of its trade tax in return for 14 percent of the income tax, to be distributed by the federal government. As a result, the federal government was able to place the local governments on a fiscal base that would be more sensitive to incomes and, therefore, more responsive to national economic objectives. The local governments, in exchange, were given an easier way to collect taxes and assured that their revenues would benefit from increased incomes.

A similar transformation has occurred in France. In 1968, France decided to replace the *taxe locale,* a locally levied indirect tax, and to terminate the *taxe salaire.* Neither was a popular tax, and the imposition of value-added tax on local government transactions, accompanied with the refund (the VRTS), seemed to be the acceptable solution. In fact, it has become the center of an intense struggle between communes and Paris. French mayors are furious and, in effect, have lost control over indirect local taxes. Their complaints have some justification because the proportion of direct taxes has gradually but steadily increased from 45 percent of local revenues in 1960 to 53 percent in 1974. The VRTS has not sustained the earlier proportionate share of indirect taxes. At the time of the change the *taxe locale* was 89 percent of indirect taxes. In 1974 the VRTS provided only 82 percent of indirect taxes. While the mayors have been relieved from imposing unpopular indirect taxes, there is some reason to think that they welcomed this change and no reason to assume they would have increased the indirect taxes as much as the VRTS. The state has intervened to use the transfer system to limit local spending and to bring local government in line with national economic objectives.

The French and German cases lead us to believe that where transfers can be kept relatively stable in relation to local spending, the reorganization of transfers will concentrate on fiscal problems. In this respect the two illustrations are particularly important, for the federal government of Germany has none of the explicit control over local government that France has. Bonn is constitutionally prohibited from raising revenues for local government, and the procedures to enter this domain are demanding, requiring either a majority vote of the Bundesrat or unanimous consent of all states. In 1976 a proposal to provide 4.5 billion deutsche marks for energy-saving devices died because two states refused consent. Although the absolute level of influence, measured either in budgetary or organizational terms, is very different in the two systems, the stability of the relationship appears to have made a fiscal reorganization possible.

There has been much less fiscal reorganization in Britain, the Netherlands, and the United States, even though there has also been major change in the size of the transfer. From 1950 to 1974 the British general grant increased from 34 percent to 45 percent of all local government income. In the three major reorganizations of local fiscal policy—1929, 1948, and 1958—there is a continuous shift to less-restricted forms of support but no change in the fiscal base of local government. Ever since Goschen unsuccessfully proposed allocating certain taxes to localities in the 1870s, the British government has refused to broaden the local tax base, which is still confined to the property tax. The Layfield Committee has proposed giving a portion of the income tax to local government, but this is unlikely to be approved while the country also confronts the explosive issue of financial autonomy for Scotland.

The growth of transfers in the United States is even more dramatic than in the British and Dutch cases. In 1954 federal grants to states and cities totaled $3 billion; for 1977 the estimated transfer is over $72 billion. In the past decade alone there has been a fivefold increase in the transfer, so that in 1976 federal grants constituted over 20 percent of state and local income. Despite the increases in state and local income and property taxes, the American government's contribution to local revenues compares with that of Germany or Sweden. Although the reasons for the refusal to alter local fiscal structures differ in Britain and the United States, the consequences are similar. In both instances the center was forced to come to the rescue of the city, in Britain because the increasing responsibilities placed on towns and cities left no alternative and the grant system is essentially open-ended (Layfield Committee 1976), and in the United States because pluralist politics at both the national and urban levels of government made multiplication of programmatic assistance desirable. Dillon's rule had the same effect as Exchequer vulnerability.

TERRITORIAL REORGANIZATION AND RESOURCE ALLOCATION

If transfers are to be interpreted as an independent variable in the structuring of intergovernmental relationships, a reasonable place to expect to find their influence would be in the reorganization of local government areas. Although it is not possible to establish the direction of causality between reorganization and the structure of transfers, there is interesting evidence that cities can be provided with larger resource bases by increasing their areas. If Sweden is added to the countries discussed in this volume, then in three of six cases, there have been important territorial changes.

In Germany the changes have been confined to the reforms each state could agree to, but it was estimated in 1968 that 24,182 units of local government had been reduced to 14,928. The federal system, of course, provides opportunities for regionally adjusted solutions that are more difficult to arrange in unitary systems. In the Rhineland-Palatinate, the consolidation law requires the merging of small communes to form communal unions *(Verbandsgemeinden)* of at least 7,500 persons. Lower Saxony established a target of communes of 5,000 persons, while Schleswig-Holstein planned special districts of communes containing 10,000 persons. In the most populous state, North Rhine-Westphalia, there is an adjustable target of 8,000 persons for rural areas and 30,000 for densely populated ones (Weiler 1972, p. 30). Since 1950 a series of parliamentary acts in Sweden have gradually reduced the number of local governments from about 3,000 to 277 (as of 1974). Though a careful study of the process is lacking, it appears to have been accomplished through the meticulous process of administrative consultation used in the reorganization of Stockholm (Anton 1975). In a more precipitous decision, the Local Government Act of 1972 completely overhauled the territorial structure of British local government. Aside from parishes, the 1,348 counties and boroughs of England and Wales were transformed into 454 varied units, ranging from counties, districts, and the city of London (which had been reorganized in

1963). Reorganization proposals had been gestating for nearly thirty years in various boundary commissions. The Wilson government forced the issue, only to see the Heath government dilute its plans for strong urban-based units when legislation was finally passed.

The anomalies in the territorial reorganization process are the United States, France, and Japan. In Japan there have been no major boundary changes since World War II, except for metropolitan regions forced on the local government system by the growth of Tokyo and Osaka. There has been almost no reduction in local government units in the United States, unless one wishes to include school districts, where there has been sub-stantial consolidation. From 1957 to 1972 only 3 of 3,047 counties have disappeared, and over a 1,000 new municipalities have been formed to make a total of 18,517 city governments. Townships have declined by 207, but there were still 16,991 in 1972 (Maxwell & Aronson 1977, p. 78). Fifteen years of determined effort by the allegedly powerful Gaullist gov-ernment of France has managed only to reduce the number of communes from 37,962 in 1962 to 36,435 in 1975. The fact that about two-thirds of the French population and roughly half the national income can be located in several thousand communes has not penetrated revolutionary logic. Despite the ideological spectrum of French parties, in neither the municipal elections of 1977 nor the national elections of 1978 have any of the parties suggested that the communes be required to merge.

The analysis to this point has introduced two major dimensions along which the transformation of local government systems might be viewed. The state has two primary ways of changing local level policy making: fiscal and territorial reorganization. The countries we are considering are arranged in this way on table 13-2. It should be underscored that concern at this point is not with whether either form of reorganization was effec-tive but only with how the state exercised influence over the system to induce change. The French fiscal reforms of 1968 and 1973, for example, made little difference to the communes and, in fact, local taxes are still rooted in the tax principles created during the Revolution. The territorial reorganization of Britain has been widely criticized, and over the past year the Labour party's Local Government Committee launched new propos-als. The nine counties containing cities over 200,000 that were demoted to districts in the 1972 reorganization recently met in London to resist any effort to restore county-level powers to these cities (London *Times* 1977). But our first concern is how political systems initiate change using both forms of leverage on lower level government. As table 13-2 shows, the United States is the only country in our sample that has not made a major reorganization effort of some kind, though Japan would be a second likely candidate. West Germany is the only country that undertook reorganiza-tion along both lines, though the Swedish Royal Commission on the Politi-cal Economy of Local Government, appointed in 1976, may recommend changes in the grant system that would add Sweden to this category.

Table 13-2   Fiscal and Territorial Reorganization by States

Territorial Reorganization		Fiscal Reorganization	
		Yes	No
	Yes	West Germany	Britain
			Sweden
	No	France	United States
			Japan

Arranging the changes that most concern us in table 13-2 provides a matrix, not an explanatory design. For a number of reasons, however, the effort at reclassification is important if we are to understand the interface of politics and policy. Undoubtedly socioeconomic changes are also occurring that predispose governments to the various policies described, and it would not be difficult to enumerate political differences that enhance or impede each course of action. But our interest is in advancing a policy-based theory of how transfers are used in the modern state. In discussion the most important point of agreement was that the policies described in table 13-2 are to some extent substitutes for each other. Each state seeks a policy to "mix" that enables it to redesign territorial and fiscal relationships across levels of government within a unique set of constraints. These could be standardized were we to embark on an ecological or demographic analysis, but the critical shortcoming of such standardization, although it enables one to use more precise, quantitative techniques, is that it also smothers precisely those decisional variations that contribute to the observed course of action. Quantitative evidence may exclude what we most need to compare: how choices are made within each country. In all the cases national and local government had their own objectives and their own interpretation of why the particular form of reorganization was acceptable or unacceptable, and these distinctions become essential in understanding a policy-making process.

The choice between territorial and fiscal reorganization is not only a problem of dealing with important social and economic problems, but it is a policy problem in itself. As cities become artifacts of the national system, the historical meanings of both fiscal and territorial relationships in government become ambiguous. Major national crisis, as Elkin shows, can work to sustain the status quo. There is ample evidence that location no longer defines political interaction, although elections must be held within well-defined territories for physical reasons. Much the same can be said about the social and economic problems of cities. While economic dislocations and social inequities are more acute in cities, it is no longer possible for cities alone to respond to these issues. Put slightly differently, socioeconomic structures may no longer help a state define policies. The sprawling mass found in a modern metropolis debases the political and social currency of the tidy, self-sufficient cities we once knew.

For a century or more cities have fought to get their problems and needs on the national agenda. Now that they are there, the cities are in an interesting way unable to state what their needs are (Williams 1977). At all levels of government the policy problem is not to either relieve racial tensions or provide jobs or build housing or improve transportation, etc., but to do *all* of these. The usefulness of the matrix in table 13-2 is that it permits us to visualize how each country, though different from the others in how advanced its urban system has become, must seek a policy most appropriate to its urban system. By this we mean something very close to what Jacob and Lipsky (1968, p. 519) called the "conversion process" of urban and national policy. The interdependence of fiscal and territorial policy is how states construct policies in a setting where urban needs are ambiguous and where cities themselves are less effective policy makers. Again, it should be stressed that this is not to say that for each country one could not plausibly select "the most pressing issue," but to do so would vastly simplify the multilevel and the multipurpose aspects of transfers. Precisely those parameters of policy making that we see as movable and changing would have to be arbitrarily "held constant." In brief, intergovernmental transfers are a policy of every advanced industrial society. Their existence and their use is of less immediate interest to the politics of policy making than how fiscal and territorial constraints influence their organization in each country.

RESOURCE ALLOCATION AS AN EXPLANATORY VARIABLE

The relationships portrayed in table 13-2 must, of course, be interpreted with caution. Japan, France, and Germany have, for example, all pursued conservative economic policies, so that the absolute amounts being transferred to the local governments are smaller in proportion to national income than in the other countries. Even so, when countries are arranged to illustrate their capacity to undertake important restructuring of intergovernmental relationships, many of the more obvious structural characteristics do not appear to be determinant. There does not appear to be, for example, a clear separation between unitary and federal governments. Indeed, one of the major reasons why this traditionally important structural difference seems to be diminishing in importance is that resource transfers blur the legal powers of subordinate provinces and states. On the other hand, there is growing evidence that the unitary governments, especially where they cannot consolidate overarticulated local government systems, turn to regionally defined policies as a way of improving central government control of local decisions (Ashford 1977). If the earlier federal distinction is fading, while the unitary government needs to re-shape areas to meet the needs of new policies and programs, intergovern-mental influences are certain to become increasingly important.

Considering the problem of how to transfer funds to local governments from the central government's perspective, there are two major possibili-ties. Organize the new areas of central government to meet the needs of the policy itself or reorganize the areas of existing local governments more appropriately to fit with the policy objectives of the center. Though less is known about the relative powers of the Japanese prefect and the municipalities, in most countries the decision to create new, functionally defined areas for meeting national policy objectives is quite clear. Unable to change either the local tax systems or the federal constraints, the Ameri-can territorial system has undergone an explosion of special districts, what Bollens (1957) calls the "dark continent" of American government. In fifteen years special districts have nearly doubled from 14,405 in 1957 to 23,885 in 1972 (Maxwell & Aronson 1977). The American transfer explo-sion was accompanied by an organizational explosion. The emphasis on specific grants both required and supported the creation of thousands of new areas for the implementation of public policy. The Comprehensive Employment Training Act will, for example, provide $13 billion of local assistance for the fiscal year of 1979.

In the absence of agreement among levels of government over the objectives of fiscal policy and with the multiplication of functionally defined territories, the politics of transfers in the United States becomes increasingly incoherent. At the local level, states move toward limiting the fiscal incapabilities of local government, and twenty-three states now have "lids" on local tax powers. Nearly all programs are allocated by formula, often being initiated, justified, and evaluated by their own constituency, not by the competitive political process. The curious effect is that with the explosion of transfers in the United States, it becomes more rather than less difficult to specify what the overall objectives are, either in terms of the territorial units or the fiscal adjustments. The effect is both centraliz-ing and decentralizing. The Office of Management and Budget (and the Federal Reserve Bank) become more important in determining fiscal pol-icy, while lower levels of government rarely coincide with the actual territories to which the transfers apply. How long such a simultaneous implosion and explosion of American policy making can continue is un-known, but it stems from a pattern of intergovernmental relationships where neither fiscal nor territorial reorganization can effectively relate to the transfer.

A very similar situation exists in France. The Guichard Commission report (1976, p. 133) provides a picture of a department that varies consid-erably from the standard version of the French territorial hierarchy. The Department of Bordurie is subdivided along fifteen dimensions—many of them carving out a number of functional units—for water supply, schools, electrification, and so forth, that have no bearing on the formal territorial divisions of commune, canton, and department. There are also eight additional subdivisions of the department, many of them for proliferating semipublic corporations for developmental purposes. The best estimate of French officials is that about four-fifths of the Ministry of Finance budget is now channeled through agencies that have no direct bearing on the territorial organization of the state. This does not include the myriad of additional funding agencies and semipublic organizations established by other ministries.

The legal framework for nearly all the organizations spawned by the fiscal and financial machinery of the state is the *établissement public*, a device created in 1901 to facilitate secondary school construction. These agencies have all the legal rights of state organizations; that is, they can enter into contracts, utilize state funds, and exercise rights to claim land. A report of the Conseil d'Etat (France 1971) lists about 3,000 such agencies; not all, of course, have to do with intergovernmental relationships. They range from the Comédie Française to the Crédit Foncier, the 1972 regional governments, and the *sociétés d'économie mixte*, which are urban development agencies of many kinds. In fact, it appears that no one in the presumably tidy world of French administration knows how many *établissements publics* exist. A best guess is that the "new" territories have budgets roughly equal to the formal territories, making the proportion of public expenditure taking place at the local level in France about the same as that in Britain. The immediate importance of these agencies is that they become the instruments of fiscal policy making that are divorced from the French political and administrative framework. Unable to restructure intergovernmental relationships through formal territorial reorganization, the French state has found a substitute by redirecting huge sums of money through development agencies. Not only are major projects like Fos and Dunkerque organized in this way, but there is also the array of *agences d'urbanisme*, zonal development agencies for industry, housing, urban renewal, and most of the land use planning organizations. Nearly every major policy innovation over the past decade has produced another version of the semipublic corporation aimed at simplifying the problems of working with the elaborate commune structure.

In Britain the intergovernmental relationship has changed in a curious way because there has, on the one hand, been no change in the fiscal base of local government (limited to the property tax), while direct central controls over spending have become increasingly rigid with the country's economic problems. On the other hand, Britain opted for a major local government reorganization that reduced the number of municipal and rural units of government from more than 1,400 to about 450. Within five years of the territorial changes, demands for new local reorganization appeared, most notably from what are called the "Big Nine" cities, which found their powers diminished under the Local Government Act of 1972.

The dilemma is curious because cities cannot increase their revenues or intervene very easily in national politics to influence the objectives of transfers or other national programs (Ashford 1976). Although the Conservative government, which passed the reform, made important changes in Labour's plans for new local government areas, the results show how the search for an ideal territorial organization in the absence of a way to redirect resources to policy problems can compound the difficulties of aligning transfers with local government. The inference is that where central government refuses to permit a degree of local initiative in raising resources, as happens in the diverse circumstances of American cities using income and sales taxes, the allocation of resources to new programs becomes a decision reserved wholly to central government.

The complexity of intergovernmental relationships does not permit a totally persuasive demonstration of whether fiscal and financial exchanges have more influence over territorial reorganization, or the reverse. What we can see is that in the British case, if not in the Swedish one, territorial reorganization without changing fiscal relationships among levels of government does little to relieve the problems of the preexisting structure. Confusing as the multiplication of areas defined by the needs of central government's policies may be, it also represents a compromise between placing impossible demands on the cities and completely isolating cities from the decision-making process. The alternatives do not seem likely to be acceptable. National governments will no doubt continue to provide more funds for local problems but will want some assurance they will achieve their objectives. Cities want to improve services and are increasingly involved with fundamental issues of economic development, but they have difficulty changing their areas and their tax structures. Intergovernmental relationships between cities and the center will, therefore, probably grow in complexity, for they are the acceptable mixture of the politically feasible and programmatically desirable. While it may be true, as the Layfield report argued for British local government finances, that "who pays the piper calls the tune," it is also becoming more difficult to identify who is indeed playing the music. The purpose of this volume has been to show how some of these variations work in the modern industrial democracies and to argue that fiscal and financial issues have become the most important dimension of center-local relationships.

REFERENCES

Advisory Commission on Intergovernmental Relations (ACIR). 1968. *Urban and Rural America: Policies for Future Growth.* Washington, D.C.

Anton, Tom. 1975. *Governing Greater Stockholm: A study of policy development and systems changes.* Berkeley and Los Angeles: University of California Press.

Ashford, D. E. 1976. *Limits of consensus.* Center for International Studies, Western Societies Occasional Paper no. 6. Ithaca, N.Y.: Cornell University Press.

————. 1977. Are Britain and France "Unitary"? *Comparative Politics* 9 (July): 483–99.

Beer, S. H. 1976. The adoption of General Revenue Sharing: A case study in public sector politics. *Public Policy* 24 (spring): 127–95.

Bollens, J. C. 1957. *Special district governments in the United States.* Berkeley & Los Angeles: University of California Press.

Caro, R. A. 1975. *The power broker.* New York: Random House.

France. Conseil d'Etat. 1971. *La Réforme des établissements publics.* Paris: Documentation Française.

Great Britain. 1976. *Public expenditure to 1979–80.* London: HMSO, cmnd 6393.

Grémion, P. 1976. *Le Pouvoir périphérique.* Paris: Editions du Seuil.

Guichard Commission (Rapport de la Commission de Développement des Responsabilités Locales). 1976. *Vivre ensemble.* Paris: Documentation Française.

Haider, D. H. 1974. *When governments come to Washington.* New York: Free Press.

Hawley, W. D. 1973. *Non-partisan elections and the case for party politics.* New York: Wiley.

Jacob, H., and Lipsky, M. 1968. Outputs, structure, and power: An assessment of changes in the study of state and local politics. *Journal of Politics* 30 (May): 510–38.

Layfield Committee. 1976. *Local government finance.* London: HMSO, cmnd 6453.

London *Times;* 14 October 1977.

Maxwell, J. A., and Aronson, J. R. 1977. *Financing state and local governments.* 3d. ed. Washington, D. C.: Brookings Institution.

Meltsner, A. J. 1970. Local revenue: A political problem. In J. P. Crecine, ed. *Financing the metropolis,* pp. 103–35. Beverly Hills, Calif.: Sage.

Mitchell, A. 1974. Clay Cross. *Political Quarterly* 45: 165–77.

Mollenkopf, J. H. 1975. The post-war politics of urban development. *Politics and Society* 5: 257–85.

Netzer, D. 1966. *Economics of the property tax.* Washington, D.C.: Brookings Institution.

Priouret, R. 1966. *La Caisse des Dépôts: Cent-cinquante ans d'histoire financière.* Paris: Presses Universitaires de France.

Thoenig, J.-C. 1973. *L'Ere des technocrates.* Paris: Editions d'Organisation.

Weiler, C. J., Jr. 1972. Metropolitan reorganization in West Germany. *Publius* 2 (spring): 26–68.

Williams, O. 1977. Towards a comparative urban politics. *Ms.*

Wright, D. S. 1972. The state and intergovernmental relations. *Publius* 6 (winter).

SELECT BIBLIOGRAPHY:
ALLOCATION OF
URBAN RESOURCES AND
INTERGOVERNMENTAL TRANSFERS

THE UNITED STATES

Theoretical and Conceptual Writings on the Changing Relationship Between the Cities and the Political System

Advisory Commission on Intergovernmental Relations (ACIR). 1977. *Federal grants: Their effects on state/local expenditures, employment levels, wage rates.* Washington, D.C.
———. 1977. *The state and intergovernmental aids.* Washington, D.C.
———. 1976. *Significant features of fiscal federalism.* Washington, D.C.
———. 1973. *City financial emergencies: The intergovernmental dimension.* Washington, D.C.
———. 1968. *Urban and rural America: Policies for future growth.* Washington, D.C.
Funigiello, Phillip. 1978. *The challenge to urban liberalism.* Memphis: University of Tennessee.
Gelfand, Mark. 1975. *A nation of cities: The federal government in urban America, 1933–1965.* New York: Oxford University Press.
Jones, Charles O., and Thomas, Robert D. 1976. *Public policy making in a federal system.* Sage Yearbooks in Politics and Public Policy. Vol. 3. Beverly Hills, Calif.: Sage.
Lucy, William H. 1975. Metropolitan dynamics: A cross-national framework for analyzing public policy effects in metropolitan areas. *Urban Affairs Quarterly* 11 (December): 155–85.
McLoughlin, J. B., and Webster, J. N. 1970. Cybernetic and general system approaches to urban and regional research: A review of the literature. *Environment and Planning* 2: 369–408.
Margolis, Julius. 1961. Metropolitan finance problems: Territories, functions, and growth. In National Bureau of Economic Research. *Public finances: Needs, sources, and utilization.* Princeton: Princeton University Press.
———. 1957. Municipal fiscal structure in a metropolitan region. *Journal of Political Economy* 65: 225–36.
Mollenkopf, J. H. 1975. The post-war politics of urban development. *Politics and Society* 5: 257–85.
Newton, Ken. 1975. American urban politics: Social class, political structure in public goods. *Urban Affairs Quarterly* 11 (December): 241–64.
Olson, Mancur, Jr. 1965. *The logic of collective action.* Cambridge: Harvard University Press.

Pestieau, Pierre. 1977. The optimality limits of the Tiebout Model. In W. E. Oates, ed. *The political economy of fiscal federalism*, pp. 173–86. Lexington, Mass.: Lexington Books.

Pommerehne, Werner N. 1977. Quantitative aspects of federalism: A study of six countries. In W. E. Oates, ed. *The political economy of fiscal federalism*, pp. 275–355. Lexington, Mass.: Lexington Books.

Sacks, S., and Sullivan, P. J. 1975. The large city as fiscal artifact. In *Urban Affairs Annual Review*. Vol. 9, *The social economy of cities*, pp. 69–113. Ed. G. Gappert and H. Rose. Beverly Hills, Calif.: Sage.

Tarrow, S.; Katzenstein, P.; and Graziano, L., eds. 1978. *Territorial politics in industrial nations*. New York: Praeger.

Thompson, Wilbur R. 1972. The national system of cities as an object of public policy. *Urban Studies* 9 (February): 99–116.

Tiebout, C. M. 1956. A pure theory of local expenditure. *Journal of Political Economy* 64, no. 5 (October): 416–24.

Wingo, Lowdon. 1972. Issues in a national urban development strategy for the United States. *Urban Studies* 8 (February): 3–27.

General Works on Urban Economics and the Control of Public Expenditure

Barr, J. L., and Davis, O. A. 1966. An elementary political and economic theory of the expenditures of local government. *Southern Economic Journal* 33, no. 2 (October): 149–65.

Bird, R. M. 1971. Wagner's "Law" of expanding state activity. *Public Finance* 26, no. 1: 1–25.

Booms, B. H., and Hu, Teh-Wei. 1971. Towards a positive theory of state and local public expenditures: An empirical example. *Public Finance* 26, no. 4: 419–36.

Borcherding, T. E., and Deacon, R. T. 1972. The demand for the services of non-federal governments. *American Economic Review* 62: 891–901.

Burkhead, Jesse, and Miner, Jerry. 1971. *Public expenditure*. Chicago: Aldine.

Gandhi, V. P. 1971. Wagner's Law of Public Expenditure: Do recent cross-section studies confirm it? *Public Finance* 26, no. 1: 44–55.

Goffman, I. J. 1968. On the empirical testing of "Wagner's Law": A technical note. *Public Finance* 23, no. 3: 359–64.

Harrison, Anthony, and Jackman, Richard. 1978. Rate support grant. *CES Review*, no. 4, September, pp. 22–26.

Haveman, R. H., and Margolis, J., eds. 1970. *Public expenditures and policy analysis*. Chicago: Markham.

Jackman, Richard, and Sellars, Mary. 1977. The distribution of RSG: The hows and whys of the New Needs formula. *CES Review*, no. 1, July, pp. 19–30.

Lynch, Barry, and Perlman, Morris. 1978. Local authority predictions of expenditure in income. *CES Review*, no. 3, May, pp. 12–24.

Musgrave, R. A., and Musgrave, P. B. 1973. *Public finance in theory and practice*. New York: McGraw-Hill.

Musgrave, R. A., and Peacock, A. T., eds. 1958. *Classics in the theory of public finance*. New York: Macmillan.

National Bureau of Economic Research. 1961. *Public finances: Needs, sources and utilisation*. Princeton: Princeton University Press.

Pauly, M. V. 1970. Optimality, public goods and local government: A general theory analysis. *Journal of Political Economy* 78 (May): 572–85.

Perloff, H. S., and Wingo, Lowdon, eds. 1968. *Issues in urban economics*. Baltimore: Johns Hopkins Press.

Rafuse, R. W. 1965. Cyclical behaviour of state-local finances. In R. A. Musgrave, ed. *Essays in fiscal federalism*, pp. 63–121. Washington, D.C.: Brookings Institution.

Thompson, W. R. 1965. *A preface to urban economics*. Baltimore: Johns Hopkins Press.

Wagner, A. 1958. Three extracts on public finance. Trans. Nancy Cooke. In R. A. Musgrave and A. T. Peacock, eds. *Classics in the theory of public finance*, pp. 1–15. New York: Macmillan.

Williams, Alan. 1966. The optimal process of public goods in a system of local government. *Journal of Political Economy* 74 (fall): 18–33.

Major Writings on "Fiscal Federalism" and the Relation of the States in the Transfer Process

Bingham, Richard D.; Hawkins, Brett W.; and Hebert, F. Ted. 1978. *The politics of raising state and local revenue.* New York: Praeger.
Buchanan, J. M. 1950. Federalism and fiscal equity. *American Economic Review* 40: 583–99.
Campbell, A. K., ed. 1970. *The states and the urban crisis.* New York: Prentice-Hall, Columbia University Press.
Cohen, J., and Grodzins, M. 1963. How much economic sharing in American federalism? *American Political Science Review* 57 (March): 5–23.
Cole, S., ed. 1976. *Partnership within the states: Local self-government in a federal system.* Urbana: University of Illinois Press.
Coulter, P. B. 1970. Comparative community politics in public policy: Problems in theory and research. *Polity* 3 (fall): 22–43.
David, E. L. 1967. Public preferences and state-local taxes. In H. E. Braser, ed. *Essays in state and local finance.* Ann Arbor: University of Michigan Institute of Public Administration.
Dye, T. R. 1966. *Politics, economics and the public: Policy outcomes in the American states.* Chicago: Rand McNally.
Financing the New Federalism. 1975. Ed. Wallace E. Oates. Baltimore: Johns Hopkins Press.
Fisher, G. W. 1964. Interstate variation in state and local government expenditure. *National Tax Journal* 14, no. 1 (March): 57–74.
Gramlich, E. M. 1968. State and local governments and their budget constraints. *International Economic Review* 10: 163–82.
Hansen, N., and Perloff, H. S. 1944. *State and local finance in the national economy.* New York: Norton.
Maxwell, J. 1965. *Financing state and local government.* Washington, D.C.: Brookings Institution.
Musgrave, R. A. 1961. Approaches to a fiscal theory of political federalism. In National Bureau of Economic Research. *Public finance: Needs, sources, and utilization.* Princeton: Princeton University Press.
Musgrave, R. A., ed. 1965. *Essays in fiscal federalism.* Washington, D.C.: Brookings Institution.
Mushkin, S. J., and Cotton, J. F. 1968. *Functional federalism: Grants in aid and PPB systems.* George Washington University State-Local Finances Project.
Netzer, D. 1974. State-local finance and intergovernmental fiscal relations. In A. S. Blinder et al. *The economics of public finance.* Washington, D.C.: Brookings Institution.
Oates, W. E. 1968. The dual impact of federal aid on state and local expenditures: A comment. *National Tax Journal* 21: 220–23.
Olson, Mancur, Jr. 1969. The principle of "financial equivalency": The division of responsibility among different levels of government. *American Economic Review* 59 (May): 479–87.
Passell, Peter, and Ross, Leonard. 1978. *State policies and federal programs: Priorities and constraints.* A Twentieth Century Fund Report. New York: Praeger.
Sanford, Harry. 1967. *Storm over the states.* New York: McGraw-Hill.
Smith, D. L. 1968. The response of state and local governments to federal grants. *National Tax Journal* 21: 349–57.
Sullivan, J. L. 1973. Political correlates of social, economic and religious diversity in the American state. *Journal of Politics* 35 (February): 70–84.

Political and Economic Considerations Concerning Transfers, Grants, and Revenue Sharing

Anton, T. J.; Larkey, P. D.; and Linton, T. 1975. *Understanding the fiscal impact of General Revenue Sharing.* Ann Arbor: University of Michigan Institute of Public Policy Studies.
Beer, S. H. 1976. The adoption of General Revenue Sharing: A case study in public sector politics. *Public Policy* 24 (spring): 127–95.
Boulding, K. E.; Pfaff, A.; and Pfaff, M., eds. 1973. *Transfers in an urbanized economy.* Belmont, Calif.: Wadsworth.

Braser, H. E. 1967. The federal government and state local finances. *National Tax Journal* 20 (June): 155–64.

Davies, David. 1970. The concentration process and the growing importance of non-central governments in federal states. *Public Policy,* fall, pp. 649–57.

Dommel, P. R. 1974. *The politics of revenue sharing.* Bloomington: Indiana University Press.

Gramlich, E. M. 1977. Intergovernmental grants: A review of the empirical literature. In W. E. Oates, ed. *The political economy of fiscal federalism,* pp. 219–40. Lexington, Mass.: Lexington Books.

———. 1969. The effect of federal grants on state-local expenditures: A review of the econometric literature. *National Tax Association Papers and Proceedings,* pp. 569–93.

Gramlich, E. M., and Glaper, H. 1973. State and local fiscal behavior and federal grant policy. *Brookings Papers on Economic Activity* 1: 15–58.

Juster, F. T. 1977. *The economical and political impact of General Revenue Sharing.* Ann Arbor: University of Michigan Survey Research Center.

Juster, F. T., ed. 1976. *The economic and political impact of General Revenue Sharing.* Ann Arbor, Mich.: Institute for Social Research.

Lampman, R. 1972. Discussion of new transfer plans. In K. E. Boulding and M. Pfaff, eds. *Redistribution to the rich and the poor,* pp. 342–47. Belmont, Calif.: Wadsworth.

———. 1972. Public and private transfers as a social process. In K. E. Boulding and M. Pfaff, eds. *Redistribution to the rich and the poor.* Belmont, Calif.: Wadsworth.

Larkey, Patrick D. 1979. *Evaluating public programs: The impact of General Revenue-Sharing on municipal government.* Princeton: Princeton University Press.

Moneypenny, Phillip. 1960. Federal grants-in-aid to state governments: A political analysis. *National Tax Journal* 13 (March): 1–16.

Nathan, R. P., and Adams, Charles F. 1977. *Revenue sharing: The second round.* Washington, D.C.: Brookings Institution.

Nathan, R. P.; Manvel, A. D.; and Calkins, Susannah E. 1975. *Monitoring revenue sharing.* Washington, D.C.: Brookings Institution.

Osman, J. 1966. The dual impact of federal aid on state and local government expenditures. *National Tax Journal* 19, no. 4 (December): 362–72.

Perloff, H. S., and Richard, N., eds. 1968. *Revenue sharing in the city.* Baltimore: Johns Hopkins Press.

Pfaff, Abe. 1972. Transfer payments to large metropolitan poverty areas: The distribution and poverty reducing effects. In K. E. Boulding and M. Pfaff, eds. *Redistribution to the rich and the poor,* pp. 93–129. Belmont, Calif.: Wadsworth.

Pfaff, M., and Pfaff, A. 1972. How equitable are implicit public grants? The case of the individual income tax. In K. E. Boulding and M. Pfaff, eds. *Redistribution to the rich and the poor,* pp. 181–203. Belmont, Calif.: Wadsworth.

Savage, Harold V. 1978. *Urban policy and the exterior city: Federal, state and corporate policies.* Oxford: Pergamon Press.

Scott, A. D. 1952. Federal grants and resource allocation. *Journal of Political Economy* 60 (December): 334–36.

Stenberg, C. W. 1977. Block grants: The middle man and the federal aid system. *Intergovernmental Perspective* 3 (spring): 8–13.

Thurow, L. C. 1966. The theory of grants-in-aid. *National Tax Journal* 19: 373–77.

Walker, D. B. 1977. Categorical grants: Some clarifications and continuing concerns. *Intergovernmental Perspective* 3 (spring): 14–19.

Wright, D. S. 1972. The state and intergovernmental relations. *Publius* 6 (winter): 7–68.

Urban Spending and Finance

Alcaly, Roger E., and Mermelstein, David. 1977. *The fiscal crisis of American cities: Essays on the political economy of urban America with special reference to New York.* New York: Random House.

Booms, B. H. 1966. City governmental form and public expenditure levels. *National Tax Journal* 19, no. 2 (June): 187–99.

Braser, H. E. 1959. *City expenditures in the United States.* National Bureau of Economic Research Occasional Paper no. 66. New York.

Caraley, Demetrios. 1977. *City governments and urban problems.* Englewood Cliffs, N.J.: Prentice-Hall.

Crecine, J. P., ed. 1970. *Financing the metropolis: Public policy and urban economics.* Beverly Hills, Calif.: Sage.

Davis, O. A., and Haines, G. H., Jr. 1966. A political approach to a theory of public expenditure: The case of municipality budgets. *National Tax Journal* 19 (September): 259–75.

Froman, L. A., Jr. 1967. Analysis of public policy in cities. *Journal of Politics* 29: 94–108.

Hawley, A. H. 1951. Metropolitan population and municipal government expenditures in central cities. *Journal of Social Issues* 7, nos. 1; 2, pp. 100–108.

Jacob, H., and Lipsky, M. 1968. Outputs, structure and power: An assessment of the changes in the study of state and local politics. *Journal of Politics* 30 (May): 510–38.

McGuire, M., and Garn, H. 1972. The integration of equity in efficiency criteria in public project selection. In K. E. Boulding and M. Pfaff, eds. *Redistribution to the rich and the poor,* pp. 357–68. Belmont, Calif.: Wadsworth.

Meltsner, A. J., and Wildavsky, Aaron. 1970. Leave city budgeting alone! A survey, case study, and recommendations for reform. In J. P. Crecine, ed. *Financing the metropolis,* pp. 311–58. Beverly Hills, Calif.: Sage.

Moynihan, D. P., ed. 1970. *Toward a national urban policy.* New York: Basic Books.

Neenan, W. B. 1972. *Political economy of urban areas.* Chicago: Markham.

Netzer, D. 1968. Federal, state, and local finance in a metropolitan context. In H. S. Perloff and L. Wingo, Jr., eds. *Issues in urban economics.* Baltimore: Johns Hopkins Press.

Reischauer, R. D. 1979. Fiscal problems of cities. In *Setting the national priorities: The 1973 budget,* pp. 291–317. Washington, D.C.: Brookings Institution.

Richardson, Harry W. 1972. Optimality in city size, systems of cities and urban policy: A skeptic's view. *Urban Studies* 8 (February): 29–48.

Roscoe, M. C. 1965. *The cities in the federal system.* New York: Atherton.

Scott, S., and Feder, E. L. 1957. *Factors associated with variations in municipal expenditures levels.* Berkeley & Los Angeles: University of California Bureau of Public Administration.

Sharkansky, I. 1967. Government expenditures and public services in the American states. *American Political Science Review* 61, no. 4 (December): 1066–77.

Steven, David. 1976. *Urban politics and public policy: Cities in crisis.* New York: Praeger.

Wildavsky, Aaron. 1976. Bias toward federalism: Confronting the conventional wisdom on the delivery of government services. *Publius* 6 (spring): 95–120.

Wilensky, G. 1970. Determinants of local government expenditure. In J. P. Crecine, ed. *Financing the metropolis,* pp. 197–218. Beverly Hills, Calif.: Sage.

The Determinants of Urban Expenditure and the Urban "Crisis"

Alcaly, Roger E., and Mermelstein, David. 1977. *The fiscal crisis of American cities: Essays on the political economy of urban America with special reference to New York.* New York: Random House.

Bahl, R. W., and Saunders, R. J. 1966. Factors associated with variations in state and local government spending. *Journal of Finance* 21: 523–34.

Bollens, J. C. 1957. *Special district governments in the United States.* Berkeley & Los Angeles: University of California Press.

Braser, H. E. 1964. Some fiscal implications of metropolitanism. In B. Chenowitz, ed. *City and suburb: The economics of metropolitan growth.* Englewood Cliffs, N.J.: Prentice-Hall.

Campbell, A. K., and Sacks, Seymour. 1967. *Metropolitan America: Fiscal patterns in government systems.* New York: Free Press.

Derthick, M. 1975. *Uncontrollable spending for social services grants.* Washington, D.C.: Brookings Institution.

Fisher, G. W. 1961. Determinants of state and local government expenditures: A preliminary analysis. *National Tax Journal* 14, no. 4 (December): 349–55.

Gale, Stephen, and Moore, Eric, eds. 1975. *The manipulated city.* Chicago: Maaroufa Press.

Hansen, N. M. 1965. The structure and determinants of local public investment expenditures. *Review of Economics and Statistics* 47, no. 2 (May): 150–62.

Hansen, W. L., and Weisbrod, B. 1972. Distributional effects of public expenditure programs. *Public Finance,* pp. 414–20.

Kurnow, E. 1963. Determinants of state and local expenditures reexamined. *National Tax Journal* 16: 252–55.

Lindblom, C. E. 1961. Decision making in taxation and expenditures. In National Bureau of Economic Research. *Public finances: Needs, sources and utilisation,* pp. 295–329. Princeton: Princeton University Press.

Margolis, Julius. 1968. The demand for urban public services. In H. S. Perloff and Lowdon Wingo, eds. *Issues in urban economics,* pp. 527–64. Baltimore: Johns Hopkins Press.

Maxwell, J. A., and Aronson, J. R. 1977. *Financing state and local governments.* 3d ed. Washington, D.C.: Brookings Institution.

Morss, E. R. 1966. Some thoughts on the determinants of state and local expenditures. *National Tax Journal* 19, no. 1 (March): 95–103.

Nathan, R. P., and Dommel, P. R. 1979. The cities. In *Setting national priorities: The 1978 budget,* ch. 9. Washington, D.C.: Brookings Institution.

Sacks, Seymour, and Harris, Robert. 1964. The determinants of state and local expenditures and intergovernmental flows of funds. *National Tax Journal* 17, no. 1 (March): 75–85.

Schussheim, Morton J. 1974. *The modern commitment to cities.* Lexington, Mass.: Lexington Books.

Scott, C. 1972. *Forecasting local government spending.* Washington, D.C.: Urban Institute.

Sharkansky, I. 1967. Some more thoughts about the determinants of government expenditure. *National Tax Journal* 20, no. 2 (June): 171–79.

GREAT BRITAIN

General Writings on the British Political System As It Relates to Urban Spending and Subsidies

Cannan, Edwin. 1912. *The history of local rates in England.* London: King.

Chartered Institute of Public Finance and Accountancy (CIPFA, formerly Institute of Municipal Treasurers and Accountants). Annual. *Local government trends.* Annual report since 1973 gives details of Rate Support Grant negotiations and distribution. London.

―――. 1977. *Local government finance and macro-economic policy.* London.

Chester, D. N. 1966. Local finance. *Political Quarterly* 37: 180–91.

―――. 1951. *Central and local government: Financial and administrative relations.* London: Macmillan.

Dow, J. C. R. 1964. *Management of the British economy.* Cambridge: At the University Press.

Eversley, D. E. C. 1972. Rising costs and static incomes: Some economic consequences of regional planning in London. *Urban Studies* 8 (October): 347–68.

Foster, C. D. 1977. *Central governments' response to the Layfield Report.* London: Center for Environmental Studies.

―――. 1972. Public financial aspects of national settlement patterns. *Urban Studies* 8 (February): 79–97.

Goschen, Sir George. 1872. *Reports and speeches on taxation.* A report by the Exchequer that anticipated the necessity for local-financial reorganization in Britain. London: MacMillan.

Great Britain. 1976. Local government finance. Report of the Committee of Enquiry (Layfield Report). The 9 appendixes deal with local taxation, central government department evidence, testimony of local government, and other pertinent matters. *Parliamentary command papers.* London: HMSO, cmnd 6453.

―――. 1971. The future shape of local government finance. *Parliamentary command papers.* London: HMSO, cmnd 4741.

―――. Royal Commission on Local Government in England. 1969. Report. *Parliamentary command papers.* London: HMSO, cmnd 4040.

―――. Committee on the Management of Local Government. 1967. Report. *Parliamentary command papers.* London: HMSO.

―――. 1963. Local authority borrowing. *Parliamentary command papers.* London: HMSO, cmnd 2162.

―――. 1961. Control of public expenditure. Fulton Report. *Parliamentary command papers.* London: HMSO, cmnd 1432.

————. 1960. Public investment in Great Britain. *Parliamentary command papers.* London: HMSO, cmnd 1203.

————. Royal Commission on Local Taxation. 1901. Report. Also see the commission's 11 earlier reports between 1898 and 1901. *Parliamentary command papers.* London: HMSO.

Grice, J. Watson. 1910. *National and local finance.* London: King.

Griffith, J. A. G. 1966. *Central departments and local authorities.* London: Allen & Unwin.

Hartley, O. A. 1971. The relationship between central and local authorities. *Public Administration* 49 (winter): 439–56.

Hepworth, N. P. 1976. The real issues facing Layfield and their implications. *Local Government Studies,* new ser., 2: 1–14.

Hutchinson, T. W. 1968. *Economics and economic policy in Britain, 1946–1966.* London: Allen & Unwin.

McLoughlin, J. B. 1969. *Urban and regional planning: A systems approach.* London: Faber & Faber.

Marshall, A. H. 1974. *Financial management in local government.* London: Allen & Unwin.

Oliver, F. R., and Stanyer, J. 1970. Local government finance. In H. V. Weissman, ed. *Local government in England, 1958–1969,* pp. 145–76. London: Routledge & Kegan-Paul.

Peacock, A. T., and Wiseman, J. 1967. *The growth of public expenditure in the United Kingdom.* London: Allen & Unwin.

Pred, Allan R. 1977. *City systems in advanced economies: Past growth, present processes, and future development options.* London: Hutchinson.

Vaizey, J., and Sheehan, J. 1968. *Resources for education: An economic study of education in the United Kingdom, 1920–1965.* London: Allen & Unwin.

Micro-level Studies of Urban Expenditure and Budgeting

Alt, James E. 1971. Social and political correlates of county-borough expenditures. *British Journal of Political Science* 1 (January): 49–62.

Ashford, D. E. 1978. French pragmatism and British idealism: Financial aspects of local reorganization. *Comparative Political Studies* 11 (July): 231–54.

————. 1975. Resources, spending and party politics in British local government. *Administration Society* 6 (November): 286–311.

————. 1974. The effects of central finance on British local government systems. *British Journal of Political Science* 4: 305–22.

Ashford, D. E.; Berne, R.; and Schramm, R. 1976. The expenditure-financing decision in British local government. *Policy and Politics* 5: 5–24.

Boaden, Noel T. 1971. *Urban policy making: Influences on county boroughs in England and Wales.* Cambridge: At the University Press.

————. 1970. Central departments and local authorities: The relationship examined. *Political Studies* 18: 175–86.

Boaden, N. T., and Alford, R. T. 1969. Sources of diversity in English local government decisions. *Public Administration* 47 (summer): 203–23.

Boyle, L. 1966. *Equalisation and the future of local government finance.* London: Oliver & Boyd.

Corden, I. A., and Curley, J. M. 1974. Control over the capital investment of local authorities. *Public Finance and Accountancy* 1: 231–33.

Danziger, James N. 1978. *Making budgets: Public resource allocation.* Sage Library of Social Research no. 63. Beverly Hills, Calif.: Sage.

————. 1976. Assessing incrementalism in British municipal budgeting. *British Journal of Political Science* 6 (July): 335–50.

————. 1976. Twenty-six outputs in search of a taxonomy. *Policy and Politics* 5 (December): 201–12.

Greenwood, R.; Hinings, C. R.; and Ransom, S. 1977. The politics of the budgetary process in English local government. *Political Studies* 25 (March): 25–47.

Lynch, Barry, and Perlman, Morris. 1978. Local authority predictions of expenditure and income. *CES Review,* no. 3, May, pp. 12–24.

Nevitt, Della Adam. 1973. The "burden" of domestic rates. *Policy and Politics* 2: 1–25.

Newton, K., and Sharpe, L. J. 1977. Local output research: Some reflections and proposals. *Policy and Politics* 5 (March): 61–82.

Nicholson, R. J., and Thopham, N. 1971. The determinants of investment in housing by local authorities: An econometric approach. *Journal of the Royal Statistical Society,* ser. A, 134, pt. 3: 272–320.

Nicholson, R. J., and Topham, J. 1972. Investment decisions and the size of local authorities. *Policy and Politics* 1, no. 1 (September): 23–44.

Oliver, F. R., and Stanyer, J. 1969. Some aspects of the financial behaviour of county boroughs. *Public Administration* 47 (summer): 169–84.

Stone, P. A. 1970. *Urban development in Britain: Standards, costs and resources, 1964–2004.* Vol. 1. Cambridge, Eng.: National Institute of Social and Economic Research.

FRANCE

General Writings on the French Political System As It Relates to Urban Spending and Subsidies

Barberye, René. 1973. Les interventions financières de la Caisse des Dépôts dans la domaine de l'équipement local et du logement social. *Bulletin Economique et Financière,* pp. 139–68.

Chambon, Guy. 1975. *Les utopistes et l'urbanisation: La croissance urbaine.* Paris: Centre d'Etudes des Techniques Economiques Modernes.

Commisariat Générale du Plan. Intergroupe des Finances Locales. 1971. *Rapport.* Paris: Documentation Française.

D'Arcy, François. 1968. *Structures administratives et urbanisation: La Société Centrale pour l'Equipement du Territoire.* Paris: Berger-Levrault.

D'Arcy, François, and Jobert, Bruno. 1975. Urban planning in France. In J. Hayward and M. Watson, eds. *Planning, politics and public policy: The British, French and Italian experience,* pp. 295–315. Cambridge: At the University Press.

Duplouy, Joseph. 1967. *Le crédit aux collectivités locales.* Paris: Berger-Levrault.

Flecher, D., and Fort, H. 1977. *Les finances locales.* Paris: Masson.

France. 1968. *Inégalité de ressources des collectivités locales.* Paris: Notes et études documentaires, no. 3543. December 9.

———. Ministry of Finance. Annual. *Le secteur public local.* Annual financial and spending reports since the early 1960s on the French local government, with comments on policy changes. Paris: Imprimerie Nationale.

Guerrier, Paul, and Bauchard, Denis. 1972. *Economie financière des collectivités locales.* Paris: Colin.

Guichard Report (Rapport de la Commission de Développement des Responsabilités Locales). 1976. *Vivre ensemble.* Paris: Documentation Française.

Lhermet, Pierre-Yves. 1978. *Les communes face à la TVA.* Paris: Librairie Techniques.

Loïc, Philip. 1976. Les finances locales et l'imperitif de décentralisation: Bilan et perspectifs. In C. Debbasch, ed. *La déconcentration pour la renovation de l'Etat,* pp. 157–66. Paris: Presses Universitaires de France.

Micro-level Studies of Urban Expenditure and Budgeting

Auffrey, M., and Mény, Y. 1972. La déconcentration des investissements publics. *Administration,* no. 72, pp. 99–119.

Bouinot, Jean, et al. 1976. *L'influence des finances municipales sur le processus de croissance urbaine.* Paris: Centre National de la Recherche Scientifique.

Bourdon, J., and Ponteir, J. M. 1973. Les collectivités locales et la TVA. *Revue de Science Financière,* pp. 509–22.

de Préneuf, Jean-Marc. 1971. Finances locales: Les projets Pompidou. *Revue Politique et Parlementaire,* no. 818, February, pp. 46–55.

Flecher-Bourjol, D. 1976. Essai de typologie fonctionnelle des contrats passés entre l'Etat et les collectivités locales et établissements publics territoriaux. *Bulletin de l'Institut International de l'Administration Publique*, no. 38, April/June, pp. 57–90.

Fréville, Yves. 1978. VRTS et équité. *Cahiers du CFPC*, no. 2, pp. 34–67.

———. 1976. La redistribution spatiale des fonds publics en France. Study Group on the Role of Public Finance and the Process of European Integration Paper no. 12. Mimeograph.

———. 1973. L'évolution de finances des grandes villes depuis 1967. *Revue de Science Financière* 4: 725–58.

Hourticq, J. 1974. La réforme des régimes des subventions d'investissement de l'Etat, aux collectivités locales. *Revue Administrative* 26 (January/February): 65–68.

Isaac, Guy, and Moliner, Joel. 1975. L'exercice par les nouvelles institutions régionales de leurs pouvoirs financiers. *Bulletin de l'Institut International de l'Administration Publique*, no. 34, April/June, pp. 341–403.

Knaub, G. 1974. De l'incidence de regroupement des communes sur leur autonomie financière. *Revue du Droit Public* 90 (January/February): 155–68.

Nault, M. 1976. L'Etat et les collectivités locales: Un nouveau style de relations? *Revue Politique et Parlementaire* 78: 44–53.

Paul-Dubois, L. 1898. *Essai sur les finances communales*. Paris: Librairie Perrin.

Pimont, Y. 1971. Les contrats du plan. *Revue de Science Financière* 63: 697–746.

Prud'homme, Rémy. 1977. France: Central-government control over public investment expenditures. In W. E. Oates, ed. *The political economy of fiscal federalism*, pp. 65–74. Lexington, Mass.: Lexington Books.

———. 1973. Costs and financing of urban development in France. *Urban Studies* 10, no. 2 (June): 189–98.

Prud'homme, Rémy, et al. 1975. La repartition spatiale des fonds budgétaires. *Revue d'Economie Politique* 65: 38–59.

WEST GERMANY

Bertram, J. 1967. *Staatspolitik und Kommunalpolitik* (National and local politics). Stuttgart: Kohlhammer.

Frey, R. L. 1974. Der schweizerische Föderalismus—wirtschaftlich durchleuchtet (Swiss federalism—the economy examined). *Zeitschrift für schweizerisches Recht* 93: 359–78.

Fuchs, M. 1969. Zweckgebundene Zuweisungen—Hilfe oder Last für die Gemeinden? (Specific purpose grants—Aid or burden for the municipalities?). *Der Gemeindehaushalt* 70 (July/August): 145–48; 169–72.

Gellen, H. M. 1971. *Zweckzuweisungen und kommunale Selbstverwaltung: Eine verfassungsrechtliche Untersuchung* (Specific purpose grants and community self-administration: A constitutional inquiry). Cologne: Deutscher Gemeindeverlag.

Gneist, Rudolf. 1881. *Die preussische Finanzreform durch Regulierung der Gemeindesteuern* (The Prussian fiscal reform through the regulation of local taxes). Berlin: Springer.

———. 1863. *Geschichte und heutige Gestalt der englischen Communalverfassung oder des Selfgovernment* (History and current form of the British local constitution or of self-government). Berlin: Springer.

Gunlicks, Arthur B. 1977. Restructuring service delivery systems in West Germany. In V. Ostrom and R. L. Bish, eds. *Comparing urban service delivery systems*, pp. 173–96. Urban Affairs Annual Review no. 12. Beverly Hills, Calif.: Sage.

Haller, H. 1969. Der Finanzausgleich in der Bundesrepublik Deutschland und in der schweizerischen Eidgenossenschaft (Fiscal compensation in the Federal Republic of Germany and in the Swiss confederation). *Schweizerische Zeitschrift für Volkswirtschaft und Statistik* 105: 121–37.

Hansmeyer, K. H. 1970. Zweckzuweisungen an Gemeinden als Mittle der Wirtschaftspolitik? (Specific purpose grants to municipalities as a means of economic policy?). In H. Haller et al., eds. *Theorie und Praxis des finanzpolitischen Interventionismus* (Theory and practice of state interventionism in industry via the budget), pp. 431–50. Festschrift für Fritz Neumark. Tübingen: Mohr/Siebeck.

Hanusch, H. 1975. Einkommensumverteilung durch kommunale Haushalte: Das Beispiel der Bundesrepublik Deutschland 1963 und 1969 (Income reallocation through local households: The example of the Federal Republic of Germany). *Archiv für Kommunal-wissenschaften* 14: 219–39.

Hunter, J. S. H. 1973. *Revenue sharing in the Federal Republic of Germany.* Centre for Research on Federal Financial Relations Research Monograph no. 2. Canberra.

Knott, J. 1977. Stabilization policy, grants-in-aid, and the federal system in West Germany. In W. E. Oates, ed. *The political economy of fiscal federalism,* pp. 75–92. Lexington, Mass.: Lexington Books.

Kock, H. 1975. *Stabilitätspolitik im föderalistischen System der Bundesrepublik Deutsch-land* (Business-cycle policy in the federal system of the Federal Republic of Germany). Cologne: Bund.

Krause, P. 1974. Die Gebiets- und Verwaltungsreform im Saarland (District and administrative reform in Saar). *Archiv für Kommunalwissenschaften, 1974* 13, no. 2: 277–90.

Laux, E. 1973. Die kommunale Gebietsreform: Ein Literaturbericht (Local district reform: A report on the literature). *Archiv für Kommunalwissenschaften* 12, no. 2: 231–56.

Mathews, R. L., ed. 1975. *Responsibility sharing in a federal system.* Centre for Research on Federal Financial Relations Research Monograph no. 8. Canberra.

Petri, W. 1977. *Die staatlichen Zweckzuweisungen im kommunalen Finanzsystem, darge-stellt am Beispiel des Landes Niedersachsen* (Specific purpose grants in the local fiscal system, the case of the state of Lower Saxony). Berlin: Duncker & Humblot.

Pommerehne, W. W. 1975. Budgetäre Umverteilung in der Demokratie: Ein empirischer Test alternativer Hypothesen (Budgetary reallocation in a democracy: An empirical test of alternative hypotheses). *Zeitschrift für Wirtschafts- und Sozialwissenschaften,* pp. 327–64.

Reissert, B. 1978. Federal and state grants to local governments: Some descriptive material on the West German case. Berlin: IIM papers 78–1, publication series of the International Institute of Management.

Scharpf, F. W.; Reissert, B.; and Schnabel, F. 1978. Policy effectiveness and conflict avoidance in intergovernmental policy formation. In K. Hanf and F. W. Scharpf, eds. *Interorganizational policy making,* pp. 57–112. London: Sage.

Spahn, P. B. 1976. *Issues of municipal reform and the future role of local governments in West Germany.* Reprint ser. Australian National University Centre for Research on Federal Financial Relations. Canberra.

Zielinski, H. 1976. *Kommunale Selbstverwaltung und ihre Grenzen. Über den Einfluß von Staat und Wirtschaft auf die Gemeinden* (Local self-administration and its boundaries. Concerning the influence of nation and economy on the municipalities). Frankfurt & New York: Campus.